PASSION AND DEFIANCE

PASSION

MIRA LIEHM

AND DEFIANCE

Film in Italy from 1942 to the Present

UNIVERSITY OF CALIFORNIA PRESS   *Berkeley   Los Angeles   London*

University of California Press
Berkeley and Los Angeles, California

University of California Press, Ltd.
London, England

© 1984 by
The Regents of the University of California

Printed in the United States of America

1 2 3 4 5 6 7 8 9

Library of Congress Cataloging in Publication Data

Liehm, Mira.
  Passion and defiance.

  Bibliography: p.
  Includes index.
  1. Moving-pictures — Italy — History. 2. Moving-picture
plays — History and criticism. I. Title.
PN1993.5.I88L44 1984   791.43'0945 83-6667
ISBN 0-520-05020-7

To the memory of Luchino Visconti

Contents

Illustrations

Titles of illustrated films that did not receive significant distribution outside Italy are given in Italian. Other titles are given in their familiar English forms.

For their kind assistance in providing illustrations, grateful thanks are due to Freddy Buache, Cinémathèque suisse; Ugo Casiraghi; Erika and Ulrich Gregor; Cineteca nazionale, Rome; Marcel Martin; Jean A. Gili; and *Film Quarterly*.

Preface

Alberto Lattuada once pointed out: "Even if you think you know Italy well, you do not know her." This is my third book about Italian cinema, and I can only concur with Lattuada's contention. In this book, the first I have written in English, I have chosen to concentrate on the period following 1942 and to restrict my discussion to fiction films. My introduction ("First Encounters") is offered as a preface to the text and simply attempts to outline the essential features of prewar Italian cinema.

Above all, I wish to express my sincere gratitude to my husband, A. J. Liehm, who patiently read the manuscript and whose remarks—as well as our endless discussions on the subject of Italy—proved invaluable. I am also very grateful to Ugo and Licia Casiraghi, my dear friends and loving connoisseurs of the Italian film scene, who provided the Italian counterbalance to my outsider's view, reading and discussing the manuscript with enormous dedication.

I also extend my thanks to the Rockefeller Foundation and to the National Endowment for the Humanities whose fellowships made the writing of this book possible. Very particular thanks are due to Beverly Michaels, who made extensive revisions in the manuscript to clarify my English; to Andrew Dickos, Archie Perlmutter, and David Packman, who read portions of the manuscript and provided helpful editorial remarks; to Ernest Callenbach, my long-time publisher, who never stopped encouraging me in my project; to Estelle Jelinek who edited the manuscript.

In various ways the following friends also helped to make this work a reality: Mino Argentieri, Freddy Buache (Cinémathèque Suisse), Eileen Bowser (Museum of Modern Art), Dr. Guido Cincotti (Cineteca nazionale), John Gillet (British Film Institute), Erika and Ulrich Gregor, Marcel Martin, Lino Miccichè, Jean-Loup Passek, Eva Rensky, Charles Silver (Museum of Modern Art), Bruno Torri (Italnoleggio Cinematografico), Virgilio Tosi, and Fee Vaillant. My gratitude also goes to Dr. Lodoletta Lupo and the entire staff of the Rome Film Archive, who enabled me to view hundreds of films.

Philadelphia, August 1982

FIRST ENCOUNTERS (BEFORE 1942)

Date: Easter 1940, a few months before Mussolini's declaration of war upon Britain and France. Place: A ship bound for Capri. Two men meet for the first time. The older is extremely good-looking, tall and slender, with dark hair. His finely chiseled features and tormented expression are reminiscent of Italian Renaissance portraits. He is in his mid-thirties. The other man is short and broad-shouldered, a smiling, extremely outgoing peasant type whose ancestors "abandoned their wives to the lust of the Turkish, Arab and Saracen conquerors."[1] Their names: Luchino Visconti and Giuseppe De Santis. Result of this encounter: a film, a milestone—*Ossessione*.

Visconti was an aristocrat, privileged by his wealth and social position to do whatever he wished. Like the majority of the Italian aristocracy, he was hostile to the fascist regime, despising the plebeian Mussolini. He had spent several years in France working with Jean Renoir and in 1940 had just returned from the United States. He had everything De Santis did not have.

De Santis, just twenty-three years old, was an eager newcomer to Rome. He was making his way in journalism, fiercely attacking the current film production in his articles for the journal *Cinema*. In the circle that formed around this journal in the early 1940s, Visconti was the potential Maecenas whereas De Santis was the "enfant terrible." All the members of the circle shared an unlimited passion for film and a desire to find new forms of expression for the medium. It is one of the inconsistencies of Italian fascism that this journal, with its increasingly overt antifascism, was run by Mussolini's son Vittorio.

Italian fascism, lacking the organizational perfection that characterized Hitler's Nazism, was more tolerant toward its adversaries and less demanding of its partisans. Fascist Italy managed to retain the nominal allegiance of more of its intellectuals and cultural leaders than Germany did; fewer emigrated from Italy than from Germany and Russia. There were no extermination camps. Many could travel abroad. The tolerance toward nonfascist intellectuals went so far that the Marxist theoretician Umberto Barbaro was able not only to teach at the Centro Sperimentale di Cinematografia but also to show the best films of the Russian avant-garde to his class of young enthusiasts (among them De Santis) and to translate Pudovkin's

1

writings. Antonio Gramsci, the secretary of the Communist party and its leading theoretician, was able to write the major part of his huge work in prison. In 1938, while the holocaust in Germany was approaching its peak, Gertrude Stein's *The Autobiography of Alice B. Toklas* was published in Rome with an enthusiastic preface by Cesare Pavese. At the same time, open admiration for American literature dominated the Italian literary scene. (A 1,000-page anthology of American literature was published as late as 1942.)

Cesare Pavese, one of the leading Italian novelists, wrote in 1948 in his *Diaries:* "Fundamentally, humanistic intelligence—the fine arts and letters—did not suffer under fascism; they managed to follow their own bent, cynically accepting the game as it was. Where fascism exercised vigilance was in preventing intercourse between the intelligentsia and the people, keeping the people uninformed."[2]

Gramsci and many others never returned from prison. In 1938, anti-Semitic laws were enacted excluding Jews from political activities and from some professions. Many authors were not allowed to publish, and censorship was strict. Fascist Italy was a dictatorship "Italian style," but it was a dictatorship. Its leaders, "gerarchi," lacked the drive and professional competence of a Josef Goebbels or an Alfred Rosenberg, who concocted a Nazi ideological concept and in its name blacklisted hundreds of books, plays, paintings, and films, setting up norms for "true German culture" in all fields. In Italy, Galeazzo Ciano, Dino Alfieri, and Luigi Freddi never managed to enforce cultural controls and never really fused the professional film organizations with the organs of political authority. By design they allowed a limited amount of criticism on specific matters, a policy that has been called "repressive tolerance."

"What is Italian fascism?" asked Antonio Gramsci as early as 1921. "It is the insurrection of the lowest stratum of the Italian bourgeoisie, the stratum of layabouts, of the ignorant, of the adventurers to whom the war has given the illusion of being good for something and truly counting for something, those who had been carried forward by the state of political and moral decadence."[3]

The fascists never succeeded in changing the people's attitudes regarding two important issues of the late thirties: racism and the alliance with Nazi Germany. Both these policies went against the historically determined Italian national character, which was neither anti-Semitic nor pro-German.

Not many nations are as basically different from one another as Germany and Italy. Few nations dislike each other so frankly as the Germans and the Italians. Yet in 1936, through the treaty that created the Rome-Berlin axis, they were drawn willy-nilly into an alliance.

Juxtaposed with the Germans' inclination toward an often tragic mythology of duty and discipline was the indulgent, easygoing attitude of the Italians: "die Schicksalstragödie" (the tragedy of destiny) of Wagner and the "bel canto" (beautiful singing) of Verdi. The ascetic faces of Albrecht Dürer and the joyful roundness of Raphael's bodies. Hitler and Mussolini. Conquerors and their imitators.

There was one attitude Mussolini could rely upon: the traditional Italian appetite for victory, the love of victory, even if it was only a disguised defeat. Never was Mussolini's popularity greater than after the 1936 conquest of Ethiopia, Eritrea, and Somalia and the 1938 annexation of Albania, presented to the indifferent world as a logical reconquest of Roman territories. At these moments he was cheered by the majority of the Italian people, to whom he gave a flattering image of their country as victorious, powerful, and free at last from those features that had generated a sense of national defeat after World War I.

Did this occasional enthusiasm mean that the majority of Italian filmmakers were profascist? that they became antifascists only at the last minute, when the victory started changing sides?

"Don't forget what happened in America during the McCarthy period," said director Renato Castellani in an interview.

> When somebody is immersed in a certain world, he cannot see things clearly, he cannot see things outside this world, have ideas beyond this world. . . . He is like a canary born in a cage. He has no idea of what is outside: maybe the cage for him is what is outside and not what is inside. Similarly, we had no political problems. We lived in a world organized in a certain way, we were marching forward, and we could more or less approve of the things this world was doing. Very often our approval was wrong. . . . You know, fascism in Italy was bland, there was no excessive toughness or violence.[4]

"Italy is a strange country," director Alberto Lattuada pointed out, when asked about fascism in Italy. "It is the only country where the religious power, the monarchic power, and a dictatorship existed as a unique triumvirate. I do not think that we had ever before seen the head of the church, a monarch and a dictator living together and loving each other. Even if you think you know Italy well, you do not know her. It is impossible to really know Italy."[5]

"You know, Rossellini is Catholic," said Sergio Amidei (scriptwriter of films such as *Open City, Paisan,* and *Anni difficili* [Difficult Years]) when asked whether Roberto Rossellini was a fascist.

> And Catholics are used to being forgiven. The more they sin, the more they are loved because they have something for which to ask forgiveness. The priests do not like people who have nothing to ask forgiveness for. . . . Fascism did not have the characteristics of Nazism, its blind faith in the destiny of a nation. In Italy there was a sense of compromise.[6]

"There was once a colonel in Cinecittà," recalls the film historian Luigi Chiarini, who, during the fascist period, was director of the Centro Sperimentale di Cinematografia.

> In each of the agencies there was a fascist. And this colonel came to the Centro to protest because it was October 28,[7] and the doorman was not in the fascist uniform. I told him: 'But I'm in plain clothes, too. If you want to yell at somebody, start with me.' And that was it. He laughed and left. He was a fascist for show. The majority of them were.[8]

"Freddi was a party bureaucrat, an obedient person," remarks Cesare Zavattini, recalling his association with Luigi Freddi, director of the General Film Management under the fascist regime.

He was a man who was happy to be a self-described servant. This was a beautiful quality in him and that's how it should have been. We cannot even hold it against him because this was his work, his duty. He fulfilled it consistently and sometimes even with a certain joy that made all the inherent oppressiveness disappear. The political element appeared almost as a kind of relationship between friends, a nice tap on the shoulder; and we were not aware of it, because our state of mind resisted such awareness. That was the true manifestation of a regime, of a dictatorship in the full meaning of the word. But we even accommodated ourselves to other things. This was our daily life, a way of life for the whole nation, not only for the intellectuals. The intellectuals and the people were in the same boat. Intellectuals made some indirect attempts at antifascism. Literature enables one to contest things from the inside of the situation. When Pirandello was writing *Six Characters in Search of an Author,* he certainly was not a fascist, even if he later joined the Fascist party.[9]

In the newspaper *Corriere Padano* on October 26, 1938, there appeared an article entitled "A Heroic Story on the Screen." It was a review of a new film, *Luciano Serra, pilota* (Pilot Luciano Serra). Directed by Goffredo Alessandrini, coscripted by Roberto Rossellini, and personally supervised by Vittorio Mussolini, the film glorifies the life of a pilot who dies in the Ethiopian campaign. The review was written by Michelangelo Antonioni, a prominent film critic of the late thirties and early forties. "*Luciano Serra* is undoubtedly the first great Italian film, which will find a place among the most respected works of our time," writes Antonioni. "And for that," he concludes, "we have to be grateful to Vittorio Mussolini."[10]

Vitaliano Brancati, the Sicilian writer who coscripted many important Italian films, offered one of the best explanations for the youthful fascist enthusiasm:

When I was twenty, I was a fascist, down to my hair roots. Fascism for me was a wondrous credo. I experienced the joy of a herded animal: the joy of being in accord with millions of people—to feel what they felt. An optimism of a third order invested me. I felt like a giant of the group even in my solitude. . . . I experienced deeply in 1927 what it is like for a twenty-year-old, inclined to meditation, fantasy, and sloth to admire a man of action and violence: to believe that a new delightful morality was about to be born. It tasted like a glass of wine. All ideological abortions . . . are as intoxicating as wine because like wine they bring us outside laws of reality into a sphere that we call 'the new world.' I experienced also the shame that follows upon such drunkenness, the boredom of 1936 and 1937, when it was necessary to look back and write: "At certain times, we should never be twenty."[11]

FILM IN A CORPORATE STATE

From 1930 to 1939, some 722 fiction films were produced in Italy.[12] With the fascists paying more and more attention to the film medium, production rose sharply: 12 films in 1931, 34 in 1933, 67 in 1938, 89 in 1941, and 119 in 1942. The fascists quickly realized the propagandistic power of film and the necessity for state subsidies and control. From the beginning they tried to centralize all cinematic activities under one authority. Between 1925 and 1929, L'Unione Cinematografica Educativa (LUCE) was created to promote educational films, and one of its first ventures was a three-part documentary, *Il Duce,* depicting Mussolini's ascent. Following Lenin's example and the shrewd use of the cinema for the benefit of the Soviet state, Mussolini proclaimed film to be "the most powerful weapon," thus paraphrasing the famous Soviet slogan "film—the most important art."

"Since the very beginning, film struck us as an important element of progress not only because of its artistic achievements but because of its capacity to become a mighty instrument of the dissemination of ideas, of culture, of the instruction and education of people." This is how the introduction to the book about LUCE, published in 1934, characterized the role of cinema in Mussolini's corporate state.[13]

In 1932, Alessandro Sardi, president of LUCE, traveled to Russia where he met with representatives of the film industry. He returned with detailed information about the Soviet film organization and published an enthusiastic article about it in the daily *Il Popolo d'Italia* (August 25, 1932). Meanwhile, Luigi Freddi, Mussolini's adviser on questions of film, went to Hollywood. It was, however, the Soviet experience that provided the original inspiration for the fascist centralization of all activities connected with film. At that time, the Italian press was flooded by articles concerned with the organization of the film industry. All stressed the educational importance of film and the close relationship between film and politics.[14] They spoke repeatedly about "film consciousness," a term that later frequently appeared in articles written by the neorealists.

Corrado Pavolini, an influential journalist of the time, wrote in the official fascist daily *Tevere* (May 5, 1930):

> We affirm that, in the present situation, the Italian production, even if good— which is the first problem—could by far not resolve the most important issue: to create a national film consciousness. . . . Film, which is both art and an instrument of propaganda, needs a collective consciousness in order to achieve all its potentials. . . . The American, German, and Russian productions are successful because film in these countries is based on a collective feeling, expressed in an appropriate cinematic form. . . . In Moscow, there is such a close and spontaneous relationship between the nation and film that these two merge into one. The Russian filmmaker has the same feeling toward the masses and the soil as the saddest of the workers and the most naive of the peasants. . . . Cinema is not a transposition of the bourgeois theater, which is approximately the same in all countries, but a unique, modern expression of national collectivity, profoundly differentiated from one race to another.[15]

Commenting on Pavolini's article, Adriano Aprà, the contemporary Italian film historian, wrote forty-five years later:

> The argument about the Russian (Soviet) film appears frequently in the articles of the thirties. At that moment, when a model for the rebirth (birth from the fascist viewpoint) of the cinema was being sought, many reservations arose in

connection with the American and German film industries (the leading powers on the market) that vanished before the model of the Russian cinema. Not only did the unity between nation and film, which the fascists were eager to attain, speak in favor of the Russian production, but also its aesthetic basis (Pudovkin was about to be translated and everybody had heard about Eisenstein's montage). Russian film was both politics and art, which was a combination representing the highest aspiration of the more knowledgeable fascist film critics.[16]

Mussolini himself said in an interview: "The Russian film is at the foremost post. In Italy, we shall in no time have the means for that too."

Beginning in 1933, a powerful state organization was progressively brought to life and generously subsidized. Luigi Freddi became the head of the Direzione Generale per la Cinematografia (General Film Management) and surrounded himself with well-chosen experts (such as Alessandro Blasetti, Mario Camerini, Mario Soldati). Under his auspices, a board of censors began reviewing film scripts and projects, distributing prizes and regulating international film exchanges. The board included representatives of the interior and war ministries, the Fascist party, and others. No Italian-made film was ever suppressed entirely, but many had to be reedited. Certain foreign films were banned for glorifying values such as pacifism (*La grande illusion*) or gangsterism (*Scarface*).

At the same time, a film section was opened at the state-controlled "Banco del Lavoro," and was authorized to advance 60 percent of the capital needed for any film with a script approved by the censorship board. In some cases, films with a strong profascist message received complete funding (e.g., *Scipione l'Africano*, which glorified the war in Africa).

Following the example of the American Legion of Decency, the Centro Cattolico Cinematografico (Catholic Film Center) was established with the task of cataloguing all films according to their moral content. Pope Pius XI stated in his encyclical of June 29, 1936: "It is necessary that the bishops create permanent offices in all regions with the aim of promoting honest films, to classify the others, and to communicate the right opinion to the priests and believers."

The first film school in Italy opened its doors in 1934. Originally it was incorporated into the Accademia Musicale di S. Cecilia (St. Cecilia Music Academy) in Rome and managed by Alessandro Blasetti. A year later, the prestigious Centro Sperimentale di Cinematografia (Experimental Film Center) was created. It was first located in an old building but later transferred into its own well-equipped facilities on the outskirts of Rome. Luigi Chiarini, the well-known critic and historian, became its first president. Among its professors were Umberto Barbaro and Blasettti, and its students included Roberto Rossellini, Michelangelo Antonioni, Guiseppe De Santis, Luigi Zampa, Pietro Germi, Luciano Emmer, Dino De Laurentiis, etc. In 1936, the theoretical journal *Cinema* came into being. (In 1938, its editor-in-chief became Vittorio Mussolini.) At the same time, the Centro started editing its own magazine *Bianco e Nero*, with Chiarini at its head. Concentrating mainly on theory, *Bianco e Nero* published articles by Rudolf Arnheim, Béla Balázs, Umberto Barbaro, Luigi Chiarini, and other established theoreticians, and *Cinema* opened its pages to the younger generation.[17]

Scipione l'Africano

A law enacted in 1933 forbade the dubbing of Italian films into foreign languages, thus making the film policy a part of the colonization efforts in Albania, Africa, and Alto Adige (a part of Italy that belonged to Austria before World War I). On the other hand, the dubbing of foreign films became obligatory. The tax collected from production companies for the dubbing of their films was invested in native production. This policy protected the market against American pictures and was an effective incentive for Italian producers. Moreover, the impersonal literary language used in dubbed films helped the official policy of linguistic unification of the country.

In 1934, Galeazzo Ciano, Mussolini's son-in-law, then the undersecretary of the press and propaganda office, declared in the Senate: "The movie industry must be placed under strict control, under an even more careful and efficacious vigilance." With the foundation of the Ente Nazionale Industrie Cinematografiche (ENIC) (National Agency for Film Industry) in 1935, the fascist takeover of various film companies was more or less completed. ENIC acquired an important chain of theaters, especially first-run theaters situated in ten key cities. It also governed a chain of subagencies both in Italy and abroad. In 1938, the National Agency for Importation of Foreign Film (ENAIPE) was attached to the giant body of the now state-controlled film industry and held a monopoly on the purchasing of foreign films, which it then resold to local distributors.[18]

In 1937, Mussolini personally opened the new studios, Cinecittà, referred to as "the artistic laboratory of Mussolini's time." The magnificent conglomerate of sixteen studios spread over an area of 140,000 square meters, facing the Centro Sperimentale on the Via Tuscolana. (By June 1943, it produced nearly 300 fiction films, 85 shorts, and 248 dubbed versions of fiction films.)[19] Meanwhile, the capital invested in the film production increased by 8 percent. State film production was centered in the CINES, a corporation built on the ashes of the original CINES run by Emilio Cecchi, which burned down in 1935. By 1942, attendance reached 477 million with 5,236 movie theaters around the country.

An example of the official fascist view on what should and should not be shown in films was offered in the following excerpt from Luigi Freddi's report to Mussolini in 1937 opposing the joint Italo-American production of opera films:

> Some people suggest that we should bring on the screen operatic spectacles such as *Rigoletto*, *Tosca*, *Cavalleria Rusticana*, and *Aida*. Is it really possible that today anyone could seriously think of bringing on the screen *Rigoletto*, that brutal story of a provincial tyrant using and abusing his subjects, of a local satrap who amused himself by abductions and murders? . . . Are they not aware of the possible political and moral impact that such a film could have on the large masses of cinemagoers, outnumbering hundreds of times those who attend the opera? Is it indeed conceivable that in a Catholic country such as Italy one might seriously propose for the education of the masses the filming of *Tosca*, a gloomy and wicked drama immersed in blood? . . . Is it really possible that in Italy, which strives to set up a moral code for relations between the white race and the colored race, anyone should think of producing an *Aida*, which—it seems to me, although I have never really understood the story—proposes a union between a white man and a Negress whose father only lacks the backing of the League of Nations in order to appear as the Negus? And there were even suggestions to film *The Passion of Jesus Christ*. It might be interesting to see whether such a creation would be more anti-Roman or anti-Catholic.[20]

MYTHOLOGICAL GENRE

The fascist efforts to use film as a popular medium could not find a more fertile soil than in Italy.[21] From the beginning, movies were accepted as the genuine continuation of the Roman *circenses* (games), as the primary popular entertainment, accessible to everybody and offering for ten to twelve *centesimi* stories of love, revenge, and heroism that the Italians are so fond of.

Public presentations—theater, opera, circus—have always been extremely popular in Italy. Plays were staged in front of churches (another popular meeting place) and, later, in any town or village square, or in taverns. Outdoor theaters could hold greater audiences than the theater houses, not counting those spectators who were just leaning out of their windows and porches. Films were often screened the same way. Well into the fifties there was a large number of outdoor cinemas with films projected on the wall of a backyard, in a garden, or almost anywhere.

The impact of visual entertainment was increased by widespread illiteracy. In 1914, Italy already had 1,500 movie houses, and with the annual production of about 500 films (the average length about 3,000 feet), the country was on its way to becoming a cinematic superpower. The main reason for this unexpected conquest of the world was the so-called mythological genre—the gigantic productions employing thousands of extras and hundreds of elephants—forerunners of the later historical and biblical spectacles made in Hollywood. Their heart-breaking stories evoked the heroic deeds of the ancient Romans, Greeks, and early Christians. Favored by the local climate and the quality of natural light, they were filmed on location (Roman ruins, Sicilian Greek temples, mountains and coasts) or in elaborate studio settings, which were used for one film after another.

The most important technician of the crew was the art director, who designed the film sets and costumes. His importance gradually grew, especially in the late thirties when decor became an important creative element of the filmic structure. Detailed descriptions of man and his environment have been characteristic of Italian art for centuries. Man's outward appearance was the subject of entirely different interest from that shown, for example, by the northern Europeans. Beginning, at the latest, with Boccaccio, the descriptions of characters and their surroundings formed an important part in the structure of both prosaic and dramatic works. The art of sketching man's picture, familiar to all Italians, was from the beginning used and abused by the film industry.

Many directors of the silent era were originally trained as art designers (which in Italy was a more honorable profession than directing). The film director was, first of all, expected to direct the actors and to execute the orders of the producer, who was always at his side and was more influential in shaping the story.

The most famous director-designer was Enrico Guazzoni (1876–1949), who in 1912 made *Quo Vadis?* one of the great mythological films, where, in his own words, "even the smallest detail will be in conformity with the strictest historical truth."[22] The film had larger sets and a larger cast than any film made before World War I and achieved the greatest international success of any picture at that time. About 300 prints were sold worldwide, and in major cities special presentations were organized with full orchestra accompaniments and inflated seat prices. The story followed the plot of Henryk Sienkiewicz's novel stressing the fatality of all kinds of love.[23]

Giovanni Pastrone's (1883–1959) *Cabiria* (1914) became another big hit worldwide not only because of its spectacular settings with 2,000 extras or because of D'Annunzio's participation in rewriting the intertitles but also because of its story of a great, desperate love. Love, as a screen subject, remained with the Italian film ever since and has become its strongest asset.

Gabriele D'Annunzio was one of the greatest expositors of the subject of passion in his time. His relationship to cinema was ambiguous. The contemporary evaluations of his film work range from strictly negative to reasonably positive. Some stress his purely financial motivations; others underline his serious interest in the potential of the new medium. He was, in fact, the only Italian writer of his time to consider film the art of the future. He received 50,000 lire for the rewriting of the intertitles of *Cabiria,* an unheard of sum for this kind of work. They are immersed in lyrical bathos, sometimes contradicting the primitive plot with emphasis on the unbearable suffering brought about by love.[24]

In an interview promoting *Cabiria,* D'Annunzio said: "In Milan, a few years ago, I was attracted toward a new invention, which, it seems to me, suggests a new aesthetics of movement. . . . It came to my mind that a new kind of pleasure might be born out of the cinematograph, the essential element of which would be 'miraculous.'"[25] D'Annunzio's cooperation with the new medium was always veiled in a haze of ambiguity with its pecuniary aspect not to be underestimated.

Cabiria is frequently discussed for its first use of certain cinematic effects. Its director, Giovanni Pastrone, retired from filmmaking in 1920, making it difficult to judge whether his contribution to the evolution of the art of film would have been of more permanent value. *Cabiria* was undoubtedly a unique achievement, influencing both D. W. Griffith and Cecil B. DeMille. The use of tracking shots in quasi-static scenes remains its significant contribution to the evolution of film language. Pastrone's stated intention was that the tracking shots should show the scale of the sets, which were frequently a daring combination of real-life settings and decor. (Tracking shots taken at a fixed distance between moving camera and moving actors were used before 1914.)

The story of Cabiria, the little girl from Catania who is sold to the Carthaginians and rescued by a Roman patrician, has strong nationalistic overtones. Its background—the second Punic war, the campaign against Hannibal, and the destruction of the Sicilian city of Syracuse—provided a justification for the Italian colonial expeditions in Africa, appealing with patriotic fire to the Italian sense of honor—"the enigmatic mixture of conscience and egoism."[26]

The exaltation of nationalistic feelings remained the backbone of the mythological genre, gaining in strength after the fascist takeover. In 1926, the fourth remake of the *Ultimi giorni di Pompei* (The Last Days of Pompeii) was released, directed by Amleto Palermi (1889–1941) and Carmine Gallone (1886–1973). The glorification of the Roman superpower permeates the whole story, emphasizing the racist element present in E. Bulwer Lytton's novel (written in 1834). The bad guys have dark skin, the good ones white. Arbuce, the Egyptian, is a tyrannical monster while the Athenian Glauco represents the very essence of innocence. He is sent into the lion's cage by Arbuce, but the beast simply refuses to devour him. In the final scenes, with lava covering the city, while everyone flees, a Roman legionnaire remains at his post unflinchingly and sacrifices himself under the boiling element. His heroic death (he dies with his eyes turned toward Rome) saves him from God's punishment, which, according to the script, was the cause of the tragedy. The continuity between the Rome of Caesar and that of Mussolini was established, yet the film was a commercial flop. The deficient acting is overwhelmed by the extraordinary pictorial composition of the mass movements in open spaces. The merit belongs to Carmine Gallone, a man of strong visual sensitivity who gave a helping hand to Palermi. The attempt to capture an authentic atmosphere of the city of

Ultimi giorni di Pompei

Pompeii is clearly visible, and the setting of the town square forms an impressive architectural landscape revealed by a moving camera and rhythmical editing. The direction of the hundreds of extras demanding Glauco's death ("al'leone"—to the lion) belongs to the best artistic achievements of this genre.

Two elements distinguish these late mythological films from their predecessors: their outspoken eroticism and their sadistic violence. The 1926 remake of *Quo Vadis?* contains a drastic scene of flagellation, its menacing atmosphere suggesting the violence of rape and extremely brutal fighting. The orgy scene in *The Last Days of Pompeii,* surprising with its audacious nudity, culminates in a well-staged striptease of a mummy. Fascism, officially as prudish as all totalitarian regimes, put an end to honest Italian eroticism.[27] It reappeared on the screen the very minute Mussolini lost power.

COMMEDIA

Italian films of all periods, whatever their genre, contain more or less hidden elements of the eternal "commedia all'italiana" (comedy Italian style). Since the early seventeenth century, which gave birth to the tradition of the "commedia dell'arte" and Italian opera, literature and theater in Italy lived with stereotypes and structures of comedy. Tragedy, on the other hand, turned into melodrama. "Shakespeare could not have been Italian," said Jakob Burckhardt, who called the Italian tendency toward the farcical portrayal of life "the corrective of the modern desire for fame and of all highly developed individuality."[28]

In some Latin farces there were already comic types: Bucco, the fat man; Dossennus, the glutton; Pappus, the old father; Maccus, the fool. Film adopted all of them, including the "double plot" (A loves B who loves C who loves D who loves A), the "multiple plot" (the great chain of lovers), and the "recognition" (at the end it turns out that A was the brother of D while B was the sister of C, etc.). It could probably be proved, if it served any purpose, that all Italian films, with few later exceptions, are "commedie all'italiana."

In the early years, practically every film had its most dramatic moments punctuated by comic shots: a servant falling into a well at a moment of high dramatic tension, a fat jailor who could not fit into a cell, a guest who would bump into things during an orgy. The use of cinematic tricks in these early Italian comedies was poor. The entire genre lagged behind the international average. In the mid-twenties, the stagnation was complete, and an already established dramatic structure became an iron-clad formula.

After the fascist takeover, the country's tendency toward provincialism was intensified by the official mistrust of anything foreign. The evolution of Italian art came to a halt; and, except for Futurism, there was no avant-garde movement, neither of surrealistic nor expressionist influence (the dominant movements in the arts of the time). The European theatrical avant-garde too found little echo on the Italian stage. The theater remained locked in nineteenth-century patterns offering the worst possible example to the film art. Indeed, during the great upsurge of the European cinematic avant-garde, the Italian cinema was living through years of both economic and aesthetic decline.

NAPLES

The most original films of this period were produced by the Neapolitan school. Some of them are landmarks of Italian production in their elements of crude realism and authentic environment. This genre was the only one to retain its originality until the late twenties.

The city of Naples has always considered itself a special place, nonintegrated into the young Neapolitan kingdom. All artistic endeavors originating in Naples differed to a greater or lesser degree from other Italian works. Nineteenth-century Neapolitan painting, for example, based its approach to subject matter on the evocation of a strong illusion of reality, centering its attention on the famous Neapolitan landscape. Film followed this tradition, using landscape as a predominant element of formal structure and as a component of dramatic action.

The most important Neapolitan films, Nino Martoglio's (1870–1921) *Sperduti nel buio* (Lost in the Darkness, 1914) and Gustavo Serena's (b. 1881) *Assunta Spina* (1915), are considered by film historians as first sources of the neorealist style.[29] Vlada Petric compares their significance to "that of the first Lupu-Pick films in Germany, which are conceived in the 'Kammerspiel' style, as opposed to the spectacular expressionist stylization of the period."[30]

Lost in the Darkness transposes the drama written by the veristic Neapolitan playwright Roberto Bracco, in 1901. (It tells the story of Nunzio and Paolina, a blind boy and a girl who live in squalid Neapolitan quarters and whose relationship is interrupted by adverse fate.) The film was discovered in 1933 during a retrospective organized by Umberto Barbaro, Luigi Chiarini, and Luigi Freddi on the occasion of the fortieth anniversary of the Italian film industry. Ten years later, during the war evacuation of the Centro, the fim disappeared and no one has seen it since.[31] This led a group of young Italian film historians in the early seventies to question the validity of Barbaro's judgment, which was automatically accepted by many film historians during the 1950s and 1960s.[32] Barbaro thought highly of the picture, especially of its parallel editing, which alternates, in the Griffith manner, shots of slums with the scenes of the palace. This alternation was already suggested, according to Barbaro, in the opening title, which reads: "People who enjoy themselves and people who suffer." In his 1935 review of *Lost in the Darkness,* Barbaro wrote: "The film is outstanding for its merging of visual values with an ethical approach. The choice of the costumes and all the details testify to a great and deep human sympathy. We see poor cotton-checked clothes, heavy but icy blankets, striped trousers of the young Neapolitan loafers . . . and in contrast to that, veils and pillows of Maria Carmi wrapped in her long flowing hair. The presentation of two contrasting environments led the director to use, from the prologue on, parallel editing in the Griffith manner. With perfect stylistic coherence the realism becomes more marked during the story until it goes beyond the story to become metaphor and signification."[33]

Sperduti nel buio

On the other hand, the French film historian Henri Langlois, who might have seen the film during the retrospective, recognized the use of natural lighting as a trait common to many Neapolitan films ("a natural light that we have never seen in any film before, not even in Buñuel").[34] An important critical assessment of Martoglio's disputed film comes from Antonio Pietrangeli, who wrote in 1942 about "the description of the squalid milieu of the Neapolitan lowest strata, full of love for the cracks and signs on the wall, for the homeless people, for greasy hair, and for the cotton-checked clothes, all of which anticipated the realism of the Russian and the French films."[35]

Barbaro's view is mainly sustained by another important, extant Neapolitan film, *Assunta Spina*. Its acknowledged high artistic qualities testify to the existence of a significant trend in Neapolitan silent production. The film transcribes the popular Neapolitan drama by Salvatore Di Giacomo (1910), a typical Italian story of passion, seduction, and bloody revenge. The most effective scenes of *Assunta Spina* are filmed on the streets amid the traffic, with bright light emphasizing the dramatic conflict interwoven into the natural setting, creating a strong visual impact on the screen. These scenes, according to Vlada Petric, can be matched "only by Griffith's concern for the ontological impact of photography, so ingeniously demonstrated in his Biograph one reelers."[36] The character of Assunta (played by Francesca Bertini, the most famous Italian star of the silent era) combines traditional feminine submissiveness with a heightened sensuality and a need for freedom. Yet Assunta accepts man as the supreme judge of all her deeds.

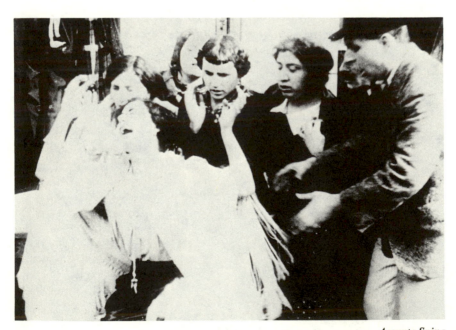

Assunta Spina

This attitude was challenged by Elvira Notari (b. 1875), the first Italian woman director. Her Neapolitan films are excellent examples of filmmaking with a unique handling of social themes. In 1921, she shot *A santa notte* (A Holy Night) centering again on the harsh life of a woman of the people. Its heroine, Nanninella, conceived probably as a continuation of Assunta, surpasses Assunta's model with her independence, displayed in many ways, and her overpowering her male counterparts. The story offers unusual insights into the lives of abused women in the poorest Italian social strata. The men in the story eventually destroy Nanninella out of fear and powerlessness. The film was shot entirely on location in wretched pubs and squalid apartments, with the camera returning repeatedly to the streets and outdoor cafés. One of its most impressive characters is the shoeshine boy, Gennariello, played by Notari's son. Notari succeeded in creating a personality type, a product of the Neapolitan streets, living and dying from poverty, who was immortalized twenty-five years later in De Sica's *Shoeshine*.

The most telling scene of Notari's films is the "table of the poor" in *E piccerella* (1922) (*piccerella* is a typical Neapolitan word designating a strong-willed, loving, and outspoken girl). In a sequence shot in an authentic setting, Notari captures the hunger of the city, reflected in the faces of the poor who gather for a charity dinner during the festival of Carmine. The toothless, emaciated faces chewing and gulping down the food belong in the gallery of the most accomplished images of the period and probably inspired the imagery of Alessandro Blasetti's 1932 film *La tavola dei poveri* (The Table of the Poor).[37] Elvira Notari, together with her husband and son,

E piccerella

shot many films. Judging from those that are still extant, she emerges as a director of exceptional talent, confirming the originality of the Neapolitan school.[38]

None of the later Neapolitan films achieved the authenticity of Notari's productions. Worth mentioning are the films by Ubaldo Maria Del Colle (b. 1883), one of the most active directors of the time. In 1926, he shot for the Italo-American company Any-film the movie *Te lasso!* (I'm Leaving You!) following the tradition of Neapolitan realism. The film contains a stunning sequence in an outdoor restaurant where the culminating drama draws heavily from the impact of the authentic settings. *I'm Leaving You!* belongs to the so-called "Mamma films," a subgenre centering around the character of a mother who dominates the plot as a good fairy and messenger of God.[39]

The Neapolitan trend was stopped by the fascist centralization efforts. Mussolini, preoccupied with the belated completion of Italy's unification, opposed any development of autonomous regional culture. The use of regional dialects in literature, on stage, and in film intertitles was viewed as a potential threat to the unity of the fascist state. The advent of sound and the continuing isolation of fascist Italy facilitated the decline of the Neapolitan school, which depended to a great extent on ethnic audiences in the United States and Latin America.[40]

FUTURISM

When tracing the affinities between the neorealists and the early artistic Italian movements, the Futurists cannot be ignored. Cesare Zavattini made the connection between neorealism and Futurism in 1954. "In the field of spiritual activity, there is always a precedent," he claimed.

The Futurists of the 1910s and the neorealists of the 1940s not only shared the predilection for authenticity and an aversion to values resulting from bourgeois attitudes; they shared, as well, a deep interest in the Italian landscape and in the visualization of subject matter in a real-life atmosphere which resulted in the effort to substitute the "I" of psychology with a "lyrical obsession with the substance," according to F. T. Marinetti, in the 1912 "Technical Manifesto of Futurist Literature." Both Futurists and neorealists considered the work of art a closed entity whose first premise was a sufficient amount of internal force that allowed it to speak for itself. They all rejected any work that required completion by a second person (viewer) and thus opposed some of the major avant-garde theories especially about the theater. As a matter of fact, both the Futurists and neorealists rejected all dependence on the theater or on the various literary forms of the novel, advocating full autonomy for the film medium. They stressed the capacity of the cinematic image to express emotions, feelings, and contemplation. The Futurist film manifesto is often discussed in connection with the Soviet poetics of montage, which, in its turn, influenced the structure of the neorealist films.[41]

The Futurists have the oldest tradition of artistic rebellion in this century, dating back to Marinetti's 1909 "Manifesto on Futurism." In 1912, Marinetti proclaimed: "Courage, audacity, rebellion are to be the essentials of poetry. Literature has hitherto exalted pensive immobility, rapture, and sleep; we shall exalt aggressive movement, hectic sleeplessness, the quickstep, the summersault, the slap, the blow."[42]

This artistic and social aggressiveness led the Futurists into the fascist ranks. Their identification with fascism went so far that in 1942 Benedetto Croce saw the origins of Futurism in its infatuation with violence.[43] Antonio Gramsci's evaluation of the Futurist movement was more favorable. "The Futurists," he wrote, "had a clear and well-defined conception that our age, the age of industry, of the great working-class city, of intense and tumultuous life, had to have new forms of art, philosophy, social habits, language." Gramsci believed, with the Futurists, that Italy needed to take a great leap forward into the mechanized world of the twentieth century.[44]

The Futurists acclaimed Mussolini's coup as the destruction of the bourgeois values they were fighting. "Destroy, destroy, in order to rebuild consciousness and opinion, culture, and the genesis of art," wrote the painter and sculptor Enrico Prampolini, one of the most prominent Futurists.[45]

The Italian art historian Umbro Apollonio sees in the Futurist movement the origins of the twentieth-century avant-garde. He pointed out:

> They threw off the shackles of the nineteenth century in order to exploit the resources of the imagination. Relations with the Cubists, with Delaunay, Villon, and Duchamps, with Larionov, Goncharova, Tatlin, and Malevich, with Wyndham Lewis and Nevinson; with Stella, the German Expressionists and Dada, all came through their mediation. On the level of ideas, interactions were even more widespread and involved many other collaborators. As result, the new movement spread from painting and sculpture to poetry, theater, architecture, stage design, music, ballet, photography, the cinema, topography, furnishing, and fashion.[46]

The Futurist desire to penetrate all aspects of life and their enchantment with movement evoked in them a passionate interest in film. In 1916, Marinetti and his group wrote their first "Manifesto on Futurist Film," in which they called the cinema an "eminently Futurist art and the most expressively adaptable to the complex sensibility of a Futurist artist." "Except for interesting films of travel, hunting, wars, and so on," their manifesto continued,

> filmmakers have done no more than inflict on us the most backward looking dramas, great and small. The same scenario, whose brevity and variety may make it seem advanced, is, in most cases, nothing but the tritest and most pious analysis. Therefore, all the immense artistic possibilities in the cinema still rest entirely in the future. . . . The cinema is an autonomous art. It must therefore never copy the stage. The cinema, being essentially visual, must above all fulfill the evolution of the painting.[47]

Many articles by Futurists concern themselves with different aspects of cinema, especially with the possibilities of movement and montage. The painter Anton Giulo Bragaglia analyzed the perspectives of movement in his "Futurist Photodynamism" (1911), and the sculptor Giacomo Balla tried to set rules for "movementism" in his "Cane al guinzaglio" (1912) (Dog on the Leash). The "Technical Manifesto on Futurist Painting" (1912) stated, among other things: "Everything is moving, everything is running. Before our eyes, a figure is never motionless; it appears and disappears continuously."[48] The echo of these and other articles and their practical results can be found, for example, in painter and experimental photographer Laszlo Moholy-Nagy's theory on the relationship between shapes in movement and controlled light, in the sculptures by Archipenko and Picasso. The Futurist theory of a "montage of objects and concepts" was even more influential (Dada collages by Jean Arp, Max Ernst, Kurt Schwitters, etc.). The Futurists proclaimed the necessity of a "montage of words" in poetry, objects in sculpture, different materials in collage, pieces of film in a movie, considering the "analogy of an analogy" as the genuine resource of montage.

Marinetti, the leader of the Futurist movement, wrote in 1912: "In order to develop and capture the most passing and imperceptible elements of a substance, we must form tight nets of analogies and images. . . . Cinematography presents us with a dancing object that divides and recomposes itself without the intervention of a human being."[49]

The Futurists made several films. "The abstract film is an Italian invention," wrote Marinetti in the magazine *L'Impero* (December 1, 1926), an extreme rightwing journal influential in its time both in Italy and abroad.[50] *Perfido Incanto* (Treacherous Enchantment, 1916), directed by Anton Giulio Bragaglia (1890–1960) with Enrico Prampolini as its art designer, was the most important Futurist film. Considered as a forerunner to *The Cabinet of Dr. Caligari* (whose art designers, Hermann Warm, Walter Reimann, and Walter Röhrig, drew inspiration from the Futurist statement about film as "living paintings" and employed comparable lighting effects), *Treacherous Enchantment* also adopted some ideas from the theatrical ventures of Erwin Piscator and Vsevolod Meyerhold.

The father of Dadaism, Hans Richter, one of the most important creators of experimental films, confirmed Marinetti's assertion about Futurism's primacy. Summing up the cinematic avant-garde of the twenties and the parallel movement in the fine arts (Expressionism, Cubism, Futurism, and Dadaism), Richter placed Italy at the top of the eleven European countries with an active avant-garde. According to Richter, thanks to Futurist films, Italy had a primacy in the field of experimental films.[51]

After *Treacherous Enchantment* or the "drama about modern magic," Bragaglia shot *Thaïs* (1916) and *Il mio cadavere* (My Dead Body, 1916). The latter was a horror story based on the emotional impact of settings, which still more than *Treacherous Enchantment* deserves mention as *Caligari's* forerunner.

The Futurists regarded film as a synthesis of all the arts, as much as Ricciotto Canudo, the first Italian film theoretician, did. In "Futurist Cinema" they wrote: "Painting + sculpture + plastic dynamism + words in freedom + composed noises + architecture + synthetic theater = Futurist film. This is how we decompose and recompose the universe according to our marvelous whims, to centuple the powers of the Italian creative genius and its absolute predominance in the world."[52]

In 1916, Arnaldo Gina financed and shot a 3,000-foot-long film *Vita futurista* (Futurist Life) with Marinetti and other Futurists appearing as actors. It transposed on the screen the Futurist predilection for the authentic, the concrete, and the immediate impact of image. *Futurist Life* was comprised of nine sequences rejecting all plot and capturing "real life," as the Futurists understood it. Prominent among them is the first episode, which features an old man sitting in a restaurant. A group of Futurists criticize his way of eating and attack him as a symbol of outdated bourgeois patterns. It was mainly these images, reflecting a distaste for old moral values as well as for plot-oriented cinema, that led Zavattini to regard Futurism as one of the precursors of neorealism.

GABRIELE D'ANNUNZIO AND THE "FEMME FATALE"

The Futurists were not the only important artists who followed the fascist movement. Gabriele D'Annunzio also joined the so-called fascist revolution and eventually ended his life (1938) as Mussolini's clown. From the very beginning, D'Annunzio was attracted to the film medium, but he never really exploited its possibilities. The literary and cultural forms of his work, though, along with its moral codes, left deep imprints on the entire prewar Italian film production.

As early as 1911, D'Annunzio sold the film rights to six of his novels and plays, all of which were turned into mediocre films. In 1921, his son Gabriellino (1890–1945), who spent his life trying to establish himself as an actor or film director, transcribed for the screen his father's most famous tragedy *La nave* (The Ship), a tale of the founding of the city of Venice. Gabriellino succeeded in capturing the unique claustrophobic atmosphere of the D'Annunziesque "kingdom of elitistic morality" ruled over by many codes of honor. D'Annunzio's misogyny permeates the whole story, showing its heroine, Basiliola, as a "fierce and untamable female beast," who uses her beauty to destroy the work of noble men. At the end, she provokes a fatal duel between two brothers, both of whom love her. Venice is founded in spite of everything, and Basiliola, "the woman who could love no one," perishes in the flames.[53]

D'Annunzio loved to make women suffer and saw in them the main reason for man's despair. At the same time, he could not live without them. He always had several mistresses, possibly the only people to give him the unconditional admiration he so desperately craved. It was eventually his pathological need for applause that brought him into the ranks of the fascist movement.

D'Annunzio's *oeuvre* brings to a climax the ancient Italian predilection for stories expressing violent passions. Many of them revolve around the "femme fatale," the most prominent figure in Italian movies of all times. The Italian "femme fatale" differs strongly from her European and American counterpart. By making men suffer, she suffers more than they do, and she is the one who dies at the end of most of these films. As the product of a matriarchal society, impressed with a strong psychic image of the Virgin Mary, she is not a vamp, the luscious beast of the German and American films, but the sufferer (la dolente).

In *La serpe* (The Serpent, 1920), the heroine (Francesca Bertini) is literally torn apart by her passion. She wants to kill her lover, a musician (another stock figure of Italian movies), in order to avenge her father's death. She kills herself at the end, though, confessing her great love to him. Anticipating the metaphoric montage, the scenes are intercut with shots of a serpent devouring a white mouse. Nino Frank writes:

Woman upon a pedestal, woman the bringer of dreams and the breaker of hearts, woman the cause of men's ruin and her own, the femme fatale—the Italians were the first to make a series of steps in characterization, giving the final product an original form. In so doing, they blurred the frontiers between fiction and reality, and created the mythological figure "the star."[54]

Ma l' amor mio non muore (But My Love Will Never Die, 1913), starring Lyda Borelli (along with Bertini, the most famous Italian diva of the time), was a picture that inspired a whole school of filmmaking. The title became a plot-setting epigram for a whole genre where everything goes wrong except love: love survives all adversities, including death. As a popular Italian song puts it:

Guardando le rose	Looking at roses
fiorite stamani	blossoming this morning
io penso: domani	I think tomorrow
saranno appassite . . .	they will fade . . .
E come le rose	Alike the roses
son tutte le cose	are all things
che durano un giorno, a poi più . . .	which last one day and never more . . .
Ma l'amore no.	Except love.

La serpe

A woman had to go through much distress to deserve this kind of love. Together with theater and literature, film taught her to suffer because this was considered the best way for a woman to live (to suffer was something to be proud of). In accordance with the behavioral code of Italian society, a woman was told that by suffering she would not become equal to men (who suffer too but differently) but that she would be better than women who did not suffer. On the other hand, by making men suffer, Italian film heroines offered to Italian women some compensation for the subordinate status they held.

An example of a "great sufferer," bearing many resemblances to the Virgin Mary, was Myrian, protagonist of *Il fauno di marmo* (The Marble Faun, 1920), loosely based on Nathaniel Hawthorne's novel. Myrian saw her husband murdered, was rejected by her lover, went through a series of tragedies, and found consolation only in religion. Even when her lover was imprisoned, she kept her composure, behaving as a model to follow. In the last scene, we see her majestic figure leaving for an unknown destination, alone, abandoned, but stronger and more beautiful than ever.

WHITE TELEPHONES

The colors of the films made under fascism were "pink" and "black." The pink productions—sentimental comedies and romantic melodramas—far outnumbered the black "truly" fascist films. Of the approximately eighty films produced yearly in the late thirties, some ten openly propagandized fascism.[55] The huge pink productions were nicknamed "white telephone" films and had many operatic features.[56] They tried to convey strong emotions without intending to have much in common with life. The origins of the "white telephones" go back to Cecil B. De-Mille films, which were considered as models of elegant productions with luxurious settings and impeccably attired characters. DeMille's *Male and Female*, made in 1919, contains all the classical ingredients of high society comedy, including the relationship of masters and servants and servants and masters, typical conventions of the later "white telephones." A second source of the pink productions was the German film of the thirties, generally referred to as "the UFA film," which combined the style of the German drawing room comedy and operetta with glamorous Hollywood comedy. The third ingredient that influenced the Italian "white telephones" was the old Austro-Hungarian "Budapest style" light genres.

The advent of sound changed the Italian film industry. Annual production fell from 150 fiction films produced in the twenties to less than ten. The mythological genre totally disappeared during the economic crisis. In the thirties, mammoth historical films were produced only sporadically and cast in a new form. Their naïveté was gone, and their good guys became fervent partisans of fascism defending the ideals of the Roman Empire both at home and in the colonies (*Scipione l'Africano*). The costume film turned into a passionate bearer of nationalistic intolerance (*Condottieri*).

Together with the good Glaucos and bad Nerones, the athletic-acrobatic genre disappeared with its sporting heroes Ajax, Samson, and the famous giant, Maciste, first seen in *Cabiria* as early as in 1914. Fascism, fond of vigorous and muscular bodies, did everything to save him. In *Il gigante delle Dolomiti* (The Dolomite Giant) shot by Guido Brignone (1887–1957) in 1926, Maciste, defending the moral values of the present society, bore a striking resemblance to Mussolini's storm troops, the "Black Shirts."

Neapolitan production came to a halt too, a victim of the financial crisis and of Mussolini's efforts toward linguistic unification. Its few remnants were found in some of the pink productions where they degenerated into poorly made musical films: *Napoli che canta* (Singing Naples, 1930), *Napoli verde-blu* (Naples in Green and Blue, 1935), *Napoli d'altri tempi* (Naples of the Old Days, 1938), and *Napoli che non muore* (Naples Will Never Die, 1939).[57]

The official fascist attitudes were virile, chaste, revolutionary, and celebrative. Gone were the days of the striptease in *The Last Days of Pompeii.* Nude breasts were covered, and all suicides became accidents, even in the newspapers. Femmes fatales became bad creatures, and purification through love was reserved for women with a strong moral sense, who would always forsake the husband to his legal wife and children. Isa Miranda, the diva of the thirties, a perfect femme fatale, and a dignified successor to Francesca Bertini, played roles of heroic Italian women (*Passaporto rosso* [Red Passport], 1935). The only time she could commit suicide and behave like a real D'Annunziesque female beast in a film set in fascist Italy was in *La signora di tutti* (Everybody's Lady) made in 1934 by a foreigner, Max Ophüls. It was her best part, and the film stands clearly above the standard production that surrounded it.[58]

The actresses of the corporate film were stylized as models of joyful girls with healthy minds and healthy bodies, the prevailing female role in the Italian comedy production of the time. This became the only genre that remained indestructible. Its patterns were enriched by Hollywood and Berlin, and especially with elements from "la rivista" (variety theater or cabaret), which in the 1930s became an important part of the Italian stage and life.

Comedy did not negate the relationship between film and reality. It expressed it through comic sentimentality, which made all dramatic harshness disappear. All details of the plot paid tribute to common sense, the guarantee of an orderly and quiet life. Timid young men, impertinent but naïve girls, and surly yet loving fathers populated this world where love reigned as long as the limits of decency were not transgressed. The mirror Italy faced reflected her burning need for a beautiful reality.

Some of the best comedies were written by Cesare Zavattini (b. 1902), one of the most active scriptwriters of the fascist period, who at that time was deeply influenced by Frank Capra. He was a steady collaborator with some of the experts of comedy, especially Mario Camerini, for whom he wrote the story for *Darò un milione* (I'll Give a Million) in 1935,[59] and Camillo Mastrocinque (1901–1969), who directed Zavattini's script *Bionda sottochiave* (The Locked In Blond, 1939). Second to Zavattini was Luigi Zampa (b. 1905), another great admirer of Hollywood comedy. Zampa entered filmmaking as one of the first graduates of the Centro Sperimentale di Cinematografia. In 1939, he wrote the script for *Mille lire al mese* (A Thousand Lire a Month) directed by Max Neufeld (b. 1887) and often mentioned as a typical "white telephone" film and comedy of errors. The same year, Zampa worked with Mario Soldati on *Dora Nelson*, centering again on the interchangeability of two couples, and in 1940 he wrote *La danza dei milioni* (The Dance of Millions) for Camillo Mastrocinque, a tale based on double identity. Zampa made his directorial debut in 1940 with a crazy comedy *L'attore scomparso* (An Actor Disappears), one of the "first Italian suspense films with a satirical and comical background."[60] This genre remained Zampa's favorite during his long career, briefly interrupted by his neorealist experience.

ALESSANDRO BLASETTI

No matter what point of view we adopt toward the productions of 1930–1942, the most important personality to emerge is Alessandro Blasetti (b. 1900). He was the only significant Italian director who continued to attract the interest of critics after World War II, and he remained one of the leading figures of the film scene until the mid-sixties. In a way, Blasetti is a man of genius.[61] This truly prolific and eclectic director shot the best film of the thirties, *1860* (1934), which the future generation of neorealists viewed over and over again in the small screening room of the Centro Sperimentale. The film is an attempt to portray Garibaldi's " Expedition of the 1,000" (*ll mille di Garibaldi*) from the point of view of the ordinary Sicilians. Its protagonist, a Sicilian peasant, travels north to Genoa to serve as an intermediary between Garibaldi and the Sicilian insurrection. During his travels he meets different kinds of people: aristocrats, intellectuals, priests, and businessmen. Eventually he joins Garibaldi's expedition and takes part in the victorious battle at Calatafimi.

1860 is remarkable for its use of Sicilian locations and nonprofessional actors. As in the neorealist films, the script was conceived for nonactors, with short condensed lines, and long silences between the dialogues. The contrasting structure between the sequences showing Sicilian peasants—especially the scenes between the two lovers—and those in which politicians decide on the peasants' future creates an atmosphere of interlaced physical and social realities.

The film culminates with scenes of the battle at Calatafimi, shot with extremely mobile subjective cameras overlooking the tragically beautiful Sicilian landscape. (One camera was placed on a hill, giving the perspective of the heroine as she looks at the battlefield; another was placed in the middle of the action, eventually following the heroine searching for her husband among the dead bodies, etc.) Most of the final sequence is composed of depth-of-field shots with parallel action scenes and extensive cross-cutting.

Blasetti was very successful in his choice of faces (typage), which seem to overflow in his images. A figure is seldom alone but always a part of the landscape (there are hardly any close-ups). Faces of Sicilian women clad in black often appear against the white backdrop of the countryside, foreshadowing the images of the neorealist films set in Sicily (e.g., *The Path of Hope*, *La terra trema*).

The editing of the battlefield sequences reveals the influence of the Soviet cinema of the thirties. It consists mostly of short shots linked with rapid movement.

These brief images (jumping horses, falling soldiers, raised arms with guns, shouting officers, etc.) have a spellbinding effect on the viewer, allowing the filmmaker to lead him in any ideological direction he chose.

The general outline of *1860* is in keeping with fascist mythology. Individual scenes, and even shots, are carefully composed to illustrate one or another of the axioms of the political and moral philosophy of the time. The ultimate mythological apotheosis has Mussolini being a direct heir to Garibaldi. Blasetti stresses Garibaldi's contributions to the unification of Italy, leaving aside his fight against the Papacy.[62] The film ends with a vision of the Foro Mussolini in Rome, where soldiers in fascist uniforms parade among the ranks of the Garibaldian veterans.[63] Such incongruous images of the victories to come were often used in costume films as a protection against possible official criticism. In the case of *1860*, indignation of the authorities might have been aroused by the film's appeal for freedom and its depiction of the spontaneous revolt of the Sicilian peasants. According to film director Carlo Lizzani, such thematic submotivation was the intention of Blasetti. Lizzani wrote: "The more seriously he took fascism, the further his generous temperament led him from the paths of conformism."[64] However, Emilio Cecchi, who put the finishing touches on the final version of the script, was probably responsible for the nonconformist overtones of the film.

1860

1860 was produced by the short-lived, semiprivate company, Cines. This company, subsidized by the state, was headed by Emilio Cecchi, the most important literary critic of the time, a well-read and much-traveled person, "one of the first-born sons of modern Italy," as Jakob Burckhardt might have put it. In 1933, Cecchi asked Luigi Pirandello to write a film treatment and invited Walter Ruttmann, the famous German director, to direct it (*Acciaio* [Steel, 1933]). In 1934, Cecchi co-scripted *1860*, which was another of his efforts to revitalize the film industry by filming realistically treated historical themes based on literary sources. Blasetti shared Cecchi's opinions, insisting always on the "Italianity" of the subject matter, which was also one of Mussolini's pet concerns.

Mussolini loved film and loved to make critical judgments. He was especially fond of Blasetti's first film, *Sole* (Sun, 1929), which he called "the dawn of the fascist film." It is a typical Italian paradox that the subject for *Sun*, a crude peasant drama, was provided by Aldo Vergano (1891–1957), one of the true antifascists of the time. *Sun* was enthusiastically received by critics as an attempt at joining the world's film avant-garde. In *Vita Cinematografica* (Rome, June 23, 1929) and *L'Italia Letteraria*, it was compared to Dreyer's *The Passion of Joan of Arc*. At the same time, the press praised its Italian-ness and its emphasis on love for the Italian soil. Only the very fascist *L'Impero* (to whose staff Blasetti had once belonged) did not like the story, noting that it "was unfortunately written by a certain Aldo Vergano, whose mentality still reveals certain democratic vices."[65]

Blasetti was always a good public relations man. He knew not only when to shoot a particular subject but also with whom to do so. He was the only director of the "old guard" in whom the critics did not lose interest after the appearance of neorealism.

Blasetti's technique is the antithesis of any theory that stresses the director's responsibility for the final outcome of the film. His collaborators, especially the scriptwriters, cameramen, and art designers, were often almost as important as the director himself. Among them we find names that became well known during the neorealist period, thus establishing a certain continuity between the fascist period films and those of the postwar era.

The neorealists did not start from scratch, as the myth would have it. The preceding period laid a good foundation for them, preparing highly qualified artistic teams. In 1945, well-trained directors, scriptwriters and technicians simply picked up the thread that had been interrupted by the events of 1943–1944. In the thirties, thanks to state subsidies, the material conditions for an artistic renaissance had been created. Only one more thing was needed for the full upsurge of "the most efficient weapon": freedom.

Blasetti was one of the first Italian directors to introduce the system of collective scriptwriting, which has become a mainstay of Italian production. For example, one of Blasetti's best films, *The Table of the Poor* was scripted by Raffaele Viviani, the author of the original literary work (a popular Neapolitan comedy), in collaboration with Emilio Cecchi, Alessandro De Stefani, Blasetti, and Mario Soldati (who had just returned from a two-year stay in the United States and was one of Blasetti's best recruitments). Subsequently, teams of scriptwriters (quasi-workshops) came into being. One such group centered around Cesare Zavattini, another around Mario Soldati and Mario Camerini, a third around Ennio Flaiano, etc. This praxis continued after the war, sometimes involving the same people.

In 1937, Blasetti gathered a group of extraordinary collaborators to make a comedy Italian style, *La contessa di Parma* (The Countess of Parma). His assistant was Mario Soldati; his scriptwriters included the playwright Aldo De Benedetti and Libero Solaroli, a brilliant executive producer and film economist. The cinematographer was Otello Martelli, and the score was composed by Giovanni Fusco, one of the prodigies of Italian film music. In the hands of these people, a very conventional subject was shaped into a likable film, which communicates Blasetti's evident enjoyment of picturesque detail.

Blasetti worked often with Otello Martelli, who photographed some of the best neorealist films (*Paisan, Tragic Hunt*, etc.). There were many extraordinary cinematographers in Italy in the 1930s who continued their work after 1945. For example, their dean, Ubaldo Arata, one of the busiest technicians during the fascist era, photographed *Pilot Luciano Serra* in 1937 and *Open City* in 1944. One of the most talented cameramen was Aldo Tonti: in 1939, he shot *Abuna Messias*, in which Goffredo Alessandrini presented an apologetic picture of Mussolini's Ethiopian war; later he shot *Ossessione* with Visconti and *The Sun Rises Again* with Vergano. Also important were Anchise Brizzi (the cinematographer of *The White Squadron* and De Sica's *Shoeshine*); Carlo Montuori (who worked with the Austrian director Luis Trenker on *Condottieri* in 1937 and, after the war, on *Bicycle Thief*); and others.

The center of Blasetti's work lay in mythological films and films with an openly profascist tendency. In the years 1938–1941, he shot a generally overvalued costume tetralogy, which represents a transition between his fascist films and his work after 1942. It consists of *Ettore Fieramosca* (1938), still imbued with the fascist ideology; *Un'avventura di Salvator Rosa* (Salvator Rosa's Adventure, 1940); *La cena delle beffe* (The Jesters' Banquet, 1940); and *La corona di ferro* (The Iron Crown, 1941). A newcomer who was soon to become a well-known director, Renato Castellani (b. 1913), was Blasetti's assistant on *Salvator Rosa* and his scriptwriter for the next two films. The films were edited by Mario Serandrei, who for thirty-five years (he died in 1966) was the most active editor the Italian film industry has ever had.

The most important film of Blasetti's tetralogy is *The Iron Crown*, a pseudohistorical fantasy based on a naïve plot (concocted by Blasetti and Castellani), which tried unsuccessfully to create a kind of Italian saga in the style of the *Nibelungenlied*. Blasetti, the true eclectic, mixed in everything he could think of, including Ariosto and the Grimm brothers, while his directing drew heavily on early Fritz Lang. The film's main interest lies in the visual impact of its meticulous decor. Likewise, *The Jesters' Banquet*, a rather tedious story set in Renaissance Florence, placed a primary interest on its settings and costumes, which were designed by one of the best Italian craftsmen, Virgilio Marchi (who worked with Rossellini and De Sica after the war). Both films offer some of the worst examples of Italian film acting. As the Italians say about their actors: "They do not talk, they sing."

Immediately after the completion of his masterpiece *1860*, Blasetti produced
Vecchia guardia (The Old Guard, 1934), the film which became a symbol of Mussolini's reign. Already in *Terra madre* (Mother Earth, 1930) Blasetti had become a
spokesman for fascist nationalism and its myth of the "native soil." "This land is
mine and will remain mine," says the count after returning to his native village. The
film concludes with images of a joyful future when there will be tractors and dancing everywhere. *Mother Earth* has some strong visual moments, full of lyricism and
pictorial impact, evidently influenced by the Soviet cinema. On the other hand, this
awkward paraphrase of the Nazi slogan "Blut und Boden" (blood and soil) is an
ideological forerunner of the post-World War II Soviet cinematic fairy tales about
happy people in a happy country.

In *The Old Guard*, Blasetti put his political commitment to work in a straightforward exaltation of "squadrism" (storm-trooper attitudes) in a small town preceding the 1922 march on Rome. The story, a western-style conflict between good
guys and bad guys, depicts the rivalry between a group of innocent and brave
fascists and a bunch of mean and cowardly "Reds." In the closing scenes, the "Reds"
kill the youngest of the fascist group, thus making him a martyr. Suddenly, the
whole town joins the fascists, with people bringing flowers to the boy's family,
while the camera tracks around his room showing his books, pictures, and gadgets.
Mario's place does not remain empty. His father joins the march on Rome, and the
viewers can be sure that he will avenge his son's death. *The Old Guard* was photographed by Otello Martelli and acclaimed by the press.[66]

Vecchia guardia

Cinematically, it is a poorly made film. Its language is unimaginative, but Blasetti was again successful, this time ironically, in casting his protagonists. They are prototypes of human vulgarity, which their smiling faces cannot hide. The "Reds" are caricatures, but the fascists are true to life, illustrating well Gramsci's characterization of fascism written in 1924: "The characteristic fact of fascism consists in having succeeded in constituting a mass organization of petty bourgeoisie. This is the first time in history that this had occurred."[67] Gramsci compared the fascist petty bourgeois to the "bandar-logs" and the "ruthless and destructive monkeys" in Kipling's *Jungle Book*.

The Old Guard became one of Hitler's favorite films. It was provided with a stormy German commentary and was shown all over Germany. Blasetti was invited to Berlin and congratulated by Hitler personally.

TRULY FASCIST FILMS

The Old Guard had some forerunners. During the months following the march on Rome, the first truly fascist film was made, *Il grido dell' aquila* (the Eagle's Cry, 1923). Its director, Mario Volpe, was one of the marginal figures of the local cinema production. (His later career led him to France and Egypt where he shot the first Egyptian sound film.) *The Eagle's Cry* is an unbelieveably naïve but quite impressive story concocted by people who probably truly believed in the fascist cause. Made with modest means by a small company, it is more persuasive than *The Old Guard* (with its unlimited budget provided by the state). The straightforward story centers on the unity between the veterans of the Garibaldi war, the victims of World War I (the role of the blind lieutenant is played by Gustavo Serena, director of *Assunta Spina*), and the new fascist generation. The "Reds" are shown as a bunch of bad guys, who, by organizing strikes, disrupt the possibility of a happy coexistence between the workers and the owners of the factory. The final sequence of *The Eagle's Cry* symbolizes the indestructibility of the fascist "revolution." A small boy waves the fascist flag in an empty square. The camera approaches, men come marching along, and the boy disappears in the middle of an endless crowd in black shirts. People come into the frame from all sides, creating the impression of an entire nation in movement and of imminent victory. There is just one outcry: "Roma o morte!" (Rome or death!).[68]

To celebrate the tenth anniversary of the fascist takeover, the Institute LUCE produced *Camicia nera* (Black Shirt, 1933). Directed by a second-rate playwright, Giovacchino Forzano, it retraces the events in Italy from 1914 to 1932 as seen through the eyes of a peasant family. The film critic from Rome's *Messaggero* spoke about its "Italian-ness," the "blood of the native land," and was particularly enthusiastic about a scene, which, in retrospect, is considered one of the most unintentionally comic scenes of Italian cinema: a blacksmith, who was wounded in World War I and lost his memory, finds himself in a German hospital where the staff tries to find out his nationality. When the doctor projects on a screen a bulletin announcing the Italian victory, he jumps to his feet, shouts "Italia!" and passes out.[69]

Many of the "black" films, as fascist films are sometimes called, dealt with

Mussolini's colonial politics, looking for valid reasons for the Italian presence in Albania and Africa. *Squadrone bianco* (The White Squadron, 1936) is the most significant among them, developing another cherished theme of the fascist cinema, spiritual and moral rebirth through love for the fatherland. Here the rebirth takes place in Tripoli, where a lieutenant fighting the African rebels forgets his unhappy love and becomes a tough and hardened soldier. Directed by the Italian "man for all seasons" Augusto Genina (1892–1957), it contains all the elements of an impressive tear-jerker, set against the backdrop of romanticized soldiering in Africa. In 1940, Genina made his best film, *L'assedio del Alcazar* (The Siege of Alcazar), centering on a Spanish fascist colonel and his defense of the fortress at Toledo until the arrival of Franco's troops. Michelangelo Antonioni wrote in his review of the picture: "A robust film, not at all sophisticated, with its roots solidly planted in recent history. . . . Genina did not neglect the civil aspect of the story. What is happening inside Alcazar is a kind of a life in a small town, with people being born and dying (that happens more often) and with their love stories."[70]

While film apologies for the annexation of Albania were rather sporadic (*Il Cavaliere di Kruja* [The Cavalier from Kruja] directed by Carlo Campogalliani and coscripted by Aldo Vergano), African stories abounded. The government had to find more reasons for its occupation of the African territory than that of Albania, which had more public support. In 1936, an ambitious crew left for Africa in search of justification for the African war. The group was led by the director Mario Camerini (1895–1981), the scriptwriters Mario Soldati and Libero Solaroli, and joined on the set by director Renato Castellani, who was then serving in Africa and was made available to the film production. Their *Il grande appello* (The Great Call), set during the Ethiopian war, is a romantic drama centered around the theme of personal sacrifices for the Italian cause. When the son repudiates his father's collaboration with the enemy, the father, conscience-stricken, gives his life for Italy's victory. "The direction is great," wrote the daily *Corriere della Sera* on November 27, 1936, and it was not entirely wrong.

A similar subject was treated in *Pilot Luciano Serra*, directed by Goffredo Alessandrini, coscripted by Roberto Rossellini (1907–1977), and supervised by Vittorio Mussolini. Here the father dies in a plane crash while returning home after a long period abroad in order to join the Italian army at the moment of war. His son goes to Africa as a volunteer, makes a forced landing on the enemy's territory, but manages, though fatally wounded, to bring the plane back to his unit.

Many of these films were heavily inspired by American westerns. The bad Africans took the place of redskins, and brave Italians replaced the white heroes. Vittorio Mussolini was known as a great admirer of Hollywood.

The omnipresent Carmine Gallone shot his *Scipione l'Africano* (1937) in the tradition of the 1920s mythological films. With a cast of thousands, photographed by Ubaldo Arata, and portraying the Roman struggle against the African leader Hannibal, this was a truly spectacular Italian production, clad in heavy-handed fascist ideology. Gallone's Scipio, the Roman conqueror of Africa in the third century B.C., paraphrases Mussolini's famous proclamation: "What I once acquired in war, I will never let go!"

MARIO CAMERINI AND THE CALLIGRAPHERS

Mario Camerini was the second prominent director of the fascist era. After 1945, unlike the more versatile Blasetti, however, he lost his admirers among the critics as well as audiences. Referred to as "the confessor of the middle class" and as a "director of nostalgia," Camerini was known mainly for his "white telephone" comedies made with a dash of melancholy and a considerable cinematic talent. They were skillful entertainments aimed at immediate popular success and imitative of Hollywood productions. The satirical hints, pointed at the wealthy middle class, were in keeping with the requirements of the times. The shy revolts of their protagonists always ended with a timely and happy acceptance of daily life. Camerini's comedies, with Vittorio De Sica as their protagonist, belong to the best of this genre produced during the thirties: *Gli uomini, che mascalzoni!* (What Rascals Men Are, 1932), *Il Signor Max* (1937), *I'll Give a Million* (1935), *Grandi Magazzini* (Department Stores, 1939), etc.

In the late thirties and early forties, Camerini belonged to the so-called "Calligraphers," a label coined by Giuseppe De Santis in one of his journalistic attacks against the "bello scrivere" (beautiful writing) in cinema. Calligraphism denoted certain formalist preoccupations linked with the retreat to the past and resulting in films with a meticulously reconstructed decor and "beautiful" photography. The Calligraphers hoped to derive an original cinematographic style from literature (especially that of the nineteenth century), which led to essentially decorative results.

The calligraphic trend was started by Camerini's films in the mid-thirties. In 1934, he made *Come le foglie* (As Do the Leaves), an adaptation of a sentimental drama by Giuseppe Giacosa, which was a theatrical success in 1900.[71] Its images of the sadness of life and love, crowned by a halo of faith in mankind, fitted perfectly into the "Camerini line" with its "little man's" philosophy of survival. Camerini's next film, *Il cappello a tre punte* (The Three-Cornered Hat, 1935), based on the Spanish novel by Pedro de Alarcón, re-created the period of the Spanish occupation of Naples. (The film encountered the problems with the censors, and Camerini had to cut a few scenes showing the discontent of the Neapolitan people.)

Formalist tendencies already prevailed in Camerini's first film *Rotaie* (Rails, 1929) shot silent and later synchronized. This ambitious work draws heavily on the experiments of the world's avant-garde, notably German Expressionism. *Rails* emerges in a sense as an anthology of cinematic expression in the silent era by indulging in long takes of rails running, in interplays of light and shadow and in a parallel rhythmical montage that creates an intensely emotional mood. The opening scenes of Marcel Carné's *Hôtel du Nord* (1938) bear a striking resemblance to the beginning of *Rails:* the stifling atmosphere of a sleazy hotel room is evoked through the symbolic montage while the photography subverts reality by capturing the loneliness and fears of a young couple (emphasized by lights and sounds coming from outside).

The significance of *Rails* for Italian cinema parallels Blasetti's *Sun*. In a country where the avant-garde disappeared in the early twenties and experiments were limited to a very few, these two films, together with Walter Ruttmann's *Steel*, rep-

Il Signor Max

resented the only noteworthy attempts at something different from the current production of the late twenties.

The Calligraphers' endeavor in the early forties has to be appreciated for their efforts to escape the dead end of the sterile fascist film industry. The sensuously chiseled atmosphere of the calligraphist production, its psychological realism, and its stylistic precision brought to mind certain aspects of D'Annunzio's writings, which were contradictory to the ideas the young generation of critics had in mind for the Italian cinema. The Calligraphers, appreciated by the "official" critics and generally well accepted by film historians, saw most of their films torn to pieces by the "Cinema group," which was becoming increasingly influential. In discussing Renato Castellani's first film, an ambitious and visually impressive *Un colpo di pistola* (The Pistol Shot, 1942), De Santis wrote: "It is probably the saddest and most desolate flirtation we have ever witnessed. A flirtation of somebody with a cold, rarified experience and without any emotional resources: somebody who is left alone with his troublesome uselessness, who possesses just a meager talent of a beautiful calligraphy, the only human activity he felt like choosing among so many others."[72]

In the constrictive atmosphere of Mussolini's pink and black productions, the formalist cultivations of the Calligraphers were probably the only innovative experiments the censorship board would tolerate. But even these attempts remained tame and eclectic and without any great formal discoveries. Their visual style was derivative, and their main interest focused on the creation of atmosphere.

Calligraphism was primarily an attempt to isolate cinema from politics through an escape into the past, into literature, and into formal beauty. It was analogous to the hermetic trend in the poetry of the time represented by Salvatore Quasimodo, Eugenio Montale, and Alfonso Gatto. Their poems worshipped isolation and moral integrity and refused contact with the fascist reality.[73] Similarly, the Calligraphers approached their work without any reference to the prevailing social and cultural conventions.

CENTRO SPERIMENTALE AND THE CALLIGRAPHERS

The formalist trend reached its peak in the late thirties and early forties when a group of critics, primarily from the Centro Sperimentale, hoped to revive picture-book aesthetics in film production by shifting attention from content to form. In 1938, the year his anthology *L'attore* was published, Umberto Barbaro directed his first and only film *L'ultima nemica* (The Last Enemy), coscripted by Francesco Pasinetti—a tearful story about the fight of a young physician against a fatal disease. The result was embarrassing. Barbaro and Pasinetti were respectable theoreticians and historians, but the film lacked any creative spark, the insipidity of its dialogue running counter to its attempts at visual dynamism.

In 1940, Amleto Palermi shot *La peccatrice* (The Sinner) in the studios of the Centro. *The Sinner* was scripted by Barbaro, Pasinetti, and Chiarini. Palermi, an experienced craftsman of the period, succeeded in transforming a maudlin story (a prostitute returns home with an illegitimate child and is forgiven by her mother) into an acceptable film, which was dealt with politely by the press. The truly Italian duo of a seduced, honest girl and a forgiving mother pleased Michelangelo Antonioni, who appreciated the internal force of the protagonist: "It is the first time in our cinema," he wrote, "that somebody tried to create a complex and purely cinematic character."[74]

The films directed by Luigi Chiarini (1900–1975) in 1942—*Via delle cinque Lune* (The Five Moon Street) and *La bella addormentata* (The Sleeping Beauty)—are often mentioned as classic examples of Calligraphism. Chiarini was among the most cultured and controversial personalities of the Italian film scene. He became the editor of the prewar journal *Bianco e Nero* and later, after the war, of *Rivista del Cinema Italiano*; he was the first director of the Centro, director of the Venice International Film Festival (1963–1968), and author of several outstanding books on film theory.[75] His closest collaborator during the first eight years at the Centro was Umberto Barbaro, the Marxist theoretician and a communist, who coscripted *The Five Moon Street* and *The Sleeping Beauty*.[76]

The films were flops. *The Five Moon Street* and *The Sleeping Beauty* were heavy-handed melodramas with crude naturalistic elements. The first was inspired by a nineteenth-century novel by Matilde Serao; the second adapted the theatrical play by Rosso di San Secondo. The naturalistic aspect revealed the influence Barbaro had on Chiarini and the importance these two personalities attributed to Italian veristic literature as a source of postwar film. *The Sleeping Beauty*, which takes place in a Sicilian village (again the story centers on a seduced and abandoned girl), was conceived as a challenge to the aesthetics of the "white telephone" films. The environment was selected in real-life settings with the intention of reviving authentic images of rural life. However, the rustic tragedy remains confined to the narrow range of provincial populism permeated with nineteenth-century fatalism, and the film is so beautifully photographed that it appears contrived.

FERDINANDO M. POGGIOLI

At the beginning of the 1940s, the use of authentic settings was becoming more frequent as a part of the general quest for "a style to be coined" (uno stile da fare). The feeling for a realistic atmosphere especially characterized the films of Ferdinando M. Poggioli (1897–1945), who might have become a significant contributor to postwar film evolution had it not been for his premature death. His *Addio, giovinezza* (Good-Bye, Youth, 1940) and *Gelosia* (Jealousy, 1942) use real-life settings to re-create the decor and the flagrance of the turn-of-the-century era.[77] Compared to some other films mentioned in film histories as forerunners of neorealism (Mario Soldati's *Little Old-Fashioned World* or Vittorio De Sica's *Teresa Venerdì*), Poggioli's work definitely was underestimated. His stories remained on the level of conventional melodramas, but his use of real-life settings and his direction of actors were remarkable.

Jealousy was based on a well-known veristic novel by the Sicilian writer Luigi Capuana (1835–1915), a keen student of female psychology.[78] *Jealousy* was the first Italian film to show a Sicily different from the mystical island as portrayed in films until then. A few months before the landing of the allied armies on the Sicilian beach of Gela, Mino Doletti wrote in his review of *Jealousy*: "Sicily is a profoundly enchanting, generous, virgin country with immediate sentiments, a burning sun, and a silence that resounds in the huge, boundless spaces of a country that still has a veiled face and walks with downcast eyes. . . . I think that Ferdinando Poggioli merits an A plus for the perfect setting of his drama."[79]

The most memorable scene in all of Poggioli's films is the Sunday ball in *Sissignora* (Yes, Ma'am, 1940). Poggioli captures a tangle of faces, fragments of conversation, details set against a meticulously described popular neighborhood, Genoa's porches, with laundry flying in the wind, the open-air markets, sunny slopes overgrown with basil, and the magnificent port. The script of *Yes, Ma'am*, centering around the character of a servant girl, was influenced by Emilio Cecchi, who, after leaving the company CINES in 1934, made occasional comebacks. Another member of the crew was Alberto Lattuada (b. 1914), Poggioli's assistant. It was his second assistantship; the first was on Soldati's *Piccolo mondo antico* (Little Old-Fashioned World, 1941).

MARIO SOLDATI

Little Old-Fashioned World became a legend and was considered by some as a direct forerunner of neorealism.[80] The critical reaction at the time, however, was split. On April 25, 1941, *Cinema* published two reviews, one by De Santis and the other by Gianni Puccini (1914–1968). While the film was hailed by De Santis,[81] Puccini compared *Little Old-Fashioned World* to William Wyler's filming of *Wuthering Heights* (which he called marvelously narrative and emotional) and referred to it as "illustrative." At the same time, he summed up Soldati's artistic profile: "If Soldati has appeared as an insecure narrator, he has revealed himself as a man of good taste."[82]

After forty years, *Little Old-Fashioned World* remains a cultured and well-made film, cool, distant, and full of intellectual arabesques. It recalls its literary model, a novel by Antonio Fogazzaro (of whom—like D'Annunzio—everybody in Italy today knows but no one reads). Its images of the habits and manners of nineteenth-century Lombardy, occupied by the Austrians, are the backdrop of a certain social world populated by withdrawn, suffering women, by heroic strong men, and by model children. The camera seeks out the most unusual angles, polishing the surfaces of all the shots. Thus, the discussion between Franco and Luisa about reconciling with Franco's mother (who disinherited him after their marriage) is shot through bars, which, even in a 1941 film, appears unbearably pretentious. On the other hand, the realistic settings are used with a sense for the needs of psychological naturalism, creating a balanced unity between the characters and their feelings (Luisa in mourning visiting the grave of her drowned daughter). The impact of authentic settings even saved the last scene, imbued with picture-book sentiments shown through conventional parallel montage. Franco, a born Italian winner (played by the popular romantic lead Massimo Serato), is off on another mission to liberate the country, leaving Luisa on shore; then cut to Franco on the ship singing a patriotic song, a shot of Luisa (Alida Valli) smiling for the first time after six years, a cut back to Franco seen among the other liberators, and then back to Luisa. Even this withdrawn woman, "closed in her pain" (so reads the intertitle), has been overcome by the all-Italian trust in victory.

After the success of *Little Old-Fashioned World*, Soldati shot two films in 1942, *Tragica notte* (Tragic Night), a gloomy rustic tragedy, and *Malombra,* an adaptation of another Fogazzaro novel with Isa Miranda in the role of the baroness Marina haunted by the vision of her dead aunt. This time, the critics were less patient. Antonio Pietrangeli wrote in *Si Gira*: "We have to acknowledge a certain progress Soldati made with respect to *Little Old-Fashioned World*. In particular, the use of the camera is more restricted and less theatrical."[83] In *Cinema*, De Santis hoped that "tomorrow he [Soldati] may give us works built on a solid basis. But he should forget the different decorative means that often form the basis of his language: written letters that fill the screen, windows that close on one season and open on another, trees and the sky that change their appearance in order to mark the passing of time."[84] Soldati continued to make one to three films a year until 1959. However, it is doubtful that De Santis's wishful thinking ever came true.

AMERICA: FIRST LOVE

In 1935, Mario Soldati published his book *America primo amore*, a kind of diary commenting on his two-year stay in the United States (the first year living on a fellow-

Malombra

ship from Columbia University, the second on menial jobs). His book is full of detailed observations of American life with much space given to a discussion of film. What takes place in the "accomplice obscurity of the screening room," Soldati wrote,

> does not basically differ from what is going on outside. . . . In America, violent and fatal passions, kidnappings, getaways, fires, lynching, crimes, suicides are not inventions of the Hollywood scenarists. They [the films] are not works of art. They are works of taste. Works that grow out of collective collaboration and craftsmanship. But they are made, made, made. One after another, there is no rest. One is a comedy, the other a tragedy. A kiss and a gun. A prayer and a chase.[85]

America First Love is a lucid portrait of an industry and a country seen with a mixture of irony and love.[86] It was one of the most important books of the so-called "American myth," which marked the Italian cultural scene of the thirties, referred to as the "decade of translations." One of its products was *Ossessione*, the film that came out of the 1940 encounter between Visconti and De Santis. To adapt an American novel in 1942, with pink and black production in full bloom, was a statement of faith. In addition, the subplot, which Visconti added to James Cain's story, belonged to a familiar theme in American literature and film: the story of a friendship between two men. Visconti put this relationship on a pedestal as something that reaches beyond the love shared between a man and a woman. Visconti's Gino and Spagnolo are brothers in the tradition of American male couples—Fitzgerald's Gatsby and Nick, Steinbeck's George and Lennie, Twain's Huck and Jim, and others. The resemblance between Cain's novel and Visconti's film is more important than usually admitted. Most often, film history books contain variations on the theory that the book was for Visconti just a pretext. The truth is more complex. The pretext theory neglects the spiritual bonds that existed at that time between American literature and Italian intellectuals.

The "American myth" had four expositors who translated thousands and thousands of pages of American literature into Italian, Cesare Pavese and Elio Vittorini on one hand and Emilio Cecchi and Mario Praz on the other. They represented two generations with different attitudes. The divergence between them was not mainly because of their age (Pavese and Vittorini were twenty years younger than Cecchi's generation) but in their different American experience. Pavese and Vittorini never set foot on American soil. Pavese's application for a fellowship to the United States was rejected in 1930, and he never reapplied or attempted to cross the ocean after the war, apparently afraid of being disillusioned. Vittorini only had an elementary school education and "learned" English by translation. Cecchi and Praz, on the other hand, were born into well-off middle-class families where knowledge of English was understood as part of a general cultural upbringing. They were both well traveled. Cecchi went to the United States twice, and his observations about the American way of life were ambiguous if not negative. The younger generation wanted to see just one side of the coin. They worshipped America without knowing it. Europe, even without fascism, did not seem to them capable of dealing with the problems arising before "the new man"; so they sought solutions in American literature. To them, the characters in the novels of Steinbeck, Caldwell, and especially Melville symbolized freedom and an antidote against fascist oppression.[87]

The American myth was always part of Italian life. A sublimated American dream, it was kept alive through the letters of more than 4 million immigrants who settled in the United States between 1880 and 1920.[88] The leftist intelligentsia, as Dominique Fernandez puts it, chose America "out of a sentimental solidarity with the poor immigrants from Sicily and Calabria, and as reaction against the fascist propaganda aimed against the New York Jewish plutocracy."[89] Giaime Pintor, the youngest among the writers of the new generation, wrote in 1942: "This America does not need a Columbus. She is discovered inside ourselves as a country toward which we look with the hope and confidence of the first immigrants and of everyone who has decided to defend human dignity at the cost of errors and fatigue."[90] Pavese himself summed up the feelings of his generation in his postwar review of Richard Wright's *Black Boy:*

[In the thirties] American culture became for us something very serious and precious, a sort of great laboratory where others were working, under different conditions of liberty and with different means, on the same task of creating a style, a modern world, as the best of our writers were—perhaps with less immediacy, but with the same stubborn will. And so, this culture seemed to us an ideal place for work and experiment, a strenuous and embattled experiment, rather than a mere Babel of clamorous efficiency, of cruel neon-light that stunned and blinded the naive—an image that even our provincial-minded rulers found of some use when they came across it in certain hypocritical novels. After several years of study, we comprehended that America was not another land, another historical beginning, but merely the gigantic theater, where, with more frankness than was possible elsewhere, the universal drama was being reenacted.[91]

The "myth" started in 1930 with Pavese's essay on Sinclair Lewis. Here, the theme of an escape from the drabness of daily life and the glorification of tramps appeared for the first time. Through his analysis of *Babbitt*, Pavese spelled out his own literary program, which had influenced the development of his writer-peers: the search for life in the provinces, the discovery of a national character, the superiority of the spoken language over the written one, the importance of dialect (slang), and the rupture with the existing literary rules. For him, the aim of literary creation was an objectivity attained through the prism of poetic synthesis. Edgar Lee Masters and Walt Whitman, the subject of his doctoral dissertation, helped Pavese to repudiate the influence of D'Annunzio, while Melville (who in Italy became an object of cult admiration) and Sherwood Anderson taught him how to replace Verga's naturalism with a multidimensional symbolism, a method that he passed on to Michelangelo Antonioni.

In the 1930s, Italy was flooded with American literature. There are few nations where American literature made such an impact on an entire generation. The harshness of Pintor's reaction to Cecchi's book *America amara* (1939) (Bitter America), calling it "a museum of horrors," testifies to the inviolability of the myth. The translations were done by some of the best writers, who during the thirties were not allowed to publish or preferred not to. The first translation of Hemingway[92] (*The Killers*) was by Alberto Moravia, whose first novel *Time of Indifference* (1929) was fiercely attacked by the fascist press. In the following years, Moravia translated Theodore Dreiser, Ring Lardner, James Cain, etc. The poet Eugenio Montale translated Ezra Pound, for whose poetry he felt great affinity, and, later, Melville's *Billy Budd*, Steinbeck's *In Dubious Battle*, Fitzgerald, and others.[93] Saroyan and Caldwell, who left deep imprints on modern Italian literature, were introduced to Italy by Elio Vittorini, who was, with Pavese and Moravia, the most important Italian writer of the thirties and forties. Not only was the first true forerunner of neorealism (*Ossessione*) based on an American novel, but also the first postwar film depicting the Italian partisan fighters bore the Hemingwayan title *Il sole sorge ancora* (The Sun Rises Again).

The new Italian literature, born during the thirties, eschewed D'Annunzio's superheroes and Fogazzaro's cultivated middle-class men. Its heroes came from the country: some were primitives, some half-wits, and some tramps—characters close to those of Faulkner's *Sanctuary* and of Melville's *Billy Budd* and *Moby Dick*. They all appear in the keywork of this period, in Vittorini's masterpiece *Conversazione in Sicilia* (*In Sicily*, 1941), a book that became a bible to the neorealists. Some of the early neorealist films portray similar characters of social outcasts:

Alberto in De Santis's *Caccia tragica* (Tragic Hunt, 1947), Ernesto in Lattuada's *Il Bandito* (The Bandit, 1946), Zavattini's happy innocents in *Miracolo a Milano* (Miracle in Milan, 1950), etc.

The censorship board tried to restrict the publishing of American literature, especially during the late thirties and the war years. The original edition of the first large anthology of American literature, *Americana* (1941), was seized and could be republished only after Vittorini had made substantial changes in his general survey of American literature. James Cain's novel *The Postman Always Rings Twice*, on which Visconti based his *Ossessione*, was published in Italy only in 1945, ten years later than in France. Both Pavese's and Cecchi's generation found Cain "false and unoriginal."

The myth of American film was more ambiguous. Pavese (who, already in 1931, had proposed to a publisher to write an essay on American film, but he never did) claimed later that American film and jazz influenced his generation as much as American literature. Pintor called the American cinema the great messenger of his youth, stressing the importance of the film medium for large audiences. Discussion about American film, however, remained more limited than that on literature, sometimes overshadowed by the interest in the Soviet cinematic avant-garde. In the forties, interest in a national cinema free of any foreign influences gradually prevailed. The theoretical foundations of the postwar Italian film were sought in the works of Italian authors, the Sicilian writer Giovanni Verga, the literary historian Francesco De Sanctis, and later in the Marxist theoretician Antonio Gramsci.

The infatuation with films by Frank Capra, John Ford, William Wyler, and especially King Vidor (*The Crowd* and *Hallelujah!*) was followed by the rediscovery of French film by Marcel Carné, Julien Duvivier, Jean Renoir, and Pierre Chenal.[94] But it was the American film that stood at the beginning of the "journey" that led to the new Italian cinema, to neorealism. Antonioni, a close, often very severe and officious observer of the American film scene, expressed his feeling in *Cinema* when he wrote: "The old America, born out of the fusing of the puritans' and pioneers' spirit, tormented by the need for creating its own truth, is present in John Ford's *Stagecoach*. The stagecoach leaves Arizona, this marvelous puritan country captured in a few shots, and the journey begins."[95]

At certain moments, the influence of the American cinema was overtaken by the Soviet avant-garde. Its impact can be traced from Blasetti (the aesthetics of long shots and rapid montage in *Sun* and *1860,* certain subplot elements in *The Old Guard,* the ideological links between the form and content of the shots) and Barbaro to De Santis and his peers. Nevertheless, Italy's contacts with the Soviet Union were mostly indirect, limited to the economic field. Only a small part of the huge Soviet production and fragments of film theory were accessible to filmmakers, and Soviet literature of the twenties and thirties remained practically unknown until the postwar period. Gian Piero Brunetta wrote in his comprehensive study of Italian criticism of the thirties:

American films were—more than the Soviet films, which constituted an important ideological reference but were not directly known—a true model for a different life. Just imagine . . . that thanks to American films a whole forbidden paradise of eros was opened, making it possible to dream about women of not just a mercenary type and of love relationships not determined by all kinds of taboos and antiquated moral principles.[96]

This hindsight evaluation is in keeping with the critics of the time. For example, Fernando De Narzi, whose articles were published in the influential magazine *Il Bo,* edited by the Fascist University Group of Padua,[97] wrote:

For us the Russian film is still locked up in an almost mysterious atmosphere generating a lot of curiosity. We did not see many of their products, but we admired what we saw, mainly during the two Venice Film Festivals. This convinced us that Russian film is not a myth, but a true artistic expression. It not only takes up reality, it reflects it. The first and the greatest merit of the Russian concept lies in its collective character. The Soviets have understood that film is a universal language that can be comprehended by the learned as well as by the illiterate, that it is not a pastime but a search for an art guided by scientific, political, and human considerations.[98]

The three film cultures—American, Russian, and French—found their exponents in the two men meeting on a ship bound for Capri in 1940. Visconti, with his deep background in French culture, and De Santis, an ardent lover of American film and of Renoir, as well as a diligent student of the Soviet film scene, were ready to set out on a long journey through new Italian cinema. After 1940, the fourth and most important of its components was coming to life, born from the very essence of the "tragic country with the smiling face"—the Italian component would emerge from the historical events that marked the end of an era. The lesson in history these two men and their peers had learned became the motivating power of their artistic evolution. "The most precious thing one gets from history is the enthusiasm it inspires," said Arnold Toynbee. These words never sounded truer than in the Italy of the early forties. In November 1943, Giaime Pintor wrote in his farewell letter to his brother:

Some of my friends, more gifted for immediately perceiving the political situation, had many years since taken part in the fight against fascism. As much as I always felt very close to them, I am not sure that I would have ever decided to follow them along that very path. Somewhere at the bottom there was always in me too much indifference, too much strong independent taste, and too solid a critical spirit to allow me to abandon all that for a collective faith. It was only the war that resolved this problem, brushing away some obstacles, clearing the ground of some too-easy excuses, and bringing me, in a brutal way, in vital touch with an inacceptable world.

I believe that such a transition was quite natural for the majority of my generation. In some of its best representatives, I have observed the same fast movement toward politics that took place in Germany when the last romantic generation exhausted its possibilities. These kinds of phenomena reemerge again and again whenever politics ceases to limit itself to simply ordinary administration and thus has all the social forces involved in an attempt to save society from a terrible disease, to answer a mortal danger. Modern society is based on many different specifications, but it can only survive if, at a certain moment, it is capable of dismissing all of them, to sacrifice everything for the one and only revolutionary postulate. . . .

We, the musicians and the writers, have to renounce our privileges and to contribute toward the liberation of all. As far as I am concerned, I can assure you that at this stage of my life, I find it hardly amusing to join the partisans. I do not think of it any more highly than I do of the pleasures of civilian life. I know I am an excellent translator and a good diplomat, but most probably only a mediocre partisan. This is nevertheless the only possibility and I embrace it. . . .[99]

I

OBSESSION (1942–1944)

Our sacrifice and the duty we accomplish probably are the benefits we derive from war. Individuals and nations both learn to suffer, resist, and to be more modest, to live with more dignity, fraternity, and religious simplicity. But, on the other hand, war is sheer loss—a sorrow, a waste, an enormous and useless distress. Let the Germans and their friends do what they want, and can. We can come up only with one thing to compensate for all the injustices of the world: our Christianity which lost its God and its hope, but which did not lose its sadness and its yearning for eternity. And we live because we cannot afford not to, because that is life. And maybe we "make literature." Why not? It is, among other things, one of the most dignified things to do.[1]

These words were written by Renato Serra in 1915, in the middle of World War I, and were published by the prestigious journal *La Voce,* edited by Benedetto Croce. One of the most promising personalities of the Italian literary scene, Serra died on the battlefields of the first world war at the age of thirty-one. The same words might have been written twenty-five years later by any of the members of the pre-neorealist generation—those tormented young people who lived "because they could not afford not to" and who wanted "to make films." They too wanted to find the lost God, the lost hope, knowing that they had to "see the truth and emerge from insanity"[2] in order to be able to make the films they wanted.

The struggle for a new artistic truth could not be initiated by the literary scene, which was too disorganized, too frustrated, and too scattered all about the country. The struggle had to originate where the "strongest weapon" was, carried out by film artists whose work was centered in the major cities, mainly in Rome. After twenty years of fascism, no other medium had the stamina to create a social context for a new artistic movement. Unlike their literary counterparts, the young film critics and future filmmakers were not inhibited by any inferiority complex. They were full of self-assurance and confidence in their potential. In 1944, Moravia analyzed the reasons for the paralysis of the literary scene:

If, alongside a general history of literature, a history of Italian literature could be written, it would become obvious that the reading public in all older societies was made up of the courtly section of the community. In Italy, it was not replaced by any other reading public, either bourgeois or popular. . . . Reading now, in its best sense, is representative of an increase in individual culture—rather disparate and anarchic—and, at worst, nothing more than an entertainment with little real informative value. The lack of social climate, in which culture is a social fact, comes from the failure of our bourgeoisie to establish a democracy in our country; a failure not only moral, but political, economic, and consequently, cultural as well.[3]

Support for the pre-neorealists from literary figures was marginal. The impact of the Italian philosophical leaders, Benedetto Croce (1866–1954) and Antonio Gramsci (1891–1937), opponents of fascism, was more stimulating. Even if they both disappeared from the public eye in the mid-twenties, their work left deep imprints in all fields of Italian cultural activity. (Gramsci was arrested and Croce retired to his home in Naples, spending most of his remaining years in semi-seclusion.)[4]

For Croce, as for the neorealists, "all history was contemporary history," with every human being situated in a particular point in time. Croce preached the importance of a subjective and intuitive understanding in the interpretation of art and of human history in terms of achieved liberty. The primary value of Croce's philosophy lay in the impulse it gave to studies in history. Its historic orientation is so dominant that his conclusions lead to an identification of philosophy with history. This approach, shared and developed on a different ideological and political basis by Antonio Gramsci, was influential in shaping the neorealist generation.

Croce's philosophical system emphasizes the history of philosophy, leaving no space for religion. According to Croce, the science of history examines the spirit in its evolution whereas the science of philosophy examines the possibilities of this evolution. Croce divided these possibilities into four categories: economics, logic, ethics, and aesthetics. He also applied this theory to the history of art and criticism. Croce's "Manifesto of the Antifascist Intellectuals" was one of the few articles of faith remaining to the antifascist front. He wrote:

> For this chaotic and elusive religion (fascism) we are in no mood to give up our old faith that for two and a half centuries has been the spirit of a resurgent modern Italy—the faith that consists of love and truth, of aspiration toward justice, of a generous and refined human feeling, of a solicitude for freedom, of the force and guarantee of every progress.[5]

Throughout his entire creative life, Gramsci discussed Croce's philosophy, opposing his own Marxism to Croce's idealism. He shared Croce's belief in history as an intellectual activity that dominates all others, including ethics, politics, and art, one which ties the past to the present, the present to the future. In his *History of Italy* and *History of Europe*, written in seclusion, Croce turned his attention to nineteenth-century liberal society, leaving aside the reasons for the fascist ascent. Gramsci, on the other hand, spelled out an analysis of Mussolini's regime and outlined some perspectives for post-fascist society. He attempted to interpret the contemporary world in articles and essays written during his eleven-year imprisonment and struggle with a fatal illness. According to Gramsci, fascism was the most brutal expression of the industrial, agrarian, and bourgeois complex, which had occupied the top level of the Italian social structure. Gramsci's analysis of capitalist society was in keeping with the basic thoughts of Leninism, but most of his thinking was incompatible with the orthodox Soviet line initiated at the end of the twenties.

He wrote to the Soviet leaders in 1926: "You are destroying your work, you are degrading the party and running the risk of destroying the directing role which the Communist party had acquired under the impulse of Lenin."[6] Gramsci's thoughts about the specific Italian path to a postcapitalist society had a decisive influence on the Italian Communist party from the very beginning. His writings inspired not only the communist members of the neorealist scene (Giuseppe De Santis, Mario Alicata, Umberto Barbaro, Gianni and Massimo Puccini) but also, for example, Luchino Visconti. Through Gramsci, Visconti discovered the hidden social structures of the Italian south and adopted his belief that the most important Italian revolutionary forces were the northern urban workers and the southern peasantry (*La terra trema, Rocco and His Brothers*).

The analysis of the relations between the northern proletariat and southern peasantry attracted Gramsci's attention to the role of intellectuals in society. His concept of the intellectual as an organizer who must actively participate in practical life left deep imprints on the Italian intelligentsia. Gramsci thus contributed, along with others, to the emphasis on politics and ideology apparent in all domains of artistic creation in postwar Italy and, quite specifically, in cinema.

The neorealist movement adopted many of Gramsci's ideas about "collective will" expressed in his essay "The Modern Prince."[7] He wrote:

> The modern prince, the myth-prince, cannot be a real person, a concrete individual; it can only be an organism: a complex element of society in which the cementing of a collective will—recognized and partially asserted in action—has already begun. . . . It is presupposed that there is an already existing collective will that is enervated and dispersed, which has suffered a dangerous and threatening but not decisive and catastrophic collapse, and which it is necessary to reconstitute and strengthen, and not that a collective will is to be created ex novo, originally, and to be directed toward very concrete and rational ends. It is to be directed toward ends whose concreteness and rationality have not yet been verified and criticized by any effective and universally known historical experience.[8]

Owing to the most diverse and contradictory circumstances (as discussed in my introduction), the first neorealists appeared on the historical and cultural scene precisely as a familiar and dedicated group—an already existing collective will—equipped with necessary production means and determined to emerge from insanity.

Around them, insanity was rampant.

ROBERTO ROSSELLINI

All the countries participating in World War II turned out films on the war—pompous, eulogistic, but sometimes deeply human. Prominent among Italian war films were those by Francesco De Robertis (1902–1959) and Roberto Rossellini. De

Uomini sul fondo

Robertis, a naval officer and the head of the Navy's film unit, made *Uomini sul fondo* (SOS Submarine, 1941), which is traditionally mentioned as one of the fore-runners of neorealism. He shot it on a submarine in authentic settings with nonprofessional actors. Yet the story about a submarine that collides with a ship and is rescued remained within the limits of the conventional semidocumentary narrative. The style did not result from an aesthetic choice but from the necessity of the subject, which was the opposite of the neorealist method. Among the "white telephone" films and the calligraphic films of the early forties, De Robertis's picture represented an interesting experiment with seminarrative structure and a low-key, antirhetorical style. De Robertis tried to broaden his method in later films, *Alfa Tau!* (1942) and others, with little success. However, his films were hailed by some critics as genuine experimental works and examples for other filmmakers to follow.[9] Later, some film historians and filmmakers (first of all Rossellini himself) found in them the first signs of neorealism.[10]

The sequel to *SOS Submarine* was signed by Roberto Rossellini in collaboration with De Robertis. *La nave bianca* (Hospital Ship, 1942), the first film of Rossellini's so-called "Fascist Trilogy," followed the lead of *SOS Submarine* in its semi-documentary style and its expressive sentimentality. It mixes elements of dramatic tension, heroics, and a romantic love story between a wounded soldier and a nurse. This pertinent episode was included in the film by Rossellini, who, as the son of an affluent Roman builder of movie houses, literally grew up on popular Italian movies. ("The only classics I could see at that time were Vidor's *The Crowd* and *Halle-lujah!*" he said in 1952.)[11] Rossellini's attempt at a "style to be coined" was carried out through his stand against traditional cinematic codes that had enslaved him in his early films and through his efforts to reintroduce into the film medium its original realism.

The two other films that belong to Rossellini's "Fascist Trilogy"—*Un pilota ritorna* (A Pilot Returns, 1942) and *L'uomo della croce* (Man with the Cross, 1943)—are products of a team of collaborators, including Michelangelo Antonioni, Vittorio Mussolini (his penname was Tito Silvio Mursino), and Massimo Mida.[12] Rossellini did not like to talk about *A Pilot Returns,* which takes place during the unfortunate campaign in Greece. Thanks to Antonioni, the film tries hard to create a believable Italian hero, which is its greatest asset. Nevertheless, it was torn to pieces by De Santis in *Cinema,* published by Vittorio Mussolini himself.[13]

In *Man with the Cross,* the main character, an army chaplain, is not a winner as the protagonists of the earlier war films were. The most heroic deed he can accomplish is to die for the sake of the others. The film is permeated with a deep faith in God, seen as the ultimate salvation and the only hope at the moment of death (and a lost war). Death, one of the main motifs of Rossellini's films, is omnipresent in this picture, shot at a moment when everything was falling apart. The sequence of the Russian attack captured in extreme long shots and intercut with medium shots of

L'uomo della croce

houses on fire, is an effective piece of cinematic rhetoric. However, the pompousness takes over again: in the very last shots, the galloping Italian cavalry appears on the horizon—the very image of the ancient "condottieri" and legendary knights; the lost village is reconquered, the Russians defeated, the chaplain dies, but Italy lives. The film ends with a title spelling out a dedication to "all army chaplains who died in action fighting the barbaric enemy and people without faith."[14] The style of *Man with the Cross* is banal with only rare moments of cinematic originality (long shots of the endless Russian plains with small figures of Italian soldiers and Russian fugitives living together in a kind of Christian collectivity; the rhythmical editing of the battle scenes; the panoramic shots of the landscape intercut with medium shots of soldiers resting and close-ups of their faces, etc.).

Rossellini always insisted on a certain coherence in his entire work, expressed, above all, by its spiritual essence. He usually began interviews on his career by claiming it began in 1945 (*Open City*). Sometimes however, he liked to stress the continuity of his career, mentioning also the first and third parts of his fascist trilogy. In an interview with Mario Verdone, he maintained:

> No one can deny that the same spirituality is present in *Hospital Ship, Man with the Cross, Paisan, The Flowers of St. Francis,* and in the final sequence of *Stromboli.* The same applies to the choral element of my films. The sailors from the *Hospital Ship* have the same spiritual meaning as the refugees in *Man with the Cross,* the people in *Open City,* the resistance fighters in *Paisan,* and the friars in *The Flowers of St. Francis.*[15]

VITTORIO DE SICA AND CESARE ZAVATTINI

Along with Rossellini, another of the founding fathers of neorealism started his directorial career. Nothing is more misleading than to view Vittorio De Sica (1901–1974) in the light of his neorealist masterpieces and to deplore his later decline. His neorealist experience should, on the contrary, be regarded as an interlude in his fifty-year-long career—the career of a unique entertainer.

The descriptions of De Sica's career usually start with his encounter with Cesare Zavattini in 1935. When they met on the location of Camerini's comedy *I'll Give a Million,* De Sica was already the number one Italian actor. He was the "Vittorio nazionale," the very symbol of Italian qualities: "sentimental and slightly cynical, with an unfailing sense for images, an ability to move audiences, and a diffidence toward intellectual rationalism; a man who loved women, beautiful clothes, and gambling and hated to pay taxes. De Sica was a hard-working man with an easy-going attitude toward work, a man with a passion for titles, proud of being called 'a commendatore,' and with a tendency to nepotism, in love with words like 'compassion,' 'humanity,' 'goodness,' and 'love.' His assessment of himself was very Italian too. He said in 1974: 'Of course, I have made many mistakes in my life, but I don't think that I have ever harmed anybody. I consider myself a very decent person [un oumo per bene].'"[16]

In the twenties, De Sica was the second and later the first romantic lead in several theater companies. He traveled all over Italy and occasionally worked in movies. But it was only "la rivista" that made him famous. This particularly Italian type of variety theater was born at the end of the nineteenth century as a "review" (rivista) of political, literary, social, theatrical, and sports news. Only later did it become a "show," a visual spectacle with settings, costumes, and dance. De Sica, with his pleasing tenor and good looks, acquired great fame as a popular song stylist in these shows. The song he sung originally in the "rivista" and later in his first important film, Camerini's *What Rascals Men Are,* became one of the biggest European hits of the early thirties. With his "Parlami d'amore, Mariù," De Sica reached the peak of his fame. He excelled in portraying the Italian "little man" lost in the big city (the delivery boy in *What Rascals Men Are,* the young newspaper seller in *Signor Max*), striving to climb the social ladder and ending up accepting the dullness of his destiny. A certain social stratum of the Italian population completely identified with this figure.[17] De Sica played it instinctively, developing from 1930 on a subtle satirical attitude toward the wealthy middle class.

There are sympathetic legends, and De Sica is one of them. Even the young Italian film critics of the seventies, who contest the merits of neorealism, challenging its very essence, find kind words for him: "If Rossellini and Visconti, the two authors who started the new Italian cinema in 1945, represent today 'the film of our fathers,' De Sica represents 'the film of our grandfathers.' A grandfather is less contested, one has the feeling that to contest him is more gratuitous and ungrateful."[18]

Between 1940 and 1944, De Sica directed six pictures. The switch in his career was provoked by an artistic crisis that he hoped to overcome with the help of the theater; at that time, he considered the movies merely a means of making money. Early in 1933, he formed his own theater company, staging primarily drawing-room comedies by Italian authors. After 1940, his repertoire became more challenging. De Sica appeared in plays by Shaw (*The Doctor's Dilemma*), Sheridan (*School for Scandal*), Noel Coward (*Easy Virtue*), and others. In 1940, De Sica wrote:

> Thanks to some songs and to the financial security from the movie fame, I have some reasons to consider myself the most loved and the best known star in Italy. But whenever I think of the theater, my smile fades away. When I shave and watch my own face in the mirror, I see that my eyes became desperately sad. I do not like the person who gave me the wealth: I am his slave. But I am considering a revolt. I was betrayed by the easy clowning and a ready smile. Calmly, implacably, and definitely I will now betray them.[19]

It was finally the despised cinematic medium that enabled De Sica to develop all his potential. The first films he directed—*Rose scarlatte* (Red Roses, 1940), *Teresa Venerdì* (1941), *Maddalena zero in condotta* (Maddalena, F in Conduct, 1941), and *Un Garibaldino al convento* (A Garibaldian in a Monastery, 1942)—were Italian-style comedies using the double identity plot and the standard types of sentimental characters. While *Red Roses* was an adaptation of a comedy by Aldo De Benedetti, staged the same year by De Sica's theater company, *Teresa Venerdì* marked the first step in collaboration with Cesare Zavattini, even if Zavattini's name does not appear in the credits. (He revised the script.) Some film historians consider *Teresa Venerdì*

De Sica's first attempt at a critique of social manners, citing, among others, the scene in which a patroness visits the squalid premises of an orphanage.[20] Focusing on the underprivileged (abandoned children), De Sica tried to switch from sentimental comedies to comedies of manners. Yet this attempt remained within the limits of the well-intentioned Camerini films, suffusing everything with a layer of heart-breaking sentimentality.

I bambini ci guardano (The Children Are Watching Us, 1943) is the first film in which De Sica did not act and Zavattini's name appeared in the credits.[21] De Sica was always interested in the problems of the couple and in the causes of separation. He picked up the theme treated in *Red Roses* (marriage, adultery, forgiveness, repentance) and developed a family crisis ending with the mother's departure and the father's suicide. His attention was concentrated on their child, who, as much as the small heroes of his *Shoeshine,* was the victim of the situation. *The Children Are Watching Us* followed in the tradition set by one of the most read books in Italy and Europe before World War II, Edmondo De Amicis's *The Heart.* However, De Sica's motivations were different. While De Amicis told a lugubrious story of a child's distress in terms of detached realism, De Sica sketched the death of a marriage as a dead-end originating in empty social values. The woman is young and bored, the man weak and boring—both are slaves to the drabness of a daily routine viewed as the road toward their destruction. The woman is torn between the love for her son and the passion for her lover, and her husband is neither capable of understanding her yearning for something different (which by no means has to be the lover) nor able to look for solutions to their problems. The woman is labeled "unfaithful" and rejected by society (represented by the tenants of an apartment house). The emptiness of her life is shown through a careful depiction of the daily routine in Alassio,

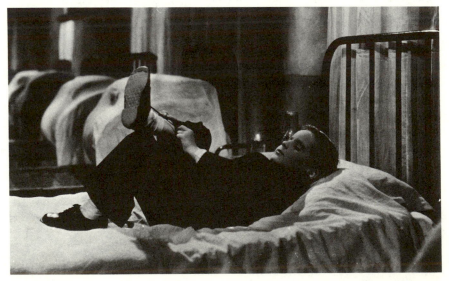

I bambini ci guardano

a popular Italian family seaside resort. Here, the woman spends a few weeks with her son in order to "forget her lover." By insisting on the dullness of family life, De Sica reveals his feeling that the romantic adventure was just a substitute for a more meaningful life.[22]

The film's ambiguity becomes apparent in the description of the story published in the influential Catholic Film Center's *Film Recommendations*. It said: "The adventure of a dishonest woman, the wife of a hard-working bank employee and the mother of a beautiful child. After having scandalously left the family to be later forgiven by her husband, she escapes with her lover, thus provoking the suicide of her husband and the distress of the child."[23]

In *The Children Are Watching Us,* De Sica and Zavattini developed certain themes that Camerini's films only touched on: those of an unhappy childhood, a dead marriage, and suicide. All of them challenged the official fascist propaganda, according to which there were no unhappy children in a fascist state, no adulteresses (only men could have extramarital relationships while women had to suffer), and, above all, no suicides: suicide was antifascist, possible only in a corrupt Western society.[24] *The Children Are Watching Us* remained largely confined to the conventional production style of the period. However, its themes transgressed the limits of the fascist cinema and provided a transition to De Sica's neorealist period.

De Sica's predilection for nonprofessional actors started long before his neorealist works, probably originating in his hesitation to direct professionals. *Maddalena, F in Conduct* was the first role of the future neorealist star Carla Del Poggio; in *Teresa Venerdì* Adriana Benetti debuted (the part of the orphanage director in the latter film was played by a nonprofessional Austrian woman), etc. *Red Roses* was the only picture that used famous actors, but here De Sica shared the direction with the experienced director Giuseppe Amato.

Another moral and social taboo was challenged by Zavattini's script *Quattro passi fra le nuvole* (Four Steps in the Clouds, 1942) directed by Alessandro Blasetti. De Sica's sensitivity was replaced by the condescending attitudes of the Italian comedies of the period. To the harshness of life, Zavattini counterposed his formula "poverty equals happiness" and managed to find a happy ending for the story of a poor, pregnant, and unwed peasant girl. Once again—sensing with preciseness the historical significance of the situation—Blasetti knew exactly what to do and shot Zavattini's script according to the demands formulated by the upcoming generation: real people and real problems. The first half of the film presents characters and situations that the Italian cinema ignored for a long time: ordinary people traveling on a bus across a real Italian landscape. They are tired and not at all glamorous: the bus is old and dirty, the roads bumpy, and the villages destitute. The girl is unhappy, afraid of facing her parents, and the man, a traveling salesman, is resigned to the dull life of somebody who works hard and seldom makes ends meet. During the second half, comic interludes prevail. But not even the happy ending sweeps away the feeling that not everything in life can be so easily resolved. De Santis wrote in *Cinema:* "We welcome enthusiastically Blasetti's return to a direct realistic language."[25]

Although it was far too early to speak about realism, *Four Steps in the Clouds*

Quattro passi fra le nuvole

was one of the first attempts to change the direction of Italian cinema. The camera, used to exploit the past and beautify the present, began to look more closely at the world around it, challenging the Pirandellian concept of the incompatibility between life and illusion. The early pre-neorealists especially challenged Pirandello's theory about the immobility of art and its unchangeable principles. At variance with his insistence on the subjective perception of reality, they postulated an objective approach, denying the Pirandellian cosmic vision of the world.

Pirandello's work, centered on portrayals of people imprisoned within themselves, influenced the first films by Alberto Lattuada (b. 1914), a talented scriptwriter who made his directorial debut in 1943. A contemporary of De Santis and Gianni Puccini, he never really joined the pre-neorealists, feeling from the outset closer to the Calligraphist experience. A lonely and well-read figure, he was largely under the spell of romantic literature. His first film, *Giacomo l'idealista* (Jacob, the Idealist, 1943), based on a novel by Emilio De Marchi and scripted by Emilio Cecchi, was enclosed in a "Pirandellian reality" with its absurd extensions. Its rigorous style exerts a strong visual impact unconcerned with intellectual interpretations.

Throughout his long career, Lattuada kept narrating stories of unhappy love. Pirandellian pessimism permeated his second film, *La freccia nel fianco* (An Arrow in the Flank, 1943), scripted by Zavattini and Moravia. Its characters live their frustrated lives from a distance, as if they were other people. In the same impersonal manner the director viewed the tragic end of the heroine unhappily married to a man she never loved.

In the turbulent time between 1943 and 1944, Lattuada remained outside the mainstream of events. The real protagonists of the new epoch were emerging elsewhere in the country and were already waiting for "something" new to begin. They did not know exactly what it would be or how it might affect them. All they knew was that it was to come.

THE END OF AN ERA — *OSSESSIONE*

The new intelligentsia answered the Pirandellian question "What is reality?" with an ambiguous "This is reality," the finger pointed at the country in which they lived: Italy ravaged by war. There was no victory in sight. The official propaganda policy was exposed with the first news about Italian soldiers abandoned without help on the Russian front by their German allies. The letters they were sending home did not talk about the sweetness of a patriotic death, as shown in so many "white telephone" films.[26] At Stalingrad, there was no time for heroic deeds: the 3,000 Italians who fought there froze to death, died of hunger, of wounds, or were taken prisoners. The African adventure was coming to an end with little room left for victorious pilots. At home, the price index was rising (100 in 1938, 120 in 1940, 153 in 1942), and morals were sinking. The end of an era was accompanied by a profound crisis of conscience. Alberto Lattuada, whose writings were at that time more interesting than his directorial ventures, wrote in 1941:

> The absence of love brought many tragedies that might have been averted. Instead of the golden rain of love, a black cape of indifference fell upon the people. And people have lost the eye for love: they are incapable of seeing clearly; they are staggering in the obscurity of death. The disintegration of all moral values started here, together with the destruction of conscience. It is a long chain anchored at the devil's feet.[27]

The establishment reacted against the growing discontent with increased censorship. In 1941, both Moravia's *The Fancy Dress Party*, a satire of a dictatorship, and the first edition of Vittorini's anthology, *Americana*, were banned. At the same time the authorities rejected the first script of the "Cinema group" based on a short story by Giovanni Verga; the new generation had chosen to follow Verga as an anti-D'Annunzian and anti-Pirandellian model. Somebody—apparently the censor minister Pavolini himself—wrote on the script with red ink: "No more bandits!" Verga's story, "L'Amante di Gramigna" (Gramigna's Mistress), about a fatalistic love between a Sicilian girl and a rebel, evolved against the backdrop of the exploited Sicilian peasantry. The "Cinema group" chose it mainly for Verga's preface, which became one of the first credos of neorealism. In this preface, Verga, echoing the French nineteenth-century realists, wrote:

> When in the novel the affinity and the cohesion of its every part will be so complete that the process of creation remains a mystery like the development of

human passions themselves, and the harmony of its forms will be so perfect, the sincerity of its reality so evident . . . that the hand of the artist will remain absolutely invisible, then it will have the stamp of a real happening.[28]

Gramigna's Mistress was Visconti's first completed script, written together with De Santis and Gianni Puccini and rendered into Sicilian by Mario Alicata and Rosario Assunto. The actors were chosen (Massimo Girotti for the role of Gramigna), and Visconti traveled to Sicily to search for locations. The "no" in red ink changed all his plans. Visconti gave vent to his disappointment in the article "Corpses," published in *Cinema* on June 10, 1941. He wrote:

While visiting certain film companies, we often trip over corpses which stubbornly believe to be alive. It happened to me, and it will happen to others, that when we meet them face to face, we do not recognize immediately that they are dead: they circulate among us, dressed like you and me. . . . And it is more than sad that young people, as impatient as they are to express so many things, have to live for the time being only on hope, finding as an obstacle in their path numerous, hostile, and resistant corpses. But the day will come of which we dream. Then the young forces in our film will be allowed to state clearly and loudly: "The corpses to the cemetery!" And on that day you will see us all rushing in search of those imprudent enough to stay behind. With all due respect we will help them (we would not like to hurt them) get their other leg into the grave as well.[29]

Visconti's collaboration with De Santis began with a treatment based on the novel by the French writer Alain-Fournier *Le Grand Meaulnes*. Then they wrote adaptations of Melville's *Billy Budd*, Thomas Mann's *Disorder and Early Sorrow*, and Julien Green's *Adrienne Mesurat*. All four treatments were based on foreign material and were written with the purpose of challenging the "formalist-intellectual-pictorial" trend that De Santis had been stubbornly fighting against in his film reviews.

The choice of James Cain's novel *The Postman Always Rings Twice* for their next collaboration was in keeping with the spirit of the "Cinema group." Visconti received its translation from Jean Renoir, for whom he had worked in the 1930s.[30] He was quite fond of the book's French film version by Pierre Chenal *Le dernier tournant* (1939). For De Santis, Renoir was God. "Nobody but Renoir understood everything that film and its specific means of expression can offer to the arts," he wrote in his review of *La bête humaine*.[31]

Thus, a film was planned with the original title *Palude* (Marsh). Originally, the setting was more important than the style. It had to be the valley of the Po, which, according to the expectations of the antifascists, would become the site of the historical turning point. This anticipation was based on the belief that both the first antifascist strikes and the fight to overthrow fascism would take place in this working-class stronghold.

From the outset, the film was conceived as a manifesto. The script was signed by Visconti, Alicata, Pietrangeli, Puccini and De Santis and revised by Moravia. Pietro Ingrao, one of the postwar leaders of the Italian Communist party, also belonged to the group.[32] Their activity was not limited to theory. They were all active in the underground antifascist movement, and it was during the shooting of *Ossessione* that the secret police opened an investigation of the group, which led to the imprisonment of Alicata, Puccini, and Visconti. "The real 'text' of *Ossessione* starts before the opening establishing shot of the film," writes Lino Miccichè, the Italian film critic and historian, alluding to the conspiratorial activity of the film's authors during its shooting, editing, and after its completion. "And in a way it continues long after Gino's despair over Giovanna's dead body."[33]

The change of the title from *Marsh* to *Ossessione* was the first step toward a change in the whole concept. A film manifesto, which foreshadowed the antifascist resistance, became also the first image of Visconti's "lost paradise"—not so much Milton's as that of Marcel Proust. "Maybe in the course of history the real paradise is the lost paradise," wrote Proust in *Remembrance of Things Past. Ossessione* is Visconti's first story about people who have lost their struggle with life and yet are not defeated because "somewhere" hope never dies.

Visconti was thirty-six years old when he directed *Ossessione*, his first film. He was the oldest of the group and the most affluent. He had some film and theater experience and a diverse education. He was, above all, a man of complete artistic integrity, who always did what he wanted and how he wanted it done. The credits of his films include a whole group of scriptwriters, but he never accepted any suggestion that did not fit his own vision. The man to whom he probably listened most carefully was Mario Serandrei, the editor of all his films.

The "Cinema group" encountered no problems in having the story, based on James Cain's novel, approved by the censors. A pretty young woman married to a much older husband falls for a handsome younger man; they murder the husband, she gets the insurance, but eventually the crime does not pay.[34] Mario Alicata and others after him liked to pretend that the film shared with Cain's book only the central plot. However, the analogies of the narrative are much more important, mainly in the first part of the film: the arrival of Frank/Gino, who is hired by the husband (Nick in the book, Bragana in the film); the common meal; the scene of seduction after the husband leaves for an errand; the picture Cora/Giovanna draws of her marriage; the planned escape of the lovers; the discussion about the baby Nick/Bragana wants from his wife, etc.

The Cain novel gives much space to the insurance subplot and develops with more precision the investigation by the local police, which in *Ossessione* is quite marginal. If the film does not have the judge Sackett and the lawyer Katz, it has, on the other hand, the character of Spagnolo (the Spaniard). Here is where the difference lies, the main reason why *Ossessione* shares, in the final analysis, only the narrative elements of Cain's novel. Spagnolo is a traveling showman whom Gino meets on the train when he attempts to escape from Giovanna. He becomes Gino's friend, his only friend, who finally betrays him. He represents the "something else" that Gino has been searching for and that the film is about: a world beyond the fascist reality in the immediate meaning, and a world of unattainable distances in its larger sense of Visconti's vision.

The incompatibility of the two concepts—the one of Alicata/Puccini and that of Visconti—is the most visible in the character of the Spaniard. Visconti's script-

Ossessione

writers wanted him to be a fighter for a better world with a clear vision of the future. Visconti made him into his most nostalgic character, a romantic tramp who will never find either love or friendship. The homosexual overtones are first apparent in the scene of their encounter when the Spaniard "picks up" Gino on the train, offering to pay his fare. All shots depicting Gino with Spagnolo are composed with utmost care: the splendid horizons behind them at their arrival in Ancona; their conversation in the port, most of the space being occupied by the cathedral of San Ciriaco with men working on it in broad light; the emotion-charged scene in the hotel room when Spagnolo's eyes caress Gino with a look full of sadness while Gino is stretched on the bed. The visual beauty of these scenes contrasts with the eroticism of the scenes between Gino and Giovanna situated in Bragana's kitchen around dirty dishes and leftovers or in the bedroom—dusky and untidy—with the always unmade bed whose sheets seem to exhale the odor of unwashed bodies. Gino refused Spagnolo's friendship, went back to Giovanna and his own destruction. In the original full version, Spagnolo follows his friend and reports him to the police, thus completing the cycle of betrayals started by Gino's betrayal of Bragana and Spagnolo, and Giovanna's unfaithfulness to her husband.[35]

The Spaniard—a nickname with a clear reminiscence of the Spanish civil war (1936–1939)—was the only positive alternative to the destructive passion of a woman. He symbolized the yearnings of the young Visconti for a world free of social and sexual oppression. This yearning informed all Visconti's films and was generally expressed through characters bearing some resemblance to the Spaniard,

Ossessione

an ambiguous and not altogether agreeable character. In him are already foreshad-owed 'Ntoni Valastro from *La terra trema*, Franz from *Senso*, Mario from *The White Nights*, Gianni from *Sandra*, and Bruno from *Conversation Piece*, whose death concludes the gallery of Visconti's solitary heroes, reaching for the stars and ending with betrayal.[36]

The character of Spagnolo links *Ossessione* to the most openly antifascist novel published during the fascist era, Vittorini's *In Sicily*. In it, the Spanish tragedy is constantly present, not only through the hints at the newspaper headlines shrilling at Silvestro, the protagonist, on his journey to Syracuse but mainly through Vit-torini's reference to some of the characters in Spanish as "más hombres" (more than men). Two of them, the knife grinder and the harness maker, solitary tramps in the Sicilian "doomed world," closed off in their nonexistence, share with Spagnolo the search for "something else" and a denial of the existing world. They are incarna-tions of a state of mind and attitudes toward human problems carrying in them-selves the possibility of antifascism. The harness maker says to Silvestro: "The world is big and beautiful. But it has been greatly outraged. Everyone suffers for himself, but not for the world that has been outraged, and so the world continues to be outraged."[37]

In Sicily and *Ossessione* are permeated with the most profound despair. It was their authors' intention to react against the obligatory optimism of Mussolini's em-pire and its fairy tales about a happy Italy populated with healthy minds in healthy bodies. Visconti stressed the solitude of his heroes by the ugliness of their environment—bumpy roads with cracked gas stations, pubs with greasy tables, the end-less banks of the Po river with dirty grass and troubled water, the apathetic, indif-ferent, and tired faces of people. Only once do they seem joyful and relaxed: during the singing contest in Ancona—itself a small masterpiece—followed by Bragana's murder. No one ever saw this face of Italy on the fascist screen. None of the films of the fascist era showed a character more alone than Giovanna at the end of the film. She is in the kitchen, dirty dishes piled on the sink, eating. Gino is gone; she moves about slowly, reads a newspaper; the camera captures her from behind, revealing all the objects around her so that she finally seems to suffocate under their repul-sive clutter. No one in a fascist film was ever so desperate as Gino in the final sequence, compared to the ending of Hemingway's *A Farewell to Arms*. The cam-era tracks toward Gino, creating the illusion of space (the world of unattainable distances) and with long shots of the seemingly endless banks of the Po river, brings back to mind the "something" Spagnolo offered him and Gino did not take. He now holds in his stiff arms Giovanna's dead body. The camera follows him as he walks in the water, carrying the woman, crying, with the police waiting in the background. Gino puts Giovanna down and embraces her as the camera pans over their bodies. Then we see a long shot of the Po valley where those who are alive can feel the "northern wind" down to the marrow of their bones. The composition of the landscape has the same dramatic purpose as the arrangement of the objects in the kitchen scene: the actors move amidst the "things" in the foreground to the background and vice versa, creating the illusion of solitude.

No film made during the fascist era ever showed unemployment. The concern with labor and capital is an important supporting theme in *Ossessione*. Seen in retrospect, it even motivates the murder of Bragana (conceived as Spagnolo's op-posite, i.e., as the representative of the pecuniary system of values). While Spagnolo professes his lack of interest in the power of money (the same as Vit-torini's "more than men" do), Bragana says during the night in Ancona, shortly before his murder: "It is not important to work, but to know how to make money." This motif opens up the whole film, being one of the basic differences between Frank and Gino. Gino is not only a tramp; he is unemployed. "What were you doing up on that truck?" asks Bragana in the opening sequence. "I don't know. I'm out of work," answers Gino. The motif comes back in the conversation between Gino and Giovanna. "Once I worked on a farm in Piacenza," she says. "I was always a sea-sonal worker. Then I lost my job, and I let men take me out to dinner." The motif of the gap between people who have money and those who do not keeps returning throughout the first half of the film. "People who have money take the train," re-marks Gino, explaining why he walks from one place to the next.

The character of Giovanna in the story represents the disruption of the family, another recurrent theme of Visconti's films. In the early 1940s, it formed a bridge between *Ossessione* and two other important films of the time, De Sica's *The Chil-dren Are Watching Us* and Blasetti's *Four Steps in the Clouds*, both based on the absence of family. While Blasetti's film centered on unconsummated adultery and the impossibility of escaping from the routine of the daily life, De Sica and Vis-conti showed a consummated adultery, a disintegration of the nuclear family and the inability to find a more valid basis than conventional social structures. Although different in many respects, these three films, which marked a turning point in Italian filmmaking, challenged the institution of marriage, considered one of the cornerstones of the establishment.

The style of *Ossessione* continued the line of French prewar populism and psychological realism represented by Renoir, Carné, Duvivier, Chenal, Prévert, and others. *Ossessione* is Visconti's most realistic film. It subverts reality as little as possible and excludes explicit judgment by substituting contextual metaphors. It suffices to see the squalidness of the streets and pubs, with their prostitutes and unemployed, to understand why a woman married a man she did not love and why a man had to dream of alternatives to keep from suffocating in a decaying atmosphere.[38] "I was drawn to film because I wanted, above all, to tell stories of living people," wrote Visconti in 1943, "of living people among things, not of things *per se*. What I am interested in is an 'anthropomorphic' film."[39]

Visconti and his group also wanted to reopen Italian film to foreign influences and to reestablish contacts with the world culture disrupted by the fascist isolationism. This "emergency cosmopolitism," as it was referred to, did not exist solely within the realistic trend of the "Cinema group" but also in the Calligraphist works and in other art forms.

In *Ossessione*, which opens with a tracking shot similar to the one in Renoir's *La bête humaine*, Visconti drew from Stroheim's visually conceived narrative style, Pabst's expressionistic objectivity, and Vigo's multisensory structure (*Atalante*). But his great master remained Renoir, connected with Visconti's recollections of the feverish years spent in prewar Paris of the Popular Front, of strikes, and of antifascist demonstrations. *The Postman Always Rings Twice* attracted Visconti's attention also because of its resemblance to *La bête humaine*. Both stories have the same triangle, the same passionate woman, rude husband, and lover—*vagabondo* in Italy, *l' homme traqué* in France. On the other hand, the structural composition of *Ossessione* (mainly the interdependence between the environment and the characters) derives more from Renoir's *Toni*, which influenced Visconti's art of creating dramatic intensity by the arrangement of objects within the shot.

Renoir's influence can also be traced in Visconti's work with actors. "Until now, the Italian cinema had to endure actors," he wrote in "Cinema antropomorfico." "It had let them free to magnify their vanity and errors while the real problem is to use the originality and actuality of their true nature." Giovanna and Gino are portrayed by Clara Calamai, the femme fatale of the time, and Massimo Girotti, who later became the leading actor in Visconti's theatrical group and a famous neorealist actor.[40]

"This is not Italy," shouted Vittorio Mussolini during the special premiere of *Ossessione* organized by the "Cinema group," and he walked out slamming the door of his box. On July 15, 1943 the Bologna daily *Avvenire d'Italia* wrote:

We wish to direct the attention of the authorities toward a movie which has already been forbidden or discontinued elsewhere and which has now surfaced in our town. We do not wish to apply to it any aesthetic criteria. The only conclusion to arrive at might be that the film is just imitating the French kind of realism that must not be transferred to Italy. The movie is a concoction of repulsive passions, humiliation and decay. It is an offense to the Italian people, the life of which it pretends to portray on a thoroughly imaginary and impossible level.[41]

The Catholic Film Center condemned the film, the priests preached against it, and most of the press attacked it. It was cut and recut until it disappeared from movie theaters only to reemerge in a Roman premiere in 1945. The young critics answered these attacks with enthusiastic paeans, which in retrospect may seem exaggerated but which at that time justly recognized the historical importance of Visconti's cinematic debut—referred to metaphorically as the "July 25 of the Italian cinema." This day, on which in 1943 Mussolini's government fell, marked the end of an era and the beginning of a new one. So did *Ossessione*, with its "X-ray reading of the bone structure of a society."[42]

THE TIME OF SALO

And around them insanity continued. . . . On September 8, 1943, the armistice was proclaimed, signed on September 3 by the new government headed by Marshal Badoglio. On September 10, Rome was occupied by the Germans and declared an "open city." On September 12, Mussolini, liberated by German paratroopers from captivity in the Abruzzi mountains, announced the creation of the Italian Social Republic (Repubblica Sociale Italiana). Its government, led by Marshal Rodolfo Graziani, was seated in the town of Salò on Lake Garda in northern Italy. On October 13, Badoglio's government declared war upon Germany. During these events, the equipment of Cinecittà and the Centro Sperimentale di Cinematografia was dismantled and partly transported to Germany. The rest went to Venice where a new Cinecittà, ironically called Cinevillaggio (film village), was set in the Giardini della Biennale, the gardens where the art exhibits of the Venice Biennale had taken place. The new studios were solemnly opened on February 22, 1944. In May 1944, production also started in the Scalera studios, which were transferred to Venice from Rome early in 1942 in order to escape bombing. However, for this to happen, Luigi Freddi had to threaten the owners with the requisition of the premises. The Scalera studios were located on the island of Giudecca, one of the poorest in the Venice lagoon. Francesco De Robertis became the head of the Venice production.

During the existence of the short-lived and notorious Republic of Salò, twenty-one films were produced (seventeen in 1944 and four in 1945). The first one among them, entitled *Un fatto di cronaca* (News Item), was made by a third-rate director, Piero Ballerini (1901–1955), and was a conventional "white telephone" film. So were the remaining twenty. Only one, *L'aeroporto* (Airport, 1944), carried an overtly fascist message.

During the German occupation, three films were produced in Rome. One of them was made by Vittorio De Sica, to whom Freddi had previously offered the management of the Venice productions. To avoid any contact with the Salò republic, De Sica accepted a commission from the Catholic Film Center and shot *La porta del cielo* (Gate to Heaven, 1944). He employed as many people as possible, thus saving them from the Venice threat. *Gate to Heaven*, scripted by Zavattini and released only after the liberation of Rome, depicts the journey of a group of religious pilgrims from Rome to Loreto. The train on which they travel becomes a kind of microcosm of human misery where the war, never even mentioned, is constantly present. For the first time, people of modest origin appeared in a film by De Sica, whose attention had been until then focused on the milieu of the bourgeoisie. The characters of *Gate to Heaven* are blue-collar workers, a young boy from the proletarian part of Salerno, a girl from the lower middle-class, etc. Through them, the director and the scriptwriter came closer to the problems of social injustice, which became the focus of their best postwar films. And the film was shot in the basement of the church of San Bellarmino and in the basilica of San Paolo—far from any studio.

De Sica, reflecting about this time, wrote: "The war experience was crucial for all of us. We were bursting with an overwhelming desire to throw out of the window the old stories of the Italian cinema, to place the camera into the mainstream of real life, of everything that struck our horrified eyes."[43] While shooting *Gate to Heaven*, De Sica was profoundly influenced by *Ossessione*, which he had seen in a private screening.

It was Roberto Rossellini, however, on whom *Ossessione* made the greatest impact. He started shooting *Desiderio* (Desire) in the summer of 1943, based on a story similar to that of Giovanna and Gino. De Santis wrote the script and worked as Rossellini's assistant, and Massimo Girotti starred. The original title of the picture was *Scalo merci* (Freight Station), and it was to have been shot in authentic settings among the railwaymen of the proletarian quarter of San Lorenzo in Rome. After a bombing leveled San Lorenzo, Rossellini moved his crew to the country, changing the title and the story (*Rinuncia* [Renunciation]). After the September 8 armistice, shooting was interrupted for the second time, and the film was finally completed in 1945 by Marcello Pagliero (1907–1981).[44] *Desire*, inspired by *Ossessione*, is just its poor copy. Centering on the same fatalistic passions, the story evolves in a heavy erotic atmosphere, which was becoming De Santis's speciality (unmade beds, hot nights, black underwear, seminude bodies, etc.). But its backdrop remained empty. *Desire* turned into another trite story of a femme fatale, a sinner, and a sufferer—a prisoner of her senses who destroys the men around her and finally commits suicide. As in *Ossessione*, the main theme is the disruption of the family, symbolized by an adulterous affair between the heroine and her brother-in-law (who looked as if he had just stepped out of *Ossessione*).[45]

The insanity around them was coming to an end. After July 25, 1943, came April 25, 1945, when the National Liberation Committee of Northern Italy (Comitato di Liberazione Nazionale Alta Italia) proclaimed a general insurrection against the Germans. If *Ossessione* can be referred to as the "July 25 of the Italian cinema," then *Open City* is its April 25, the day on which a new Italy was born and with it a new realism.

II

LACRIMAE RERUM   (1944–1948)

The historic center of Rome is among the world's most beautiful sites. Here it is not easy to find an ugly street, a place of no interest. The Via del Traforo, however, at the end of Largo di Tritone, has little charm. There, in house number 133, postwar Italian film production had its beginning. The first films made after 1944 were certainly not preoccupied with beauty. There were not many beautifully composed images; there was very little beautiful photography. These films were light years away from the "white telephones" and the elegant language of D'Annunzio's writings. The style had become crude, and the stories focused on a ravaged, humiliated country: Italy after the 1943 defeat. It was a tragic country, hungry and desperate, occupied by foreign soldiers who bought its women for a few pieces of candy. These first postwar films were bursting with "tears shed by things": *lacrimae rerum* (a term used by Francesco De Sanctis in his *History of Italian Literature* to characterize the nineteenth-century veristic movement). In the 1960s, Roberto Rossellini summed up the postwar Italian situation: "In 1944, everything was destroyed in Italy. The film, and everything else."[1]

Anybody who ever wants to know the immediate reactions to the human implications of World War II will not find a more telling testimony than the first postwar Italian films: *Open City, Days of Glory, The Sun Rises Again, Without Pity, Shoeshine, Paisan, Germany, Year Zero,* etc.—all films born of insanity and the will to fight back.

Even while Rome was still occupied by the Germans, some Italian filmmakers were secretly meeting in the Via del Traforo to discuss the cinematic future of a country on the brink of becoming an American film colony. Among those present were Rossellini, Aldo Vergano, Alfredo Guarini, and the representatives of four underground political movements (the Socialist party, the Communist party, the Party of Action and the Movement of Communist Catholics). In June 1944 when the Germans left and the allied armies marched in, these filmmakers—united in the newly founded Union of Film Technicians (Sindacato Lavoratori del cinema)— were ready to face the victors and to defend the Italian film industry. During the first meeting among the representatives of the allied armies and the Italian film industry, U.S. Rear Admiral Emery W. Stone declared:

The so-called Italian film was invented by the fascists, therefore it has to be suppressed. The instruments which created this invention have to be suppressed too. All of them, including the Cinecittà. There has never been a film industry in Italy. There have never been Italian film industrialists. Who are these industrialists? Speculators and adventurers, yes, that's what they are. Anyway, Italy is an agricultural country. What would she need a film industry for?[2]

Among those listening to this historical proclamation were Stephen Pallos, former assistant to Alexander Korda (representing the British army), Pilade Levi (representing the U.S. army), and Alfredo Guarini, an Italian producer and director. Thanks to Guarini and many others, Admiral Stone was proven wrong. Italian film was alive, well, and destined to get even better. The admiral may even have helped, by expropriating the premises of Cinecittà and turning them into a refugee camp. Thus, even the little that had remained after the German loitering did not survive; those adventurers who, in spite of everything, wanted to make films had nowhere to turn and nothing to work with. And so they went out "into the streets" (according to a favorite description of the origins of neorealism) and shot their films there.

By 1944–1945, Italian film could no longer be "suppressed." Rossellini was in the streets shooting *Roma città aperta* (Open City), assisted by his old friend, scriptwriter Sergio Amidei, and by a young man from Rimini—an eager and enterprising newcomer to Rome—Federico Fellini (b. 1920). Antonioni had just returned from the shooting of his first short, *Gente del Po* (People of the Po River): the war prevented him from completing it, but he was already captivated by filmmaking and resolved to carry on.[3] Blasetti, always ready to join a current trend, was preparing a film about the resistance (*Un giorno nella vita* [One Day in a Life]). Mario Soldati was writing another of his nostalgic films (*Le miserie del Signor Travet* [Mr. Travet's Troubles]). Guiseppe De Santis was producing one script after another and was attempting, along with Gianni Puccini, to create a new film journal. Life in Rome was not yet sweet—"la dolce vita" was still far away—but it was extremely interesting, hectic, and fertile.

When Milan was eventually liberated and the war was really over, cinematic activities started there too. In June 1945, the first issue of a new film magazine *Film d'oggi* was published, following the tradition of *Cinema* (which had ceased to exist in December 1943). De Santis, Carlo Lizzani (b. 1922), and Massimo Mida-Puccini became members of the journal's Milan staff, and Gianni Puccini and Antonioni worked as its Rome correspondents. In his article about the first film made by the Milan group, *Il sole sorge ancora* (The Sun Rises Again), De Santis insisted: "This film shows Italian cinema the path to follow: the path of realism."

Meanwhile in Rome, Visconti, who had narrowly escaped death,[4] was working on several scripts. Collaborating with Visconti were Puccini, Antonioni, Antonio Pietrangeli, and Vasco Pratolini, the rising star of Italian literature. In one of these scripts, "Pensione Oltremare" (The Boarding House Oltremare), Visconti sought to evoke his own experience in a German prison. Another Visconti script told the story of a women's orchestra playing on the front during World War II. Antonioni later said: "What a shame that this film was not made. In my opinion, it might have taken the place of *Open City*."[5]

In 1945, Visconti directed one of the episodes in the composite film *Giorni di gloria* (Days of Glory), which combined war newsreel footage with documentary material shot after the war.[6] The other episodes were directed by De Santis and Marcello Pagliero, and the commentary was written by Umberto Barbaro, who since 1944 had been president of the Centro Sperimentale. (Mario Serandrei was the film's editor and general supervisor.) The visual expressiveness and simplicity of the crude images in *Days of Glory*—the tired faces of the partisans, women protecting their children and lining up for bread, hostages taken away by the Germans, etc.—became a source of inspiration for later neorealist films. Visconti's episode in *Days of Glory* records the trial of Pietro Caruso (the police chief of Rome during the German occupation), the lynching of the police superintendent Garetta, and the execution of Caruso and Pietro Koch.[7] It is an impressive piece of filmmaking, with particularly outstanding scenes showing the court proceedings. These scenes were shot with direct sound and edited in an elaborate montage that alternated close-ups and long shots. The continuously moving camera draws the viewer into the action by carefully juxtaposing striking details: a twisted mouth, the face of a screaming woman, a raised hand, an angry gesture by the judge, Caruso's face, which dominates the entire screen for a long moment, the seething crowd in the courtroom. The authenticity of the situation and people create the impression that the event is taking place "before the viewer's eyes." Such authenticity became one of the most impressive features of the style that "was being coined."[8]

There was one thing missing from *Days of Glory* and other films to come: Italy's own role in the war and its perpetuation, Italy's own fascism, fascism as a way of life. With the exception of Zampa's *Anni difficili* (Difficult Years, 1948) and Lizzani's *Cronache di poveri amanti* (Chronicle of Poor Lovers, 1953), such themes had to wait for a new generation to emerge in the early sixties—a generation that required at least some reckoning with the past. In the meantime, the villains held responsible for Italy's tragedy were the Germans, together with a handful of collaborators and fascist big shots.[9] In *Days of Glory*, women who had slept with the Germans (and had their hair cut by the patriots for their "treason") also shared the blame.

MOMENTS OF UNITY:
OPEN CITY, THE SUN RISES AGAIN, PAISAN

The first film of the neorealist movement was made by Rossellini, an outsider to the "Cinema group," an impulsive filmmaker and film addict, with little interest in theoretical problems. While Visconti was frantically preparing his theatrical calendar in an attempt to fill a quarter-of-a-century void[10] and while the others were writing scripts and articles, Rossellini borrowed some money and shot *Open City*.

He started shooting as early as the spring of 1944 while the Germans were still in the city. The film was premiered in the fall of 1945. Its critical response was divided, but it became a hit with audiences.[11] (In the 1945–1946 season, the film headed the list of the best-grossing pictures.) Its fame grew slowly, mainly after its 1946 premieres in France and the United States where it was hailed as the best film of the year.[12]

Open City is a film about death and an awareness of the tragic in ordinary life. Death has always been a major theme in Italian art. With *Open City* this theme entered Italian cinema and subsequently became one of its most important concerns. In Rossellini's films, death is linked with martyrdom inspired by a Christian interpretation of life. The army chaplain in *Man with the Cross,* who dies somewhere in Russia with his lips pressed to the cross, represents similar ideals as Don Pietro (the priest) and Manfredi (the communist) in *Open City.* The image of the chaplain's body lying on the battlefield is reminiscent of the famous close-up of Don Pietro looking at Manfredi's mutilated body, his eyes full of tears. His face remains on the screen for a few seconds; then the camera returns to the torture chamber, and Don Pietro's voice is heard off-screen: "You wanted to kill his soul, but you have only killed his body."

In retrospect, the plot of *Open City* is of limited interest. It depicts the underground activities of a group of workers in Rome during 1943–1944 when it was declared an "open city" by the Germans. Just before Francesco's marriage to Pina, his pregnant girl-friend, Manfredi hides from the Gestapo in Francesco's home. Manfredi has Don Pietro deliver some money to the underground. The Gestapo raids the apartment block. Francesco is arrested, and Pina, as she rushes after him, is shot. Francesco escapes and rejoins Manfredi, who is hiding in the apartment of his mistress, Marina. Marina is a drug addict, and her supplier is a woman Gestapo

Open City

agent. Marina betrays Manfredi, and he and Don Pietro are arrested. Manfredi dies under torture; Don Pietro is shot.[13]

In the years immediately following the war and for a quarter of a century, dozens—maybe hundreds—of similar stories were filmed all over Europe: in Prague, Rome, Athens, Warsaw, Paris, Sofia, and Belgrade. They featured partisans and resistance fighters on one side, and the Germans on the other portrayed as a tight-knit group of murderous beasts.

As its original title, *Storie d'ieri* (Yesterday's Stories), indicates, *Open City* is composed of several episodes linked by the atmosphere of a precise historical moment. Originally, Rossellini wanted to tell just the story of Don Morosini, a priest, who had actually lived in Rome and was shot by the Germans. In *Open City*, Rossellini portrayed Morosini in the character of Don Pietro and then gradually added episodes depicting the experiences of other people. These episodes were scripted mainly by Fellini and were improvised on the set by Rossellini and Amidei with changes inspired by immediate circumstances.[14]

The narrative structure of the film drew heavily on the patterns of "la rivista." Both Anna Magnani and Aldo Fabrizi (Don Pietro) were famous rivista stars, and both Fellini and Amidei occasionally wrote sketches for rivista shows. The characters of *Open City* blend the traditions of "la rivista" with those of Italian popular comedy (comedy Italian style). There is the bad woman causing the man's tragedy; there is the good priest endowed with some comical traits of the "fatso"; his servant (the sexton); there is "la mamma" (Pina), a woman who suffers and dies for love; and, finally, there are the stereotypes of eternal damnation, the Gestapo man Bergman and his lesbian assistant Ingrid.

The characters of the film are symbolic representations of nationalism, Christianity, unity, moralism, existentialism, Catholicism, etc. But Rossellini uses them mainly as components of his "choral" story of a city in a crucial moment of its existence.[15] The film is at its best when it emphasizes dozens of seemingly unimportant details. The facts of life under the German occupation and the people who really lived this life are engulfed in an atmosphere of continuous tension: the tenants of Pina's house discussing daily events, believers praying in church, a German patrol crossing the Piazza di Spagna, soldiers surrounding the house where Francesco and Manfredi are hidden, Don Pietro walking the streets "among things" with money for the underground movement in his hand, children returning toward the city with the dome of St. Peter's visible in the valley below and with Don Pietro dying a few steps away from them, etc.

The dramatic force of Rossellini's films originates in the authenticity of "the things." There is Pina's apartment and its table with plates never full enough to appease a child's hunger; her worn jacket and checkered scarf; Don Pietro's rectory with its shaky wood-burning stove, a pot of thin cabbage soup, and old newspapers; there is the printer's shop; the overcrowded double streetcar; the greasy, slovenly coat of the waiter who serves spaghetti to Marina, Francesco, and Manfredi; Andreina's face in the scene preceding Pina's death, a face of a poor Roman woman as she rushes to inform the priest of the approaching catastrophe, etc. Such details— which might have appeared occasionally in earlier films as part of a set or decor or

Open City

as elements of montage—became for Rossellini the very basis of the narrative and visual texture, the very source of the dramatic impulse.[16]

When he made *Open City,* Rossellini already saw film as an instrument of a modern vision, a way of seeing things "with one's own eyes." He used film as a mass medium to disseminate to a wider audience information that previous techniques could communicate only to the happy few. The novelty of *Open City* lies in its transformation of art into information. Rossellini provides the viewer with a real memory of something the viewer has not actually experienced.

At the end of 1945, the clients of a brothel in the Via San Pietro all'Orto in Milan went through a moment of horror. Entering the establishment, they found themselves in the midst of soldiers in German uniforms. Some ran out and called the police, who actually came to the scene. All the policemen found was Aldo Vergano and his crew, trying to put into practice their theories about shooting films in an authentic environment.[17] Their film entitled *Il sole sorge ancora* (The Sun Rises Again) was the first attempt to analyze the social and historical structure of Italian society at the time of the partisan struggle of 1943–1945.[18] The story takes place on a large agricultural estate in Lombardy after the events of September 1943. Its characters are divided into clear-cut groups: the landowners on one side, the exploited peasants on the other. The protagonist, a young villager who tries to join the partisans in the mountains, is arrested by the Germans and executed along with the village priest. At the moment of the execution, when death is again viewed as resurrection, the partisans appear on the horizon and annihilate the German unit.

The film was conceived as a manifesto for the new movement. It was shot in places where similar events had really occurred not long before. Only the leading roles were played by actors, and the supporting parts and the extras were played by people who had lived through similar situations. The script was written by De Santis, Carlo Lizzani, and Guido Aristarco, who was later to become a prominent film theoretician. The extras included several journalists and a keen newcomer to the film scene, Gillo Pontecorvo (b. 1919).

The director of the picture, Aldo Vergano, was an intriguing personality, a man with a complicated past and an uncertain future. He was one of three perpetrators of the assassination attempt on Mussolini in 1925. During the fascist regime, he was active as a scriptwriter and associate producer. In 1938, he directed his first feature film, *Pietro Micca,* a mediocre costume story about a young rebel who died for the freedom of Italy. During the German occupation, Vergano was arrested for another assassination plot; he managed to escape and went into hiding. He played an active part in the creation of the first Union of Italian Film Technicians, and it was no coincidence that this experienced filmmaker, close to both the unions and the National Association of Italian Partisans (who produced the film), found himself at the head of the Milan group. A loner, mistrusted by the leftists as well as by the conservatives, Vergano entered film history as the director of just one film: *The Sun Rises Again.*[19]

Il sole sorge ancora

The Sun Rises Again blends religious feelings with leftist political activism. The crude picture of Italy at war, re-created while "still hot," remains the greatest asset of the film, which tries to inspire a belief in an alliance between the church and the communists. The people who found themselves working together on the set came from different political directions. Yet all of them felt that the only hope for the rebirth of their country lay in this unity, symbolized by a peasant boy (played by Gillo Pontecorvo, himself later a director) and a priest (played by Carlo Lizzani, an ardent communist), who face a firing squad together.

After the completion of the film, the Milan group fell apart. The journal *Film d'Oggi* ceased publication. The moment of unity that had given birth to *Days of Glory, Open City,* and *The Sun Rises Again* was coming to an end.

Paul Eluard, the French poet, described *Paisà* (Paisan) as "a film in which we are impatient rubber-neckers and greedy voyeurs; but one in which, like all good rubber-neckers, we are both actors and spectators. We see and we are seen, and this upsets us. Life surrounds us, involves us, and overwhelms us."[20]

Paisan is considered to be Rossellini's most important film, and in a way it is the most impressive film of the entire neorealist movement.[21] Art and information again become one, and the melodramatic patterns are weakened by a new type of narrative, stemming from a direct confrontation with life. A sentimental approach still dominates at some climactic points, but the overall impact is no longer based solely on the interdependence between characters and "things." In *Paisan* Rossellini gained control over his own blend of realism and subjectivity, combining the personal philosophy of his previous films with a structure built on verisimilitude.

At the time Rossellini started shooting *Paisan* in the first months of 1946, he tried to set up an Association of Independent Filmmakers, but, according to him, nobody wanted to be associated with the director of *Open City*.[22] Still, he received some American financial backing and was able to shoot *Paisan* under much better conditions.

Paisan opens in southern Sicily, on the most "African" coast of Italy—the arid and desolate shore between Gela and Marina di Ragusa not far from Syracuse. There in June 1943, the Allies had landed. Rossellini intended to re-create their advance toward the north while their presence was still fresh in the minds of the "paisans" and to express the mixed feelings these events evoked in the population. Rossellini was fascinated by the country's first encounters with the "American myth," personified by the G.I.'s who appeared like creatures from another planet in the middle of the Italian countryside. Stories of these encounters were easy to find. As Fellini put it: "After the war, our subjects were ready-made. They were problems of a very simple kind: survival, war, peace. These problems were preordained, they stood out a mile."[23]

The characters were preordained too: a Sicilian girl, the sweet innocent Carmela, who shows an American patrol the way and is killed by the Germans; a black American soldier who has his boots stolen by a Neapolitan shoeshine boy; a G.I. who encounters a prostitute in Rome and does not recognize in her the innocent girl whom he had met earlier; a British nurse in Florence searching for the man she loved in the middle of ferocious fighting; three army chaplains, a Catholic, a Jew, and a Protestant, who find themselves in a monastery, treated with distrust by the "all-Catholic" Italian monks; and two allied soldiers who follow Italian partisans to their death. In *Paisan*, the clash of two civilizations, which became the central conflict in Rossellini's later film *Voyage in Italy,* is overcome by an all-embracing humanism and a belief in the solidarity among people as utterly different as the Italians, the British, and the Americans.

The script was based on personal reminiscences and stories told by Rossellini's friends Amidei, Pagliero, Pratolini, Klaus Mann (the son of Thomas Mann), and others. The dialogues, though carefully scripted, were changed and improvised on the set. All the shooting was done on location, and many characters were played by nonprofessionals. Later, Rossellini pointed out:

> Too many believe that the secret of neorealism rests in having an unemployed man play the role of an unemployed man. I select my performers on the basis of their physical appearance. You can pick up anybody in the street. I prefer non-professionals because they do not have preconceived ideas. I watch a man in his day-to-day life and get him embedded in my memory. Facing the camera, he will no longer be himself. He will be confused and will try to act; which has to be avoided at any cost. A nonprofessional always repeats the same gestures, his muscles work like that. In front of the camera, he is as though he were para-lyzed. He forgets who he is, thinking that he was chosen for the role because he has become an exceptional human being. I have to bring him back to his real nature, to reconstruct him, to teach him again his usual gestures.[24]

Paisan is explicitly and implicitly suffused with the theme of waiting. According to Rossellini, the representation of waiting provides an ideal opportunity for reality to manifest itself in either real or fictitious time. In each episode of *Paisan,* some-one is expecting an important event to take place, a hidden truth to become appar-ent, an anguish to disappear. The death of Carmela in the first episode puts an end to the confused emotions between her and the American soldier. In the final scene of the Neapolitan episode, which is built on hesitations, dreams, and uncertainty, a black soldier finds himself in the worst shantytown he has ever seen. In the Roman episode, the G.I. tears up the piece of paper with the girl's address and thus marks the end of an illusion. The Florentine story, that of an anguished search, comes to an end when it is revealed that the man who the woman has been looking for is dead. The episode in the monastery focuses on tensions that build while the protag-onists wait for a common dinner, which the Italian monks will ultimately refuse to eat, deciding to fast for the salvation of the two non-Catholics. And the last episode is simply a waiting for death.

Continuity among the six episodes is established by newsreel footage and by the off-screen voice of a radio announcer covering the allied advance into Italian terri-tory. *Paisan* is not a chronicle of war events. Nor is it a cinematic *Decameron*—a collection of stories told by different people at a certain historical moment—as is so frequently the case in Italian literature and cinema. The film transcends mere authenticity of events by revealing unique human attitudes. In *Open City,* such

Paisan

attitudes were paradigmatic, but in *Paisan* they reach beyond the given fact. Rossellini's own anguish, desires, and fears, which were later manifested in *Germany, Year Zero,* are already reflected in some of *Paisan's* characters, who are photographed so as to appear as part of the landscape. They are almost never shown without their surroundings, as if imprisoned by the film's frame itself. The premise of Sartre's *No Exit* has never been truer than in *Paisan:* there is no escape from the encounter with truth. Rossellini later observed:

> Usually, in the traditional film, a scene is composed as follows: a long shot, we see the milieu, the character, we approach it; then a medium shot, a three-quarter view, a close-up; and then the story of the character is told. I proceed in an opposite way: a person moves and his movements make us discover his surroundings. I begin always with a close-up; then the movements of the camera, as it follows the actor, reveal the milieu. The actor must never be left alone; he must move in a complex and comprehensive way.[25]

The Neapolitan story and the last episode, which is set in the Po region in the north, are the best parts of the film. The Po episode, reminiscent of the unpolished images in *Days of Glory,* first reveals the eerie countryside along the river. The

Paisan

calm is broken by the sound of shouted orders as the Germans bind the hands of the captive partisans and tie rocks to them. Soon the river will carry them away. In the atmosphere thus created, two allied soldiers are inspired to join the partisans in their death. The final scenes of *Paisan* show the soldiers being shot and the bodies of the Italians disappearing under the water's surface while a voice is heard off-screen: "This happened in the winter of 1944. At the beginning of spring, the war was over."

GERMANY

Paradoxically, one of the first three postwar films to capture the atmosphere of Germany at the moment of her defeat was made by an Italian.[26] *Germania anno zero* (Germany, Year Zero), shot by Rossellini in 1947, has as many disparagers as advocates. Most German film historians belong to the first category. In their *History of Cinema,* the most important such work written in West Germany, Ulrich Gregor and Enno Patalas state:

> Rossellini's method of improvisation could not deal with an alien or alienated reality. In a documentary style, his film recorded the backdrop of a Berlin reduced to rubble, with overcrowded streetcars and black marketeers. To all that, however, Rossellini added a narrative rooted in the world of fiction rather than in the real world.[27]

Unintentionally, the German film historians had touched upon the heart of the matter. The postwar Italian filmmakers never intended to reduce their narratives to mere depiction of the "real world," to "record and reveal the physical reality" as advocated by Cesare Zavattini and, to some extent, also by Siegfried Kracauer. Kracauer was basically right when he pointed out that "Rossellini of *Open City, Paisan,* and *Germany, Year Zero* develops his scenes on locale, with only rudimentary story serving as a guide."[28]

On the other hand, Rossellini, considered the founding father of true neorealism, was from the outset more concerned with subjective issues than with a faithful rendering of physical reality. He used the so-called neorealist method as a moral weapon aimed at the artistic conventions of the past. He was not interested in "things" for their own sake but for the emotions they evoked—their tears. He never really believed in the autonomy of external reality, understanding only too well how treacherous and easily deformed outward phenomena can become. As a matter of fact, all the major postwar Italian directors shared this attitude. The discussions about neorealist films as "true pictures of facts" and "slices of life" were based on a misunderstanding of the technique, which ultimately contributed to neorealism's premature demise.

The narrative of *Germany, Year Zero* was inspired by the death of Rossellini's first-born son in 1946. The intensifying agent of the story is again the idea of martyrdom, coupled with a belief in grace as the only source of true faith. Twelve-year-old Edmund is the foremost example of Rossellini's absorption with the fundamental sentiments of Christianity. The film chronicles the boy's maturing through exposure to a series of extreme situations. In a film by Rossellini, the

Germany Year Zero

maturing of a child in Berlin in 1945, in a family wrecked by war, must inevitably lead to death. The final sequence captures Edmund walking through the desolate streets of Berlin, among "the things." The fusion of the landscape with the human element of the narrative is reminiscent of Don Pietro's walk through occupied Rome, leading to the same destiny. Edmund passes a church that towers over the rubble. We hear music, which the boy seems not to hear. We see the priest inside; he does not. The camera changes repeatedly from Edmund's viewpoint to the objective one and back. The church music is still heard as Edmund disappears into a bombed-out house. He makes his way up the stairs, looks down to the street below from each floor, plays with his toy pistol, and finally jumps. Before killing himself, he confesses to his former teacher, an ardent Nazi, that he has acted according to the teacher's principles and killed his ailing father. "The weak are always eliminated by the strong," the teacher had often told him.[29] Edmund's "I killed my father!"—words that will be heard so often in later Italian films—resound against the background of the destroyed city, laying bare the absurdity of the world in which they originated.

Rossellini's narration has many flaws. As in his other films, he is not concerned about "telling a story well." Unlike the majority of Italian filmmakers (including Visconti, De Sica, Zavattini, Fellini, and Lattuada) Rossellini was never a storyteller. He never worried about the flow of events. His characters are sketchy and incongruous, and their motivations can be understood only in light of the dominating idea. Ironically enough, this disregard for the narrative became one of Rossellini's major assets and an important element of his style.

After *Germany, Year Zero* was first shown, remarks were made about Rossellini's decline. Fortunately, Rossellini was an artist of strong integrity, a true film adventurer who constantly sought contact with the phenomena around him. He continued on his own path, stubbornly and consistently until eventually he saw his work reevaluated (in the mid-fifties, initially in France).[30] In 1947, when Rossellini returned from Germany with Carlo Lizzani (at that time his assistant) and Anna Magnani (then his passionate love), the protagonists on the Italian film scene had changed, and the moment of unity—in culture and in politics—was definitely over.

In the film world, it was at this time Cesare Zavattini who started to work out a theory that diverged in many ways from Rossellini's approach. Literature, on the other hand, was slowly catching up with film and rivaling the impact of the first postwar films. Writers could deal more openly with the fascist past than filmmakers.[31] In 1948, the year of the premiere of *Germany, Year Zero,* Vasco Pratolini wrote one of his best novels, *A Hero of Our Time,* in a way a companion piece to Rossellini's film. With a keen sense for his characters' state of mind, Pratolini traces the scars that the past had left on the mind of a young boy. Unlike Rossellini's film, however, *A Hero of Our Time* takes place not in Germany but in Italy. The story is set in 1946, and its protaganist, Sandro, is a typical product of a fascist upbringing. At a moment when many former Italian fascists were trying to shed all responsibility for the past—and some films were echoing this attitude—Pratolini's reckoning was an act of extreme importance. Sandro does not commit suicide—he kills in cold blood. At the end of the novel, a key dialogue takes place between him and Virginia, the woman who loves him and whom he kills. Virginia says: "You do evil without realizing it. As father wrote about Nora, you set fire to everything without realizing that you're setting fire to yourself. I think that's what fascism is." "What makes you say that?" he asked her, and went on, without waiting for an answer. "Perhaps it's true that I'm the one who gets burned, but it has always been others who lit the fire. . . . I've only just realized that I've never completed any of the things that I set out to do. And I've always paid for them a hundred times more than if I had." "There you are," she interrupted him. "Listen to what you've just said. You always consider that you're the victim. . . . You'll end by believing that you were never in the marò."[32]

DE SICA'S HUMAN REALITY

The three major Italian film directors of the post-World War II period—Rossellini, De Sica, and Visconti—had one thing in common: "a hunger for reality, an urgent need to attach oneself to reality after having been nourished for decades by sophisticated codes of literary exclusiveness."[33] Their individual aesthetic concepts are widely divergent, and each of the three is an original creator in his own right. But this shared "hunger for reality" gave birth to a style that became, as much as a deep moral commitment, the unifying agent of the movement referred to as the neorealist school. As time went on, the neorealists' "style commitment" or "style as ethics" was to influence all the major Italian directors (including Antonioni and Fellini) and many of the minor ones (e.g., Lattuada and Castellani).

Rossellini's personal, spiritual concept of reality and Visconti's stylized understanding of reality as history and culture long outlived the neorealist period (usually confined to the years 1944–1953). De Sica's humanistic perception of reality, however, was more attached to the postwar cultural and political atmosphere and exhausted its potential as soon as its model—Italian society marked by collective tragedy—became more diversified and complex. In 1945, the situation appeared simple: there were the oppressors and the oppressed, the victors and the vanquished. The coin had just two sides, and the relationship between men and reality seemed amenable to ontological cognition. This apparent transparency of the phenomenological state became the basis for Zavattini's theory of "the necessity to render facts as they are."

The congruence between the neorealist concept of cinema and the concept of life, resulting in 1945 from an identical social content, had already disappeared by 1948. After 1951, when De Sica and Zavattini made their last major film, *Umberto D.*, the art of "naked reality" was no longer possible. The simplified perceptions were increasingly obscured by a complex network of new references. The country was heading toward a split not only in its politics but also in its human matrix, which had been the very essence of De Sica's *oeuvre*.

In Italy, the words *human, human being, man* have a slightly different meaning. Dominique Fernandez pointed out the difference between Italy and France:

The very notion of "human being" in a poor country like Italy just cannot be the same as in France. In France, a human being that is of any interest to the writer, a human being that triggers a novel, is from the beginning a psychological creature, provided with a special identity, or a metaphysical one. In any case, it is a being who tries to escape the brutally immediate human condition. Such a human being is, in a certain way, rich in his inner self; and it is on this richness that classical occidental culture focused, and rightly so. In Italy, the word *human being* embodies its full literal meaning. The kind of culture that begins to take root in Italy does not attempt in any way to bring to the forefront some new type of human being. It just tries to discover the simple, immediate, and unshakable content of these simple words: a human being, a man, a woman.[34]

In the years 1946–1948, De Sica made two films with Zavattini: *Sciuscià (Shoeshine)* and *Ladri di biciclette (Bicycle Thief)*.[35] Both are permeated with the bitter statement—later labeled as "De Sica's and Zavattini's pessimism"—that few things had changed in the new society. While Rossellini was searching for subjective freedom of facts and Visconti for the freedom to interpret them, De Sica tried to find their human face. He discovered it not in the exceptional sorrow of the war but in the misery of daily life where war was just one aspect of the human lot.

Shoeshine is imbued with De Sica's compassion for the oppressed and with his genuine sentimentalism.[36] What is new in this film is the authenticity of the atmosphere and of the overall perspective. De Sica's and Zavattini's method consisted in a preliminary investigation of the characters and their ambience and in the group-

Shoeshine

ing of documentary elements around fictitious situations rich with ethical and poetical implications. In *Shoeshine*, the authentic milieu—the streets of Rome, the black market, the poor apartments, the prison—forms a telling setting for the film's statement that dreams are incompatible with certain social conditions.

As in some of Zavattini's previous stories, the dream in *Shoeshine* is symbolized by a horse, the object of desire for Giuseppe and Pasquale, the two little "sciusciàs" who make their living in the streets. Together they manage to buy a white horse, but their black-marketeering lands them in prison where one of them is tricked into informing and the other betrays his friend in revenge. Giuseppe escapes; Pasquale leads the police to his hiding place; eventually Giuseppe kills his friend. In the final scene, with Giuseppe crying over his friend's body, the white horse wanders away, disappearing into the morning fog.

The structural weakness of *Shoeshine* stems from the incongruity between the authenticity of scenes shot in actual settings and those staged in the studio or composed in the traditional manner (close-ups of innocent childish faces; close-ups of little hands whose fingerprints are being recorded; the composition of the scene showing Giuseppe's mother's visit to the prison, etc.). In spite of these inconsistencies, *Shoeshine* is one of those films that has "a persistent life" (as Malcolm Cowley once said about Ignazio Silone's novel *Fontamara*). Both De Sica and Zavattini were excellent storytellers who managed to endow the most contrived images with an extraordinary cogency, appealing to the audience's emotions. Their endeavor to render a message through epic metaphors allowed them to transcend the mere replication of reality. De Sica was probably not the greatest Italian narrator (as Cesare Pavese once called him), but he had a genuine talent for soliciting emotional response from the most banal stories.[37]

There could hardly be anything more trite than the story of *Bicycle Thief*. Based on a 1947 novella by Luigi Bartolini,[38] it was cast exclusively with nonprofessional actors. (The main character was played by a blue-collar worker.) The words De Sica wrote about his film in 1948 testify to his artistic credo and are as touchingly sincere—and as overwhelmingly self-assertive—as his films themselves:

> Why seek extraordinary adventures when we are presented daily with artless people who are filled with real distress? It has been a long time since literature first discovered that modern dimension of small things, that state of mind once considered too "common." Thanks to the camera, the cinema has the means to capture that dimension. This is how I understand realism, which cannot be, in my opinion, mere documentation. If there is any absurdity in this theory, it is the absurdity of those social contradictions that society wants to ignore. It is the absurdity of incomprehension, through which it is difficult for truth and good to penetrate. Thus, my film is dedicated to the suffering of the humble.[39]

Completed at the same time as neorealism's masterpiece *La terra trema*, *Bicycle Thief* became the most famous neorealist message, understood and accepted by the whole world. De Sica's so-called "small-scale psychology" produced two perfect Zavattinian characters, symbolic of a world forever divided between rich and poor. An unemployed man finds a job posting municipal bills; he needs a bicycle for the job, so he pawns his sheets to get one. The bicycle is stolen. He spends the day in the streets of Rome with his son searching for the thief. Finally, he himself resorts to stealing a bicycle, but he is apprehended by passers-by. The owner lets him go, and the man and his son are again lost in the crowd.

The story is typical of the "news items" (fatti di cronaca) that Zavattini considered an important source for film subjects. In 1953 he wrote: "I believe in imagination, but I have more faith in reality, in people. I am not interested in prearranged encounters, in the drama of things that happen to come together."[40] In the same year he pointed out:

> Imagination is allowed, but only on the condition that it exercise itself within reality and not on the periphery. Let me be clear: I do not intend to give the impression that only "news items" matter to me. I have tried to concentrate on these with the intention of reconstructing them in the most faithful way, using a bit of imagination that comes from the perfect understanding of the event, the situation, of the fact itself.[41]

The effect of *Bicycle Thief* depends, paradoxically, upon the calculated absence of a complex story. By insisting on the utter banality of the narrative, Zavattini and De Sica created a unique dramatic plot that relies by way of compensation on an extremely elaborate script and mise-en-scène. André Bazin called *Bicycle Thief* "one of the first examples of pure cinema": "No more actors, no more story, no more sets, which is to say that in the perfect aesthetic illusion of reality there is no more cinema."[42] This statement may be perfectly justified, but conversely, *Bicycle Thief*, like *La terra trema*, is among the most carefully crafted and also the most costly neorealist films.[43]

All available resources were put to work to produce a perfect model of Zavattini's theory, and De Sica traveled all over Europe to get the funding.[44] The composition of the film, and of each shot within it, was formulated down to the smallest detail, with nothing left to last-minute decisions. The film's imagery concentrates on the representation of a man trapped in closed spaces. These spaces represent the enemy—the class society. The climactic scenes showing Ricci's rebellion against his misfortune are composed against a background of anonymous geometric lines (walls, windows, balconies), which isolate the man from his environment and suggest his basic alienation. Through a highly stylized presentation of an authentic environment (the entire film takes place in the streets, stores, and apartments of Rome), the filmmakers transcend the descriptive dimensions of the narrative, engendering in the audience a feeling of great empathy, which replaces the usual identification with the characters. In the absence of a story and the apparent absence of any mise-en-scène, the film generates a net of images that are projections of the characters' emotions. From these images, symbolic messages begin to emerge (the unity of the family, the indifference of the crowd, the loneliness of a human being, etc.). The meticulously chosen authentic settings create an imagery with strong emotional overtones (slums, flea markets, and brothels of Rome; the picturesque Piazza Vittorio; the atmosphere of the sports stadium; etc.). The story, which "would not deserve two lines in a stray dog column,"[45] eventually emerges

Bicycle Thief

with tremendous dramatic impact and uniqueness; De Sica's instinctive mistrust of historicity allowed him to transcend Zavattini's conception of *Bicycle Thief* as a chronicle of a precise time period and set of social circumstances.

A new style had clearly been coined in *Bicycle Thief*; it had both limitations (a belief in the omnipotence of facts) and assets (an imagination rooted in reality). Each filmmaker took from it what he wanted, adapting it to his own artistic vision.

GIUSEPPE DE SANTIS'S BITTER HUNT

When Giuseppe De Santis first met with Visconti in 1940, he was twenty-three years old, and his most precious asset was his youthful enthusiasm. Seven years later when he made his first film, he had everything a beginning director could dream of. He had experience, authority, a name, and a talent that had matured during years of apprenticeship. He also had a group of excellent collaborators: Antonioni, Lizzani, Barbaro, Zavattini, the editor Mario Serandrei, and the two best Italian cinematographers of the postwar decades—Otello Martelli and his assistant Gianni Di Venanzo. With this group, De Santis set out to accomplish the messianic mission of neorealism: to create a link between people and cinema, to make a "populist" film in the best sense of the word. He failed. *Caccia tragica* (Tragic Hunt, 1947) is an almost unknown masterpiece, which no distributor ever really attempted to exhibit properly. De Santis was defeated by the films that he had been fighting during his entire journalistic career: the "white telephone" films of both Italian and American origin. He found himself in the best of company. Other such dramatic flops were *Shoeshine, La terra trema, Days of Glory, Germany, Year Zero*, Antonioni's first feature *Chronicle of a Love*, and *Variety Lights*, the first feature codirected by Fellini.[46]

Tragic Hunt opens with a long tracking shot of a man on a moving truck (Massimo Girotti), intended as another tribute to *Ossessione*. The man kisses the woman, but the opening shot quickly changes into a long view of the surroundings. The director makes his intention clear from the outset. His primary interest is not the couple but the environment, the endless fields of the Po valley and the crowds on the roads. The plot of *Tragic Hunt* is just a part of a dramatically presented landscape, which was not permitted on the screen during the fascist regime. De Santis, its most eloquent advocate, wrote as early as 1941:

> If we consider that a great number of films among those most valued belong to a genre in which a landscape has a primordial importance—*White Shadows in the South Seas, Tabu, Que Viva Mexico, Storm Over Asia*—then it is clear that the cinema has an even greater need to use the same element of landscape that communicates almost immediately with the spectators who above all want to "see."[47]

The structure of *Tragic Hunt* is based on parallel action scenes. The plot, involving four protagonists, develops in parallel to the story of the postwar peasant movement with its strikes, occupation of land, and police raids.[48] The main visual component of the film consists of open spaces continuously occupied by dramatically important crowds. The camera was mounted on a crane (the only one left in Italy), allowing for extremely vivid photography that seems to suggest the changes occurring in the country under the current pressure for agrarian reform.

The kissing couple at the beginning of the film are Michele and Giovanna, newly married peasants. In the following scene a group of fascists, led by Michele's former friend Alberto and Daniela, Alberto's lesbian lover, take Giovanna hostage.[49] Pursued by peasants, the fascists attempt to flee the country. Depicting the chase provided De Santis many opportunities for long tracking shots of the 1947 Italian landscape, still marked by the war. (The film was shot from a train crossing the country on a whistle-stop election campaign trip.) Daniela is killed by Alberto, and Giovanna is reunited with Michele. In a splendid scene, shot in a packed assembly room of the agrarian cooperative, the peasants forgive Alberto. Here, the camera, placed in the middle of the room, tracks on the crowd, fusing all individual movements into one and creating a tense atmosphere expressive of the general state of mind.[50]

De Santis's next film, *Riso Amaro* (Bitter Rice, 1948), challenged the prudishness of the neorealist period. Drawing heavily on cinematic eroticism, it marked, above all, the return of the diva, the star, the femme fatale. The rice farm worker

Silvana is a true Italian prototype of the diabolical seductress who destroys the men around her and dooms herself to destruction. Silvana Mangano, a stately counterpart of Rita Hayworth, was glamorous, sexy, and provocative, exhibiting her black-stockinged legs and her bare breasts with an inborn defiance. Her legs entered film history whereas the frames showing her breasts disappeared from practically all prints of the film, falling prey to the interest of projectionists.

In *Bitter Rice* De Santis tried to fuse a populist melodrama of love and death with a socially committed subject. He was accused by the press of imitating American westerns, of stylistic extravagances and other offenses. But such criticism did not prevent the film from becoming extremely popular, ranking fifth among the top-grossing movies of the 1949–1950 season. (*Bitter Rice* was a commercial success worldwide, surpassing even *Paisan*.)

Bitter Rice captured one aspect of the postwar atmosphere better than any other film: the "Americanization" of Italian life, the superficial merger of two civilizations, and their clash. Silvana was a product of this subculture. She was addicted to American music, film, fashion, and cartoons. She loved chewing gum and adventures. De Santis punished her with death, but the film could not hide his own infatuation with jazz, radio, and American movies. He spent months editing the famous scene that shows Mangano and Vittorio Gassman dancing boogie-woogie in a squalid railway station, filled with the noise of loudspeakers and crowded with rice farm workers.

Bitter Rice

Like *Tragic Hunt*, *Bitter Rice* is visually based on a background-foreground composition. The rhythmic structure, created by a meticulous montage that changes to the beat of the boogie-woogie music, is extremely effective. While Giovanna of *Tragic Hunt* was completely asexual, Silvana is the personification of sexual desire. Attracted to the gangster Walter, she lures him away from Francesca. When she kills him in the end, as Alberto kills Daniela, it is not because she no longer loves him, not because he has stolen rice from the warehouse—as some critics pretended and as the tradition of the Italian melodrama required—but because she discovers that he has betrayed her. Having killed Walter, Silvana leaps to her own death.

Behind Silvana's story, there is another one: the story of women slaving in the rice fields for paltry wages, of their small pleasures and great misfortunes. Along with Mangano's black stockings, other images from *Bitter Rice* entered film history: images of endless rows of women in broad hats, toiling in the knee-deep water of the rice paddies for twelve hours a day; and images of the northern Italian marshes, not far away from the place where in 1942 De Santis had assisted Visconti in shooting *Ossessione*.

After making *Days of Glory*, the two men never worked together again. While De Santis was filming *Bitter Rice*, Visconti was far to the south, in Sicily, trying to realize his own great dream—a film based on Verga. The two were never again to collaborate artistically. But they were reunited symbolically after 1948 when both became targets from the same political quarters: Visconti for his alleged "aristocraticism" and "aestheticism," De Santis for his "eroticism," "formalism," and "indebtedness to American movies." Visconti, the aristocrat, did not pay much attention. De Santis, "the broad-shouldered peasant type," unfortunately was deeply marked by the criticism, falling victim to the spirit he himself had helped to unleash through his early writings.

VERGA AND VISCONTI, VISCONTI AND VERGA

The writings of Giovanni Verga, with their broad social implications, had long attracted Visconti, and in 1947–1948 he finally set out to film one of Verga's works. *La terra trema* (The Earth Quakes)[51] is based on Verga's most famous novel, *The House by the Medlar Tree*. It depicts the destructive power of ardent passions, a dominant theme in the work of both Visconti and Verga.[52]

It is easy to see why the early neorealists chose Verga's writings as models. Giovanni Verga (1840–1926) followed the realist tradition in Italian art, focusing his interest on the less privileged social strata. The trend toward realism has always been the most important of the Italian artistic endeavors. Beginning in the early Renaissance, with Petrarch, Boccaccio, and Ariosto and followed later by Goldoni and others, Italian artists had sought to render the flow of life rather than indulge in the kind of meditative creation, typical, for example, of German literature. Fascination with the landscape, a perspective that was the most treasured heritage of the neorealists, was inherent in this tradition. Landscape emerges as a dominant trait in the work of many Italian poets and painters, together with sensuously rendered human bodies. The significance of nature is clearly displayed in Verga's work, a massive array of short stories and novels, amounting to many thousands of pages. Emile Zola and the whole of nineteenth-century French naturalism stood as close to the Italian "verismo" (*verità* in Italian means "the truth") as Jean Renoir and the French populist cinema of the thirties did to the first neorealist attempts.[53]

Having opted for Verga and his "compassion without mercy," the neorealists turned their backs on official Italian literature, represented in their time by Alessandro Manzoni, Giosuè Carducci, Gabriele D'Annunzio, and Luigi Pirandello. As early as 1941, Mario Alicata and Giuseppe De Santis wrote:

> Our argument leads us necessarily to one name: Giovanni Verga. Not only did he create a great body of poetry, but he created a country as well, an epoch, a society. Since we believe in an art that above all creates truth, the Homeric, legendary Sicily of *The House by the Medlar Tree*, *Mastro Don Gesualdo*, "Gramigna's Mistress," and "Jeli, the Shepherd" offers us both the human experience and a concrete atmosphere. Miraculously stark and real, it could give inspiration to an imagination of our cinema that seeks things in the space-time of reality, to redeem itself from the easy suggestions of a moribund bourgeois state.[54]

In August 1947, there was a violent clash between Sicilian peasants and the police,[55] and three months later Visconti left for Sicily with a small crew. His team included Francesco Rosi and Franco Zeffirelli, both of whom were to become distinguished artists in their own right (one in film, the other in theater). Visconti had a contract with Alfredo Guarini and some financial backing from the Italian Communist party, which wanted him to make a propaganda film for use in the electoral campaign. Instead he produced *La terra trema*.[56]

La terra trema differs from Visconti's other pictures in its closed visual structure with tightly framed shots, which are closely allied to the story line. Abandoning the long tracking shot that opens *Ossessione* and most of the neorealist films, Visconti begins *La terra trema* with a pan that reveals the village square and suggests its main role in the story. The camera never leaves the village, never escapes the strict boundaries delimited on one side by the bus stop and on the other by the oddly shaped rocks (faraglioni) looming out of the sea just offshore. The men of the village leave only to serve in the army and to go fishing. The women stay behind, waiting. The stagnation, the efforts to break free of it, and the endless waiting with no expectations are the main themes of Visconti's film.

In Verga's book, the central character is the grandfather, and the plot focuses on his struggle to help his grandchildren after his son dies at sea. He is defeated by the elements and by the same fates that dominate Greek and Roman mythology. Visconti's main character is the grandson, 'Ntoni, who fights the exploitation of the fishermen by the wholesale dealers and decides to operate as an independent. A storm wrecks his boat, his house is seized, and he has to return to the dealers. He too is defeated but not as a defenseless victim of immutable social conditions and an implacable destiny. 'Ntoni is a rebel who lives a moment of liberty and has to pay for it. The price is high, more than he can afford to pay. It is not the vain adventure

La terra trema

he regrets but a paradise lost. Beyond Verga's eternal sea, changeless villages, and olive groves of misery, Visconti traces the destiny of man, which he views as an open-ended road. Visconti has transcended Zola's fatalism and Renoir's determinism and made 'Ntoni into one of the "vanquished victors" so characteristic of his work. A scene toward the end of the film, while too literary to sound true, expresses Visconti's deeply felt conviction. 'Ntoni says: "They should have understood that I did it for everybody, not just for myself. But one day, they'll realize I was right. Then it will be a blessing for everybody to lose everything as I did. We have to learn to stand up for each other, to stick together. Only then we can move forward." The theme of betrayal and lack of solidarity again emerges here, to be developed more fully in Visconti's subsequent films.

Male characters are the vehicles of Visconti's intellectual convictions, but his love and compassion go to the female characters. Here, the downfall of the male character is not brought about by a woman but by his own actions. It is 'Ntoni who destroys the family, and he does not do it because of a woman. He sacrifices everything for his revolt, searching for something that may not exist. While 'Ntoni is the bearer of the social commitment, he seems less persuasive than the major female characters, his mother and his sisters. The women, condemned to eternal sadness, represent the poetic component of the film. The lyricism of the imagery is built upon the graceful movements of their black-clad figures: the Valastro women waiting on the cliffs, surveying the stormy sea where the men fight for their lives; feminine hands packing the family property, caressing the white sheets, black scarves, and family photographs; women walking to and fro within the white walls of the family house and sitting on the steps under the medlar tree, eating its bitter-sweet fruit. *La terra trema*'s superb photography is by G. R. Aldo, who has often been compared to E. Tisse. He was assisted by Gianni Di Venanzo, at that time a young novice, who had joined the crew in Sicily the moment he finished shooting *Tragic Hunt*.

While following strictly some proclaimed neorealist rules (the fishermen and their wives play themselves in their own villages, and they speak their own dialect),

La terra trema

La terra trema is stylized down to the smallest detail. It was prearranged to a far greater extent than *Bicycle Thief*, which summed up the neorealist method without attempting to redefine its confines. The script was written in such a way as to sound improvised and to induce the fishermen to utter naturally exactly the words Visconti wanted them to. The overwhelming impact of the character stems from Visconti's basic concept that they were not to make a single movement that would not be their own; they were not to express anything they would not say in real life. This method required an even more careful staging of each scene than is necessary for a film scripted to the last detail. In *La terra trema* Visconti's interest shifts toward scrutinizing faces and delineating atmosphere through the play of expressions. Dialogue is less important than in other Visconti works, and the film is structured around emotions reflected on faces. One of the major scenes depicts the salting of the first catch of fish, which 'Ntoni intends to sell directly, by-passing the dealers. The scene is based entirely on the facial expressions of the Valastros and their friends, revealing joy, expectation, and eagerness. Here the influence of Dreyer and of the Soviet cinematic avant-garde overshadows the impact of Renoir's psychological objectivism. This same influence, however, also leads to rhetorical camera movements. A clear example is the scene showing 'Ntoni's humiliation and the dealers' victory, with high and low angles used symbolically.[57] Visconti does not work with close-ups but rather uses close shots, thus achieving an effective synthesis of his previous method (showing characters in an accentuated environment) and a new emphasis on the human face in the composition of the frame.

La terra trema is a film of infinite visual beauty and intense emotional impact, which originates in the re-creation of the authentic through stylized cinematic means. The best description comes from André Bazin:

> It is the merit of Visconti to have managed a dialectical integration of the achievements of recent Italian films with a larger, richer aesthetics for which the term *realism* has not too much meaning now. I am not saying that *La terra trema* is superior to *Paisà* or *Caccia tragica* but that is does, at least, have the merit of having left them behind from a historical standpoint. Seeing the best Italian films of 1948, I had the impression that Italian cinema was doomed to repeat itself to its utter exhaustion. *La terra trema* is the only original way out of the aesthetic impasse, and in that sense, one supposes, it bears the burden of our hopes.[58]

Visconti spent several months filming *La terra trema* at Aci Trezza, a small fishing village near Catania, Verga's birthplace. After the shooting was finished and it became clear that the planned trilogy would remain incomplete, he returned to Rome. There he found himself, like 'Ntoni, in the hands of dealers, middlemen, and swindlers. After *La terra trema* was shown at the 1948 International Venice Film Festival (where it received only a minor prize), the film was cut by 4,000 feet (1,300 meters), the Sicilian dialogue was dubbed in Italian, and the film was released in second-rate theaters.[59] Although Visconti personally supervised this whole operation, he never accepted the mutilated version as the original one. Embittered by the cavalier treatment of his most beloved film, he abandoned filmmaking for four years.

La terra trema was not only doomed to the obscure existence of a "film maudit"; it also encountered, especially in Italy, a predominantly hostile reception. Many of the critics eventually changed their opinion and years later acclaimed *La terra trema* as the most accomplished film of the period. In 1958, Oreste Del Buono wrote: "My judgment, the label which I put on the film years ago, became inadequate, ridiculous, sophomoric, inadmissible. *La terra trema* was getting greater and greater as we grew older. In discussing the film, one must talk not of beauty but of greatness."[60]

FOLLOWERS AND IMITATORS: LUIGI ZAMPA, ALBERTO LATTUADA, PIETRO GERMI, AND OTHERS

In 1947–1948, after more than a quarter-century of artistic isolation, Italy began increasingly to attract the attention of the cultural world. This time, however, it was not a literary school or a movement in fine arts that won the world's esteem but Italy's films: movies from a poor, defeated postfascist country became one of the most talked about European artistic phenomena of the postwar period. Italian films were winning awards at international festivals, and in addition to receiving critical attention, some of them became top-grossing pictures. France and the United States were the most enthusiastic in their praise of the early neorealists.

Almost every Italian director experimented with the so-called neorealist method, applying it to his own style or filming a topical subject. One such experiment resulted in the most successful film of the time: Luigi Zampa's *Vivere in pace* (To Live in Peace, 1946), which was shown worldwide. (In 1947, it was awarded the New York film critics prize for the best foreign film.) The film is set in a small Italian village still occupied by the Germans, and the story revolves around the unexpected appearance of two American soldiers, fugitives from a POW camp. A typical Italian-style comedy, partially adopting neorealist patterns, *To Live in Peace* was structured as a "rivista" around a series of sketches performed by well-known actors. The film is unified by an appealing humanistic message: "Let's love each other, we are all brothers!" Zampa suggests at the end, and that was exactly what the postwar world wanted to hear.

Zampa's best film remains *Anni difficili* (Difficult Years, 1948). It marks the beginning of his association with the Sicilian writer Vitaliano Brancati, which lasted until Brancati's death in 1954. *Difficult Years* contains some strong moments, particularly when Zampa succeeds in enriching his former style through the neorealist approach. It relates the story of a petty clerk in a Sicilian village who is the only person punished for his fascist past while the mayor and other former fascist dignitaries continue their careers under the new regime. This was the first film of the neorealist period to provoke a discussion in the Italian parliament about movies dealing with inappropriate themes, compromising "the smooth transition from fascism to a new society."

Whereas Zampa fused the neorealist approach with his own predilection for farcical comedy, Alberto Lattuada adapted the neorealist principles to his favorite genre, tales of unhappy love. His protagonists, pursuing visions of undying passions, were transferred to authentic environments, and their sorrows unfolded

Anni difficili

against the backdrop of postwar Italy and social unrest. Lattuada's basic convictions about the goodness of people and the destructiveness of society were not in conflict with neorealist humanism, making his films appear as typical examples of the neorealist approach. Until the reevaluation of neorealism in the mid-seventies, Lattuada was regarded as one of the leading neorealists, more important than De Santis.

A sensitive artist with a broad capacity for selecting the best cultural impulses, Lattuada considered the neorealist approach a moral and cultural challenge, capable of giving more relevance to his stories, which were oriented mainly toward the past. In 1948, he directed the only neorealist costume film, *Il mulino del Po* (Mill on the River Po), which turned out to be his best work and one of the most outstanding films of the postwar period. It is based on a novel by Riccardo Bacchelli, whose main characters, struggling against all kinds of misfortune, belong to Lattuada's gallery of the "insulted and injured." The story, set on the shores of the Po River toward the end of the nineteenth century, is conceived in the manner of populist melodramas, drawing its main impact from the realistic depiction of the authentic environment. The film develops on two levels. One, a metaphorical story of two lovers and a murder, progresses by means of literary dialogues, theatrical performances, and sentimental music. The other level consists in the construction of a telling social background, based on a dramatically conceived landscape, artfully composed mass scenes (the ball on the village square), and the faces of the film's nonprofessional extras. The film culminates in the sequence of a clash between striking peasants and an army unit, shown in a montage that juxtaposes shots of faces and long shots of the countryside, thus underlining the film's choral aspect. Women in broad hats, an old man shaking a stick, a fragile girl shouting a threat, a lady under an umbrella, a woman crying, a villager with deep wrinkles—these random figures lend the film an authenticity that eventually emerges as its principal asset.

Il bandito (The Bandit, 1946) and *Senza pietà* (Without Pity, 1947), two previous Lattuada films acclaimed in their time, appear in retrospect primarily as moralistic stories about good people in a cruel world, a world that is sometimes rendered with a striking sense of reality. *Without Pity* was shot in Tombolo and Livorno, postwar centers of smuggling, drug trafficking, and prostitution. Lattuada captures the atmosphere of a big port populated with black-marketeers and parasites, all of whom are out to get his protagonist, Angela. She is an innocent girl, infatuated with a black G. I. named Jerry. Together they dream of departing for the United States. Jerry's assertion "We could live there and be happy," is, in 1947, an unintentionally ironic line for a poor black American who wants to marry a white girl.

Because of Lattuada, Zampa, and others, the subject range of the neorealist cinema was considerably broadened, and an increasing number of topical problems were tackled. These films offer no comprehensive analysis, and most just touch upon various aspects of life in postwar Italy. However, the fact that they bore witness to the existence of the problems was important. Not only the neorealists and their fellow travelers were infected by the prevailing desire to render as many aspects of life as possible in film. This trait extended beyond the early postwar years to become a permanent feature of Italian cinema.

The exploration of new aspects of Italian life was typical of Pietro Germi (1914–1974). Germi became one of the most controversial directors. He was referred to as

Il mulino del Po

Il bandito

"the director of compromise," and his role in the neorealist movement was questioned. Germi tried to implant the neorealist trend into the mainstream of the film industry. Using elements of traditional action films, he strove to attract a wide audience to socially committed pictures. The film that made him known was *In nome della legge* (In the Name of the Law, 1948). Like Germi's earlier film *Gioventù perduta* (Lost Youth, 1946) depicting the delinquency of the younger generation during the postwar period, *In the Name of the Law* was structured along the lines of detective stories and westerns. It is set in a Sicilian village, which provides the background for the clash between a young magistrate endowed with the qualities of a valiant sheriff (played by the attractive Massimo Girotti) and evil forces. The good peasants support his fight for the law. However, they are under the control of the Mafiosi, who are shown from time to time galloping on the horizon like a group of mounted Indians. Reality is glossed over, and there is a fairy-tale ending when justice prevails and the two parties shake hands.[61] And yet this picture helped to uncover part of the hidden face of Sicily, a country torn apart by contradictory interests, poverty, and fear, which paralyzed the people so completely that they would sooner die than speak out. Germi's imagery, showing the whiteness of the barren mountains as a protective barrier against the outside world,

In nome della legge

has since become a commonplace in Italian cinema—part of a code of signs along with the sinuous streets and dusty roads, the houses with closed shutters, and the villagers with inscrutable faces. In 1948, all this was new, and to capture it on the screen was an act of courage.

Neorealism had its rose-colored aspect too. "Pink neorealism," as it was later called, originated in Renato Castellani's film *Sotto il sole di Roma* (Under the Roman Sun, 1948), which disclosed the barrenness of the neorealist aesthetic canon if deprived of its humanistic component. Castellani reduced the neorealist approach to subject matter only. His film has all the paraphernalia of neorealism: a poor boy living in the colorful neighborhood of Porta San Giovanni, squalid apartments, innocent hearts, the German occupation of Rome, the familiar details of everyday life, the boy's encounter with wartime reality, etc. What is missing is the ethical spark, the facts behind the things, their tears.

Films of "pink neorealism" presented important problems in such a way as to make them appear less serious and less difficult to solve, and their style, aiming at authenticity, made people believe that the problems as well as the offered solutions were real. *Under the Roman Sun* introduced a new kind of comedy Italian style. It forced its way into the middle of the neorealist trend, splitting it wide open.

III

NEOREALISM, ACT II (1948–1953)

In 1948, Cinecittà reopened its doors. One of the first pictures produced in the renovated studios was *Fabiola,* a remake of Enrico Guazzoni's 1917 blockbuster. *Fabiola* marked the comeback of both a director and a genre: its director, Alessandro Blasetti, had made only one film, the mediocre *Un giorno nella vita* (One Day in a Life, 1946), in the previous four years; and the mythological genre, once the backbone of the Italian film industry, had received little attention in the past decade. Now the Italian producers, deprived of state subsidies and unable to compete with Hollywood, viewed the revival of this genre as a possible salvation.[1] Blasetti's *Fabiola* surpassed all expectations. In 1948–1949, it headed the list of top-grossing films in Italy and was soon followed by a whole series of mythological and historical epics. Their success opened a new chapter in Italian film history, characterized by historical superproductions and coproductions. These projects eventually attracted American producers and transformed Cinecittà into a "Hollywood on the Tiber."

The production of *Fabiola* followed the path of Blasetti's prewar costume tetralogy—particularly *Ettore Fieramosca* and *Iron Crown.* Even the crew remained unchanged. It included Corrado Pavolini, Emilio Cecchi, and Cesare Zavattini, joined by Antonio Pietrangeli and Vitaliano Brancati as representatives of the neorealist movement. The cinematographer was Mario Craveri, who had been second cameraman for *Iron Crown.* Massimo Girotti again played one of the major roles, and Franco Interlenghi (the little "sciuscià" whom De Sica had found in the streets of Rome three years earlier) appeared in a small part. Did all this suggest a possible fusion between the film industry and the neorealist movement? Would the most glorious moment in the history of Italian cinema end in a glorious merger?

For the time being, it did not seem likely. The neorealists were engaged in a battle against the institutions of the new republic, which in 1949 enacted a film law severely restricting artistic freedom.[2] The law was introduced by Giulio Andreotti, then a member of the government, a man close to Prime Minister Alcide De Gasperi. On the one hand, the law protected the national movie industry against American competition by taxing imported films and by imposing compulsory programming of Italian films for eighty days a year in every theater, thus tripling the distribution of Italian productions on the home market.[3] On the other hand, "la legge Andreotti" reintroduced strict precensorship, putting the state in control of the movie industry. All scripts were to be submitted to a special ministerial commission, and only those that met with official approval were granted production loans. (Thus, typically, the farcical comedy *Don Camillo* was allotted 216 million lire whereas *La terra trema* received only 6 million.) This system drastically reduced attempts at filming controversial subjects and discouraged producers from supporting films that were unlikely to receive financial assistance.[4]

Although the number of Italian films kept growing in the early fifties (161 in 1953), their overall artistic level declined considerably. As early as 1955, the government—faced with the disastrous effects of the Andreotti law—eased the censorship rules, but it was four more years before any substantial change occurred.

Of 313 feature films produced in Italy between 1945 and 1950, approximately forty showed neorealist influence and about twenty were genuinely neorealist.[5] They put Italian cinema on the map and opened the doors to foreign markets. And yet it was these twenty or thirty neorealist films that became the prime targets for Italy's new government policy. They were accused of "washing dirty linen in public" and of "slandering Italy abroad." Under the Andreotti law, a film could be denied an export license on the pretext that it "slandered Italy." This policy cut off some of the foreign returns on which many neorealists depended.

Vittorio De Sica, one of the few who continued to make socially committed films even after 1950, became Andreotti's number one target. Next on the list was Giuseppe De Santis—in at least one case the ministry vetoed a film project merely because he was the proposed director.[6] Similarly, Pietro Germi encountered problems with one of his best films, *Il Cammino della speranza* (The Path of Hope, 1950).

Andreotti himself summed up the accusations against neorealism in an open letter addressed to De Sica, published on February 24, 1952, in *Libertà*, the weekly of the Christian Democratic party. According to Andreotti, neorealist films were slandering Italy abroad, presenting her as a country of social conflicts and flaunting her unemployed and underprivileged. In his letter, Andreotti asked De Sica to "assume his social responsibility, which cannot be limited to a description of the poverty and abuses of a system and of a generation but which must help to overcome them." "We ask De Sica," Andreotti continued, "not to forget the minimal commitment toward a healthy and constructive optimism that can help humanity to move forward and to gain some hope. It seems to us that the world fame that our directors have rightly acquired gives us the right to demand that he accept his duty and fulfill this task."[7]

The conflict between Andreotti and the neorealists was representative of a pervasive tension in postwar Italy. This mood was described by Albert Moravia, writing in *Europeo*:

> At a party of Roman high society, I once met a well-traveled lady who complained that the neorealist films were slandering us, showing us as a country of people in rags. 'There are so many lovely countrysides in Italy,' this lady said. 'Why don't we make films about our lovely countrysides?' My answer was that the best way to

make films about poverty disappear was to make poverty disappear from life—to make poor people into rich ones. But I did not convince the lady.[8]

Part of the Italian film industry was sympathetic toward the government's protectionist measures. For a time, the financial returns on Italian films were increasing, and so was production. The majority of filmmakers, however, joined in a wave of demonstrations, meetings, and polemical articles against Andreotti's policy. In December 1947, thirty-five directors signed a letter to Andreotti and distributed copies to the press. The letter expressed their opposition to government measures aimed at suppressing Pietro Germi's *Lost Youth* and other films. In February 1948, the Movement for the Defense of Italian Cinema was created, and ten prominent filmmakers attacked Andreotti's law in a group of articles published in the communist weekly *Rinascita* on March 3, 1949. There, Germi summed up the situation as follows:

> Neorealism is not a fashion or a craze. It does not spring from casual or contingent sources. If it is so for some, such people will be left behind and will finish by betraying the art. Others have achieved their ambition after years of toil. They will not move backwards; they will move forward. The current Italian cinema is taking part in a long and difficult struggle for a new modern Italy. Its works represent the "lists of grievances" of a period. The Italian cinema has discovered a new language, an inexhaustible source of inspiration. But it is a discovery that has just begun and whose development cannot be planned or imagined. To smother that ferment would be a crime not simply against Italian culture but against world culture. In conclusion I declare that any measure intended to protect production without protecting quality is useless.[9]

This confrontation within the film industry coincided with the beginning of the Cold War, which separated many who had been allies during the years of struggle against fascism or in the early postwar reconstruction period. In the developing atmosphere of bitterness and hatred, "Zhdanovism," the cultural form of Stalinism, made its appearance. At the 1948 congress of the communist-dominated peace movement, held in Poland, the Cold War and its ideology were first carried into the realm of culture on an international scale.[10] One of the leaders of the peace movement, the Italian communist Emilio Sereni, wrote in *Rinascita* in the fall of 1948: "Zhdanov offered an essential and fundamental contribution to the renaissance of Italian culture."[11] A year later, Vsevolod Pudovkin gave a fiery speech at the International Film Congress in Perugia, in which he exhorted the participants to disregard the problems of form in favor of content and to use the film medium in the struggle against capitalism. Part of his speech concerned the necessity for creating "positive heroes" embodying the people's fight for freedom.

Thus, while the neorealists were defending themselves against the assault by the Christian Democratic government, their films also came under attack by some Marxist critics, who accused them of formalism, pessimism, subjectivism, and insufficient social commitment. In October 1948, the communist daily *L'Unità* ran a polemic about De Santis's *Bitter Rice*—mainly about Mangano's breasts and legs.

Admittedly, neither Silvana nor Walter was a "positive hero," and they could not possibly withstand the Zhdanovist scrutiny. The reproach, addressed to De Santis, questioned how breasts and legs could contribute to the promotion of such noble issues as socialism and the class struggle. And in the standard Zhdanovist terminology, the critics also objected that Silvana was not "typical" of the Italian working woman. "It is in the healthy men and women—mothers, wives, husbands, sons— who fight for their daily bread that truth appears the richest," wrote Antonello Trombadori in *L'Unità*. The polemic was summed up by Davide Lajolo, editor-in-chief of *L'Unità*'s Turin edition. Referring to the Soviet films presented at the festival in Milan, Lajolo stated that "they have shown us how to proceed on the road toward socialism." De Santis tried to defend himself, arguing that *Bitter Rice* was intended to denounce the American ideology that "had managed to diffuse its poison among the healthy strata of the population, especially the young generation, to whom it showed the pleasant face of boogie-woogie, chewing gun, and easy luxury."[12] Yet this claim did not convince his critics, who demanded that he prove with his new films what he had learned from their criticism. De Santis's next two pictures, *Non c'è pace tra gli ulivi* (No Peace Under the Olives, 1950) and *Roma ore undici* (Rome, 11 O'Clock, 1951), lost the richness of style and the complexity of characterization that marked *Tragic Hunt* and *Bitter Rice*. The new protagonists were unmistakably either positive or negative, and the neorealist formula was used merely to produce simplified pictures of the class struggle.

At the Perugia congress, the attacks against "bourgeois and cosmopolitan" influences were launched mainly by Vsevolod Pudovkin (the distinguished Soviet guest) and by Umberto Barbaro, at that time a visiting professor at the Polish Film Academy at Lodz.[13] As an inspiring teacher at the Centro Sperimentale di Cinematografia during the fascist era, Barbaro helped to coin the neorealist style. But now he claimed:

> It is true that there is an affinity between Visconti's films and the prewar French cinema. But Visconti picked up its worst and most condemnable aspects: for example, the erotic ambiance of Renoir's films, which tarnished him mainly in *Ossessione*. When he tried to free himself from this, Visconti came close to the flatness of Rouquier's *Farrebique*. *La terra trema* is a result of this effort. It is a film which lacks any lucid idea.

With these words Barbaro had translated the latest Soviet political line into Italian.[14] His words reflected the spirit of two resolutions adopted in 1948 by the Italian Communist party. The first, called "For the Preservation of Italian Culture," postulated an increased ideological control over the intellectuals. The other, published under the title "Against Imperialist and Clerical Obscurantism," assigned to culture one and only one role, to serve political goals.

Attacks against nonconformist Italian film continued for years, culminating in the 1954 discussion of Fellini's *La strada*. Hardly anyone was spared. After De Santis and Visconti, it was De Sica's and Zavattini's turn (they had allegedly fallen prey to pessimism and had described everyday reality "without clear judgment").[15] Later came Rossellini, Antonioni, and others. Since virtually all neorealists had leftist sympathies, they naturally resented the leftist attacks far more than those by the government and the rightist press.

In order to understand the strong impact that the views of the Marxist critics had on Italian filmmakers, we have to keep in mind that during the entire post-World War II period, between 30 and 50 percent of Italian voters voted for the parties of the Left. Among these parties, the Communist became the strongest, representing almost 40 percent of the electorate at the peak of their influence (in the seventies). Italy went to the Left for several reasons. There was the structural poverty of the country, the late industrialization, and the underdevelopment of the south. Furthermore, Marxism had offered the only consistent antifascist ideology during the twenty years of fascism; and it had in Antonio Gramsci an original theoretician who made Italian Marxism to some extent independent of foreign philosophical and ideological impulses. Nor should it be forgotten that the armed resistance against the Germans and the Republic of Salò was to a large degree manned by forces sympathetic to the Italian Left. The reason critical opinion in general has always carried such weight with Italian filmmakers lies in the great importance that the Italian press, and later television, attaches to culture in general and to film in particular. Numerous Italian dailies, national and regional, devote pages to the discussions of the problems of film as culture, as well as to the glamorous trappings of the movies. Critics rooted in the Marxist tradition and associated with the Left have always exercised great influence. The same can be said of filmmakers and their professional organizations. Finally, it should not be forgotten that a centuries-old Catholic tradition has accustomed the Italians to the translation of most problems, including those of art and culture, into ideological terms.

To those two fires of criticism, from the right and from the left, a third was added, that of the church. The Catholic Film Center's journal, *La Rivista del cinematografo*, often warned against the influence of neorealist films. Its "Recommendations to Believers" classified the neorealist films as follows: Dangerous for children: *Open City*. For adults with restrictions: *The Sun Rises Again, Mill on the River Po, In the Name of the Law, Umberto D., Bicycle Thief, La terra trema*. Forbidden for all believers: *Bitter Rice, No Peace Under the Olives, Rome, 11 O'Clock*.

Unlike the government and the church, the Marxists were not unified in their judgment of Italian cinema. Many of them were aware of the danger that Zhdanovism represented to the arts. Some spoke out to warn of its consequences. The opposition came mainly from the field of literature, where Zhdanovists had launched a major offensive against the influence of American writers. These attacks provoked a fierce reaction from two leading writers, Cesare Pavese and Elio Vittorini, both members of the Communist party.[16] Vittorini, responding to an article by Mario Alicata in which Ernest Hemingway was called "a reactionary scribbler," engaged in a public dispute with the Italian Communist leader Palmiro Togliatti. Vittorini's letter to Togliatti, anticipating the spirit that was to prevail in the Italian Communist party a quarter of a century later, ends with the following words:

Soviet literature . . . is a part of an Arcady of the weakest kind, although it partakes of the best sort of lyricism; a fact that demonstrates that the crisis of culture is worldwide, in capitalism's "insufficient politicization" as well as in socialism's "political saturation." In one society, one runs the risk of becoming involved in reactionary politics, and in the other, of being drawn into a no less serious automatism. The revolutionary writers in a capitalist country must be awake to both dangers. The revolutionary writers who support our party will have to refuse the aesthetic tendencies of the USSR because, as Italians, they come from a Western country in a different phase of socialist construction and because the Russian way is not the way of the Italian or French socialist construction. . . . We know what happened to politics and culture during every great revolution: poetry became Arcadian, and the culture became the handmaiden of politics.[17]

FILMS OF ACT II

After 1948, De Santis abandoned his tales of social unrest and carnal desire. In his next film, *No Peace Under the Olives,* he replaced his broad imagery of existential anguish and his formal experimentation with symbolic living pictures, resembling socialist realist paintings. The seduction of the American way of life has been replaced by the myth of populist culture, and social conflicts are reduced to elemental themes. The authenticity of the actual countryside has receded to a mythical eternal landscape, populated by elemental human beings who are moved by

No Peace Under the Olives

collective feelings of revenge, passion, and solidarity. *No Peace Under the Olives* is a visually beautiful film, based on a news item. The story concerns an honest shepherd, Francesco, and his fiancée, Lucia, who are pursued by the local villain, Bonfiglio; Bonfiglio steals Francesco's sheep and has him imprisoned, but good prevails and he is punished. He dies a typical neorealist death, the fall off a cliff.[18]

In his subsequent film, *Rome, 11 O'Clock*, De Santis followed Zavattini's theory to the letter. The subject came from a news item that appeared on January 15, 1951. As more than a hundred women stood waiting to apply for a single typist's job, the staircase collapsed. Seventy-seven were injured; one died. Elio Petri (1929–1982), a young journalist and scriptwriter, later to become a well-known director, interviewed the victims for Zavattini and De Santis. Zavattini himself wrote the first draft of the script. Considering the re-creation of an event essential for capturing its reality, he placed an advertisement similar to the one that had provoked the catastrophe, and again more than a hundred women gathered at the specific address. However, Zavattini's method was foreign to De Santis, who had always been fascinated by uncommon situations and enigmatic characters. Nor was he really interested in such a blanket condemnation of capitalism presented through stereotypical characters (the wife of an unemployed worker, a girl from a poor peasant family, a prostitute who wants to change her life, a wealthy girl running away from her environment, etc.). Thus, suffering from a lack of artistic commitment, *Rome, 11 O'Clock* is unconvincing and unimaginative and resembles a well-intentioned picture book.

"What is reality?" the Pirandellian question that the first neorealists had asked in the early forties, again confronted them before the decade came to its end. This time, the answer was less simple, as the failure of *Rome, 11 O'Clock* proved. While Fellini, Rossellini, and Antonioni struggled to find a new approach corresponding to the new possibilities of the cinematic medium, De Sica and Zavattini attempted to revise the original neorealist formula, to adapt it to a more complex subject matter. Like *Bicycle Thief*, their *Miracle in Milan* (1950) and *Umberto D.* (1951) tell about people alone in the middle of a crowd. The protagonists, however, are no longer merely innocent victims of social conditions. The poor in *Miracle in Milan* are also mischievous, greedy, and egotistical. And old Umberto Domenico, with all his touching defenselessness, is completely self-centered, incapable of any real interest in other human beings. He is the product not just of social conditions but also of his own choices and attitudes.[19]

Miracle in Milan, a fable about a kingdom of the poor and the rich, is based on Zavattini's stories *Totò, the Good One* and *Let's Give Everyone a Rocking Horse*. Its protagonist, Totò, is a foundling raised by an old lady endowed with magical powers. After her death he joins a group of poor people living in a shanty town and leads them in their fight against the villain, Mobbi, who tries to evict them. In the end, thanks to the magical powers that Totò acquired from the old lady, the poor give up their search for happiness on this earth and fly away on broomsticks to "somewhere else." De Sica developed Zavattini's poetic vision—close to the sad humor of Chaplin's films—alongside a stylized imagery, mixing realistic elements

Rome, 11 O'Clock   *Miracle in Milan*

with moments of sheer fantasy. As long as the film follows the structure of a fable, its metaphoric message is perfectly at ease. When, however, the realistic dimension is expressed through special effects that are rarely used in neorealist films, (process shots, superimposition, rapid montage), we feel that De Sica's search for a new style has reached an impasse. Similarly, in sequences that attempt to portray the ideological conflict between the "Mobbists" and the "Totoists," the stylized images—betraying an inadequate fusion of neorealist techniques with old cinematic effects—prove discordant with the social argument.

Like *Miracle in Milan, Umberto D.* was a transitional work. De Sica and Zavattini, the most faithful advocates of the neorealist principles, were affirming the necessity of a new approach without abandoning basic neorealist principles. In *Umberto D.*, the narrative no longer has the simplicity of *Bicycle Thief*.[20] Here, the story is one of existential anguish, of human solitude. The social environment does not cause the isolation; it merely exacerbates it. Umberto D., a retired civil servant who must survive on a meager pension, is not only a poor man who contemplates suicide; he is also a human being who closes himself off in his solitude, resigning all contacts with the external world. As the film progresses, it becomes apparent that Zavattini's method, postulating the revelation of reality through the rendering of small details, can barely scratch the surface of Umberto's misery.

Umberto D. is an extremely touching and socially eloquent film. Its innovative narrative unfolds through a stunning visual austerity that renounces all effects and restricts the camera movement to the bare minimum. The emphasis on real time and the deletion of all "meanwhiles" anticipated the subsequent development of the cinematic language and the dedramatization of the narrative. *Umberto D.* remains a strong piece of social criticism (the demonstration of the retirees). It failed, however, to find a way of expression that could render the tragedy of a destitute man without melodramatic elements. This discovery was reserved for others. At the

Umberto D.

time of *Umberto D.,* Michelangelo Antonioni was already working on *Signora senza camelie* (Lady Without Camelias, 1951), which was to become one of the turning points in the evolution of the modern film narrative.

MINOR FILMS

The vulnerability of Zavattini's theory of "facts that speak for themselves" was confirmed in the ambitious composite film *Amore in città* (Love in the City, 1953) supervised by Zavattini. Its failure was a blow to the belief that facts are independent of their artistic interpretation. *Love in the City* anticipated the later experiments of the *cinéma vérité* method—made possible by new technology that had not been available to the neorealists. The film consists of six episodes, conceived along the lines of the Zavattinian film inquiry (film inchiesta) with its detailed re-creation of actual events reenacted by the people concerned. A new generation of filmmakers participated in this venture—Antonioni, Fellini, Lizzani, Dino Risi (b. 1916), and Francesco Maselli (b. 1930). They concentrated on various aspects and consequences of love (prostitution, matchmaking, suicide), trying to capture them in their most obvious manifestations. Outstanding among them were Fellini's and Maselli's episodes (*Agenzia matrimoniale* [A Matrimonial Agency] and *Caterina Rigoglioso*). The overall impact of the film was, however, marred by the rigor of the theoretical conception.

One of the most interesting films of 1953, sometimes labeled "the last year of neorealism," was the directorial debut of Antonio Pietrangeli (1919–1968), one of the early neorealist critics and scriptwriters. In *Il sole negli occhi* (Eyes Full of Sun) Pietrangeli attempted to create a complex portrait of a human being, drawing upon the original neorealist approach. As the story progressed, his interest in the psychological aspect prevailed over his involvement with authenticity, and the result is a visually rich and revealing account of the daily life of a housemaid, her relationship with the masters, and her own changing personality.

The first film by Carlo Lizzani, *Achtung, Banditi* (1951), also attempted to revive the neorealist principles, especially the thematic matrix of neorealism, the antifascist resistance.[21] Lizzani was a committed political filmmaker, for whom neorealism meant a complete simultaneous commitment of the artist to the world and to art. One of the early neorealists and the youngest among them, Lizzani helped to lay the groundwork of the neorealist approach to cinema and later collaborated on some of the most important neorealist films. Next to Zavattini, Lizzani was the most important spokesman for the neorealist movement. Throughout the years, he defended his concept of neorealism, blaming his demise solely on adverse political circumstances.[22]

Opposing Zavattini's theory about the present as the only source of art, Lizzani proposed the concept of history as a unifying agent of the past, the present, and the future. He hoped that neorealism could be brought back to life if it returned to its original inspiration—the resistance. In his later films, he continued to address the present through the stories set in the past. None of them, however, revealed any artistic originality.

Achtung, Banditi focused on the problem of a continuing fight, drawing a parallel between the year 1944 (when the partisans disobeyed the Badoglio government's orders to cease all armed actions) and the situation after the defeat of the Left in 1948. *Achtung, Banditi* suffered not only from an excess of ideology but also from a deficient formal structure—a pictorial composition influenced by the shot-reverse-shot aesthetics of Soviet socialist realism.[23] His next film, *Chronicle of Poor Lovers* (1953), is a more subtle work. Lizzani again turns to the antifascist movement, this time transposing to the screen a successful novel by Vasco Pratolini. But by 1953 the established approach to the antifascist theme had exhausted much of its immediate potential and impact. The past could no longer be revealed through an "objective" vision. A deeper insight into the problems and characters was needed, and new ways of expression were required.

ACTORS IN NEOREALIST FILMS

The neorealists' endeavor to break with all the canons of the traditional cinema comprised a radically different method of casting to complement the other elements of the emerging style. Already Rossellini's casting of two famous performers from "la rivista" in the two tragic roles in *Open City* delivered a blow to the reigning conventions. De Sica sought out the protagonists of *Shoeshine* and *Bicycle Thief* in the streets of Rome, applying the old "typage" principle to his own aesthetic formula. But the neorealists soon discovered that this method, with all its freshness, authenticity, and "realism," could be used only in a certain type of film and was in itself limiting. Eventually, type casting was reserved mostly for extras and for supporting roles.

De Santis and some others who realized the limitations of type casting and of actors "found in the streets" tried another way. They selected as their protagonists "natural performers"—from among their friends, participants in pageants, etc.— helping them, in many cases, to attain a professional level.[24] Here, the neorealist principle was served by having performers who were untouched by acting schools and professional clichés. Yet these performers gradually achieved a professional status within the industry.

To these two categories of untrained actors, some professionals were added. They came from the rivistas, the stage (Vittorio Gassman), and sometimes from the traditional cinema (Massimo Girotti, Carla Del Poggio, Amedeo Nazzari). Their professionalism was eventually recognized as an important contributing element in the efforts to blend the heterogeneous ingredients of a neorealist cast (e.g., in *Without Pity*).

At the beginning of the fifties, "divismo" (the star system) made a comeback, and some neorealists saw it as a possible way out of the growing artistic and economic crisis. Alberto Lattuada used Silvana Mangano's glamour as the basis for his *Anna* (1951), a tear-jerker about a bad girl who becomes a nun.[25] In *Rome, 11 O'Clock*, a film that strictly followed the neorealist canons, all the leading roles were played by the big stars of the time (Carla Del Poggio, Massimo Girotti, Lucia Bosè, Raf Vallone). Pietro Germi's *The Path of Hope*, made in 1950, was typical of efforts to combine the original neorealist commitment with the most seductive element of the cinema—the stars. The simple plot was embellished by the presence of Elena Varzi and Raf Vallone, their performances enhanced by an expressive camera and emotional music.

The Path of Hope lacks the aggressiveness of some neorealist films, but it presents an important aspect of Italian life—emigration. The film tells the story of a group of Sicilian emigrants who travel across the country to the French border hoping to find work abroad. It begins with a masterly portrayal of the Sicilian village, showing the farewell of the workers and their families, and continues with several dramatically well-balanced sequences that capture the clash between these "southerners" and the other Italy. Germi proved to be extremely adept at incorporating some of the best neorealist techniques (such as the foreground-background action juxtaposed with crowd scenes), and the influence of *La terra trema* was particularly evident. Interrupting the main plot with frequent digressions, he enhanced the verisimilitude of the characters and endowed the first part of the story with an impressive visual grandiloquence. In the second part, a melodramatic seductiveness takes over the space previously held by the authentic Sicilian environment.

Despite Germi's efforts to attract large audiences, *The Path of Hope*, distorted by the censor, was a commercial failure.[26] In his following films, Germi renounced his neorealist commitment in favor of less controversial populist simplicity. Rossellini referred to filmmakers such as Germi, Zampa, Castellani, or Comencini as "popularizers" who came "after the real innovators." "They were perhaps more important, as they spread neorealism everywhere, and possibly with greater clarity. They didn't have to change anything and were perhaps more widely understood. But then deviations and distortions crept in, with fatal consequences. But by this time, neorealism had accomplished the main part of its work."[27]

At the end of the forties, the neorealist movement was approaching its end, weakened by a severe crisis. The crisis had two aspects: an objective one (economic) and a subjective one (artistic). By 1949, the Italian film industry entered a slump, caused primarily by unlimited imports of American films and by the American control of distribution. Giulio Andreotti helped the industry to achieve a certain prosperity, at the same time crushing the neorealist movement as a threat to the restoration of the old society. Carlo Salinari, the prominent literary critic and historian, analyzed the situation as follows:

> The crisis of neorealism was rooted in an objective general fact: in the involution of the Italian society or, if we wish to use another expression, in the restoration of capitalism in Italy. It affected the arts in different ways. Film received a direct, massive, and brutal blow. The state used its entire political power and took advantage of the dependence of film on the industrial structure. All kinds of administrative measures were used to disrupt a further evolution of neorealism. The blow aimed at the cinema had a far-reaching effect.[28]

The objective reasons for the crisis had their subjective counterpart. Some spokesmen for neorealism, such as Zavattini, Barbaro, De Santis, Puccini, Lizzani, Pietrangeli, wanted to continue the neorealist impetus against all odds, without any changes whatsoever in fundamental approach. Others, such as Fellini, Amidei, Rossellini, Lattuada, and Visconti, gradually broke away from the neorealist matrix, opposing its devotion to simple, everyday reality (the already seen) and proposing the quest for a reality that remained to be discovered. The story of neorealism followed, in a way, the patterns of evolution of other art forms, which, at different historical moments, have abandoned the imitation of nature to search for their own metaphoric interpretations. The tendencies dividing the neorealist movement became fully apparent at meetings that took place at the end of the forties and the beginning of the fifties—meetings called to discuss the crisis of neorealism and to save the movement (e.g., at Perugia and Parma). But the dissensions and the clashes were too profound, the misapprehensions too obvious, and no kind of agreement could be reached. More and more, former adherents were deserting the movement that seemed to be driven underground.

As often happens with such groupings, the neorealists stayed together for only a limited period of time. They had lived together "the long journey through fascism," the antifascist resistance, the postwar struggle for social change, the defeat of their efforts in the 1948 elections. These events had coined both the poetics and the ethics of their generation. Their crushed hope in a better future was not replaced by any other perspective, any other commitment. Each of the neorealists went his own way, some toward important achievements, some, no longer supported by the enthusiasm of the others, toward obscurity.

IV

WHAT IS REALITY?

At the Perugia congress, Zavattini began his speech by dividing cinema into two trends: that of Lumière—true to life—and that of Méliès—based on fantasy and fiction. According to Zavattini: "Cinema failed completely because it did not choose Lumière but Méliès."[1] The "Lumière-Méliès dilemma" ultimately divided the neorealists. But even at Perugia, voices were heard contesting Zavattini's approach. Above all, Galvano Della Volpe[2] opposed the assertion that "verisimilitude equals reality." In his opinion, the best neorealist films, like *Bicycle Thief,* stemmed from the Méliès inspiration (which he called "documentary cinematic poetry") whereas a strict application of the Lumière approach could lead to, among other things, photographed literature, such as Cocteau's *Beauty and the Beast.* Alberto Lattuada pointed out that the "Lumière method" could produce distorted documentary films. He said:

> If it is true that Méliès can lead us to the detached perfection of Sternberg's *The Devil Is a Woman,* then Lumière brings us easily to documentaries made in Hitler's spirit. Truth appears in fairy tales as much as in rigorous chronicles. A fairy tale, however, exercises a deeper suggestive power over the audience, which means that it equips truth with an efficient weapon. I do not consider it necessary to introduce any literary references, but it would be enough to mention mythological tales or Jonathan Swift.[3]

Zavattini—stubborn, intolerant, and devilishly persuasive—never revised anything in his theory, which from the outset had been more notable for its journalistic attractiveness than its scholarly rigorousness. Along with Siegfried Kracauer, Dziga Vertov, Béla Balázs, John Grierson, and others, Zavattini would be classified as a theoretician of cinematic realism and discussed most often in connection with Kracauer. Zavattini surpassed Kracauer's aesthetics, which were based on the presumption of a photographable world. Zavattini's number-one postulate was an unconditional acceptance of "life as it is," which implied capturing reality as nearly as possible in real time. Kracauer based his theory on film's unique capacity to record and reveal physical reality, documenting it with a wide selection of films, including *Battleship Potemkin, Greed,* and the westerns, as well as the films of Renoir and

Buñuel. Zavattini, much more of a purist, rejected all of narrative cinema, believing that film would surmount the crisis of the early fifties only if it accepted altogether new codes of expression.

Whereas Kracauer recognized that filmmakers must render their own view of reality, Zavattini rejected any infiltration of photographable material by the film-makers' will, claiming that all intellectuals were conditioned by their past—in the Italian case by twenty years of fascism. Kracauer divided nonnarrative films into films of fact and experimental films, stressing the limitations of the "film of fact" (the same qualities that Zavattini viewed as its assets). In his *Theory of Film* (1960), Kracauer pointed out: "In the case of film of fact, it opens only on part of the world. Newsreels, as well as documentaries, feature not so much the individual and his inner conflicts as the world he lives in. The suspension of the story then not only benefits the documentary but puts it at a disadvantage also."[4] Meanwhile, Zavattini refused to allow any fiction and contended that the most valid cinematic form was a film based on real time that rejected all dramatic structure including artistic time. For Kracauer the ideal film was based on the so-called "found story," like the plots of *Paisan, La terra trema,* and *Bicycle Thief.* According to Kracauer, "found stories" are not products of an individual artist's imagination but products of reality: "Being discovered rather than contrived, they are inseparable from films animated by documentary intentions."[5]

A compromise between facts and "found facts" touched by the artist's will could not satisfy Zavattini. He adhered to the assertion that facts exist independently of the artistic interpretation and rejected the concept that facts cannot come into existence without the good offices of a hypothesis. Thus, in certain respects Zavattini was closer to Dziga Vertov than to Kracauer.

According to Vertov's conception of "life caught unawares," the image on the screen must conform to an objective representation of an event filmed in reality so that its ontological authenticity is preserved. Zavattini followed Vertov on three of his main points: his concern with the ontological authenticity of the shots; his belief in the artist's obligation to face reality, without hiding from the facts; and his linking of an aesthetic perception with an ethical and social concern (this third issue being probably the most important).[6]

Zavattini's radicalism went so far as to deny the importance of montage (together with all special effects) that Vertov had seen as a way to organize facts into new cinematic structures reflecting the artist's ideology. While Vertov used the Constructivist[7] concept of building films in segments, Zavattini opposed any re-arrangement of the material by means of editing, which he claimed could falsify life. Zavattini saw montage as an obstacle to the simple presentation of the facts—a technique that forced artists to make choices. Montage, with its attempted synthesis, creates historicity. And historicity, according to Zavattini, is always permeated by some kind of propaganda. For Zavattini, true historicity—and this is where he differed with Carlo Lizzani, as well as with Visconti's aforementioned concept of "anthropomorphic man"—is comprised in a human being, even just one human being captured in his temporal and spatial unity. On this point, Zavattini shared Kracauer's concept that film is more a product of photography than of editing or other formative processes. He stated:

Today a man who suffers before my eyes is absolutely different from a man who suffered a hundred years ago. I must concentrate all my attention on the man of today. The historical baggage that I carry within myself must not prevent me from being what I wish to be, neither from using the means I have at hand to deliver this man from his pain. This man—and this is one of my basic and fixed ideas—has a first and last name. He is part of society in a way that concerns us, make no mistake about that. I feel his fascination. I must feel it in such a way that I am urgently obliged to speak to him or of him, but not as a character of my imagination's invention. It is exactly at that moment one must beware, for it is then that the imagination attempts to come between reality and the self.[8]

Zavattini based his naturalistic theory on the insufficiencies of neorealism. According to him, neorealism was heir to the old culture in general and to its melodrama, populism, and sentimentalism in particular. Zavattini was aware of the weaknesses of the neorealist narrative originating in traditional cinema, his own films included, and wanted to remedy them by insisting on an immediacy of knowledge that he found lacking in neorealist films. He never stopped believing that this was the only way out of the dead end in which neorealism found itself in the early fifties. For him, the role of the scriptwriter, his own profession, was tied to old structures and hence of no use at all. Going beyond Antonio Gramsci's vision of a new culture, Zavattini postulated a struggle for a new art. He rejected the Gramscian concept of continuity between the old and the new created by the flow of history, and he denied the past as such.[9] He repeatedly demanded that all plots be burned because plots always arrive late on the scene of the crime; when "the house is on fire," there is no time to lose and "any narrative would just delay the tragedy."[10] Zavattini's projects were a challenge to Italian intellectuals, who, according to him, were always inclined to place speculation ahead of action. In 1949, Zavattini said:

Film has always cultivated the tendency to escape any radical scrutiny of one's conscience. With the rapidity of a flashing light, it succeeded in alienating the spectator from himself, and with the help of money and talent it made this escape smooth and final. One day, as we walked out of the dark screening room, we heard the newsboy shout that war had started, which meant a woman's arm torn off of her body and thrown against the telephone wires, and the head of a certain Paolo Gaj hurled into the vase of flowers in a house with the number three. And all we could do was hope that the remaining bombs would fall on the house across the street and not on ours. And when the house across the street was hit, we—superstitious, as we were—kissed each other and sang, filled with joy. . . .[11]

The importance of Zavattini's naturalistic utopianism lay in its challenge of the so-called "contenutismo" of Italian neorealism—the exaggerated importance attributed to the film's content. Zavattini postulated a radical shift in the filmmakers' attention, thus trying to avert the danger that led to "the self-corruption of neorealism."[12] In 1972, film historian Bruno Torri pointed out: "After 1948, neorealism frequently resorted to mannerism and stereotypes, indulging to a greater or lesser degree in 'chronicling,' in an anecdotal approach, in populism, provincialism, sentimentalism, and the stereotype of the dialect comedy. Some of these features, characteristic of the minor films of neorealism, can be detected in some accomplished films of the previous period."[13]

By suggesting different ways of exploring reality, Zavattini attempted to find a way out of the impasse of "mannerism" and "dialect comedy." He hoped to create a new basis for the neorealist movement, which, while it had the resources of a strong human and social matrix, lacked a firm philosophical and theoretical background. Yet neorealism, like every unified historical phenomenon, carried the seeds of its own destruction within its basic features, and Zavattini's approach became one of them. Through its prevailing interest in the underprivileged (to a large extent originating in the neglect of this stratum by the traditional cinema with its concern for the world of the affluent), Zavattini's theory generated confusion between plot and ideology, narrowing the range of the subject matter and creating the illusion that theory is self-sufficient. Moreover, the quest for truth, as proposed by Zavattini, had to touch upon the complex problem of verisimilitude. Even a truth discovered by means of Zavattini's method would necessarily appear in some prearranged form as a result of a preconceived process. In Zavattini's teachings, however, verisimilitude was institutionalized as similitude and identified with reality.

The general atmosphere of the early fifties contributed to the confusion and uncertainty. In a climate of growing political tensions, both the Marxists and the Catholics interpreted aesthetic problems in terms of political expediency, using them as weapons in political battles. Most of the critics renounced any critical reassessment of the problem, adopting a paternalistic and prevailingly defensive attitude. Insisting upon the basic validity of neorealist patterns, they merely tried to protect the movement against governmental attacks and increasing censorship.

The Marxist critics and their fellow travelers saw an additional reason for the crisis in the "betrayal" of neorealism by some filmmakers (Rossellini, Fellini), and the Catholic film theoreticians considered neorealist films lacking in spirituality and insisted on the necessity of transcending existing reality and reaching beyond social problems. Confusion prevailed at the 1953 congress on neorealism held in Parma. There, as film historians Sandro Petraglia and Stefano Rulli pointed out in 1974: "Everything was hidden under a layer of clouds as it appeared suicidal to show the public that the crisis of neorealist production was accompanied by an equally severe crisis of criteria."[14]

In the atmosphere of confusion, Zavattini's ideas, despite their aesthetic flaws, radicalism, and naturalistic utopianism, were the only theoretical framework that could sustain Italian cinema. Although these theories never generated any coherent cinematic trend, they made a significant impression on much of the production of the following years, merging with the original neorealist impulses that had engendered them.

In the quest for a more complex reality, a metaphoric vision began to prevail in the approach of several directors such as Rossellini, Fellini, and Antonioni, who, along with Visconti, emerged as leading personalities out of the disrupted neorealist generation. This was in part a reaction against a narrow interpretation of "realism Zavattini style." In fact, however, these directors could not avoid the influence of neorealism and probably did not wish to. From the outset, their metaphors were linked to sociohistorical moments through a series of clearly outlined historical, sociological, existential, and ontological codes. (Galvano Della Volpe referred to these metaphors as "rational.")

None of the first post-neorealist films bothered much with the plot. The mood and the evolution of the characters' feelings were the main elements of their structures whereas their overall approach was influenced by phenomenological attitudes. In Italy, phenomenology became increasingly popular as a kind of a third way between Kierkegaard's idealism and Marx's materialism.[15]

Antonioni, Fellini, and Visconti, each in his own way, now answered the questions about reality that had been haunting them since the early forties, not by pointing to the world around them but by examining its relationship to the state of mind of human beings and to their inner selves, which until then had been overshadowed by the insanity of the war and its consequences. Years later, Antonioni summed up their dilemma:

> The primary concern of the neorealist films was to establish the relationship with society. However, when I started making films, things were different, and my approach therefore was also different. I had arrived a little late on the scene, at a time when the first flowering of films, though still valid, was already beginning to show signs of exhaustion. Consequently, I was forced to stop and consider what subject matter was worth examining at that particular moment, what was really happening, what was the true state of things, what ideas were really being thought. And it seemed to me that perhaps it was no longer so important to examine the relationship between the individual and his environment, as it was to examine the individual himself, to look inside the individual and see, after all he had been through (the war, the immediate postwar situation, all the events that were currently taking place) what remained inside of the individual, to see, I won't say transformation of our psychological and emotional attitudes, but at least, the symptoms of that restlessness which began to outline the changes that later came about in our psychology, and feelings, and perhaps even our morality.[16]

VERISIMILITUDE AND ROSSELLINI

In 1948, Rossellini—who at that time avoided all theoretical proclamations—made a film that can be considered his contribution to the discussion in progress. In the fable *La macchina ammazzacattivi* (The Machine to Kill Bad People), he presented a metaphorical meditation on the relationship between photographed reality and the reality of moral problems. A demon bequeaths to a photographer the power to kill villains by means of his camera. The photographer, a good man preoccupied with justice, destroys the rich people and fat cats who exploit poor people, but finally he turns against the underprivileged too, for he finds that they are greedy and selfish as well. In Rossellini's portrayal, the photographer is persuaded that photography endows him with knowledge and moral judgment. While his camera captures only the visible facts, he believes that he can penetrate beneath

La macchina ammazzacattivi

the surface. The outcome of such a venture can only be catastrophic. *The Machine to Kill Bad People* dramatizes Rossellini's faith in the necessity of illusion and imagination in art as well as in life.[17]

One of the most important issues of the time concerned the aesthetics of verisimilitude—the appearance of truth and actuality. Verisimilitude has always been an important problem in Italian art, and it became increasingly pressing during the neorealist period. In the early fifties, Galvano Della Volpe challenged Zavattini's theory (verisimilitude equals reality), which rejected all the films being made at that time by Rossellini and Fellini. Della Volpe's essays in film criticism opened new paths for film appreciation, postulating the same freedom for cinema that Visconti had demanded for the theater.

Della Volpe, drawing upon Aristotelian aesthetics, approached the issue by redefining cinematic verisimilitude as nonequivalent to reality and by opposing fantasy to the "banality of authenticity." The second important issue in Della Volpe's theory was his emphasis on the analysis of formal aspects and on the necessity to choose among a variety of styles and approaches. Challenging the prevalent emphasis on content, Della Volpe was concerned with the film's capacity for symbolic representation and its ability to express abstract concepts through the technical and structural process of montage.[18] In his essay "Il verosimile filmico," Della Volpe pointed out the function of form and content together and the tension between them, claiming equal rights for films based on the possible (what has happened) and those based on the impossible (what might have happened).[19] In 1970, Edoardo Bruno wrote: "Della Volpe's foresighted lesson refuted all the insults and accusations that the so-called critical journalism had heaped upon Rossellini; these critics had questioned Rossellini's stylistic coherence, considering it an obvious infidelity to a misinterpreted content."[20]

After *Germany, Year Zero*, Rossellini moved in the direction of a cinema based upon the predominance of unfolding events over the "already seen" and of hypothetical situations over facts as such. Refusing the neorealist "contenutismo" and the narrative patterns of realism, he searched for a new "dramatic sense" that would renovate the original neorealist form—a form he claimed had been stifled by the prevailing interest in film's ideas. After six films concerned with the war (the fascist trilogy and the war trilogy), Rossellini—sometimes called "the poet of disaster"—turned to films based on ambiguous moral and emotional issues.

Among the films he made between 1948 and 1953, two stand out as quite exceptional: *Francesco, giullare di Dio* (The Flowers of St. Francis, 1950) and *Viaggio in Italia* (Voyage in Italy, 1953). Rossellini's basic approach never changed. The different microcosms and individual stories (which had been linked by an intrinsic dramatic quality of the subject matter in his war films) became independent of the background; they remained, however, enclosed in nature that was conceived as a mirror of human activities. The objectiveness of external facts continued to interest him only inasmuch as it allowed him to capture individual mannerisms, through which he could approach the inner truth of human beings.

The character of St. Francis belongs to the Fellinian gallery of pure, innocent creatures considered by others to be simple-minded or crazy. They are firmly rooted in Rossellini's concept of spiritual values as well as in Fellini's supernatural vision. (The first saint scripted by Fellini and directed by Rossellini was Nannina, the protagonist of the film *Il miracolo* [The Miracle, 1948], about a poor village woman who believed that her pregnancy was the result of a miracle.)[21] Fellini, Rossellini, and, later, Antonioni have often used the extreme sensitivity, the "sickness" or "madness" of their characters to foster their metaphors about contemporary society. The real or alleged abnormality of their protagonists, such as Irene in *Europe 51,* Gelsomina in *La strada,* the photographer in *The Machine to Kill Bad People,* served them as a prism through which they observed the world. In so doing, they joined an important trend in European literature and film that uses illness as a metaphor of our time.[22] Rossellini's protagonists bear the same message as those of Fellini: a supernatural instinct inherent to some simple or crazy creatures leads them to a surer understanding of the profound truth of human existence than can be achieved through reason, history, or science.

In *The Flowers of St. Francis,* inspired by St. Francis's life, Rossellini used the simple-mindedness of St. Francis and his brethren to render the spiritual reality emanating from the flow of facts. The world seen through the brethren's eyes is a world that reached the limits of despair because, as Rossellini put it: "It has lost its faith." The simple way of life of St. Francis, re-created through a pure neorealist method, serves as its counterpoint. Rossellini pointed out: "I was searching for a

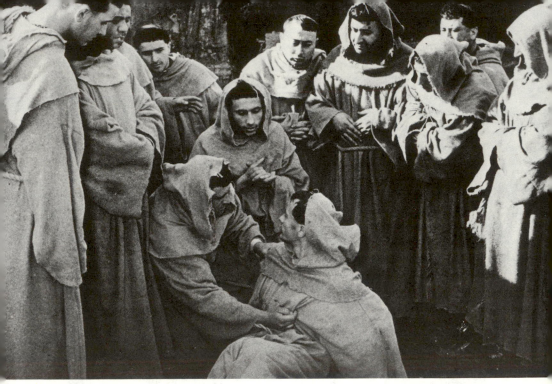

Francesco, giullare di Dio

more complex form of the ideal Christ, and I found him in the Franciscan ideal. Today's humanity, enslaved by its affluence and ambition, has forgotten about all the joys of life. Humanity needs, and desires, to be reminded of certain aspects of primitive Franciscanism."[23]

With nonprofessional actors, in authentic settings, Rossellini rendered the life of the friars, shunning all dramatic structure and stressing details and "things": the fire that went out, the tools used in the building of the cabin, the food offered to St. Claire, the routine of preparing meals and caring for pigs, the faces of the villagers, the encounters between the villagers and the monks, their dirty capes. The Renaissance era appeared without its glamour and with all its shabbiness. Rossellini recorded a lifestyle from the dim past as if he had witnessed it, giving the viewer the feeling that everything must be exactly as he showed it. The film's eleven episodes evolve against a striking landscape, which in many scenes becomes the leading component of the imagery. In the final scenes, when the Franciscans part, each taking a separate road, the landscape seems to absorb them, much as in the beginning they had emerged from the dusty roads and leafy forests. There are not many films where the effectiveness of the neorealist method—particularly in its capacity to express themes apart from factual immediacy—has been demonstrated with more strength.

Landscape plays an equally important part in *Stromboli, terra di Dio* (Stromboli, 1949), Rossellini's first film starring Ingrid Bergman.[24] Just as death was the dominant theme of the war trilogy *Open City, Paisan, Germany, Year Zero* (with the theme of solitude functioning merely as a submotivation), the stories of *Stromboli, Europe 51,* and *Voyage in Italy* are permeated with the questions of solitude and with the search for personal truth, which, in Rossellini's understanding, equals the search for God.

Stromboli was the first film in which Rossellini used sequence shots (very long takes), mainly to capture the relationship between Karin and her husband Antonio. The flow of facts was replaced by a flow of psychological symptoms while images of objects were used to reflect the development of feelings. The director elevated the characters' inner nature to the status of an independent world, thereby expressing a moral judgment. Like the method of Antonioni and Fellini, Rossellini's narration by a system of clues based on the characters' emotions was an expression of his own social disillusionment; it signaled a state of crisis and at the same time a yearning for new knowledge.

The sequence shots enabled Rossellini to follow the disintegration of a marriage through an uninterrupted flow of the couple's gestures. Karin, a Baltic refugee, marries Antonio, a peasant from the island of Stromboli, in order to escape the horrors of a camp for displaced persons. She feels isolated among the islanders and decides to return to the mainland.[25] Rossellini accentuated her self-centered solitude by the frequent use of "temps morts," when nothing happens and time seems to stop. The insertion of pauses into both real and artistic time, underscoring the symptoms of Karin's confusion, was a part of Rossellini's strategy aimed at creating a metaphoric image of life and transforming the daily reality into a mystical one.[26] In the final sequence when Karin, running away from her husband, confronts the volcano and her own anguish, time almost stops altogether. Rossellini uses images of immense spaces (mountains of lava, the endless ocean, and distant stars) to suggest Karin's state of mind when she implores God to help her. Yet the symbolic imagery, stressed by the unrestricted camera movements, becomes too allusive and

Stromboli   *Europe 51*

weakens the impact of the powerful story. *Stromboli's* most characteristic feature is the insistence on the undistorted reality of objects and gestures. Rossellini was never at ease with symbolic imagery that was meant to express metaphoric meanings. The "new dramatic sense"—which for him comprised the subconscious search for personal integrity, eros, and death—was to be found through a dedramatized narrative based on the flow of concrete events.

The opening of *Europe 51* is a superb sequence. In less than ten minutes the film draws a complex portrait of the protagonist, Irene (Ingrid Bergman), simply by following her actions as she arrives home: she enters the house, goes to her room, combs her hair and touches up her make-up, talks to her son and the maid, changes her dress, goes to the living room and pours herself a glass of wine. Already it is clear that she is a rich, self-centered woman, respecting the rules of her society, including her own empty marriage, a woman with a refined culture of a particular class. The following sequence shots depict a party at Irene's house, conveying the atmosphere of Italy at the threshold of the economic boom. Then Irene is struck by tragedy—the suicide of her young son—and her search for the sense of life begins. Like Karin, she comes to grips with a truth of her own, and when her family, not understanding the sudden change in her, places her in a mental institution, she accepts the situation. In the final scene, she stands behind a barred window looking down at her departing husband and mother. The expression in her eyes (while we overhear the dialogue between her husband and her mother) suggests that it is not she who is mad, but those who are free and who do not know what to do with their liberty.

In *The Flowers of St. Francis,* Rossellini's search for faith had returned to the original principles of Christianity. In *Europe 51,* he intimated his feeling of the inadequacy of institutionalized Catholicism in the face of profound existential and emotional crisis. "Love has to be subordinated to the reigning order" is the priest's answer to Irene's questions, thus denying her the possibility of spiritual recovery through love for "all human beings."

Some parts of *Europe 51* are marred by narrative simplifications (Irene's conversion, the depiction of the milieu of the underprivileged, etc.), and some of its ideas may seem confused. With hindsight, however, this confusion reflects to a considerable extent the spiritual atmosphere of Europe in those years.

The film with the programatic title *Dov'è la libertà?* (Where Is Freedom? 1953) was the least persuasive of Rossellini's works of that time, using an anecdotal approach to sum up the questions asked in the trilogy of solitude (*Europe 51, Stromboli, Voyage in Italy*). Structured around the powerful personality of Totò, the most famous Italian comic actor, it drew heavily on the elements of "la rivista," presenting different scenes as solo numbers by the protagonist. These were loosely tied together by a plot centering on a man who, after twenty years in prison, does not know what to do with his freedom. He finds himself surrounded by people who use their liberty solely for egoistic purposes. Finally, Salvatore, the protagonist, returns voluntarily to the jail and is put on trial for "trespassing on prison property." The trial sequence provided Rossellini with the opportunity to dwell upon the questions that preoccupied him at that time. The answers remained the same as in

Voyage in Italy

his previous films: freedom for Salvatore, Irene, Karin and Antonio can only be
found in the inner self.

Catherine, the protagonist of *Voyage in Italy,* pursued the search for freedom,
but her questions remain unanswered. In *Stromboli* and *Europe 51,* Rossellini had
still been preoccupied with the progression of the story, emphasizing the development of situations and characters. In *Voyage in Italy,* mainly static essential facts
are portrayed while the characters remain unchanged from beginning to end and
the story is left open. For the first time, Rossellini, always a poor storyteller, renounced most of the rules of narration and continued his attempts to reach the
essence of human anguish internalized and without melodrama.

Rossellini (like Antonioni) portrayed emotional crisis through female characters, for they were, in his opinion, more sensitive than men. Women, he maintained, could "feel the future" while men remained attached to the present. The
sensitivity of women, however, also implied impotence and utopianism. Even if
not a force of evil and destruction, a woman is still an elusive creature: only men
could eventually conquer the future; and the men of the future are not men victimized and enslaved by women but men like Garibaldi and Louis XIV, Lorenzo de

Medici, Socrates, and Blaise Pascal, who attracted Rossellini's attention in the 1960s and 1970s.

A prototype of Rossellini's victimized man is Alex (George Sanders), the protagonist of *Voyage in Italy,* a wealthy English lawyer who is bored with everything except his own work and who functions only through his work. He has come to Italy to sell a house that he inherited from his uncle. After arriving there, he and his wife Catherine (Ingrid Bergman) experience an acute crisis in their relationship. It is this crisis, along with the manifest clash of two cultures—the Anglo-Saxon and the Italian—that form the basis of the plot. The film is a continuing dissection of the husband-wife relationship, never taking sides or drawing conclusions. Neither Alex nor Catherine bears the greater responsibility for their problems, and both appear equally indifferent to other people and to each other. Their reconciliation at the end of the film, initiated by a surge of emotion amidst a religious procession, is as futile as everything that has preceded it. In *Voyage in Italy,* the question no longer is why something happened and what will happen next: all solutions are equally absurd. Rossellini just seems to be stating what he has seen, examining the behavior of two human beings faced with facts they had scarcely considered before: death—omnipresent and all-important in Italy; the past—hidden in art, catacombs, caves, legends, or just the imagination; the Italian mentality, which challenges the couple's life patterns. It is as if the director has thrown the characters into situations and recorded their reactions: Catherine fighting with a dish of spaghetti; Alex unable to communicate with an Italian maid; Catherine confronted with death in the museum in Naples; Catherine waiting for Alex, who had gone to Capri to escape the truth of their marital breakdown, etc.

In *Voyage in Italy,* the paradigms and metaphors of Rossellini's previous films have disappeared, giving way to direct situations. This approach does not comprise a return to objective immediacy. On the contrary, the narrative is stylized and contrived. Rather than being a forerunner of *cinéma vérité* (as *Voyage in Italy* is often described), this final part of Rossellini's trilogy of solitude anticipates what Jean-Luc Godard later called "theater truth" (théâtre vérité): a method that creates reality out of fiction, imagination, and fantasy. Gianni Rondolino, Rossellini's biographer, pointed out:

> In these years, the concept of film essay was coined, later to be used by Rossellini and others. I have in mind not only certain films by the French "new wave" directors (Godard, Rohmer, Rivette), but also Rossellini's own television films, which drew heavily upon the breakdown of the old cinematic structure. This concept of filmmaking, the origins of which can be traced back to Rossellini's previous films, manifested itself fully just at the moment when it seemed to many that Rossellini had been ruined by a hopeless crisis.[27]

SECOND ENCOUNTER: FELLINI AND ROSSELLINI

If it is true that there are as many neorealisms as there are neorealists, it could also be said that there are as many Fellinis as there are "Felliniologists." In hundreds of interviews, Fellini himself has only added to the confusion. Like the characters in his films, he loves to wear masks; and like the world of comic strips—the world that shaped him—he loves the distorted truth of illusion.

Yet there is one encounter in Fellini's life with no ambiguity attached. For the Italian cinema this encounter probably has the same kind of importance as the one in 1940 between Visconti and De Santis. In 1944, Fellini met with Rossellini and became one of his closest collaborators, working with him on *Open City, Paisan, The Flowers of St. Francis, Love,* and *Europe 51.* From the outset, however, their artistic concepts differed. Although Fellini was not shaped by the neorealist impulse as much as some of his friends and collaborators were, the turbulent years 1944–1948 had left deep imprints on his personal and artistic experience. His personality had matured in the feverish atmosphere of the first postwar years, in endless discussions about art, film, fascism and Italy's future. At that time, Rossellini was at the center of attention and would spend hours in Roman cafés arguing with De Sica, Sergio Amidei, De Santis, Antonioni, Pietrangeli, or the Puccini brothers. For Fellini, an awkward young provincial, every day in this environment brought new encounters, new friendships, travels across Italy in search for film locations, and meetings with different kinds of people, each of whom had a story to tell.

Rossellini, one generation older, helped Fellini see beyond the limited horizons of a young man from the provinces and beyond the glittering paraphernalia of the "amorous lie" (as Antonioni nicknamed the milieu of the photo-romances, the comic strips of the time).[28] When the two men first met, Fellini was twenty-four years old and yearning for glory. In 1939, he had left his native Rimini and had decided to become a journalist, "like the men in trench coats with their hats pushed back in American movies." But fame eluded him. He did everything and accomplished little, wrote sketches for "rivistas," scripts for second-rate comedies and photo-romances, drew caricatures and cartoons. After *Open City* and *Paisan,* everything changed: the "amorous lie" was abandoned, and Fellini joined the ranks of the most esteemed neorealist scriptwriters. He coscripted, among others, *Without Pity, Mill on the River Po, In the Name of the Law,* and *The Path of Hope.* His search for glory was replaced by a quest for individual artistic vision. This vision, once found, had more room for illusion than for facts and was reminiscent of Pirandello's reality, as uncertain and vague as the dream that tells of it and the mask behind which it hides.

Though it was mere coincidence that Fellini codirected his first feature film, *Luci del varietà* (Variety Lights, 1950), with Alberto Lattuada, he was at that time closer to Lattuada than to anybody else. Both of them were intrigued by the Pirandellian unknowable worlds and by the existential quest for identity that Pirandello instilled in his characters. These concerns are already manifest in the first film that Fellini scripted for Lattuada, *Il delitto de Giovanni Episcopo* (Giovanni Episcopo's Crime, 1946, based on a novel by D'Annunzio), which depicts the multiple personalities of its protagonists caught in a tangle of frustrations.

The conflict between Fellini and Lattuada over the real authorship of *Variety Lights* lasted for decades.[29] In retrospect, it appears as vain to try to solve it as to

Variety Lights

search for a one-sided Fellinian character who would be perceived the same way by everyone. The original idea of making a film about comedians—people who rarely take off their masks—might have been Fellini's as well as Lattuada's. Although there are some typical Fellinian characters and situations in *Variety Lights* (nighttime parties ending at dawn with moments of truth; empty squares and desolate parks; tired, slovenly comedians arriving in small anonymous towns, etc.), there are also features undeniably typical of Lattuada: the narrative is meticulously developed and overloaded with dialogue, the main plot depicts, as in all Lattuada's films, an unhappy love, and the film's imagery is imbued with the veneration of the star—Carla Del Poggio. Fellini filled in some episodes and supporting characters in the frame delineated by Lattuada. He also cast Giulietta Masina for the first time in the role that was to remain with her for fifteen years—the role of an unloved woman, a woman sufferer, always ready to forgive.[30]

In *Variety Lights,* Melina (Masina) is betrayed by her fiancé, Checco. Director of a third-rate vaudeville troupe, Checco is the most ambiguous character of the story. He never removes his mask. Until the very last minute, he pretends to be somebody else—a successful artist, a great lover. Even when Liliana (Carla Del Poggio) abandons him for a rich man, he sticks to the image he has created for himself and carries on in the role of a great seducer.

While Lattuada needed the patterns of a traditional melodrama to develop this story, Fellini summed up the subject in one sequence: a dinner at the house of a rich lawyer who is infatuated with Liliana's legs. The takes are filled with a true Fellinian imagery, with a persistent note of melancholy: the comedians are gulping down food, dancing and having fun, while an old actor sits by himself and stares into an empty dish; his sadness gradually permeates the whole sequence, which ends with the comedians returning to their sleazy hotel. They seem shabbier than ever before, lonely, goalless, rejected by the "high society" their host represents. The sequence closes with a shot of Melina—the innocent saint without a mask—crying as she realizes for the first time that Checco is cheating on her.

Like Rossellini's *Machine to Kill Bad People,* Fellini's next film, *Lo sceicco bianco* (The White Sheik, 1952), could be considered an attempt to resolve the basic dilemma of the time: how to move beyond realism to a new reality. In later films, Fellini was to situate his characters in the world of illusion, but in *The White Sheik* his attitude was still ambivalent. The world of Wanda, his protagonist, consists entirely of illusions. The life of Ivan, her husband, is firmly implanted in a petty social reality, and both their lives are equally dull. This time, Fellini solved the problem of illusion versus reality with a compromise. At the end of the story, Wanda agrees to accept her husband as her "white sheik," and Ivan forgives his wife's escapade into the dream world. (In Fellini's next film *I vitelloni,* the clash of dream with reality left no possibility for adjustment, and the "man made of the same stuff as dreams are" became the center of Fellini's artistic vision.)

The White Sheik was Fellini's first quantum leap on the road to fame. Edited to perfection and told with balanced ironic overtones, *The White Sheik* is a film of rare stylistic integrity. The script was written by Michelangelo Antonioni, who in 1949 directed *Amorosa menzogna* (Amorous Lie), a rather mediocre short about the stars of the "photo-romances." Antonioni's story of provincial newlyweds spending their honeymoon in Rome provided Fellini with the opportunity to bring together on the screen the two milieus that had shaped him: the kingdom of the "fotoromanzi," where Wanda, a passionate reader of the "amorous lies," meets her white sheik; and the city of Rome, which Ivan traverses in search of his wife. This is a truly Rossellinian Rome, seen through the eyes of a careful observer but dissected and reshaped by an elaborate montage. The city itself—where Fellini, like Ivan, had served his apprenticeship—is the protagonist of *The White Sheik*. It is the Rome of real things and people, lost corners and cafés unknown to the tourist, with piles of food and torrents of wine—the same city that in 1971 became the sole subject of *Fellini Roma.*

In the spirit of "la rivista," Fellini created a solo number for Masina in *The White Sheik*. She emerges at dawn at a deserted fountain and, introducing herself as Cabiria, tries to comfort the desperate Ivan with all the philosophy of her profession. The fountain sequence closes with a lonely performance by a fire-eater, which enhances the eerie melancholy of the story. (A similar effect is obtained in *Variety Lights* when the sudden apparition of a saxophone player [John Kitzmiller] as Liliana and Checco return home from a wild night out emphasizes the unreality of their existence.)[31]

The White Sheik

Following the commercial failure of *The White Sheik* (audiences rejected it because it destroyed their own illusions), Fellini turned to his past for inspiration. At this time, and later as well, this familiar ground seemed his safest refuge. *I vitelloni* (1953) was entirely inspired by the kind of life he had lived before he departed for Rome: life in a small seaside resort, nurtured on illusions and destroyed by boredom.[32] The narrative is split into episodes built around the five protagonists. The episodic structure is typical of all Fellini's films. Fellini views life as disjointed—composed of encounters, small events and incidents that seem to obstruct the coherent evolution of the story. He wants to portray "life with its inexhaustible, unforeseeable treasures of meetings, persons, events, and adventures."[33] Thus, the traditional Italian narrative form of the short story seems most appropriate for his intention.[34]

Of the three films by Fellini that are to some extent linked to the Rossellinian concept of reality (*The White Sheik, I vitelloni,* and *Il bidone*), *I vitelloni* is the most accomplished and the most "unfaithful" to real life. It represents the Rossellinian-Godardian "theater truth," creating an appealing imagery with the attributes of a perfect fake: its imaginary milieu, governed by Fellini's mythology, looks one hundred percent real. The studio scenes look as though they were shot on location. Ostia, where some of the outdoor scenes were filmed, looks like Fellini's native Rimini, and the montage re-creates the flow of events as if they had never been interrupted by any outside interference. *I vitelloni* is often mentioned as the most "neorealist" of Fellini's films whereas, in fact, the feeling of authenticity is created by illusion.

The stories of *I vitelloni* are centered around the moments of truth in the lives of five overgrown adolescents. All of them are concerned with the void inside them and around them, but only one, Moraldo, is able to realize their common dream and leave for Rome. As the setting for the stories, Fellini creates a sleepy town with a stereotypical provincial atmosphere. Beauty contests, carnival balls, and the arrival of a variety theater are the major events that trigger crises in people's lives without ever actually changing anything. The environment—which in the neorealist films was used to complement and generate the motivations of the characters—is here conceived as the expression of a state of mind. This becomes an independent, self-explanatory element, an extension of the characters' actions.

I vitelloni contains a masterful sequence showing a masked ball and a sober self-recognition at the break of dawn. Alberto, the most pathetic of the *vitelloni,* gets drunk and dances with a huge papier-mâché mask until the other guests have gone and the waiter throws him out. He staggers home, followed by a restless, subjective camera, which gives the viewer a feeling of dizziness and uneasiness. The melancholy portrait of a useless human being culminates with Alberto watching his sister, who has always provided for him, as she leaves the town together with her lover.

In 1954, Fellini wrote a second part to *I vitelloni* called "Moraldo in città" (Moraldo in the City), but it was never filmed. The treatment contains several elements of Fellini's later films, especially *Nights of Cabiria, La dolce vita,* and *8½*. In "Moraldo in the City," Fellini's Pirandellian obsession with the search for identity

I vitelloni

again becomes apparent. The treatment ends with an unmistakably Fellinian scene that shows Moraldo returning home after a riotous party:

> He does not know anything, he does not understand anything about life and people. He is obsessed with distressing questions: What do I want? Who am I? I am a little vicious but not too vicious . . . a little bourgeois but not too bourgeois. What am I waiting for, what do I want? Outside the city, Moraldo runs into a friend with whom he used to work. He says hello, keeping his distance, and remains alone. Then, seized by a mysterious change of mood, he returns to the city. First, he walks slowly, then he quickens his steps. He relaxes. An inexplicable joy begins to take hold of him. The lights around him again seem cheerful. And the faces in the crowd seem less hostile. A young woman with a full mane of black shoulder-length hair passes by him and smiles at him radiantly. . . . Further on, a shirtless boy on a bike is whistling a song. . . . He meets two lovers who are walking slowly with their arms around each other. A baby cries, a cacophony of women's voices is heard. Life with its inexhaustible, unforeseeable treasures of meetings, persons, events, and adventures. . . . Moraldo walks quickly amidst the people, smiling at everyone.[35]

THIRD ENCOUNTER: ANTONIONI AND PAVESE

On August 27, 1950, Cesare Pavese, aged forty-eight, killed himself in a hotel room in Turin not far from his home. In taking an overdose of sleeping pills, he gave up his fight with the "absurd vice," suicide. It is this "vice" that is the true protagonist of his novellette *Among Women Only,* which Antonioni, his admirer, transposed to the screen in 1955.

Pavese and Antonioni had a lot in common. Born into austere, northern bourgeois families (Pavese was born in a village near Turin in 1908, Antonioni in Ferrara in 1912) where men stayed away from family life, they were both raised by women. And women became the prisms in the imaginary worlds of their later *oeuvres.* Shy, self-centered, extremely reserved, Pavese and Antonioni longed for people and yet at the same time avoided them. They were strangers to the mentality of their Roman friends and were both tortured by a sorrow that Pavese once expressed in a remark about Fitzgerald: "I understand that Fitzgerald drank a lot and eventually became almost insane. It is clear to me that anyone who has an inner urge to say something ends up like this."[36]

Their restlessness and dissatisfaction reflected to a certain degree the dilemma of the Italian cultural world in the 1940s, torn between the stringent reality of social events and the growing need for its transfiguration through imagination. Pavese found a way out of this dilemma by combining "realism's wealth of experience with symbolism's depth of feelings."[37] Antonioni was less certain about the path he wanted to follow, though the Pavesian solution was closer to his temperament than any other. For a long time success eluded him. In the early postwar years, he lived on menial jobs and often felt discouraged. He was already thirty-eight years old when he directed his first feature film in 1950, the year of Pavese's death. A few months before his suicide, Pavese pointed out: "One does not kill oneself for the love of a woman. One kills oneself because love, any love, reveals to us our nudity, misery, defenselessness, and nullity." This could be any of Antonioni's film characters speaking.[38]

From the outset, Antonioni was fascinated by Pavese's writings, which helped him to overcome the limitations imposed on him by his previous cinematic experience. Antonioni discovered in Pavese's approach some important stylistic elements that later became the foundations of his own *oeuvre:* the transformation of the landscape into a crucial element of his vision, the inner world of the characters seen as an extension of their environment, the primacy of language (form) over content, the return to "writing well" (in film terms, beautiful photography), etc. Antonioni, like Pavese, was aware that "the artist who is not constantly analyzing and breaking down his technique is a poor one."[39] As early as 1942, when Antonioni was a film critic, he wrote:

> Film, fundamentally a visual art, should link its method of representation to the external appearance of nature and individuals because it is through this appearance that their interiority reveals itself. I said appearance, not substance. Therefore, it is essential to capture the relationship between the spiritual aspect and the emotional one. This can be achieved through the transfiguration of the real aspect of the world into a purely artistic illusion, or through color, whose nuances, shades, and transitions create an analogous transformation.[40]

The true artistic encounter between Pavese and Antonioni occurred five years after Pavese's death when Antonioni chose to film *Among Women Only,* whose subject is suicide. In *Tentato suicidio* (Attempted Suicide), an episode of the 1953 composite film *Love in the City,* Antonioni had already concerned himself with the subject of suicide, depicting its echoes and signs more than the act itself and concentrating mainly on the aftermath. It was the same approach he had used in his first feature film, *Cronaca di un amore* (Chronicle of a Love, 1950), which focused on the consequences of actions more than on the actions themselves.

Chronicle of a Love is close to the social commentary pictures of the neorealist era. It depicts the barriers between a young woman who has married money and her lover who has remained poor. Both of them are indirectly responsible for the death of their partners. Guido (Massimo Girotti), a typical product of the war years, penniless and frustrated, leaves Paola just when, after long years of waiting, they are finally both free to begin a life together. The Pavesian "revelation through love" permeates the whole film, especially in the last scenes where the camera captures Paola standing in front of her mansion ("her face riddled with tears, shivering with cold and despair")[41] and then focuses on Guido, who then leaves for good. The characters are conceived to express emotions of which they may not yet be aware and which will lead to a modification of their own moral condition. The development of feelings moves in the foreground while the social aspects gradually lose significance.

In his first fiction film, Antonioni already abandons a narrative structure with beginnings and ends, turning instead to the inner flow of emotions.[42] The camera often follows the characters even after everything has been said, favoring extremely long takes (sequence shots). Antonioni's attempt to break with the formula of the traditional script is apparent in his rendition of the past. Avoiding conventional flashbacks, he makes the past a part of the present, linking it to the actual state of mind of the characters and unveiling former acts through their present symptoms. (Paola's working-class past is revealed through her emotional reactions as the wife of a rich Milan businessman.)

In *Signora senza camelie* (The Lady Without Camelias, 1953), Antonioni deepened his search for a form capable of expressing "a crisis of feelings." Clara, an insignificant actress who becomes a star, is the first of his protagonists who foresees her loss of affection and the beginning of her loneliness—that Pavesian "main obstacle and crust to be broken." The Antonionian couple, fading out of an emotional relationship, also makes its first appearance here in the characters of Clara and her husband Gianni, the direct predecessors of Lidia and Giovanni in Antonioni's major film *La notte.* Gianni, a successful film producer, refuses to recognize the disappearance of the emotional bond between him and Clara whereas Clara accepts the breakdown with all its consequences. At the end, her fabulous career terminated, Clara is left alone, without even the symbolic camelias, which Paola, in *Chronicle of a Love,* always kept in a vase.[43]

Antonioni's belief that "for a human being, everything originates in a human being" is reflected in the structure of the script for *The Lady Without Camelias.* The narrative facts are not shown as parts of a separately recognizable reality; they are captured at the moment when they are conceived by human minds. For example, Clara's intention to secure her film future at any cost becomes apparent in the film's

Signora senza camelie

opening scenes when long sequence shots capture her waiting in front of the movie theater that is showing her film; thus her marriage to Gianni comes as no surprise at all. Similarly, Sergio's apprehension that his affair with Clara could damage his diplomatic career manifests itself in their very first encounter so that the further development of their relationship is clear without reference to external circumstances.

Although Antonioni renounced the basic patterns of neorealism, above all by abandoning characterization and motivation, he never gave up thorough documentation, be it of the events depicted or their suggested origins (such as the milieu of the Milan upper middle class in *Chronicle of a Love* and the film world in *The Lady Without Camelias*). In all of Antonioni's films, there is the same nostalgia for reality that was the center of gravity in his two shorts (*People of the River Po*, made in 1943–1947, and *Netezza urbana* [Trash Collectors], made in 1948).[44] For Antonioni, as for Fellini, neorealism remained the most important formative experience whereas the innovative urge of their films stemmed from the reaction against its established formulas.

In *The Lady Without Camelias*, the milieu of the film world is rendered most meticulously. One of the key scenes depicts the shooting of a picture starring Clara. Everybody is ready for action, the crew is waiting, but the newlywed Clara arrives late. Antonioni draws a stunning picture of people immersed in veneration of the star and the producer. The director is portrayed running around in disarray, the only one who does not know where his star is and whether she is coming. "Can somebody tell me what's going on here?" he keeps asking. This sequence reflects in part authentic events that accompanied the production of *The Lady Without Camelias*. The shooting dragged on for two years, the script (originally written for Gina Lollobrigida) was altered several times, and the production was constantly short of money. "Too many rumors, too many news items, too many scandals accompanied the shooting of this film," Antonioni said in 1953.[45] In this respect, the insertion of bits of real life into the story was worthy of a neorealist.[46]

Of the three films Antonioni directed in the years 1950–1953, *I vinti* (The Vanquished, 1952) bears the deepest imprint of his original creative impulse—the transfiguration of aspects of reality into artistic illusion. Richard Roud suggested that "it was an attempt to satisfy that side of him which is genuinely concerned with immediate social issues."[47] The three episodes of the film, set in France, Italy, and England, have one common denominator: an effort to determine the moral origins of crime. Antonioni's juvenile delinquents have been shaped by the war and its disruptive consequences. They all belong to the so-called "defeated" or "lost" generation, which reached maturity during the 1950s economic boom.[48] Despite its well-documented historical and social background, *The Vanquished* is again more concerned with the "enigma of facts" and with unmotivated actions. Antonioni records actions without mentioning any motivations or drawing conclusions.

I vinti

The Vanquished is Antonioni's most mutilated film. Both the producers and the censors demanded cuts and changes. Thus, the Italian episode, capturing the marks left by fascism on the young generation, was so distorted that it became incomprehensible.[49] The French episode tells a well-outlined story of a teenager murdered for money by his best friends who, like himself, come from affluent families. The booty turns out to be play money, and the murderers are left in a state of indifference and incomprehension similar to that of the protagonist of the Italian story, who kills a man without knowing why and without really caring.

The authentic origin of the English episode (a news item) is manipulated by the director's imagination to such an extent that André Bazin called the result "stylized realism." The Antonionian theme of the inscrutability of phenomena becomes the true subject of the film, immersed in an eerie atmosphere of squalid London suburbs. The takes are organized in such a way as to create the impression of a never-ending maze and to suggest the insurmountable distance between events and characters. (This kind of distant visual beauty reappeared in *Blow-Up* and in *Chung Kuo,* the 1971 documentary on China.) The murder, committed by a student obsessed with the idea of an unmotivated crime, remains a mystery even after all appearances had been unveiled and all facts shown.

VISCONTI AND THE OTHER ROAD OF ITALIAN FILM

Visconti's critico-historical approach can be referred to as the other alternative of the Italian post-neorealist cinema, as a counterpart of the metaphoric representations cherished by some other neorealists, mainly Fellini. On the one hand, there is the complex texture of Visconti's cinematic "novels," a narrative rendering of global aspects and objective relationships; on the other, we find a constant breaking up of stylistic and narrative knots that are taken out of their natural context, distorted and combined in fantastic ways as they might be in dreams.

After *La terra trema,* the masterpiece of neorealism, Visconti broke away from the principles of the movement he helped to bring to life. The slow, solemn rhythm of *La terra trema* was replaced by a form based on an extreme concentration of the dramatic material, which resulted in an opposite rhythm. The language of *Bellissima* (1951), the film that followed *La terra trema,* is aggressive, brutal, structured around violent melodramatic conflicts. The situations and relationships become more strident, filled with an overpowering intensity and an emphasis on doom rather than hope and progress. With *Bellissima* Visconti effected his escape from the rigidity of any method and prepared his way for his own critico-historical mode, which would express his concern with human destinies enclosed within precise historical circumstances. He concentrated his efforts on a few basic themes that he explored in many different ways, trying to sum up his experiences in the exploration of man and his place in the society.

Before making *Senso* in 1954, the key film of the post-neorealist period, Visconti attempted a compromise between the propositions of the neorealist movement and his own perspective. Giovanni Verga was not the only literary figure to inspire early neorealists. There was also Francesco De Sanctis (with a "c," as

Chiarini used to put it), a prominent literary critic of Verga's time, who, unlike Verga and the Verists, asserted the necessity of imagination and intuition. Above all, the neorealists were impressed by his demands for a critical reassessment of national values and attitudes, a goal that they themselves had also set out to accomplish. In the closing pages of his history of Italian literature (published in 1871), De Sanctis stated:

> We must reexamine ourselves, our customs, our ideas, our prejudices, our qualities, both good and bad; we must convert the modern world into our own world by studying it, assimilating it, changing it. We live a great deal on our past and on the work of other people. There is no life or labor we can call our own. And from our boasts, one can perceive the awareness we have of our inferiority.

De Sanctis proposed an art "sharpened in the jargon of the people, close to nature, an art with more living passions, immediate impressions, deriving its language not from rules but from impressions."[50]

At the Parma congress, Visconti followed De Sanctis's ideas in answering those who refused to change neorealist patterns by moving beyond reality. "I do not think," Visconti said, "that neorealism is a rigid stylistic form tied to the demands of a limited period. I see it as the beginning of the evolution of cinema as art. This development has to proceed on two levels: on the level of a deepened approach toward life in all its aspects and on that of a deepened knowledge of human reality."[51] Visconti's words bring to mind De Sanctis's remark aimed against the literal application of the veristic method. In his essay on Petrarch he wrote: "Those who out of fear of offending reality represent things bare and empty, such as they appear to an idiot, do not have any feeling or understanding of nature."[52]

Zavattini's and Visconti's concepts clashed in *Bellissima,* the first and only film Visconti made after a subject by Zavattini. As early as 1948, Visconti was already involved in a polemic concerning the issues of neorealism. His stage production of *Rosalinda, or As You Like It*—conceived as a fantastic fairy tale in a surrealistically designed eighteenth-century setting—was attacked for its betrayal of neorealism.[53] Visconti's reply summed up his image of the future evolution of theater and cinema. He pointed out:

> In the field of cinema, neorealism helped us to define different concepts that inspired the recent "Italian school." It comprised those who believed that poetry can be born out of reality. Today, in my opinion, it is an absurd label that has stuck to us like a tattoo and that, instead of designating a method and a reference, has become a limitation and a set of rules. . . . On the stage, we carried neorealism as far as we could. We used real objects and authentic reminiscences that had been rejected by the conventional theater. All our present efforts stem from this method, which is also at the origins of our fantasy. I said fantasy and I insist on that word. Neither realism, nor neorealism, but fantasy, a complete freedom of spectacle.[54]

In *Bellissima,* Visconti deepened the narrative level of Zavattini's subject by identifying it with his own experience. Thus, a collision ensued between demands

Bellissima

of pure objectivity and the concerns of an open narrative with its different cognitive levels. The integration of the personalized subject matter and the description of the environment gave birth to a method that eventually became the dominant agent in all Visconti's films. Zavattini's subject for *Bellissima* was similar to that of *Bicycle Thief*. A mother and her daughter were substituted for the father-son pair, and they too were portrayed as victims of social circumstances.

Visconti thoroughly desentimentalized the character of Maddalena, the mother, turning *Bellissima* into a story of Maddalena's inner anguish. Focusing on her marital crisis, he dealt with one of his major themes—the relationship between people living in the same house. However, although some of Visconti's films remain confined within the walls of a house or of a community (*La terra trema, The White Nights, Sandra, Conversation Piece, The Stranger, Ludwig, The Innocent*), *Bellissima* opens on different milieus with their various human components. In the final analysis, it is not only the many-sidedness of the protagonist that gives the film its splendor but also Zavattini's influence—his plot that had to unfold in highly expressive settings.

Bellissima's plot—the story of a mother who is ready to sacrifice everything to enter her five-year-old daughter in a film contest for the most beautiful child in Rome—had to be told amidst real things and people. In the entire narrative, Visconti's efforts to achieve the transition from neorealism to realism appear to be developed so as to scrutinize the relationships among the characters and the different manifestations of their changing feelings.

Anna Magnani was the main reason Visconti directed *Bellissima*. Throughout his career, he had wanted to work with Magnani, "a stupendous actress, an extraordinary woman with a pagan disposition," just as he always wanted to direct Maria Callas.[55] Magnani was equally eager to work with him, more so than ever in 1950 after Rossellini had left her for Ingrid Bergman.[56]

Visconti's interest in the many-sided character of a self-destructive mother, portrayed by an actress such as Magnani, helped him to transcend Zavattini's anecdotal approach and to go beyond the French objective realism.[57]

At the outset of the fifties, films by Antonioni, Fellini, Rossellini, and Visconti were instrumental in the attempt at a "transition from neorealism to realism" (as this period is referred to). For several years, however, these four directors remained men alone on an untraveled road; they did not find much critical understanding for the innovative force contained in their films. Especially Rossellini and Antonioni were the underdogs of the Italian film industry, having increasing difficulties in finding financial backing for their projects. Their full appreciation came only after years of delay.

In retrospect, the unity of the neorealist movement was an exception in the overall history of the Italian cinema. Since its end, there has not been a trend that shares a common poetics, even less an ethics. Lino Miccichè goes so far as to suggest that "after the period 1945–1950, the Italian cinema was the only one among the major film countries to lack a common denominator shared by a group of filmmakers and not to produce a group of films born out of a collective film. In our cinema personalities have always prevailed over general movements and trends."[58]

V

NEOREALISM IS LIKE...

What is neorealism? Definitions abound. "There are many kinds of neorealism; everyone has his own. Mine was a moral position, an effort to understand myself inside a phenomenon."[1] This was Rossellini talking.

The majority of film dictionaries and encyclopedias refer to neorealism as, for example, "a movement in Italy from about 1943 to 1952 which reacted against the artificiality of the prewar and fascist cinema; although its adherents were diverse and never really formed a school, most of them shared a generally left-wing attitude and relied on natural decor, unprofessional actors, and a simple direct style of direction."[2]

In the early seventies, a group of Italian film critics reacted against the very concept of neorealism as a movement. A movement, according to them, has to have a unity, which neorealism lacked. Thus, for Lino Miccichè, neorealism was not even a phenomenon because "on the level of its expressive results, namely, films, it could be decomposed and recomposed almost as desired."[3] This critical group was probably right to view neorealism as the result of previous traditions, but it underestimated the coherence of its style as it was progressively coined.[4] In his introductory paper at the 1974 conference on neorealism Miccichè said:

> Neorealism was not an aesthetics, and one of the reasons for its demise was the belief that it was and, what is worse, had the intention to be one. Neorealism was "an ethics of an aesthetics." It was the answer of a generation of filmmakers to the question asked by Vittorini: "Shall we ever have a culture capable of protecting people against suffering instead of just comforting them?" In this respect— and only in this respect—the Viscontis, De Sicas, Rossellinis, and the De Santis, aesthetically so different from one another, were ethically similar.[5]

Yet all these artists, one so unlike the other, brought to life a phenomenon with clearly defined technical and moral components that influenced almost all subsequent film trends in the West and in the East. In this respect, little doubt remains.

After *Paisà, Shoeshine, Germany, Year Zero* and *Bicycle Thief,* cinema could never be the same again. The neorealist approach became a permanent part of the filmmakers' equipment. Its influence could be seen in French cinema from Clément, Cayatte, and Clouzot to Godard and Truffaut, its influence on Japanese directors like Kinoshita, Ichikawa, and Oshima must have been considerable, and it may well be that the neorealist example encouraged Satyajit Ray when he embarked on *Pather Panchali.*[6]

Basil Wright's contention is supported by James Monaco, who wrote: "While neorealism as a movement lasted only until the early fifties, the effects of its aesthetics are still being felt. In fact, Zavattini, Rossellini, De Sica, and Visconti defined the ground rules that would operate for nearly thirty years. Aesthetically, Hollywood never quite recovered."[7] *The International Encyclopedia of Film* as well states in connection with *Open City:* "It was a way of making films which was to influence not only the postwar generation of filmmakers in Italy, but also generations to come."[8] As the French critic Louis Marcorelles contended:

Historically, neorealism in 1944–1945, the British "free cinema" of 1956–1959, and the French New Wave of 1958–1959 show the first efforts that were made to create a cinema that was not costly, that came closer to reality, and that was free from slavery to technique. The most significant films of the period bear on them, like a watermark, something that foreshadows the direct cinema of the sixties.[9]

Stephen Member emphasized mainly the influence of Zavattini:

Zavattini has to be cited as part of the aesthetic foundation of *cinéma vérité,* regardless of the failure of neorealism to fulfill this stated commitment to undirected reality. There has to be room here for a man who can say: "However great a faith I might have in imagination, in solitude, I have a greater faith in reality, in people. I am interested in the drama of things we happen to encounter, not those we plan." Here, he beautifully articulates the *cinéma vérité,* outlook.[10]

Others, such as Louis D. Giannetti, concerned themselves with the influence of neorealism on American fiction film directors, such as Elia Kazan and Samuel Fuller (*The Steel Helmet*). According to Giannetti, Kazan was influenced

particularly in the use of authentic urban location, the use of nonprofessional actors (though primarily for minor roles), and in the development of explicit sociopolitical themes. Significantly, Kazan's movies (*Boomerang! Panic in the Streets, On the Waterfront, A Face in the Crowd*) did not eschew plots. The "new look" of his films was largely confined to matters of details, not to structure.[11]

Rossellini was right. Everyone had his own neorealism according to his disposition, temperament, belief, and external circumstances. In Japan, the neorealist films provoked a real explosion in the development of cinema, linking up with prewar Japanese realism, mainly with the films of Yasujiro Ozu. Ozu's crude style (e.g., in *An Inn in Tokyo,* 1935, or *The Only Son,* 1936) and striving for authenticity anticipated especially the neorealist method found in De Sica's early work with its poetic vision of streets populated with social outcasts and an indifferent crowd.

Some postwar Japanese directors fused these traditions with the new Italian influence (Tadashi Imai, Keisuke Kinoshita, Satsuo Yamamoto).[12]

Neorealism holds a special place in the development of the East European cinema. In the mid-fifties, its influence in Hungary, Poland, and Czechoslovakia was crucial, merging with the endeavor of these productions to free themselves from Stalinist aesthetics. The neorealist experience in these countries symbolized the yearning for truth and freedom that obsessed the East European filmmakers as much as the early neorealists. The generation of Felix Máriássy and Zoltan Fábri in Hungary, of Elmar Klos, Ján Kadár, and Vojtěch Jasný in Czechoslovakia, of Andrzej Wajda, Andrzej Munk, and Jerzy Kawalerowicz in Poland saw in the neorealist struggle not only an inspiration to renovate an antiquated style, but also, in a broader sense, an impulse to deal with certain aspects of their own society. The Soviet director Mikhail Romm said about the influence of neorealism in the USSR: "I know the impression created by the Italian films. I can underline that this influence was real."[13] While in Hungary and Czechoslovakia, the attempts to follow the example of neorealism were stopped in their early stage, in Poland neorealism found a more congenial atmosphere. In 1954, Krzysztof Toeplitz, the Polish film critic, saw neorealism as "an artistic ideal for our authors and our cinema."[14] Twenty years later, Bołeslaw Michałek claimed that "Toeplitz expressed to a large degree the opinion of the Polish film scene and of mature audiences. For them, neorealism was not just an Italian phenomenon bound to a geographical, historical, and political context: it was an alternative genre—or one of the alternatives—for the Polish cinema at a moment when it was trying to find its way out of a crisis."[15] Andrzej Wajda said about his first feature film, *A Generation* (1955), whose perspective and style bear some marks of the neorealist influence: "In the neorealist films we have seen that scenes shot in studios were used only to complement scenes shot on real-life locations. In Polish productions, my film was the first where scenes took place outdoors in the rain or under covered skies. Before, similar techniques were simply inadmissible."[16]

Afraid of the impact that Italian neorealism might have on filmmakers and audiences, the authorities of the majority of the East European countries withheld several important neorealist films from public release or restricted them to film clubs and art theaters (e.g. *Open City, Paisan, Germany, Year Zero, Bitter Rice, Miracle in Milan, La terra trema, Difficult Years*).[17]

TEN POINTS

In 1952, the Parisian journal *Films et Documents* published the famous "ten points of neorealism," which, to a large degree, still remain valid.

(1) A message: for the Italian filmmakers, cinema is a way of expression and communication in the true sense of this word. (2) Topical scripts inspired by concrete events; great historical and social issues are tackled from the point of view of the common people. (3) A sense of detail as a means of authentification. (4) A sense of the masses and the ability to surprise (De Sica) or manipulate them

in front of camera (De Santis, Visconti): the protagonists are captured in their relationship to the masses. (5) Realism; but reality is filtered by a very delicate sensitivity. (6) The truth of actors, often nonprofessionals. (7) The truth of decor and a refusal of the studio. (8) The truth of the lighting. (9) Photography reminiscent of the reportage style stresses the impression of truth. (10) An extremely free camera; its unrestricted movements result from the use of postsynchronization.[18]

The last point played an important role in the shaping of neorealistic aesthetics (and of the aesthetics of the Italian cinema in general). Most of the films were shot silent and postsynchronized. Consequently, the filmmaker had an unprecedented freedom of movement, which reappeared in movie production only after the invention of light hand cameras equipped with sound recording. Because of their long distinguished tradition in dubbing, Italian sound technicians were experienced enough to re-create sounds in a studio to such perfection that hardly anybody noticed any discrepancy. (The most famous case is that of *Bicycle Thief* where Lamberto Maggiorani, a blue-collar worker who played the part of the unemployed worker, was dubbed by an actor.) In an article aptly called "Film Witness," Jacques Doniol-Valcroze, the French critic and director-to-be, observed in 1947:

> The photography of the neorealist films, austere and gray, creates the impression of having gone through changes of temperature and situations. Also, the sound (though almost always recorded in a studio) evokes the feeling of outdoors, of hasty direction, and a complete absence of a search for effects. The actors follow these movements; they "exist" modestly in front of the camera.[19]

Almost twenty years later, Giuseppe Ferrara, author of several books on Italian cinema, analyzed the points that Doniol-Valcroze noted. In his essay "Il neorealismo italiano," Ferrara wrote:

> The neorealist cinematographer simply followed the stream of light, as Caravaggio used to do. If the light entered through one window, then the lighting had only one source that illuminated objects in their most humble truth. Objects were not to be beautified—the cruder they were, the purer they appeared, the more authentic, the more "beautiful." Neorealist photography contains a luminous truth that had never before appeared in any film. Similarly, the neorealist actor did not transfer a literary reality that was beyond his reach. He was no longer just the image of a human being; he was its historical interpretation.[20]

Several critics tried to explain neorealism as an aesthetics of rejection. (Barbaro said in 1943: "If we want to reject forever historical set pieces, the heated-up nineteenth century, and the double-identity comedy, we must try out realism.")[21] The theory of rejection was fully adopted by the Soviet semiotician Jurij Lotman in his popular book *Semiotics of Cinema*. He writes:

> In its struggle against theatrical pomposity, Italian neorealism arrived at the total equation of art and extraartistic reality. Its active elements were always refusals: a refusal to use stereotyped heroes or typical scenes; a refusal to use professional actors; a refusal of the star system; a refusal to employ montage and an iron-clad scenario; a refusal to use prepared dialogues or musical accompaniment."[22]

Lotman's contention does not stand the proof of any major neorealist film. The leading neorealist filmmakers never achieved "a total equation of art and extraartistic reality" and probably never really tried. They did use elaborate montage (*Bicycle Thief, La terra trema, Bitter Rice*), as well as prepared dialogues (*Tragic Hunt, Shoeshine, Umberto D.*), dramatic musical accompaniment (*Mill on the River Po, No Peace Under the Olives, Germany, Year Zero*), and professional actors (*Open City, Bitter Rice, Without Pity*). Lotman just reduced neorealism to a simple denial of the past, which is an attitude shared by so many (e.g., the verists and Futurists went much further in this direction.)[23]

Lotman's simplification must be compared to the concept of neorealism as a movement that went beyond previous aesthetics based on the emphasis of reality— be it naturalism, verismo; or, in cinema, the French populism of the thirties or the British documentary school of John Grierson and Basil Wright. This approach, formulated mainly by Amédée Ayfre, the French philosopher and film critic, saw neorealism as a movement that used the full capacity of the film medium in order to capture not only real events but also their deeper significance. In a 1963 essay, Ayfre wrote:

As much as Merleau-Ponty—following Husserl, but in a more existential than transcendental way—elaborated the phenomenological method to reach beyond the opposition of materialism and idealism, the neorealists in cinema transcended all previous aesthetics that took for their points of departure the notion of the ultimate foundations of the real. Neorealist films presented themselves to anybody who wanted to look at them with naïve eyes as simple descriptions of appearance lacking a dominating contextual idea. In this respect, many critics of the time did not consider them art but only documents that were not interpreting a historical point of view but only chronicling. Such minimalization occurs whenever radically new works of art cannot be judged according to existing canons.[24]

Ayfre touched the heart of the matter. Neorealist films caught critics unprepared, and much of the confusion stemmed from the incongruency of the theory that accompanied them and eventually helped to bury them. And yet, its manifold qualities provoked a discussion that continued long after those who had once started it were no longer its protagonists.

Like some critics, audiences often were not prepared to accept stories basically so different from almost everything that had been presented to them until then. Films that did not attract attention with immediately understandable and topical messages (as did, e.g., *Open City, Paisan, To Live in Peace*) or with their extracinematic values (the eroticism in *Bitter Rice*) were usually financial failures.

HUMANISTS AND SOCIOHISTORIANS

Two approaches prevail in the overall evaluation of neorealism: the humanistic and the sociohistorical. In retrospect, the humanists, who explained the neorealist phenomenon in terms of its ethical content, proved more foresighted than those who tied it solely to its sociohistorical background.

André Bazin was prominent among the former. For him, what counted was cinema's way of explaining reality and not what was explained. "I am prepared to see the fundamental humanism of the current Italian films as their chief merit," he wrote in 1948. "They offer an opportunity to savor, before the time finally runs out on us, a revolutionary flavor in which terror has yet no part."[25] Bazin considered neorealism as an exemplary model of his thought about cinema, "attaining its fullness in being the art of the real." On the other hand, for Henri Agel, another of the French humanists, neorealism—as a "state of mind"—was "tied to the deep song of the Italian soul."[26] Bazin considered it a "revolution in art," another of the assessments attacked during the 1974 congress on neorealism.

The word *revolution* is often mentioned and not only in Bazin's writings, though it is without doubt an exaggerated term for a movement bound in many ways to established aesthetics and inspired by the 1930s cinema (descriptive calligraphist realism, documentarism of De Robertis's and Rossellini's war films, French populism, etc.). Yet for Bazin, neorealism was

> a revolution in a form which comes to bear on the content. For example, the priority which they accord to incidents over plot had led De Sica and Zavattini to replace plot as such with a microaction based on an infinitely divisible attention to the complexities in even the most extraordinary of events. This in itself rules out the slightest hierarchy, whether psychological, dramatic, or ideological, among the incidents portrayed.[27]

In Italy, too, Luigi Chiarini claimed that "neorealism tends, perhaps unconsciously, toward new cinematic forms that mean a real and true revolution with respect to the concept of cinema as spectacle." Chiarini belonged to the best known humanists among Italian critics. In the early fifties, he wrote one of the most pertinent analyses of the neorealist phenomenon, attacking simplified sociohistorical attitudes. He pointed out:

> The greatest misunderstanding consists in confusing neorealism with cinematic verismo and in the belief that a neorealist film can be created just by shooting on location without actors and with people picked up in real life. That was a mistake that led to the confusion between the demands postulated by a spiritual attitude and a technical fact. It is utterly arbitrary to classify as neorealist all films, and only such films, that tackle the contents of social concern and are based on certain external features such as the use of nonprofessional actors and shooting on location.[28]

One of the best definitions of neorealism was provided by Mario Gromo, one of the first Italian film critics inspired by the teachings of Benedetto Croce. In his essays on neorealism, Gromo always linked historical circumstances with the evolution of human freedom. He wrote in the early fifties:

> After the fall of fascism, when half of the country was still under German occupation, life was hard and cruel; this pain and anguish became vital for our directors. They felt free but obsessed with this suffering. Thus *Open City* and *Shoeshine* were born and were hailed almost all over the world. They appeared,

suddenly, in an atmosphere of three tired conformities: the American, predominantly industrial; the Russian, entirely political; and the French, rather literary. What came to life was less a new realism and more a new truth rooted in the search for a new freedom.[29]

Among the humanists, some read the neorealist films in terms of "stories of despair," as Basil Wright put it. In 1956, Brunello Rondi, the film critic and screenwriter for Rossellini and Fellini, anticipated the later evolution of the Italian cinema when he contended:

> The new Italian cinema is imbued with a tragic sense of human coexistence and an ethical passion that searches for the meaning of a "valid society." Films about human solitude, about gaps between individual lives separated one from the other by hatred and indifference, draw their decisive impact from the war only because war revealed the truth of the ethical passion, the sense of a lost coherence and the horrible deformations caused by man to man. Italian cinema is the only cultural expression that has sensed this urgent situation of modern humanity. It inserts it into a complex historical vision. The major Italian directors are "historians" of human solitude, not its "elegists."[30]

Umberto Barbaro in Italy and Georges Sadoul in France were the most prominent among the sociohistorians. Their theory of neorealism as an exclusive expression of the war and antifascist resistance, with an emphasis laid on social concern, proved extremely tenacious. It was more easily explainable and applicable than other concepts. This theory, departing from a just assessment about the birth of neorealism out of an exceptional moment in European history, never really went beyond its premise. Its proponents attempted to tie down all subsequent development in Italian cinema to this original impulse. Simplistic contentions, such as "neorealist films were repeatedly showing that unjust and perverted social structures threaten to warp and pervert the essential and internal human values,"[31] eventually prevailed in other countries also, especially in Germany, Switzerland, and the United States. A more careful analysis is needed to reveal that the consistent focus of major neorealist films was "not only upon social reality but also upon the dialectics of reality and appearance, usually the appearance or illusion of reality produced by artistic means."[32]

However, in such a widely read book as Georges Sadoul's *Histoire générale du cinéma* (1946) only a simplistic explanation of neorealism appears that pays a heavy tribute to the political situation of the time: "Thanks to the people, thanks to their fight for national independence, thanks also to the theoretical basis elaborated in deep clandestinity by antifascist militants, neorealism could emerge fully armed the very moment the war was over."[33] Sadoul followed the general outlines of neorealism defined by Umberto Barbaro, for whom "art was on one hand conditioned and determined (i.e., tied to an epoch), expressing a determined reality, and, on the other hand, turned toward the future, anticipating and contributing to the creation of a new epoch."[34]

The sociohistorical opinion was carried to its utmost rigidity by Raymond

Borde and André Buissy, for whom "neorealism was the first mass experience of social cinema," which "had the ambition—and only on this ambition can any definition be based—to be a cinema of content."[35]

A more differentiated attitude was adopted by Ulrich Gregor and Enno Patalas in their *Geschichte des modernen Films*. In the opening pages, they point out:

> After 1945, Italian cinema became the avant-garde of those European countries that had gone through the war. Postwar Europe found its representative style in neorealism, in its concept of crude reality, and in its documentaristic camera. Humanism and universal impact, deeply rooted in the historical and social reality, were the reasons for the exceptional success of early neorealist films, both in Italy and abroad.[36]

Siegfried Kracauer, who based large segments of his theory of cinematic realism on his experience with neorealism, defined its roots better than most of the social critics. He wrote:

> When history is made in the streets, the streets tend to move onto the screen. For all their differences in ideology and techniques, *Potemkin* and *Paisan* have this "street" quality in common; they feature environmental situations rather than private affairs, episodes involving society at large rather than stories centering upon an individual conflict. In other words, they show a tendency toward documentary. . . . These narratives serve to dramatize social conditions in general. The preference for real people on the screen and the documentary approach seem to be closely interrelated.[37]

The conflict between the humanists and the sociohistorians culminated in its time in the discussion about Rossellini ending with André Bazin's open letter to Guido Aristarco. Bazin could not admit that Rossellini be excluded from the ranks of the major Italian filmmakers only because he did not limit the use of the film medium to the confines determined by the sociohistorical demands that Aristarco upheld. Bazin rightly anticipated that by narrowing neorealism to just one side of its experience, both the future development of Italian cinema and the general image of neorealism could be jeopardized. Thus, for example, the refusal by the 1974 Pesaro group to see neorealism as a movement was based, among others, on the rejection of the formula into which neorealism had been locked after the dismissal of directors like Rossellini, Fellini, and Antonioni. The sociohistorical definition penetrated into many film histories and later created a certain mistrust of neorealism among some critics and filmmakers outside Italy who considered it a typical product of the traditional narrative cinema with no space left for formal experiments.

In his letter to Aristarco, the editor-in-chief of *Cinema Nuovo*, Bazin wrote:

> When I find you hunting for fleas in Gelsomina's tousled hair (*La strada*) or dismissing Rossellini's last film (*Voyage in Italy*) as less than nothing, I am forced to conclude that under the guise of theoretical integrity you are in the process of nipping in the bud some of the liveliest and most promising offshoots of what I persist in calling neorealism. [These two films], far from being felt

here [in France] as a break with neorealism and still less a regression, have given us the feeling of creative inventiveness deriving directly from the spirit that informs the Italian school. I have to confess to a strong dislike for a notion of neorealism that is based on the exclusion of all else, on what is only one of its present aspects, for this is to submit its future potential to a priori restriction.[38]

As early as 1952 Rossellini said:

Neorealism involves a greater interest in individuals. Modern man feels a need to tell of things as they are, to take account of reality in an uncompromisingly concrete way, which goes with today's interest in statistics and scientific results. Neorealism is also a response to the genuine need to see men for what they are, with humility and without recourse to fabricating the exceptional; it means the awareness that the exceptional is arrived at through the investigation of reality. Lastly, it is an urge for self-clarification, an urge not to ignore reality whatever it may be. This is why I have tried in my films to reach an understanding of things, and to give them their true value. It's not something easy or lightly undertaken but a highly ambitious project because to give anything its true value means grasping its real universal meaning.[39]

VI

DIFFICULT YEARS (1953–1959)

Today, a conformist atmosphere prevails which is not much different from that of the fascist period. In my opinion, this is happening because of the growing power of the governing party. Its actions against freedom of expression are not democratic and liberal but, on the contrary, conformist and backward. Unfortunately, censorship generates self-censorship. Today, nobody knows for sure what he is allowed to say; one is sure only of what he must not say. The Italian film started losing courage.

This excerpt from the autobiographical novel *Success* by Luigi Zampa, published in Rome in 1957, sums up the atmosphere of the fifties, often referred to as "the difficult years"—the title of Zampa's 1948 film. Sandro Zambetti, the Italian film critic, pointed out:

The fifties represent the worst period in the history of the Italian cinema—with the exception of fascism. It was a period of so-called pink neorealism, of "Love, Bread, and, . . ." of "Poor but Beautiful," of flat composite films put together for a fast profit. The Italian cinema was pervaded by mystifying optimism, escapism, and happy misery. ("We're not doing too well, that's true, but we have the sun, the sea, pretty women, and thus we are, in a way, a happy country.") Not too many films deserve to be remembered. Many prominent authors let themselves be dragged along with the overall decline. The cinema of the fifties was typical of De Gasperi's "centrism."[1]

NEOREALISTS AND THE DIFFICULT YEARS

After years of unity and confidence, the story of the Italian cinema became a story of mistrust and uncertainty with some of the leading neorealist personalities leaving the film scene for some time or forever. In 1949, Umberto Barbaro left the country and spent several years in exile (he died in 1959). De Santis, ostracized by the government as well as by the producers, tried to reassemble the pieces of his concept of "cinema as a national medium" in films such as *Un marito per Anna*

Zaccheo (A Husband for Anna Zaccheo, 1953) and *Giorni d' amore* (Days of Love, 1955). These tales, however, were deeply marked by the compromises of the time and were light years away from De Santis's former endeavors. Like Barbaro or Gillo Pontecorvo, De Santis too looked for work abroad, in France and in Yugoslavia where in 1958 he finally shot *La strada lunga d' un anno* (The One-Year-Long Road). As Georges Sadoul put it: "Because of the pressures and coercions, none of these films equaled *Tragic Hunt*."[2] Artistically, De Santis never recovered from the effects of "the difficult years."[3] Antonio Pietrangeli too attempted for some time to preserve the nationalist-populist line of early neorealism, but eventually he bowed to the demands of the industry and directed several finely chiseled comedies. Even the old fox Chiarini paid his due to the witch hunt. In 1949, he was fired from the editorial board of *Bianco e Nero*. De Sica, along with his faithful Zavattini, went to Hollywood but did not make any deal. At home, he returned to his acting career, starring with tremendous success in all three "Bread and Love" films, thus reassuming his place as "Vittorio nazionale," the most popular Italian actor. Zavattini went back to scriptwriting (a profession he had tried to bury a few years before), scripting as many as three films a year, films of all kind, value, and impact. But he never stopped preaching his idea about fidelity to reality, influencing deeply some members of the upcoming generation (Francesco Maselli, Gillo Pontecorvo, Paolo and Vittorio Taviani) and keeping alive, in a way, the spirit of neorealism.

In 1956, Zavattini and De Sica made another attempt to revive the neorealist idea. Their pathetic *Il tetto* (The Roof) brought the maids and bricklayers, the underemployed and exploited, back to the screen. The simple, sentimental plot revolved around the efforts of a newlywed couple to roof their illegal home in a single night before the arrival of the police. *The Roof* bears touching testimony to the impossibility of resuscitating the past. Its characters and events are presented almost exclusively in terms of one facet of life, leaving no space for a reality out of which to forge new possibilities.[4]

Pietro Germi made a similar attempt with *Il ferroviere* (The Railwayman, 1956) where he himself portrayed a railwayman struggling against poverty and injustice. The story, a predictable melodrama, transformed its social background into a convenient metaphor and idealized both the main characters and their milieu.

Those neorealists who had begun their careers in commercial production during the 1930s were soon reintegrated into the mainstream of the film industry. In 1952, Luigi Zampa directed an ambitious film, *Processo alla città* (Trial Against the City), which was subsequently mutilated by the censors. It focused on the investigation of a double murder, leading to the revelation of criminal connections in Neapolitan high society. (The story, written by Francesco Rosi, anticipated Rosi's later films in centering on the power-brokering between political groups.) With his following films, Zampa returned to the traditional comedies of his beginnings.

In 1952 Alberto Lattuada successfully blended the calligraphist notions of his early films with the neorealist method in *Il cappotto* (The Overcoat). Gogol's story of a humble provincial clerk was transposed from nineteenth-century Russia to twentieth-century Italy and thus could be comfortably adapted to the neorealist concept of reality. Renato Rascel, one of Italy's most appealing actors, played the

Processo alla città

role of the poor clerk. A fable of fascist Italy with allusions to present-day attitudes and flaws, *The Overcoat* is one of Lattuada's finest achievements.

Following *The Overcoat* there is a noticeable shift in Lattuada's career, evidence of the impact of the prevailing conditions during the "difficult years." His 1958 film, *La tempesta* (The Tempest), based on Pushkin's short story "The Captain's Daughter," is constructed along the lines of a costume blockbuster, resembling a rather flat and conventional picture postcard of a snowed-in countryside.

RETURN OF THE GENRES

During the fifties, all the genres of the thirties gradually reemerged and became standardized, eventually resulting in a boom of mass culture. The Neapolitan style was popular, with its songs, low-budget productions, and traditional formulas.[5] The mythological film, neorealism's fiercest opponent, found a powerful representative in Mario Camerini, who directed the blockbuster *Ulisse* (Ulysses, 1954), prefiguring the Italo-American superproductions of the early sixties. In the field of literary adaptations, Mario Soldati was again one of the leading figures, pursuing his lifelong preoccupation with such films as *La provinciale* (A Provincial Woman, 1954), based on Moravia's novel, and *War and Peace* (directed by King Vidor in 1956), for which he staged most of the battle scenes.[6]

As in the thirties, production in the fifties—over which Antonioni, Fellini, Rossellini, and Visconti towered like four maladjusted giants—evolved under the sign of sentimental melodramas, prettified comedies, and all kinds of pink neorealism. The neorealist interlude had never really interrupted this kind of production. It had, however, changed some of its characteristics.

PINK NEOREALISM

Pink neorealism and its prettified comedies continued in the same vein as the "Camerini line" of the thirties. Its first product was Renato Castellani's controversial film *Due soldi di speranza* (Two Cents Worth of Hope, 1952), which tastefully imitated the neorealist approach. Its setting was a poor village in southern Italy and the squalid quarters of Naples; the characters were of modest origins; the shooting was done on location; and some of the actors were nonprofessionals. The film told of two lovers' struggle against poverty and ended with the victory of pure love. Castellani's images of humble people, composed with his usual concern for visual beauty, enhance his premise that happiness results mainly from the fulfillment of emotional demands. In this respect, the world of pink neorealism is reminiscent of the old-time comedy Italian style, with its philosophy of happy resignation.

Everything was nice and rosy in the films of pink neorealism: even poverty, sickness, misfortune. Everyone looked beautiful, everything was glittering, and the establishment was pleased. The Italian cinema was no longer "slandering Italy," as neorealism did according to Giulio Andreotti.

The films of pink neorealism, such as *Bread, Love, and . . .* and *Two Cents Worth of Hope,* were inspired by a decadent antirealistic spirit and by a conservative

Two Cents Worth of Hope

Catholicism. They pretended to be realistic so as to make the viewers believe that their deformed images reflected Italian reality. To achieve this impact, these films used the technical experience of neorealism, replacing its original revolutionary significance with an escapist, edifying silent-majority content.[7]

The most famous of these "wastes of realism," as Chiarini referred to pink neorealism, was *Pane, amore e fantasia* (Bread, Love, and Fantasy, 1953), drawing on a stylized peasant mythology and a contrived anecdotal approach. Its heroine (a glamorous Gina Lollobrigida clad in a high-fashion minidress), a poor village girl, ends up living happily ever after because she is modest, goes to church, never complains about her misery, and believes in good and evil, just as the priest has always taught her. The success of *Bread, Love, and Fantasy* gave rise to a whole series of pink comedies and farces, evolving against the picturesque Italian countryside (*Bread, Love, and Jealousy, Bread, Love and . . .* , etc.). Their central characters were affable priests, charming policemen, poor and pure girls, and village villains. The neorealist heritage enlarged their scale by adding farm laborers, shepherds, prostitutes, and World War II veterans.

Pink neorealism was unthinkable without the glamour of its main protagonists and the so-called "pink vamp" as the leading lady. Dressed in sexy rags, with carefully unkempt hair and made up to look like a true poor peasant girl, the pink vamp was the Italian version of the American pin-up. The images of Gina Lollobrigida and Sophia Loren were created as a national reaction to the stardom of Rita Hayworth and Ava Gardner. (Lollobrigida was often referred to as "the most beautiful Italian housewife.")

LUIGI COMENCINI AND DINO RISI

The most successful directors of pink neorealism were Luigi Comencini (b. 1916) and Dino Risi, both originally documentarists.[8] Having been silent witnesses to the neorealist experience, they were boosted to sudden success by its economic failure. Faced with the demise of neorealism and the rising American competition, the producers turned to Comencini and Risi, who made a series of neorealist imitations, searching for forms of expression for a modern popular spectacle. Obsessed with a fidelity to reality, they concocted a successful formula through a compromise between verisimilitude and the conventions of the comedy. Their statements do not differ substantially from those of the early neorealists, and it is possible that they both believed in the truthfulness of their prearranged cinematic reality. Risi, whose models were Lubitsch and Billy Wilder, contended: "I portray things as they are. In my opinion, it is important not only to tell the truth but also to show it as profoundly as possible."[9]

Both Comencini and Risi shot several films a year. Comencini created the "Bread and Love" series, whose third installment was directed by Risi. In 1956, Risi started his own, slightly cynical, version of the pink stories with *Poveri ma belli* (Poor but Beautiful Boys) followed by *Belle ma Povere* (Beautiful but Poor Girls, 1957), *Poveri millionari* (Poor Millionaires, 1959), etc. In Risi's films, the poor but beautiful characters lost their innocence, which they harbored in the

Belle ma povere

"Bread and Love" series and were transferred to urban settings. Portrayed by actors such as Alberto Sordi, Vittorio Gassman, and Marisa Allasio (the Italian Jayne Mansfield), Risi's protagonists wandered in the streets of Rome, leaving far behind the idyllic meadows of southern Italy, which had formed the realistic setting of "Bread and Love." The neorealist tradition of nonprofessional actors continued, together with the realistic overall concept of the stories and the attempts at verisimilitude. "The real" was integrated into Italian production once and for all as a supplement to fiction. The impact of pink neorealism lay in its spontaneity and its interest, albeit superficial, in social problems.

In the area of production, the neorealist craftsmanlike and improvisational methods continued and gradually prevailed. Low-budget production techniques led to a boom in 1954: 204 feature films were made (compared with 104 in 1950); the number of spectators grew to 820 million and the number of movie theaters to 16,207. But soon the situation changed. The advent of television, the growing artistic poverty of pink neorealism and popular melodrama, combined with the poor quality of the overall production, plunged the movie industry into a deep crisis.[10]

COMEDY AND DON CAMILLO

Various elements of pink neorealism were gradually absorbed by the comedy Italian style, whose extraordinary longevity was due to its evolution parallel to changes in the social structure of Italian society. Mario Monicelli (b. 1915) was one of its most prominent directors. Monicelli began working independently in 1949, after having been for fifteen years an assistant director (to Gustav Machatý, Augusto

Genina, Pietro Germi, and others). Monicelli had worked successfully with script-writer Steno (b. 1915) and had Steno codirect his first film, starring Totò (*Totò cerca casa* [Totò Looks for an Apartment]). Monicelli's comedies have slight over-tones of social criticism directed against the bureaucracy of the judicial system and sympathetic to individuals who are defeated by absurd obstacles. In *Guardie e ladri* (Guards and Thieves, 1951), a good-hearted policeman must renounce his friendship in the interest of abstract justice; in *Totò e Carolina* (Totò and Caroline, 1955), another policeman intervenes on behalf of a girl who has been seduced and abandoned. In 1979, Monicelli pointed out: "In Italy, there has always been a ten-dency to view reality as a comedy with a touch of bitterness, a touch of vulgarity, even boorishness. Such is Italy, with our temperament originating in remote tradi-tion. It is a bitter tradition, born of misery, which takes advantage of the bad luck of others. Comedy Italian style has always been the foundation of our production."[11]

Monicelli's comedies are direct heirs to the "rivista" style, which was as com-mon in the movie production of the fifties as it had been twenty years earlier on the stage. The visual was suppressed in favor of verbal humor, and the comedy was based more on situations than on narrative. Monicelli's best comedy, *I soliti ignoti* (The Big Deal on Madonna Street, 1959)—constructed around an exceptional trio of actors: Totò, Marcello Mastroianni, and Vittorio Gassman—portrayed three petty thieves, victims of their own incapacity to be truly dishonest. Monicelli (with his scriptwriters Steno and Scarpelli) created an excellent parody of the criminal genre with its idealization of modern gangsters and master minds.[12] Audiences apparently identified with the awkward antiheroes who failed at everything they tried: *The Big Deal on Madonna Street* grossed over 1 billion lire. Vittorio Spinaz-zola pointed out:

> Monicelli put his finger on an ancient and very topical area of Italian reality. The plot transcends its space, and the whole country becomes its main protagonist: our Italy, that easy-going Italy that manages to survive against all odds, that kingdom of the approximate and the nonscientific, that country of false profes-sional dignity where it is almost honorable to have a profession for which one has not been trained.[13]

This description also holds true for Don Camillo, the most successful film series of the fifties, based on the bestseller by journalist and novelist Giovanni Guareschi. Its central characters, the village priest Don Camillo and the communist mayor Peppone, symbolize the conflict between the major powers of contemporary It-aly—the church and the Communist party. All five films featuring Don Camillo are characterized by explicitly conformist attitudes that deprive class conflicts of all seriousness: all blame is put on "dirty politics," and the natural Italian kindness of heart is given credit for eventually reunifying everyone. The Don Camillo films borrowed liberally from the patterns of pink neorealism, mixing them with ele-ments of tame political satire. The first *Don Camillo,* directed by the Frenchman Julien Duvivier, grossed 1.5 billion lire and was the most popular film of the 1951–1952 season. It was followed in 1953 by *Il ritorno di Don Camillo* (Don Camillo's Return—third place among that year's top-grossing films); in 1955 by Carmine

Gallone's *Don Camillo e l'onorevole Peppone* (Don Camillo and the Deputy Peppone); and in 1961, by *Don Camillo, monsignore ma non troppo* (Don Camillo, Almost a Monsignor); these last two films took fourth place in their respective years. And as late as 1966, Comencini's *Il compagno Don Camillo* (Comrade Don Camillo) grossed 779 million lire. (Don Camillo was portrayed by the popular French comic actor Fernandel, Peppone by Gino Cervi.)

Numerous critics and historians have tried to explain Don Camillo's unprecedented success. The main reason probably lies in the fact that in one of the most politicized countries of the world, it offered audiences a truly popular spectacle that focused on daily political issues, directly addressing the two protagonists of the political scene (the communists and the Catholics). The films touched the heart of certain Italian attitudes, especially the belief in "following the path of least resistance."[14]

FILM SOAP OPERAS

Between 1950 and 1955, the most successful genre was the populist melodrama, which later was assimilated by television and transformed into serialized soap operas. The trend was started by *Catene* (Chains), one of the greatest hits of the 1949–1950 season, which grossed 750 million lire in that one year. With this film, Raffaello Matarazzo (1909–1966) opened a new chapter in the history of Italian movie production, mixing stale conventions with some neorealist impulses. *Chains* tells the story of a happily married woman who is pressed to yield to the passion of

Catene

her former lover. Her husband, believing that she has betrayed him, kills the lover and emigrates to America; arrested, he faces a severe sentence; yet the woman, though innocent, confesses to adultery, thereby transforming his crime into a crime of honor. The husband is set free, learns of his wife's innocence, and reaches her just in time to prevent her from committing suicide.

Similar in many ways to traditional melodramas, *Chains* also contained some new elements. The story was set in the present, the atmosphere was authentic, the protagonists were common people, and issues such as emigration, poverty, and crimes of honor were mentioned. Yet the melodramatic core, the codified great sentiments, remained unchanged; and so did the protagonists, "victims of social injustice, torn by eternal passions and destroyed by blind, cruel destiny."[15]

Thanks to *Chains,* Matarazzo experienced a meteoric rise in popularity. As early as the thirties, he had been noted as one of the foremost directors of tear-jerkers. But now, in the fifties, his fame reached its peak with films such as *Tormento* (Torment, 1950), *Torna!* (Come Back! 1954), *Schiava del peccato* (Slave of Sin, 1955), etc. Working with Aldo De Benedetti, Matarazzo packed his films with the characters and situations that had formed the backbone of silent melodramas. Audiences were offered images of maternal anguish, of threatened honor, of innocent beauty menaced by worldly evil, etc.[16]

Italian melodramas competed successfully in Italy with Hollywood productions. No American film ever grossed as much as Matarazzo's movies. The Italians have always preferred portrayals of their own life—or an imitation of it—to remote fantasy. Melodramas, like the other genres of the early fifties—and all yellow journalism—were aimed primarily at female audiences. The new aspect of the melodramas was that they no longer lured women with fables of fantastic passion but instead offered an ersatz realism, which eventually became the basis of the soap operas. Codified melodramatic situations were seasoned with extramarital relationships, masculine irresponsibility, the woman's desire for sexual freedom, her longing for adventure, the problems of adolescents, etc. The influence of neorealist female characters is apparent in many of Matarazzo's heroines. But the melodramas' characters are still a far cry from women such as Pina (*Open City*), the first independent modern woman to be portrayed by an Italian film; or Silvana (*Bitter Rice*) with her sensual lust for life. Matarazzo's timid references to equality of the sexes takes place in an atmosphere that carefully preserves the notion of male superiority. In spite of all the changes, the heroines of the cinematic soap operas continue to be "good girls."

ONE DEBUT

The Italian film industry of the fifties was not hospitable to young filmmakers. In order to get backing, one had to be a known director; in order to be a director, if ever, one had to go through a long apprenticeship. Like the thirties, the fifties was a decade of veterans. After the passing of the neorealist wave, the film scene soon came to be dominated by middle-aged and older directors, with little space left for newcomers. Among the rare debuts, Francesco Maselli's was the most promising.

Deeply affected by his experience with the neorealists as Visconti's assistant and Zavattini's collaborator (he directed one of the episodes of *Love in the City*), Maselli at twenty-five, returned to the neorealist matrix in his own first feature—a story of war and resistance. Having also been an assistant to Antonioni and a fervent admirer of Kenji Mizoguchi, he linked the neorealist impulse with the attempt to probe into human emotions.

Gli sbandati (The Runaways, 1955) is set in the summer of 1943 when Italian soldiers were deserting the army following Mussolini's capitulation. Maselli focused on a character, a twenty-year-old man from an aristocratic family, and on his emotional reactions to the events. His story has the concentrated power of a parable (the indifferent attitude of some of Italian youth to fascism) ending with inner defeat. When faced with a choice between his comfortable life and the fight against the fascists, Andrea lacks the strength to overcome his indifference. The narrative is constructed in a slow rhythm with long insistent takes of incidental details so as to highlight the protagonist's qualities. Like Antonioni's films, *The Runaways* is composed of individual moments that are given meaning in relation to the protagonist's memory. In the final sequences, Maselli ceases to concentrate on the protagonist's isolation and also abandons his characteristic preoccupation with the visual, producing a straightforward finale with political overtones. The dramatic tension, rather than increasing, as Maselli obviously intended, is lost.

In Maselli's second film, *La donna del giorno* (The Woman in the News, 1957), inspired and overseen by Zavattini, the outdated neorealist approach prevailed, resulting in a static description of a young woman in search of fame who is destroyed by the world of advertising and movies.

Gli sbandati

THE BATTLE OF *SENSO*

The last battle of neorealism took place in connection with *Senso*, Visconti's fourth film, "the most relevant film of the decade"[17] and, according to Aristarco, "a great historical film, a revolutionary film that brought our cinematic history to a new peak."[18]

The film was considered by some as the ultimate proof of Visconti's desertion from the ranks of "committed" cinema and by the others as the first film to bridge the gap between neorealist chronicling and realist narrative. Along with Vasco Pratolini's 1955 novel *Metello, Senso* became the focus of the never-ending Italian polemic concerning the representation of reality. Both works aroused controversy by concentrating on their central characters rather than on the objective recording of the events. This attitude marked a significant change from works such as Pratolini's previous novels (e.g., *Chronicle of Poor Lovers* and *The Girls from San Frediano*) where the characters are viewed as secondary to the plot or the overall message.

Senso is loosely based on an undistinguished short story written in 1883 by Camillo Boito, who in his time was a fashionable Milanese writer. The story is set in 1863, in the last months of the Austrian occupation of the Venetian provinces, shortly before the unification of Italy. Its far-fetched premise—a love affair between two enemies—intrigued Visconti, who saw it as another episode of his "teatrum mundi," his tragic merry-go-round of passion and unattainable dreams.

Senso followed the artistic patterns that Visconti had set for himself as early as *Ossessione*, with some aspects of the patterns becoming more pronounced: the landscape and the interior settings are described with a sophisticated elegance and functionality; music is used as an integral part of the imagery, providing a commentary; the shaping of the characters sets into motion a whirl of insights into human souls and historical events. In comparison with Visconti's previous films, *Senso*'s "positive" figures, sometimes used to express the director's view, are less persuasive, and the controversial "negative" characters move toward the foreground. Thus, the central figure of *Senso* is not the beautiful Venetian countess and wife of a high dignitary, Livia Serpieri, but the decadent Austrian army officer, Franz Mahler. A corrupt coward and, at the same time, a vulnerable dreamer, Mahler is one of the richest figures among Visconti's doomed heroes. From the outset he is conscious of his inescapable destiny and submits to it with the passivity, and even pleasure, of Camus's or Sartre's characters. Livia and Franz are the foremost representatives of Visconti's romantic realism, inspired by Byron's and Leopardi's yearning for grandeur and their preoccupation with death, as well as by Verdi's romanticized reality.[19] In *Senso*, Visconti no longer tried to render an exact image of reality. He staged the hallucinations of this world and its most devastating passions, creating a powerful impression of reality through overt melodramatic imagery and an almost operatic character. Avoiding any attempt to reconstruct the phenomena of a historical epoch, he captured its spirit.

The film reaches its climax in the sequence of the battle of Custoza, depicted as a calamitous defeat for Italy; its needless casualties were quickly forgotten in the over-

Senso

all enthusiasm and the subsequent political victory. Acclaimed by Georges Sadoul as "the most beautiful battle to take place on the film screen since Griffith,"[20] Visconti's battle of Custoza was conceived as a picture of total confusion as witnessed by an uninvolved observer. The method is reminiscent of the way Tolstoy described the battle of Borodino in *War and Peace* and of Stendhal's account of Waterloo in *The Charterhouse of Parma*. The battle scenes are cross-cut with images of Livia's betrayal: devoured by her passion for the much younger Franz, Livia gives him money that belongs to the Italian patriots so that he can bribe a physician and get out of the army. The third act opens with Livia's journey to Verona where she hopes to find Franz. Her carriage passes wounded soldiers, refugees, the remnants of a defeated army. Livia's face ages before our eyes. The voyage is seen as a trip to hell, ending with Livia's moral annihilation and Franz's execution.

In retrospect, Visconti's attempt at the actualization of a historical subject has lost much of its meaning. In 1954, however, it provoked intervention of the censor and a protest from the Italian Ministry of Defense. Eventually, the scenes set at the headquarters of the Italian army had to be eliminated. In them, the Italian patriot Ussoni (portrayed by Massimo Girotti) offers the regular army the help of his company of volunteers and is refused. This scene, for which Visconti had historical backing, suggested parallels with the year 1944 when the Italian partisans were ordered by the provisional government to stop all actions against the Germans.[21]

Senso is the first Italian film to use color to convey human emotions and to color the landscape as these feelings change. This dynamic concept of color contradicted its traditional descriptive function and anticipated Antonioni's use of color in *Red Desert*. During Livia's trip to Verona, the prevailing color is gray with its impersonal low-key shades, occasionally intercut with the vivid green of the landscape. The first act, showing the beginning of Livia's love, is composed in large expanses of pastel tones whereas the interior of the Serpieri's summer estate, the scene of the betrayal, is toned with a dramatic crimson, contrasted by the white of Livia's gown.

Senso's theatrical conception occasionally weakens the overall impact without transgressing Visconti's original intention. As he pointed out in 1956: "It is a romantic film filled with the true essence of Italian opera. In real life, there are melodramatic people, just as there are illiterate fishermen in Sicily."[22]

Senso was followed by a strange, almost totally theatrical, experiment, *Le notti bianche* (The White Nights, 1957). Whereas in *Senso* the environment was authentic—but made to look artificial—in *The White Nights* the environment was artificial and intended to be perceived as such. The streets of Livorno were reconstructed in the studio, and the characters, reduced to their essential traits, functioned as parts of a deliberately unrealistic metaphor. All the Viscontian themes appear in the story of Natalia, a lonely girl of the fifties who waits for the return of the man she loves; and of Mario, in love with Natalia, a stranger in the town, consumed by solitude. Pervaded with the theme of expectation, *The White Nights* becomes to a certain degree an anthology of Visconti's obsessions.[23]

A minor film but the most romantic of Visconti's works, *The White Nights* was inspired by a story by Dostoyevsky. It is a rigorously directed "kammerspiel," bound by the unity of time and place. With the settings as a major structural ele-

Le notti bianche

ment, it is conceived primarily as an underscoring of the dreamlike aspect and evanescence of life.

"A formalistic nightmare" for Umberto Barbaro (but a probing of certain ways of expression for Visconti), *The White Nights* was an attempt to break away from the concept of verisimilitude, to create a mediated and reworked reality. No unity of criticism has ever been attained in the case of *The White Nights,* which testifies, to some degree, to the film's exceptionality.

THE LONERS: ROSSELLINI, ANTONIONI, FELLINI

During the fifties, the gap between the movie industry and the so-called art films deepened to such a degree that the quantitative difference became a qualitative one, affecting the overall structural balance. Amidst a heap of assembly-line productions, the few films marked by definable personalities stood out as solitary achievements. For some Italian historians, this was the reason why "the vital and live contact between the Italian cinema and society was lost, and all types of active political, cultural, and artistic testimony in film were abandoned."[24]

Rossellini's *India* is among the solitary achievements of these years. Its innovative influence was felt above all in the France of the New Wave, particularly in the mode started by Jean Rouch. Rossellini's two previous films, the last ones he made with Ingrid Bergman (*Giovanna d'Arco al rogo* [Joan of Arc at the Stake, 1954] and *La paura* [Fear, 1954]), had already contained some technical experiments that were important for the subsequent development of the film's language: slow, almost imperceptible camera movements, long takes (sequence shots), interdependence between color, background and characters, the linking of a documentaristic view to a symbol. *Joan of Arc at the Stake* re-created an oratorio by Paul Claudel and Arthur Honegger: *Fear* was based on a novella by Stefan Zweig, which, like *Stromboli,* captured the evolution of the relationship between a husband and his wife. Although both films are among Rossellini's minor achievements, critical evaluation of them as products of a period of "Rossellini's crisis" underestimates their overall qualities.

India, planned in 1955 and completed in 1958, affirmed Rossellini's belief in film as an instrument capable of restoring the truth of "things" and their inherent sacredness. Its realism transcends documentary objectivity to establish a harmonious relationship between the observed facts and the observer, thereby creating an implicit metaphysics. Rossellini intensified his rejection of plot-bound films and his urge for absolute expressive freedom by freely blending documentary with fiction and facts with reconstructed events. The film is divided into four narrative blocks: the marriage of a peasant to the daughter of a poor shopkeeper; the building of a dam and the farewells of a worker when the project is completed; a drought, during which a man dies, leaving his monkey abandoned; and one day in the life of an old man. In this last episode, the best in the film, Rossellini captures a man's gestures throughout an entire day, showing his rituals and his profound dependence on nature. The man lives with his wife in the jungle, they do not talk, expressing everything with gestures: everything has already been said between them. Their presence becomes overwhelming with scenes of their lives blending

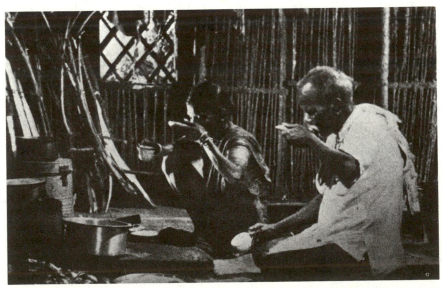

India

into a more general vision, achieved by introducing details of human work and spiritual experience in metaphoric parallels with nature.

In *India,* Rossellini renounced the leading motif of his previous films—life viewed as a road to martyrdom and ultimate hope. Fellini, however, reintroduced this theme in all three films he directed in the mid-fifties—*La strada* (The Road, 1954), *Il bidone* (The Swindler, 1955), and *Le notti di Cabiria* (Nights of Cabiria, 1956). In these three films, especially in *La strada,* Fellini tried to construct a very personal vision that would give meaning to the world. He seemed to suggest, in a Pirandellian way, that man is lost in a maze where the least trustworthy things are the common and the immediate. His allusions to the Christian yearning for redemption evoke a feeling of existential uneasiness and spiritual crisis, a crisis not only personal but much more general. The worldwide response to all three films confirmed the self-explanatory essence of Fellini's protagonists and the intensity of the desolation pervading the modern world.

La strada answers the questions posed by the protagonist of Fellini's autobiographical script "Moraldo in the City" ("What do I want? What kind of a person am I?"), expressing a basic existential fear in its search for the meaning in the life of Gelsomina, a half-witted peasant girl (portrayed by Giulietta Masina). She eventually finds her vocation in the love for another human being, in her relationship to Zampanò (Anthony Quinn), an itinerant strongman who purchases her from her mother and teaches her to accompany his circus act with drumbeats. Gelsomina's inner purity is contrasted with Zampanò's apathy toward everyone and everything except his basic physical needs—food, drink, the circus act, sex, sleep. During their pathetic union, Gelsomina finds her place in the world and her descent into

La strada

madness is mitigated by the presence of other people. Zampanò is alone—he never felt the need for any human relationship until the news of Gelsomina's death reaches him. Then, for the first time in his life, he cries because of his solitude, and perhaps because he has truly loved this creature he had rejected.

The characters are overtly symbolic, carrying a personal simplified message of basic existentialism. The symbolism is realized mainly in the character of the fool (Richard Basehart), the tightrope walker who initiates Gelsomina into the purpose-fulness of the world and who is killed by Zampanò. Conceived as a Christ figure, expressing Fellini's belief that Christ must be sought outside the church, the fool cannot be reduced to a single interpretation. The attitudes he represents are sub-ject to various readings, interpreting his apparent knowledge of the way out of the maze.

Il bidone is also a story of cognition. Its protagonist Augusto suffers almost the same fate as Zampanò, the only difference being that Augusto's hope for redemp-tion is weaker than Zampanò's and his yearning for it stronger. A great con man who has spent his life swindling people out of their money, a "vitellone" who has left his native town and failed, Augusto tries to redeem himself, but he always falls back into his former ways. Finally, he dies alone, in a wasteland, stoned by his own accomplices. Whereas Zampanò and Gelsomina move in a world of unspecified location and time, *Il bidone* evolves against the background of modern Rome and its provinces. Drawing upon his neorealist past, Fellini describes the different milieus of Augusto's various swindles, bringing to life the world of the underprivileged and the handicapped: the shantytown, reminiscent of *Miracle in Milan,* where Augusto and his gang pose as housing commissioners; the poor kitchen of two peasant women from whom the con men extort money; the desolate farm where a crippled girl falls for Augusto's impersonation of a bishop, etc. The symbolic background of these sequences, however, remains the same as in *La strada* and is created with similar visual clues. There is the desert with sparse, strangely shaped trees, the dilapidated walls, the narrow blind alleys, the grayish ocean, and the penetrating sound of the wind. The Italian landscape has lost all its beauty. Its emptiness and coldness reflect the state of mind of the characters. In Fellini's "mid-fifties trilogy," the sense of space becomes pervasive, suggesting the helplessness and dismay of the characters. Fellini often pictures them as very small, engulfed by the space of a road, a fair, or a forest or flattened against the surface of a wall.[25]

Even in this visual composition, the characters are positioned so as to be always in the center of attention. Everything that surrounds them works to focus interest on them, weakening the impact of all the objects except those directly linked to the film's message. Cabiria, for example, remains central to the action even when her tiny figure is virtually lost amidst the massive statues and high trees bordering a darkened road or crushed by the crowd in a religious pilgrimage. A sense of the overall importance of a human being is emphasized by a prevailingly subjective camera, which retains its own point of view when the character in question is ab-sent from the take.

La strada, Il bidone, and *Nights of Cabiria* are all based on three main compo-nents, which manifest themselves in each of the three films with a different degree of intensity. The "abandonment in space" imagery prevails in *La strada;* the neo-realist method in *Il bidone;* and *Nights of Cabiria* draws, above all, upon farcical elements. *Cabiria*'s episodic structure follows the pattern of "la rivista," and Cabiria, the main character, played by Masina, is conceived as the unifying agent of the fragmented action.

In *Cabiria,* Fellini's innocent saint is clad in the narrow skirt and pathetic fake fur of a whore. Her basic goodness blends the lyrical tensions and spiritual perspectives of *La strada* and *Il bidone.* In one episode, Cabiria is hypnotized by a magician and reveals her yearning for a conventional life—virginity, Sunday Mass, a husband, children. Instead, she too finds her Zampanò—a man who promises to marry her and who, after having robbed her of all her savings, does not even have the courage to kill her. The film carries less impact than *La strada* or *Il bidone,* primarily because of its static narrative, the even plane of its events (Cabiria's little adventures in a big city) and the one-dimensional nature of the supporting characters. Lacking the elaborate Gelsonima-Zampanò mythology (which was disturbed neither by the description of the environment nor by the strength of the farcical

Nights of Cabiria

elements), Cabiria's innocent smile does not communicate Fellini's message about salvation with the same power found in *La strada*.

Fellini, whose films always mirror his own state of mind, perhaps no longer believed in this message as strongly as he had in Gelsomina's time. He was not insensitive to the attacks by the Marxist press on *La strada*'s spirituality. In *Cabiria* he tried to revive some of the neorealist impulses: the shooting was preceded by a very thorough research on Roman prostitutes, and the dialogues, coscripted by Pier Paolo Pasolini, were charged with social content. But the imagery of the neo-realist style did not express Fellini's spiritual concern, and the film seems dated. Three years were to pass before Fellini directed another film—*La dolce vita*— wherein the road to salvation and hope was definitely barred.

The films Antonioni made in the mid-fifties—*Le amiche* (Girlfriends, 1955) and *Il grido* (The Cry, 1957)—were also his last films in which people were still ready to die for something—the loss of love or the pain of memories. In his later films, willingness to leave life receded in favor of indifference, of a refusal to take responsibility for one's own life in any way. Rosetta, in *The Girlfriends,* commits suicide because she does not know how to live, not unlike Giuliana in *Red Desert* (the film Antonioni made in 1964) who suffers from the same neurosis but is incap-able of making any decision at all. Likewise, Aldo in *Il grido* foreshadows Sandro in *L'avventura* and Giovanni in *La notte* in his refusal to acknowledge the fading of love. Whereas Sandro and Giovanni eventually accept the inevitable, Aldo strug-gles against it; and when he loses, he leaps to his death. The characters in

Il grido

Girlfriends and *Il grido* rebel against the changes of sentiments, against a mystery of emotions in which they are trapped.

The Girlfriends, based on a novella by Cesare Pavese, follows the lives of four young women as observed by Clelia, who has returned to Turin, her native city, after having risen to an important position in a fashion house in Rome. She becomes involved with a group of wealthy young people, only one of whom, Rosetta, questions their empty lifestyle. Clelia is "a character among characters," sharing the author's omniscience about the others and preferring like Pavese, to see isolation as a voluntary solitude.

The Girlfriends, like *Il grido,* tells of the pain of memories and the impossibility of escaping the reality of the feelings. Both Rosetta and Aldo make this attempt but return to their point of departure, only to find that their emotional core has remained unchanged. With this realization, they succumb to the Pavesian "absurd vice." Each of these films holds a special place in Antonioni's *oeuvre. The Girlfriends* is the most elaborate of his black-and-white films. By 1955, his style had already reached its peak and did not undergo any further essential changes. Loosely inspired by the Pavesian narrative, it anticipated the approach of the French *nouveau roman,* according to which the world is neither meaningful nor absurd; it just *is. The Girlfriends* reveals almost everything of Antonioni's style: the internal montage that does not follow the action and is based on temporal expansion or restriction; the insistence on "useless gestures," usually captured by sequence shots; a slow pace, creating the impression that the film does not progress; the emphasis at certain moments on sounds rather than on characters; the "stylization of emotions" (a term coined by Antonioni) created through the use of psychological time in opposition to real time. (One of the most impressive sequences captures Rosetta's walk with Lorenzo on a road outside the city, with horseback riders and cars passing by. The insistence on sounds and silence, together with the rhythmically patterned gestures and dialogue, creates the impression that the sentiments are evolving while the action stands still.)

In the overall composition of *The Girlfriends,* incidental shots become increasingly rare. Everything is subordinated to a rigorous formal structure where nothing is left to chance.[26] Above all, the meaning of the dialogue is fully revealed only in connection with the composition of the shots. As Antonioni pointed out: "Whether a line is uttered against a wall or against the background of an entire street can change the situation."[27]

The distinctive characteristic of Antonioni's style is a kind of objectivity generated by the decomposition of the environment and the events. This objectivity, however, often referred to as "coolness," is always injected with lyrical components (such as the landscape in *Il grido*), which produce interdependence between subjectivity and objectivity. The same holds true for characters. On the one hand, Antonioni sides with them (close-ups, subjective function of the landscape); on the other, he views them as aliens (the distant perspective of the camera during Aldo's frantic search for oblivion). In this respect, Antonioni's style differs from the poetics of the *nouveau roman,* which never renounces its objectivity.

Il grido has a special place in Antonioni's *oeuvre* not only because it is his only

Le amiche

Il grido

film set in a working-class milieu—as is often mentioned—but also for personal reasons. This reputedly autobiographical film was shot in the Po valley at the time of Antonioni's separation from his wife; there, fifteen years before, Antonioni had directed his first short, *People of the River Po,* which he wanted so much to make into a feature film. It is as though he wished to revive the time of his youth and with it the era of neorealism. *Il grido* draws upon some neorealist components, particularly the interdependence between the landscape and the characters and the emphasis on objects, which in Antonioni's other films seldom play a significant role. But the dramatic nucleus of *Il grido* is charged with the same sense of abandonment and dismay as *The Girlfriends* or *L'avventura*: Aldo returns home only to find Irma married to another man and his friends enclosed in an almost hostile indifference.

Il grido is one of Antonioni's own favorite films. In 1959, he contended: "When I saw *Il grido* after some time, I was stunned to find myself faced with such nudity, with such great solitude. It was like what happens on some mornings when we look in the mirror and are startled by the reflection of our own face."[28]

In 1955, in an open letter to the journal *Contemporaneo,* Fellini summed up the moral problems of the "difficult years" as reflected in both his and Antonioni's films. This letter concludes, in a way, the period of transition from neorealism to realism, answering some of its questions and suggesting the direction for the further evolution of the Italian cinema, or, at least, of one of its alternatives. *"La strada* captures an experience," Fellini wrote,

> which is, according to the philosopher Emmanuel Mounier, the most important for any social perspective: the experience of the communication between two human beings. This is what I have in mind: to learn to live with a human being is as important as to learn to live a rich sociopolitical life. If we do not resolve this humble but necessary point of departure, we may soon find ourselves in a well-organized society, where the private relationships between two human beings will be empty, indifferent, isolated, and impenetrable. Solitude will be the greatest pain of modern man. It begins somewhere very deep, at the very roots of a human being. No public delight, no political symphony can ever heal it. In my opinion, there is a way for two human beings to reach out and find one another. If a film creates a microscopic concentrated image of this evolution of feelings (in art, historical dimensions do not count) and captures the contrast between a monologue and a dialogue, then it fulfills a contemporary need, clears up and penetrates some of its aspects: this is what I call realism. Art has the duty to discover the historical process. But this process is based on a less complicated, less technical and political dialectics than some believe. Sometimes a film that captures the contradictions of contemporary feelings through an elementary dialectics is more realistic than a film that depicts the evolution of a precise sociopolitical reality.[29]

VII

THE RIFT (1959–1960)

The beginning of Italian cinema's recovery from the inertia of the 1950s is usually marked by the year 1959, more precisely from the month of September when two Italian films shared the Grand Prize at the Venice International Film Festival.[1] Amidst strong competition—Bergman's *The Face*, Preminger's *Anatomy of a Murder*, and Kawalerowicz's *Night Train*—Rossellini's *Generale Della Rovere* (General Della Rovere, 1959) and Monicelli's *La grande guerra* (The Great War, 1959), both concerned with the war, were awarded the Golden Lion. This unexpected success was immediately interpreted as the first sign of a new "neorealism" and was referred to as the Italian film miracle.

Yet not only was the jury's verdict an accidental compliance with the authority of its strong-minded president, Luigi Chiarini, but both films appear, in retrospect, to fall short of the best efforts of the Italian cinema of the time. Neither Rossellini nor Monicelli fathered Italy's return to a place among the leading film countries in the 1960s. The success of their films, however, first in Venice and later at the box office, opened the door for other films tackling nonconformist subjects. A wave of films dealing with war and antifascist resistance (subjects frowned upon during the fifties) followed. Some of their directors were newcomers kept out of the industry by overcautious production attitudes. Morando Morandini wrote in *Sight and Sound* that in "1959, Italian producers began, timidly enough, to embark on a slightly bolder policy, largely as a result of the French example. This year, films are being made in Italy, which two or three years ago could not have been attempted. Fear of censorship is an excuse that no longer holds water, and films about fascism can be made."[2]

There were several reasons for this sudden rejuvenation of the Italian cinema. The Cold War was over, as well as the witch hunt. The 1958 and 1960 elections shattered the power of the Christian Democrats with the left-wing parties getting a bigger piece of the cake. Sandro Zambetti contended: "After twelve years of an absolute immobility, it is obvious that this popular revolt against the alliance between the Christian Democrats and the fascists was not born out of nothing: it originated in the ferments that developed during these twelve years, influencing also the cinema."[3] The 1949 Andreotti law was amended, and censorship was eased. But the economic crisis

160

sweeping the film industry could no longer be stopped. As a consequence of the expansion of television, an obsolete film law, and a general artistic inertia in film production, attendance fell from 815,424 million (1955) to 747,904 million (1959), and output dropped from 210 films (1954) to 105 (1956). Several big companies went bankrupt, such as Minerva, Diana, IGI, and Excelsea.

Paradoxically, this economic decline opened up a number of opportunities for filmmakers. As Morandini put it, the producers began to realize that traditional productions were insufficient to lure people away from their television sets even though at this time television in Italy had a much smaller impact than in the United States or Great Britain. Like their counterparts in other countries, Italian producers responded to the challenge of television by broadening the range of subjects, by eliminating worn-out genres (pink neorealism, the populist melodrama, etc.) and by bringing new talents into the ailing industry. The success of the French New Wave—between 1958 and 1963, 170 French directors made their first features—linked to the emergence of the new generation, helped to end the impotent decade of the veterans in the Italian film industry.[4] Films about fascism and the resistance reappeared on Italian screens, along with films about the problems of the younger generation and shy attempts to analyze the matrix of the Italian republic, which had just completed its first decade of existence.

In Italy, however, the names in the spotlights did not change to the same extent as they did in France or England at that time. The rift of 1959–1960 was dominated by three personalities, all well established in the past decade: Antonioni, Fellini, and Visconti. Amidst the crowd of new directors, only two were to equal these three in poetic vision and personal integrity: Pier Paolo Pasolini (b. 1922) and Ermanno Olmi (b. 1931), who followed, in his way, the line abandoned by Rossellini.

GENERAL DELLA ROVERE, THE GREAT WAR, AND THEIR FOLLOWERS

General Della Rovere (along with Rossellini's four subsequent films) was merely an interlude in Rossellini's career, which subsequently was to continue with fictionalized television documentaries for the rest of his life. *General Della Rovere* was, in fact, the final attempt to integrate a genius into an industry. The subject was directly related to Rosselini's greatest success ever—*Open City*—and so, too, was the style. The German occupation served again as the background for a story of martyrdom and redemption. Rossellini's protagonist is a Fellinian "swindler," who extorts money from people jailed by the Germans; he ends up in prison himself where the Germans force him to impersonate a well-known Italian general who has sided with the anti-German provisional Italian government; they hope that one of the resistance leaders—whom they know to be among the prisoners—will reveal himself to him. But in prison, the swindler is confronted with true suffering and heroism for the first time in his wretched life, and he volunteers to join the resistance fighters when they are executed.

De Sica's presence in the main role enhances the film's attractiveness. As the false general he manipulates to perfection all the strings designed to guarantee a positive public response. The story of *General Della Rovere* counterpoints temptation and resistance, set in a carefully rendered milieu (the streets of Genoa marked by the presence of the occupation, the squalid coffeeshop where the swindler meets his victims, the prison yard filled with the sound of gunshots and the prayers of the victims, etc.). Yet the film's overall style lacks the innovative spirit of Rossellini's previous films, testifying to the director's relative lack of interest in this particular story and in narrative film in general.

After the success of his comeback, Rossellini immediately turned to another wartime story: *Era notte a Roma* (It Was Night in Rome, 1960), the adventures of three POW's in Rome during the German occupation. Again Rossellini's disinterest in the subject casts its shadow on the entire film, and this time it led to poor financial results as well as artistic ones.

The decision of the Venice jury to have Monicelli's *The Great War* share the Golden Lion with *General Della Rovere* was well founded. The films have several features in common, and both attain similar spectacular results. But whereas *General Della Rovere* is among Rossellini's less interesting films, *The Great War*, set during World War I, is Monicelli's best film. As in *General Della Rovere*, the two

The Great War

protagonists of *The Great War* are cowards whose main concern is to make the best of their humble lives and to survive at all costs. Yet at the decisive moment, in a pathetic gesture of heroism and much to their own surprise, they prefer death to treason. As in his previous comedies, Monicelli created appealing figures of two common Italians at odds with the laws of the world. This time, it is the law of war that crushed them, after having dragged them through the hell of the trenches: in mud and dirt, they remain.

The story of Monicelli's antiheroes (played by Alberto Sordi and Vittorio Gassman) takes place in the vividly displayed atmosphere of the great debacle. An apt mixture of comic and tragic aspects transcends the film's rivista structure, providing it with an appealing humanistic message.

Monicelli's film was the first to demystify Italy's controversial role and performance in World War I. From the outset, the war was glorified as a great patriotic struggle for national grandeur and gradually became a legend of unconditional Italian heroism. At first, efforts were made to prevent Monicelli from damaging this image. In 1978, Monicelli recalled:

> The Italian cinema, theater, and press were prohibited from speaking of the Great War in other than flattering terms. After the news about my film was made public, the press (*Il Giorno* and *Corriere della Sera*) published articles written by well-known journalists who demanded that the film be stopped. A huge campaign was launched: "Monicelli, [his scriptwriters] Age, and Scarpelli will dishonor the six hundred thousand dead of World War I." But the film was made, and it was the first to say that these men went to war without knowing why, that the war had nothing to do with them. They were poor devils, badly dressed and undernourished, ignorant, and illiterate, who were sent to do something that had nothing in common with their lives.[5]

Searching for a way out of the crisis, the producers were willing to break other taboos in addition to the myth of the Great War. Italy's role in World War II and the impact of fascism on the country were among the subjects that until then had been only cautiously mentioned in Italian movies. Even *General Della Rovere* did not reach far outside the usual limits: the Germans were still the ones responsible for Italy's tragedy. The theme of the oppressive aspect of Italian fascism was especially attractive to young filmmakers. In 1960, Florestano Vancini (b. 1926), at that time a successful documentarist, based his first fiction film on Giorgio Bassani's short story "La lunga notte del '43" (A Night in '43), which told of a massacre of innocent townspeople by Italian fascists. Although Vancini's film is impressive, it fails to translate the most salient features of Bassani's prose into a comparable stylistic work of filmmaking. Bassani, one of the finest Italian novelists, excels in portraying personal dramas in connection with historical events, imbuing one with the intensity of the other. Vancini's film captures the atmosphere of a city at the mercy of fascists, but the drama of his three protagonists is told according to the patterns of traditional love stories and does not successfully blend with the complex backdrop. In addition to his documentary experience, Vancini drew upon the neorealist impulse, which had been of primary importance to his generation.

A Night in '43 opens with breath-taking images of the 1942 Italian defeat in Africa: the screen is covered with rows of graves and crosses, followed by frames filled with the printed words of the fascist slogan: "We shall be back!" Then a group of fascist "black shirts" appears, preparing a raid on the city of Ferrara to avenge the assassination of a provincial fascist official. The Italian cinema had to wait fifteen years before it could show the execution of Italians by Italians and the terror spread by fascist troopers. "Who in Ferrara does not remember the night of December 15, 1943. It was an endless, anguished vigil for everyone," wrote Bassani.

Vancini centered his story of a marital triangle around the events of this night when eleven hostages were shot in retaliation for the killing of a fascist satrap. The commander of the firing squad said during the 1946 trial: "I was the soldier of an idea, not the hired assassin of a system." (Bassani based his story on a true event.) Vancini shows the commander at the end of the film, sixteen years after the night of '43: a respectable citizen of Ferrara, he welcomes Franco, the son of one of the victims, home to his native town after a long stay abroad. With a broad smile on his face, watching a soccer game out of the corner of his eye, he says: "Why, you look more and more like your father."

Before embarking on his first feature, Vancini assisted Valerio Zurlini (1926–1982) in making *Estate violenta* (The Violent Summer, 1959).[6] The film is a sensitive depiction of a love affair between a young man and a considerably older woman. Again, the setting is the war as it is perceived by a group of teenagers vacationing on the seashore. Like Maselli's *Runaways*, *The Violent Summer* centers on the events of 1943, which disrupt the carefree life of the idle rich, among them

La lunga notte del '43

the members of the fascist elite. Zurlini was an experienced scriptwriter who had debuted as a director in 1954 with a pleasant comedy *Le ragazze di San Frediano* (The Girls from San Frediano). In *The Violent Summer*, he is very successful (more so than Vancini) in drawing appealing portraits of his protagonists, particularly a war widow who breaks all the rules of her patrician milieu by becoming involved with a younger man. The contribution of both Vancini and Zurlini was limited to the introduction of new subject matter. They remained untouched by the efforts of their contemporaries in France, England, Czechoslovakia, and the United States to break through the clichés of the traditional narrative.

The resurrected war theme was eagerly picked up by the neorealist generation, who were scattered throughout the stagnating movie industry. In 1960, De Sica attempted a new film that would tie in with his postwar work. *La Ciociara* (Two Women), based on Moravia's novel, tells the story of a mother and daughter trying vainly to preserve their lives and honor amidst the horror of war. The film's impact stems from its well-directed crowd scenes (war fugitives on the roads, allied soldiers conquering Italy, etc.) and, to a lesser degree, from the presence of a deglamorized Sophia Loren (whom her influential husband-producer elevated from the ranks of the "pink vamps" to the peak of international stardom). De Sica tried hard to strip her of her star mannerisms and transform her into a lower-middle-class "mamma." But Loren was not a Magnani, and the film became what *Bicycle Thief* might have become if Cary Grant had played the role of the unemployed Roman worker.

Gillo Pontecorvo's *Kapò* (1960) was among the best films of this period by a director of the neorealist generation. Pontecorvo—a journalist, documentarist, and scriptwriter—appeared on the film scene as early as 1946 when he collaborated on *The Sun Rises Again*. Profoundly marked by the artistic experience of his youth, Pontecorvo never renounced his basic belief in the force of crude reality. The strength of all his fiction films lay in their documentaristic features rather than in the contrived narrative. In *Kapò*, his re-creation of the horrors of a concentration camp for women attains a high degree of authenticity, but he lapses into heavy-handed sentimentalism in his portrayal of a young Jewish prisoner who collaborates with the Germans.

TIME STOOD STILL

The most original film of the "rift years" was created by a newcomer uninvolved in the current polemics who always kept his distance from the film scene. Ermanno Olmi's *Il tempo si è fermato* (Time Stood Still, 1959) is the only Italian feature film of this period comparable to contemporary efforts of the young generations elsewhere in Europe.

Olmi's films are concerned with the need of human beings to reach out to one another, to establish a sense of belonging and rootedness. At a time when nearly everyone around him was analyzing the problems of human isolation and loneliness, Olmi, a straightforward peasant from northern Italy, emerged with his attempt to overcome this alienation. His films are filled with apparently simple yet universal themes: the finality of one's actions, the sense of one's presence in the

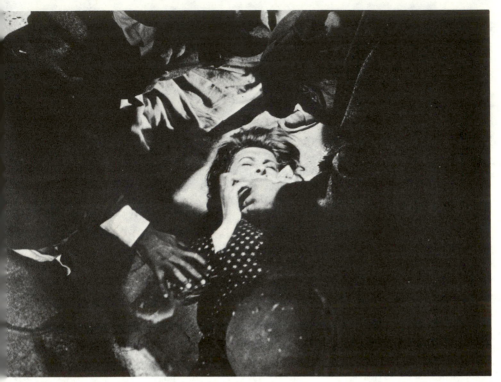

Two Women

Il tempo si è fermato

world. Olmi possesses the unique talent of the true story-teller who portrays his characters through the prism of his own personality. He went so far as to build his personal life according to his artistic beliefs, and vice versa. He never moved to Rome but remained secluded in his remote, native province, going through difficult periods of isolation.

Olmi's beginnings in cinema can be traced back to his first job with the Milan company Edisonvolta, which he joined when he was fifteen. Eight years later, he set up a film section and started making documentaries about Edisonvolta activities. By filming power stations, dams, and transformers, he assessed the meaning of the human touch and the place of work in one's life. *Time Stood Still* was started as a documentary about a dam high in the mountains and gradually developed into one of the most impressive black and white cinemascope features ever made.

Combining Olmi's own highly personal concept of cinematic structure and an objectivized spirituality inspired by Rossellini, *Time Stood Still* represents a true departure from traditional canons, following Rossellini, Fellini, and Antonioni in their attempts at dedramatization, veracity, and voluptuousness of sensations. It tends toward plotlessness, replacing allegiance to myth and traditions with allegiance to the present. Along with Antonioni, Olmi (b. 1930) is one the few Italian directors unmarked by the influence of the comedy Italian style and "la rivista."

The film's only characters are two men in the snow-covered mountains: a watchman in his forties and his youthful helper, a student who has just arrived as a holiday replacement. Olmi introduces the watchman's house, a two-room wooden cabin with creaking doors and floors, a few pieces of furniture, and an outside toilet; the dam, almost invisible in the enormous expanse of white; and absolute silence interrupted only by the ticking of the clock and the whistling of the wind, which eventually become a part of the silence. The watchman teaches his helper to survive in the solitude; his initial mistrust slowly changes into an ironic affection. The young man is clumsy, the older one set in his ways. Few words are spoken. The camera rarely approaches the faces, so the characters are isolated even from the viewer. The director's attention is centered on the objects in the cabin, on the tools the men use in their work—the maintenance of the dam—on their daily routine. At the end of the three days that the men spend together, we know the cabin as intimately as if we ourselves had lived there a long time: the shelf that the young man tries to fix up for his books, the soup plates, the wine bottle, their sweaters, the bucket. The objects are few, yet the composition of the images is based on the utmost visual richness. Olmi does not work with empty spaces. He fills his images with details of the human presence, created through a heightened perception of a world that we generally take for granted. He says very little about his protagonists (only at the end does the watchman mention that he has a wife and three children), and yet we feel we know all about them. The details Olmi shows lay bare their background, habits, personality, and feelings. The film's structure seems almost improvised, yet quite the contrary is true. The overall patterns of the entire film as well as those of the individual scenes are meticulously elaborated to evoke the impression of casualness. The result is an intricate embroidery created with thousands of little stitches by someone who is fully immersed in his work and loves every minute of it.

Seen in perspective, Olmi's inconspicuous debut was an event of quite extraordinary importance for the future. At that time, however, it was overshadowed by other first features, especially by two films directed by Francesco Rosi (b. 1922), Visconti's former assistant. *La sfida* (The Challenge, 1958) revealed a filmmaker who knew how to re-create the atmosphere of his native Naples and also how to spell out his involvement in the social issues of the day. The film tells the story of Vito, who confronts the world of swindlers and profiteers and is assassinated on their orders on his wedding day. Rosi used the narrative mainly to depict a world of corruption, sacrificing the complexity of his characters to the almost neorealist authenticity of the background. A year later, in *I magliari* (Dry Goods Dealers, 1959), he turned to the fate of the first wave of Italian journeymen who tried to find a better life in West Germany during the early years of the "economic miracle." *Dry Goods Dealers* does not have the dramatic strength of *The Challenge*. Its strong points are the originality of the subject matter, the portrait of Germany at this particular moment, and the portrait of a group of Italians in a foreign world. The film suffered, however, from compromises with the requirements of commercial production.[7]

The fiery revolutionary Francesco Maselli used film to depict characters typical of Italian bourgeois society. *I delfini* (Heirs to the Throne, 1960) returns, after six years, to the world of *The Runaways* but this time not in the context of the German occupation and the resistance. The film's protagonists are the golden boys of a provincial town, the scions of affluent families. For Maselli they represent the moral, social, and political degradation of an entire generation. But the moralizing message of *Heirs to the Throne* was too generalized to capture attention despite its interesting observation of a certain kind of life in the provinces.

La sfida

FURTHER ENCOUNTER:
MAURO BOLOGNINI AND PIER PAOLO PASOLINI

Mauro Bolognini (b. 1922) was an assistant to Luigi Zampa and debuted modestly in the early fifties, but it was only in 1959 that he began attracting attention. At that time, through his exploration of twentieth-century Italian literature, Bolognini revealed to the Italian screen the talent of Pier Paolo Pasolini, a controversial, award-winning young poet from the north.

The tradition of literary adaptation is deeply imbedded in Italian film production. Many directors, such as Visconti, had been adapting great literary works of the past for the screen, thus adding a new chapter to the interrelationship between the language of literature and the language of film. Bolognini had worked his way into the ranks of highly professional craftsmen and gradually switched from comedies to cinematic transcriptions of works by important Italian writers such as Pasolini, Brancati, Moravia, and Svevo. He had no ambition to impose his own vision or his own personality upon the works he adapted. He can best be described as an understanding, intelligent illustrator with a cultivated feeling for the visual characteristics of various Italian cities and provinces and for the heritage of certain Italian painters of the nineteenth and twentieth centuries (Signorini, Cecioni, etc.).

Bolognini embarked on his series of transcriptions with a version of Pasolini's first novel *Ragazzi di vita* (Children of Life). Pasolini had previously worked for Bolognini, and one of the films he scripted for him, *Giovani mariti* (The Young Couple, 1957), attracted attention primarily because of the daringly colloquial dialogue, which was unlike anything Italian film was accustomed to. Pasolini went to Rome in 1951 after a scandal concerning his homosexuality had forced him to abandon his position as a part-time teacher in the Friuli region of the north where he spent most of his formative years. He was also expelled from the Communist party, whose local branch he headed. The young poet was known to literary specialists for poetry written in the almost extinct Friuli language. After his arrival in Rome, he became peripherally involved in the movie industry when he discovered that he could earn a living by assisting with scripts. Then in 1955, he suddenly emerged into the limelight with his novel *Children of Life*, the most controversial book of the time. Another novel, *Una vita violenta* (A Violent Life), followed in 1959. (Already in 1957, Pasolini had won the coveted Viareggio Prize for a volume of poetry, *Le cenere di Gramsci* [Gramsci's Ashes].) A leftist radical and an avowed homosexual, Pasolini explored the world of Roman shantytowns, the realm of the Roman subproletariat, those unemployed youngsters, petty criminals, and prostitutes who became the beloved and tragic heroes of his novels and films.

In 1959, he wrote the story and the script for *La notte brava* (A Night of Audacity), inspired by *Children of Life* and again directed by Bolognini. Its international cast and Bolognini's studied camera angles ran contrary to Pasolini's style, and the film lacked any vital or informing direction. *Una giornata balorda* (A Foolish Day, 1960) better captures Pasolini's tragic vision of people who are driven to self-destruction because society has no place for them. The cast was more homogeneous, and Bolognini found a more direct approach to parallel Pasolini's crude language. The film was based on Moravia's *Roman Tales* and was scripted by Pasolini. Although it was booed by the audience at its gala premiere, *A Foolish Day* firmly established Pasolini as a force in Italian filmmaking.

The most successful result of Pasolini's collaboration with Bolognini—at least in terms of audience reception—was *Il bell'Antonio* (Antonio, the Great Lover, 1960). Based on a well-known novel of the same title by Vitaliano Brancati, it tells the tragicomic story of the impotent "bell'Antonio," using it as a pretext for an ironic portrait of a certain society and its manners. The film, situated in Catania, Sicily, shifts Brancati's narrative from fascism to the present. The film historian Gian Piero Brunetta observed: "We are taken to survey a society that still sticks to a series of myths inherited from fascism, among them that of virility, which condemns a man to play a fixed role that he can almost never escape."[8] Brancati's wit and stylized world fit with Bolognini's cinematic style much better than Pasolini's crudeness.[9] Bolognini's collaboration with Pasolini came to an end when Pasolini decided to become a filmmaker in his own right.

His "Pasolini period" over, Bolognini turned to two other works of literature: Mario Pratesi's *L'eredità* (The Heritage), which became *La viaccia* (The Trip, 1960), and Italo Svevo's famous novel *Senilità* (As a Man Grows Older, 1961). In *The Trip,* Bolognini for the first time turned toward the Italian nineteenth century. The story of a peasant family from Tuscany—utterly destroyed in the clash between town and country, between patriarchal ways of life and those of the new

La notte brava

La viaccia

ascending class—provided Bolognini with an opportunity to portray another Italian region, Tuscany, and another big city, Florence, and to develop further his own calligraphic style. Thus, Pietro Bianchi, the film critic, called him "the most Proustian among Italian directors," referring to Bolognini's astuteness in the cinematic reconstruction of "time lost."

As in *Il bell' Antonio,* Bolognini shifted the time and place of Svevo's *As a Man Grows Older* from the last years of the Austro-Hungarian empire to Trieste of the twenties. The tale of physical conflict between the sensual Angelina and the clerk Emilio, an insecure man on the threshold of his forties—told against the background of social and class conflict—suffered from an overaestheticized treatment, Bolognini's trademark and also his greatest weakness.

THE BREAKTHROUGH:
ROCCO, LA DOLCE VITA, L'AVVENTURA

After 1959 the fossilized crust of what the French labeled "cinéma de papa" was cracking all over Europe. In England, the former protagonists of the "Free Cinema" movement reemerged as the Angry Young Men. In France, the New Wave was the critics' baby, and some of those who had been busy destroying the aesthetic principles of the past came into view as the New Wave's leading directors. In literature, *l'école du regard,* with its intention "to let the reader see" via the impassive surfaces of the *nouveau roman,* was fighting its first battles. Its representatives, such as Alain Robbe-Grillet, Michel Butor, and Le Clézio, were examining the phenomenal world as it exists apart from the human mind, apart from all human influence and manipulation. In Poland, a new generation of filmmakers established itself, and the young Czechs were soon to follow. In Italy, by contrast, it was "the old ones," the representatives of the previous period, who were to achieve the decisive breakthrough.

The first features (debuts) of this period were engendered to a certain degree by the neorealist experience, primarily by its social commitment. But these were not the most stimulating results of those years. It was again on "that other road of the Italian cinema," within its metaphoric alternative, that the strongest impulses for the generation of the sixties were to be found. The attachment to the past, though neither literal nor excessive, proved more of a bridle, keeping the young Italians from adopting the modes of the different New Waves and preventing them from generating a similar movement.

In these years, however, it became obvious that the polarity between the two alternatives (the historico-critico-social and the metaphoric) had become the strongest asset of the Italian cinema and that the Italianity—that special feature distinguishing the best of the Italian cinema from other productions—rested in the meeting and in the interrelation of these two approaches. Films conceived in such a way became more frequent, especially beginning with the mid-sixties. In 1961, after the release of *La dolce vita* and *L'avventura,* Guido Aristarco, a fervent partisan of the historico-realistic alternative, complained:

> Contemporary Italian cinema refuses critical realism: the depiction of phenomena as well as the search for and the analysis of their determining circumstances. The influence of Antonioni's last film has prevailed, among younger filmmakers as well. The term *antifilm* may be added to the term *antinovel* in literature because of their destruction of characters, story, plot (refused already, but in a different sense, by Zavattini's neorealism) and their fundamental conflict between the paradoxes within a human being who has become a kind of Musil's "man without qualities" or a quality without a man.[10]

In the period 1960–1961, three films were released worldwide that left a deep mark on the international scene. Representing both alternatives and occasionally suggesting a possible blurring of their distinctions, *Rocco and His Brothers, L'avventura,* and *La dolce vita* best exemplify the endeavors of the Italian avant-garde in the years 1959–1961.

Rocco was probably the most predictable of the three. Visconti's love for Verga and his involvement with the social and human tragedy of the Italian south could be identified as the main inspiration of his film. The theme was highly topical: between 1951 and 1961, 1,800,000 Italians from the underdeveloped south emigrated to the industrialized north; in 1958 alone 13,000 settled in Milan. In the recently published collection of stories, *The Ghisolfa Bridge* by the Milanese Catholic writer Giovanni Testori, Visconti, himself a Milanese, found what he was looking for: the characters and the complex melodramatic plot for a cinematic tale that, in a way, is a continuation of *La terra trema*. This time everything begins in the far south of continental Italy, in the province of Lucania. However, the planned prologue to the film—four sons of the Parondi family bury their father at sea and then comply with their mother's decision to follow their older brother Vicenzo to the industrial north—was never made. Thus, we first meet the formidable matriarch Rosalia Parondi and her sons, Vicenzo, Simone, Ciro, Rocco, and Luca, on the platform of the enormous Milan Central Station. This encounter of the expatriated southern peasants with the impersonal symbol of Italy's largest city sets the tone. Deprived of the feeling of security (provided for generations by their fathers' land, which now can no longer feed them), each of the brothers in his own way attempts to integrate into the new, alien world. Four of them eventually succeed. It is an ironic success, for their hopes are smashed, and the family has disintegrated. Simone is in jail for having murdered Nadia, the prostitute who loved his saintly Dostoyevskian brother Rocco. At the end, Ciro, who has become part of the industrial working class, explains to the young Luca what to expect should he ever be able to return to Lucania: "Our town will become a big city too where people will

Rocco and His Brothers

learn to stick up for their rights and to impose duties. I don't know if that kind of world is nice, but that's the way it is, and if we're part of it, we have to accept its rules."

Drawing not only on Verga and Thomas Mann (he often acknowledged his indebtedness to Mann's novel *Joseph and His Brothers*) but also on Dostoyevsky, Visconti elevated Rocco's story to one of the mythical symbols of contemporary Italy. The saintly goodness of this boxing champion with Prince Mishkin's soul becomes a mirror that reflects the weariness of a society trapped in the growing emptiness of private relationships. Rocco's solitude in the middle of a 1959 booming city seems to confirm Fellini's apprehensions voiced in 1955 in connection with *La strada:* "Solitude will be the greatest pain of modern man."

Visconti created in *Rocco* his greatest "cinematic novel." Once again he proved himself a masterly director of actors. (*Rocco* was the springboard for the great careers of Alain Delon—Rocco—and Annie Girardot—Nadia.) Finally, it is in *Rocco* that Visconti developed the experience of *La terra trema* into a kind of symbolic realism, often expressed with naturalistic means.[11] Sadoul compared him with Stroheim.

Whereas Visconti was preoccupied with the new kinds of human tragedy brought about by industrialization and prosperity, Fellini's questions were somewhat different. As the years went by, he was realizing more and more that the treatment for his story "Moraldo in the City" was no longer viable because Rome was no longer the city he knew when he first arrived there: "A tiny casbah of furnished rooms around the main station, with a population of frightened immigrants, prostitutes, confidence tricksters, and Chinamen selling ties."[12] At the end of the fifties, Rome was becoming a different place: the international capital of a country embarking on a great economic adventure. Fellini was never attracted by the crowd that assembled daily in the typical nightlife settings on the luxurious Via Veneto rising steeply from the Piazza Barberini toward the arches of Porta Pinciana and the greenery of Villa Borghese.[13]

Yet in 1958 Fellini began spending his nights on Via Veneto, mostly in the company of news photographers, who would provoke situations for scandalous photos and then sell them to the yellow press. From their stories, true or false, the Moraldo treatment started taking a new shape. It preserved the basic characteristics of an episodic picaresque plot, the loose, nonnarrative "rivista structure," but the Roman world that the new script captured was very different. And so was Moraldo, given a new name—Marcello. Thus, as always with Fellini, at the outset of *La dolce vita* (1960) there was the concrete detailed visualization of a theme. Fellini felt that the next decade would change many aspects of Italian life, that Rome and its people would become very different. When he got together with his scriptwriters, Flaiano, Pinelli, and Brunello Rondi, to confirm his impressions of the material, as Fellini later recalled, they "went ahead in the vague direction of a film that would deal with the life of those years. And thus during the summer evenings of 1958, along the Via Veneto, *La dolce vita* was born.[14]

La dolce vita, a gigantic fresco of certain segments of European society in the sixties, is a series of episodes held together by two picaresque heros, a journalist

La dolce vita

who is a chronicler of scandals and a "paparazzo," his photographer. They travel through the cynical "world without love." They are first shown symbolically descending from a helicopter that is carrying an enormous statue of Christ the Redeemer above the roofs and terraces of Rome. Twelve more episodes/stations follow: Marcello meets with Maddalena, a rich industrialist's man-hungry daughter who wishes to make love with him in the bed of a prostitute; he finds out that his girlfriend Emma, an insecure, possessive woman, has attempted suicide; he rushes her to a hospital and then is off to cover a Hollywood sex bomb's visit to Rome; after a hectic day and night, culminating with the famous wading scene in the Fontana di Trevi, Marcello meets his friend Steiner, a writer, who seeks calm by playing the organ in a church; Marcello makes a short trip to the seashore where he chats with Paola, a young waitress, whose profile reminds him of little cherubs; then he is back on assignment, this time covering scenes of religious hysteria following the false appearance of the Virgin Mary to two children who are being exploited by their parents; after a visit to Steiner's snobbish literary salon, Marcello is unexpectedly visited by his father; the evening ends almost tragically when the old man

La dolce vita

follows a night club dancer home to her apartment, suddenly feels sick, and leaves
hastily to return to his quiet hometown where people grow old prematurely because of boredom; the Via Veneto's merry-go-round catapults Marcello into a castle outside the city where he finds Maddalena amidst the aristocratic decadence;
when he becomes convinced that she is willing to marry him, she disappears with
another man; next morning he learns that Steiner has killed his children and himself; he rushes to Steiner's apartment, which had seemed to him almost a refuge
from the horrors of the outside world; and a moment later he finds himself in the
street waiting for Steiner's wife, who is surrounded by a cloud of "paparazzi" trying
by fair means or foul to photograph her bewildered face. The final sequence shows
an orgy in a luxurious villa at the seashore at Fregene; in the morning Marcello
walks to the beach where some fishermen have just dragged a hideous fish out of
the ocean; a transvestite tells Marcello: "I think we shall all be like that in 1970,
completely rotten. It will be worse than the apocalypse. God, what an abomination
it will be. . . ." The little waitress Paola appears on the other side of the beach,
shouting and waving at Marcello; he cannot understand what she is saying; one of
the women from the previous night's party grabs his hand and leads him back to the
group. No more redemption, no more hope. The spiritual annihilation is complete.

The French critic Gilbert Sachalas argues in his book on Fellini that *La dolce vita* is the last of Fellini's films whose plot can be briefly summarized. It seems, however, that even in *La dolce vita* Fellini's internal world has become as important as any of the narrative episodes. The Rome of the film is just a reflection of Fellini's inner subjectivity and is only distantly related to reality (as witness the *flat* Via Veneto, which Fellini had constructed in the studio). It was during the process of writing and filming that the work kept acquiring new dimensions. In a discussion with the French director Alain Resnais, Fellini said:

> You can read a complete story in each fresco. I love paintings that show several views at the same time, for example those by Bosch and Brueghel. When I was shooting *Dolce vita,* I would have liked to be able to contain the entire film within a shot. I do not like to find myself under pressure to narrate a story with all its successive developments. I do not wish to narrate. I want to show. Film is an offspring not of literature but of painting.[15]

For the first time, Fellini filmed in cinemascope, giving the background a paradigmatic function while the characters, with almost no optical perspective, acquired a metaphysical quality. Thus, Fellini achieved a particular blend of the authentic and the imaginary. Some critics felt that *La dolce vita* tended to be an almost documentary piece of social criticism. For years, Fellini went to considerable trouble to dissipate this misconception, suggesting that the film is more than that. In 1965, he contended: "Frankly, even *Dolce vita* is completely invented. The Rome of which I speak is a city of the inner self; its topography is entirely spiritual."[16]

The enormous success of *La dolce vita* at the box office was, of course, partly a success "de scandale." Provoking the hostility of the establishment, the film was attacked almost immediately by the official press. The authorities pressured Fellini to make substantial cuts in the final version. But Fellini resisted, and the film was eventually protected by its success in Italy and all over the world. But the disputes continued. Some found the film permeated with religious spirit, a work by a man desperately seeking grace in a world deprived of it. Others attacked it as immoral, blasphemous, thoroughly antireligious. Fellini himself suggested what seems to be the best answer: "There's a priest who found a pretty good definition for *Dolce vita*. He said: 'It is when the silence of God falls upon people.'"[17]

The audience at the gala performance of the Cannes Film Festival in May 1960 received Antonioni's *L'avventura* with unmitigated hostility, which was shared by some of the critics. Some, however, recognized the nature of the event they had just witnessed, and *L'avventura* eventually won the Cannes Special Jury Award and the Critics' Award.[18] What was even more surprising was the reaction of the general audience. In France, *L'avventura* established itself as one of the biggest commercial successes of the year, and even in Italy it proved that there is a large audience for "difficult" films.

Superficially, *L'avventura* may seem to be a love story. During an excursion, a young woman disappears. For her fianceé and for one of her girl friends, the search becomes a kind of sentimental journey, at the end of which they both find themselves in a new and quite unforeseen situation. There is not much to add: a few names, Sandro, Claudia, Anna, the fact that the search fails to solve the enigma of the young woman's disappearance; the fact that Sandro's relationship to Claudia at the end of the film is as fragile as his relationship to Anna at the beginning.

L'avventura, however, is not just a restatement of Antonioni's main motif. This time Antonioni has made a step in a new direction. He does not tell a story, and he is not involved as a narrator. He simply shows. *Il grido* was, in a certain way, still a film of social criticism, a film about the alienation of feelings. Not so *L'avventura.* Antonioni declared in a statement distributed in Cannes in 1960:

> During the last few years, we have examined and studied the emotions as much as possible, to the point of exhaustion. But we have not been able to find any new emotions, not even to get an inkling of the problem. I am not a moralist. My film is neither a denunciation nor a sermon. It is a story told in images, and I hope that people will be able to see in it not only the birth of a deceptive emotion but a method through which it is possible to deceive oneself about one's feelings.

Antonioni threw his audience right into the middle of "objective art," the *nouveau roman* and the aesthetics that pervaded European literature, fine arts, and music at the time. His technique paralleled to a certain degree not only the *nouveau roman* but a whole trend in European literature starting with Flaubert and leading directly to Proust and Joyce. He renounces any stated thesis, any intervention in the flow of event, and any interpretation of the facts. He observes and describes the flow of life.

Many have established links between Antonioni and the authors of the *nouveau roman,* but in the final analysis, it was more Proust than Robbe-Grillet who influenced Antonioni's dissections of human feelings. Along with Robbe-Grillet, Antonioni adopted the early Husserlian principle to examine facts as such and to eschew all judgment about the significance of things, which had always been the main point of philosophical arguments. This basic attitude liquidated the traditional novel/film based on passions, psychology, and characters: the novel/film where all things could be explained in terms of their relationship with the protagonists.[19] Antonioni eliminated everything that produced movement, incident, conflict, or ideas. His reality is static. Anguish is the only feeling it inspires, and it is in this feeling that reality is reflected. Thus the contemplation of a space (wall, sea, road) carries more weight than a series of images edited so as to create dramatic tension. Antonioni, however, never completely rejected the use of metaphor as the *nouveau roman* did. He used the immediate significance (presence) of things to reach beyond their mere objectivity and to create out of their phenomenal existence a Proustian metaphor of oblivion (e.g., the description of Anna's cabin in *L'avventura,* Lidia's walk across Milan in *La notte,* the last sequence of *Eclipse* with its detached recording of objects).

Everything becomes landscape for Antonioni, but it is no longer landscape as a state of mind, as some of the neorealists saw it, but as a complex dramatic character composed of people, objects, and feelings. This landscape cannot be influenced

L'avventura

L'avventura

by any point of view: it can only be observed, followed, registered. "In this film," said Antonioni,

> the landscape is a component of primary importance. I felt the need to break up the action by inserting, in a good many sequences, shots that could seem banal or of a documentary nature (a whirlwind, the sea, dolphins, etc.). But in fact these shots are essential because they help the idea of the film: the observation of a state of affairs. We live today in a period of extreme instability, as much political, moral, and social as physical. I have made a film on the instability of the emotions, on their mysteries.[20]

Antonioni has said of filmmaking that "the problem is to catch a reality that is never static, is always moving toward or away from a moment of crystallization, and to present this moment, this arriving and moving on, as a new perception." For Penelope Houston this "perception" is the key term for understanding Antonioni, "as is the insistence," she pointed out "that the obvious dramatic occasion, the 'moment of crystallization' only finds significance through the continuous flow of movement toward or away. Neither life nor the cinema really stands still for big scenes; and Antonioni has of course been the cinema of nonevents, occurrences offscreen or unexplained."[21]

Antonioni has called the story of *L'avventura* "a detective story back to front." When asked what happened to Anna, he replied: "I don't know. Someone told me that she committed suicide, but I don't believe it."[22] Throughout the entire film we almost physically feel the slowness and the overwhelming presence of time (which is the agent of oblivion), the disintegration of feelings, the birth of new emotions and boredom, which again generates new involvements, crises, catastrophes.

In *L'avventura,* the strictly individual human experience is not tainted by any historical or social factor. The fact that Antonioni chose an upper-middle-class milieu had nothing to do with the attempt to make this particular kind of emotional adventure the privilege (or vice) of one social class, as has been sometimes mistakenly understood.

L'avventura has often been referred to as an expansion of possibilities of cinematic language, comparable to those works by Griffith, Murnau, the Soviet avant-garde, Orson Welles, Alain Resnais, etc. In actuality, the style of *L'avventura* shows no basic changes over that of *Girlfriends* and *Il grido.* Antonioni's approach already had fully ripened during the fifties, but during his early career, not many critics outside Italy took notice of his accomplishments. Not until the scandal at Cannes did Antonioni become one of the most talked about directors, and his style—by then fully established—was hailed as something new, as something that had been born only with *L'avventura.*

VIII

THE GLORIOUS SIXTIES (1961–1969)

With the exception of the neorealist period, the sixties were the richest decade in Italian cinema. This Italian "golden age" was without parallel in the film production of other nations of the time, offering a picture of extremely varied ambitions and efforts. After years of inertia, Rome once again became a bustling city, attracting film producers, actors, and filmmakers from all over the world. The period of the veterans was definitely over. There were new faces, new themes, new ideas. Film once again became a battleground where a long desired settling of accounts with the past and the present could take place. The situation that had been established fifteen years previously held sway again in the sixties: Italian cinema assumed the role of an observer of Italian society, exploring various facets of the nation and penetrating beneath its smiling face. The pontificate of John XXIII and the shock of the attempted de-Stalinization in the USSR shattered some ideological dogmas of the fifties and created an atmosphere favorable to more complex philosophical approaches and artistic visions. Also the increasing volume of movie production left room for more controversial subjects, tackled mainly by the members of the new generation.

The "glorious sixties" were made possible by an economic boom that offered young filmmakers the opportunity to express themselves in a variety of ways without creating, however, a consistent trend.[1]

Along with the rest of Western Europe, Italy too had an economic miracle. It was more modest, less stable, and much shorter than, for example, the German one, which took place in a more developed and more centralized country and was not from the outset weakened by profound social discrepancies. Thanks to important foreign credits, Italy lived through a period of economic modernization, based on the industrialization of a prevailingly rural country. (By 1964, only 25 percent of Italians had attained the standard of living of other Western countries.) The French historians, Serge Bernstein and Paul Milza, called the Italian economic miracle

> a child of European politics of the fifties. It rested, to a large degree, on the purchasing possibilities of foreign countries, mainly of members of the European Common Market.

Italian competitiveness relied on extremely low prices. Beginning with 1958, these competitive prices started attracting tourists from all over Europe. The Italian peninsula offered them not only its historical and natural beauty but also cheap accommodation and food. At the same time, Italian products conquered foreign markets. Until 1959, these low prices did not result from increased productivity but rather from the politics of low wages, accompanied by unemployment and underemployment. After 1959, this situation improved thanks to the help of the European Common Market. There was a general wage increase and more jobs became available. Soon afterwards, however, the industrial sectors not covered by sufficient investment started losing their competitive power. From the outset, the Italian economic miracle was accompanied by profound contradictions rooted in the general conditions of the postwar economic restoration.[2]

It was this basic situation, however, with all its maladjustments and discrepancies, that turned Italy into a mecca of international film coproduction.

ITALY—USA

Italo-American collaboration became an important part of the Italian cinematic scene in the early sixties. The thoroughly organized and prearranged Hollywood way of filmmaking merged with Italian craftsmanship, improvisation, and reliance on chance. And yet the products of this cooperation—the historical blockbusters—indicated a trend that generated innumerable imitations worldwide, even in the Soviet Union, Poland, and Japan.[3]

At the root of American producers' sudden interest in Italy were the precursors of later supermen, such as Hercules and Samson. In 1957, the revival of a typically Italian genre brought such mythological giants into the very center of Italian production, making them famous throughout the world. Pietro Francisci (b. 1906), until this time an obscure director, became a millionaire overnight when his film *Le fatiche di Ercole* (The Labors of Hercules, 1957), the first in an endless Hercules series, grossed 900 million lire in Italy. The first Hercules, like his followers, also made a fortune in the United States and thus lured American businessmen into investing in the mythological genre. Either they cofinanced historical blockbusters or provided full funding for their productions at Cinecittà (*Cleopatra*, *Ben Hur*, *The Bible*, etc.). By 1965 twenty films had been produced featuring Hercules, two dozens about Maciste (the good giant who appeared for the first time in the silent film *Cabiria*), eight with Ursus (originally a character in Henryk Sienkiewicz's novel *Quo Vadis?* which was filmed several times), and seven starring Samson. These were joined by various other characters from all kinds of mythologies, beginning with the Greek, Roman, and Christian and reaching to the Incas, Gengis Khan, Zorro, Queen Nefertiti, vampires, the Cyclops, various sheiks, the Mongols, headhunters, Amazons, etc. In the years 1957 to 1964, 170 mythological films were made, 10 percent of the entire Italian production. Their fantastic box-office success lasted until 1965. Then people tired of them, and this generation of supermen disappeared as quickly as they had emerged.[4]

Le fatiche di Ercole

But the overall situation created by these Italo-American coproductions did not change. American producers continued to come to Rome (now nicknamed Hollywood on the Tiber), especially after 1962 when Dino De Laurentiis built his "Dinocittà"—large film studios equipped to provide services for foreign companies. The Italian production partly recovered from its economic crisis and soon ranked second to the United States among the cinematic powers of the Western world. The Germans, the English, and the French joined in the deals between the Italians and the Americans, thus opening the way for the creation of multinational production companies. Films of the countries involved lost some of their nationalistic features; beginning with the late sixties, the number of innovative and artistically ambitious films substantially declined while a growing mass of impersonal and more or less monolithic international productions came to monopolize the market.

The mythological supermen—present at the very beginning of the change in filmmaking patterns—represented Italian popular entertainment at its best. Idealizing the positive hero (the good guy) and leaving no doubts about the ultimate victory of good over evil, the historical adventure films were imbued with a certain humanistic message, however simplistic and schematic. Man, though transformed into a superman, was portrayed as the measure of all things. "The escape from reality was, in a way, a criticism of reality."[5] One of the best definitions of the social impact of mythological films was provided by Vittorio Spinazzola who pointed out:

> Hercules invites the spectator to abandon completely the world of reality and human logic. On the other hand, he is not inaccessible, like a divinity, nor is he, like prophets, a mere reflection of divinity. In spite of his superhuman qualities, he remains an earthly hero and as such demands from the spectator not a passive adoration but an active process of identification. This duality is quite important for a sociological identification of the character. Hercules is the incarnation of a noble hero who does not come from the people but who is ready to fight for them, to protect the poor, and to restore order and social peace. He brought back to the screen the eternal tale of the knight errant, challenging his own class in the name of justice.[6]

The mythological film was based on an absolute hero, and historical material was used solely to bolster his existence with no regard for verisimilitude. Some of these films, continuing in the spirit of their 1920s precursors, had sadistic and erotic overtones. Female bodies were put on display as often as possible, bathing, belly dancing, or, in the first attempts at striptease, the dance of the seven veils. Battle scenes and scenes involving any kind of torture were charged with extreme cruelty. The sadistic element, absent in the first tales of Hercules and Maciste, became more pronounced in later years when the genre was approaching exhaustion.

Sadism continued to flourish in the genre that followed the mythological blockbusters—the famous and immensely successful "westerns Italian style" or, to mention just one of their various nicknames, "the spaghetti westerns." This trend began by chance in 1963: some Italian producers received an attractive offer to work in a film village in Spain that had been constructed as a location for German westerns. The following year, Sergio Leone (b. 1929) directed *Per un pugno di dollari* (A Fistful of Dollars), calling himself "Bob Robertson" and pretending that the film was a Hollywood production.[7] Within two years, *A Fistful of Dollars* had grossed 2 billion lire in Italy. It sold all over Europe and also did extremely well in the United States. In December 1964, *Il Giornale dello Spettacolo* contended:

> The phenomenon of the year is westerns. *A Fistful of Dollars* grossed 420 million lire in fifteen major cities, thus surpassing John Sturges's celebrated film *The Magnificent Seven*, which grossed a mere 280 million. It is more than probable that it will surpass Sturges's marvelous film by another 170 million by the time its first release is terminated. The success of *A Fistful of Dollars* is just spell-binding.[8]

SERGIO LEONE

The man who unleashed the rash of "spaghetti westerns" made his first appearance on a film set in 1948 at the age of nineteen; he was an extra in De Sica's *Bicycle Thief*, portraying a German seminarist in the scene at the market of Porta Portese. The son of a film director and an actress, Leone had been around movies since his

A Fistful of Dollars

early childhood. He worked as an assistant director and occasionally as an actor. In 1961 he directed his first film, the mythological *Il colosso di Rodi* (The Colossus of Rhodes). In 1964 he surprised the world with his second film, *Per un pugno di dollari* (A Fistful of Dollars), whose subject he borrowed from the Japanese film *Yojimbo* (1960) by Akira Kurosawa, who had himself borrowed it from a little-known American novel set in the prohibition era.[9] Leone's success was based on his combining elements of the American western with those of the James Bond tales, which were conquering the world at that time.[10]

Thus, Leone's films are also filled with secret agents, safe-crackers, torture, blood baths, and sex instead of love. The protagonist of *A Fistful of Dollars* (portrayed by Clint Eastwood) has nothing of the generosity of the noble cowboy. He is a dubious (unshaved and dirty) individual with only profit and pleasure on his mind. To free a bandit from prison, he does not get himself arrested and then organize the escape from inside, as a traditional good guy would do; instead, he jumps the wall with a dynamite charge. He is a cynical killer, whose double standard of morality is reminiscent of George Stevens's *Shane*—as some French and Italian critics pointed out. And, above all, he is the embodiment of the Italian philosophy of "getting by." Leone's antihero does not restrict violence to a fight against injustice. In Leone's films, violence becomes a bloody orgy, an element in the composition of overall horror. According to Lino Miccichè:

The American western tries to create an epic image of the past in order to exalt the present American way of life and to glorify the United States' choice of civilization (a true historical mission performed by an armed scout: yesterday on the Western frontier, today in the Western world). The western attributes to the Tom Mixes of yesterday a role that parallels that of the Johnsons and Nixons of today: they are all flagbearers of "an American peace." They are violent because violence is necessary. The source of the Italian western, on the other hand, is the daily internal and external violence of American civilization (or Western civilization as such).[11]

Images of violence became commonplace in the films of the 1970s, especially after Sam Peckinpah's *The Wild Bunch* (1969) and *Straw Dogs* (1970). Yet their beginnings go back to Leone, who endowed violence with the splendor of operatic stylization and choreography. In Leone's later westerns, especially *Il buono, il brutto e il cattivo* (The Good, the Bad, and the Ugly, 1971), the core of the action is conceived as a metaphoric dance with the victors and the vanquished becoming interchangeable. In *C'era una volta il West* (Once Upon a Time in the West, 1968), the idea of death loses all rationality and exhausts itself in a circle of endless killing. This story of a beautiful widow (Claudia Cardinale), who lives alone somewhere in the Far West, turns upside down the western's basic belief in the finality of one's actions. Like dancers in a macabre ballet, men come to the woman's house to die, one vengeance follows another, with dead bodies piling up before the woman's eyes, until no hope is left and no illusion has been spared. Similarly, Leone's last western, *Giù la testa* (Duck, You Sucker, 1971), set in Mexico in 1913–1914, is a variation on the theme "to kill for the sake of killing" (which became one of the leitmotifs of the seventies). Referring to one of the Mexican uprisings, *Duck, You Sucker* is permeated with the political disenchantment of the 1960s. Killing provokes more killing, revolt is followed by assassination, and people die by the hundreds. After *Duck, You Sucker*, the door to the depiction of endless violence was wide open. But those who passed through it often left behind Leone's stylistic elegance, his low-key humor, his knowledge of cinematic language, and the richness of his ideas.

Between 1964 and 1972, 300 "spaghetti westerns" were made in Italy: sixty-six in 1967 alone. Americanized names proliferated to such an extent that the *Monthly Film Bulletin* (London) listed 350 pseudonyms used by Italian filmmakers and actors: Carlo Lizzani became Lee Beaver, Florestano Vancini Stan Vance, Gian Maria Volontè John Welles, Gianni Puccini Jeff Mulligan, Camillo Mastrocinque Thomas Miller, Carlo Di Palma Charles Brown, etc. Some, like Bertolucci, Pasolini, and Damiani, worked under their own names. Most of the "spaghetti westerns" were unimaginative concoctions whose directors had shortly before been mass-producing stories about Hercules. But they were cranked out by the dozen, and their profits ran high. In 1966, the magazine *Europeo* (Rome) organized a panel to discuss the reasons behind the western fever. Scriptwriter and director Duccio Tessari provided an explanation: "Our westerns offer the spectator a product that has become a classic, but in addition they demystify the traditional West, transforming its heroes into anti-heroes. Today's masses are attracted to heroes like James Bond and Leone's 'bounty killer.'" Leone pointed out: "The hero of the American western has become too diluted. The director stops the action too often and indulges in long, sentimental digressions. In his love life, the western's hero should remain mysterious and distant. Thus, his impact would be stronger, mainly upon female audiences." And Sergio Corbucci, another star director of "spaghetti westerns," concluded: "Our westerns are more emotional and more realistic, but let's face it, they are also more perverse. There is everything: drugs, savage cruelty. We kill babies too. Soon the Americans will understand how things are. For the time being, they remain attached to honest fights and legal duels." The Americans came to understand how things were, and after 1968 this kind of violence was "made in Hollywood." But it did not take long before the "spaghetti westerns" faded out.

SEX BY NIGHT

The Italian mentality is strongly imbued with a sense of strict morality. Italians love to pass moral judgments in life as well as in art.[12] In the realm of film, Antonioni is among the few who never put characters on trial, who refrain from the manichean opposition between good and evil. Fellini's films, on the other hand, are pervaded by strict moralistic attitudes. (*La dolce vita* is basically predicated on indignation over an "immoral" way of life.)

Thus, it is all the more paradoxical that the Italians were the first to initiate a mass production of erotic films—films that were permissive to an extent unthinkable elsewhere at that time. Their eroticism reflected the typical mentality of the Italian middle-class male with, as the saying has it, "one foot in the church and the other in a brothel." These sex movies could also be regarded as an unconscious revolt against the "idolization of the family," against the sacred image of "the mamma" and the "mother-wife-sister" mythology (expressed in all its complexity in Fellini's films).

The genre was introduced by the ever-opportunistic Alessandro Blasetti. His films *Europa di notte* (Europe by Night, 1959) and *Io amo, tu ami* (I Love, You Love, 1961) exploited unabashedly the spectacular aspects of eroticism and sex. Blasetti's entries were immediately followed by others, and by 1965, Italian theaters were inundated with movies bearing titles such as *The World by Night*, *Hot World by Night*, *Sexy World by Night*, *The World by Night 3*, *America by Night*, *Hot Sex in the Orient*, *Sexy*, *Sexy Follies*, *Magic Sex*, *Naked Sex*, *Forbidden Sex*, *Sexy Africa*, etc.

Whereas the "spaghetti westerns" sometimes were imaginative and made an attempt at style, the majority of the Italian erotic films did not even attain the level of average entertainment. Their main features were low budgets and high profits. They brought an end to certain taboos without changing in any way the overall puritanistic morality of the Italian audiences. After brothels were outlawed in January 1958, the Italian male stepped with his other leg into the pornographic movie theaters, indulging in "a rite of collective masturbation."[13] By the end of the sixties, sex in film had become a commonplace, and hundreds of "adult magazines" appeared on the newstands. In the face of this competition, another successful genre died a quick death.

THE NEW ITALIAN CINEMA

A new group of filmmakers eventually emerged out of the growing power of the Italian cinema, bringing to life an extremely heterogeneous and short-lived phenomenon sometimes referred to as the New Italian Cinema. Twenty years after the neorealist revolt, another angry generation appeared in the Italian film world—this time not out of devastation and pain but out of the well-being of a consumer society. Their films were no longer full of compassion for suffering humanity; there were no attempts to capture "the tears shed by things." They were boiling with rage against a society that had developed during the past twenty years and against the older generation that had conformed to the rules—some of them well rooted in the fascist era—thus betraying, in the eyes of their children, the postwar ideals. Some of these new films were filled with explosive fury and utopian ideas already anticipating the events of 1968–1969: demonstrations by Italian students in 1968, followed by the same movement in Germany; street fighting in Paris in May, upheavals in Japan and Mexico; revolts on the American campuses challenging "not only the power of money, not only capitalism, but also the bureaucracy, the hierarchy, the division of labor, the atomization, and the mechanization of city life."[14]

The New Italian Cinema was born in this atmosphere "before the revolution." It shared with other New Waves a few common features:

1. A subjective approach that resulted from the denial of an objective reality identified with the establishment. The "He thought" of nineteenth-century literature and the traditional film was replaced by "I think." Alberto Moravia contended: "'He thinks' or 'He thought' originated in a system of values that made possible faith in an objective reality. These values shattered, 'He thought' became an empty convention. 'I think' expresses the contemporary concept of reality as something that may or may not exist. In any case, it exists differently for each human being, and it is not connected to other individual realities."[15]

2. The rejection of all closed plots. Following on the road initiated in the early fifties by Antonioni, the young filmmakers favored the "open work approach," allowing each viewer an interpretation from his own point of view and according to his own experience.

3. The concept of the film's structure as an expression of the film's idea. The film's ideology was no longer expressly proclaimed by one or more characters but was expressed through the film's language. The cinematic structure was free of all dramatic knots and became increasingly disconnected, loose, violent, shocking, restless, provocative, so as to convey the authors' discontent with established values. This new structure was based on a new concept of montage, which mainly opposed Pudovkin's notion that "film art begins when the director begins to combine and join together various pieces of film." The new films of the sixties show a ferocious contempt for film grammar, especially for traditional editing, characterized by André Bazin as a "technique of cross-cutting which, for instance in a dialogue, consists of alternate shots of the speakers according to the logic of the text." The young filmmakers of the sixties also opposed the traditional subdivision into

shots and sequences, favoring the sequence shot (*plan séquence*), used, for example, by Rossellini as early as 1951 (*Europe 51*). Each of them created, in a way, his own approach to montage, linking it directly to the film's ideology. According to Guido Oldrini, "the films of the New Cinema, not only Italian, but also European and international, share a strong avant-gardist ambition and the effort to reveal the crisis of the traditional cinematic modes. According to the filmmakers, the renewal of old forms can be achieved only through linguistic research."[16]

4. The rejection of the social and political status quo. The different New Waves can be viewed as accompanying phenomena of political events in different parts of the world in the sixties: the antiestablishment revolt and the antiwar movement in the Western world, the opposition toward bureaucratic dogmatism and Soviet hegemony in the countries of Eastern Europe, the anticolonial wars in the Third World. These and other events created a specific atmosphere during the sixties—a decade of renewed hopes for social change, for a "better world." This was a decade of young people, of the "flower children," often referred to, and justly so, as the romantic period of the twentieth century. In Italy, these years were characterized by the collapse of the politics of the center (centrism) and by efforts to open up the government to left-wing forces. After the 1963 elections, the Socialists joined the government, following the Republicans and the Social Democrats. Ten years after it had been proposed for the first time, the coalition of parties from the political center and some parties left of the center became a reality.

The new generation of Italian filmmakers had their *Ossessione* too, a film manifesto, often compared to Visconti's first film. It attacked the existing moral values and drew a ravaging picture of a segment of Italian society in an attempt to destroy its myths and to create a new style. Marco Bellocchio's *I pugni in tasca* (Fists in the Pocket, 1965) was hailed as the most important debut of the decade. It is an overwhelming moral metaphor, again using disease as a window into the world of "normality." But this time the sickness is representative of the typical, and the normal is viewed as sick. The film's title can be interpreted as a symbol for all the young men and women of the sixties who challenged the accomplishments of the preceding generation: in Italy, in France, in the United States, in Czechoslovakia, in Hungary, in England. Bellocchio (b. 1940) explained it as follows: "Everyone who keeps his fists in his pocket is inevitably heading toward the extreme consequences of his own passivity: the longer he clenches his fists in his pocket, paralyzed by his own inertia, the more obsessed he becomes with a fatal desire to revolt and with this desire a long suppressed lust for evil."[17]

Fists in the Pocket is an existential parable whose characters reflect allegorically the adversary relationships between the individual and society. Bellocchio, born into a provincial middle class, centers the film's problems in a nuclear family, making it a prototype of the 1960s moral bankruptcy. The family lives in the provinces, leading a monotonous middle-class life. All its members, except the older son, are epileptics. Sandro, the second-born, decides to eliminate the epileptic members in order to free his older brother from the family burden. He pushes his blind mother over a cliff, drowns his younger brother in a bathtub, and after having confessed his crimes to his sister Giulia (to whom he is sexually attracted and

Fists in the Pocket

whom he wants to impress), he dies in an epileptic fit. Giulia watches his agony, refusing to help him.

Bellocchio's main theme—his hatred of the established moral patterns—explodes in two masterful scenes: in the first, set during a meal, the entire family watches as a cat eats from their blind mother's plate; the second, following the mother's death, shows Sandro and Giulia destroying family souvenirs in an explosion of uncontrolled hilarity. *Fists in the Pocket* is a perfectly coordinated work of art. Its slow camera movements contrast with the violence of the plot; its dramatic musical score, evocative locations, and realistically stylized milieu create an aura of tension that is enhanced by a broad range of savage emotional mockery. It is the work of an artist who is in full command of his talent and his medium.

Bellocchio's second film, *La Cina è vicina* (China Is Near, 1967), uses far-reaching subject matter with vast political references. This was the time "before the revolution," the second half of the sixties when almost none of the Italian filmmakers kept aloof from the political discussions in which the country was immersed. This was also a time of films dealing with political subjects. The plot of *China Is Near* centered again on a deformed family, a group of misfits. But this time their malformation is less physical than psychological. Vittorio, the older brother, unsuccessfully runs for office as a Socialist party candidate; Carlo, the younger brother, wastes his energy in useless actions against Vittorio, who, in his eyes, represents the frustrated helplessness of the Italian political center. They are both ridiculous and immature, paralyzed by sexual inhibitions and dominated by their sister Elena, who enjoys every minute of their failures. Their wealthy household is eventually taken over by their maid and her lover, who trick Vittorio and Elena into marrying them.

China is Near, intended as a biting social metaphor, lacks the stylistic coherence of *Fists in the Pocket* and misses the mark with many of its well-aimed points. Too abstract and not consistent enough, it does not come close to Bellocchio's first film. However, its image of a disintegrating family dusting useless family souvenirs dealt another blow to Italy's illusions about the infallibility of its moral and political codes. After *China Is Near* and *Fists in the Pocket,* the cinematic image of the Italian family was never the same again.

BERNARDO BERTOLUCCI'S SEARCH FOR MYSTERY

Bellocchio was a graduate from the Centro Sperimentale di Cinematografia. So was Liliana Cavani, another prominent figure of the New Italian Cinema. But some of their peers, such as Bernardo Bertolucci (b. 1941), were learning the film profession on the set. Bertolucci made his first film after years of apprenticeship with some of the greatest personalities of the Italian artistic scene. Introduced by his father, Attilio, the famous Italian poet and literary critic, Bertolucci started attending regular discussion meetings of an artistic group that included Alberto Moravia, Elsa Morante, Giorgio Bassani, the brothers Sergio and Franco Citti, and P. P. Pasolini, the host. Two women, both aspiring actresses, belonged as regular guests at Pasolini's house: Laura Betti and Adriana Asti. But soon there was a rift, caused by Bertolucci, at that time an extremely attractive young man. Betti wanted to influence his life and career, but he preferred the less explosive Asti, choosing her for the leading female role of his second film *Prima della rivoluzione* (Before the Revolution, 1964) and eventually marrying her. Betti, who became one of Italy's best actresses, did not speak to them for years.[18] The encounters at Pasolini's place went on (after 1963 in his modern duplex in the Via Eufrate), but Bertolucci and Asti were rarely among the guests. In retrospect, it seems that it was not Asti who caused the split. Rather, Bertolucci wanted to free himself from the influence of Pasolini, whom he first met at the age of fifteen.[19]

Yet it took many years for Bertolucci to liberate himself from his "spiritual father." In 1975, he contended: "Pier Paolo Pasolini has always been a father figure to me. When he spoke badly about *Last Tango in Paris,* I felt a kind of liberation. The more he insisted on the film's poor qualities, the more he was destroying his image of the father figure."[20]

Years earlier, long before the success of *Last Tango* catapulted him to world fame, Bertolucci was the prodigy of his generation. At twenty he won the coveted Viareggio Award for his book of poetry entitled *In cerca di mistero* (In Search of Mystery), and at twenty-one he made his first feature film. Alberto Moravia claimed that in another historical period Bertolucci would have become a great writer. When someone objected that Bertolucci had an undeniable film sense,

Moravia said: "Vocation always results from a personal relationship to culture. The culture of our time is film."[21]

Bertolucci made two home movies at the age of sixteen, but his first true contact with cinema was on the set of *Accattone* (1961), Pasolini's first film. As Pasolini's assistant, Bertolucci tried above all to understand how a film was made. In 1973 he said: "I stopped writing poetry the moment I took the camera in hand. I was mesmerized. I knew that films were my future—and also my punishment. Because there are also many other things in life."[22]

Bertolucci's first film, *La commare secca* (The Grim Reaper, 1962), based on a subject by Pasolini, evinces a sophisticated cinematic language and a dynamic visual style that relates it to the international modernistic cinema. Together with Sergio Citti (Pasolini's proletarian friend whom he called "my living lexicon"), Bertolucci created an impressionist poem of Rome as seen by "the children of life," young men from the subproletariat who enjoy life in spite of their poverty and lack of perspective. Three features of *The Grim Reaper*—a narrative founded on an investigation, the enigmatic feature of some of the protagonists, and the pervasive presence of death—form a continuing thread in Bertolucci's subsequent films. Already in his first film, Bertolucci was assaulting the old montage in an attempt to strengthen the film's immediacy. The images are edited in a rhythmic crescendo that atomizes the cinematic structure in favor of freer improvisation.

After a breath-taking aerial shot of a Roman bridge and falling leaves in the park of San Paolo, *The Grim Reaper* begins with the murder of a prostitute by one of her clients. Then a police officer questions all the suspects, a broad array of people whose individual stories are told with meticulous attention to details, the melancholic poetry of life, and a visual richness balanced by a sensitivity for social issues. The film ends with a magnificent sequence of a dance (another narrative element typical of Bertolucci's work) and the identification of the murderer.

Like *The Grim Reaper,* Bertolucci's subsequent film, *Before the Revolution,* unfolds through a succession of semiautonomous narrative blocks while montage and a mobile camera constantly increase the ambiguity of the situations. The protagonist, Fabrizio, is torn between the comfort of his life as an upper-middle-class adolescent and his yearning to break free from it. In his search for something different, he chooses the ardent communist Cesare as his friend and mentor and has an intense love affair with his own aunt Gina (Adriana Asti). Yet eventually he renounces his dreams and marries Clelia, the choice imposed on him by his parents.

Although *Before the Revolution* borrows its setting (Bertolucci's native Parma), the protagonists' names, and some narrative elements from Stendhal's 1838 novel *The Charterhouse of Parma,* it is to no immediate avail to compare details of the two. The truly "Stendhalian" elements of the film are its attempt to evoke a "prerevolutionary" atmosphere and its portrayal of Fabrizio's indecisiveness as a phenomenon resulting from a specific historical environment: the growing impact of the Italian Left on one hand, and the fear of revolution, deeply embedded in the European bourgeoisie, on the other. The quote from Talleyrand that opens the film is the best expression of this ambiguity: "He who did not live the years before the revolution cannot understand the sweetness of living."

Before the Revolution

Before the Revolution is the most autobiographical of Bertolucci's films. It is propelled by the uninterrupted inner monologue of Fabrizio/Bernardo and could, as such, be referred to as "the confession of a child of our century." All Bertolucci's fears and hesitations are reflected in Fabrizio's dilemma, "what is to be done." Bertolucci's attraction to the Communist party (which he eventually joined) and his attachment to his own social background are gradually overshadowed by an infatuation with cinema, embodied in the film by Fabrizio's friend, a film buff in love with Rossellini (played by the film director Gianni Amico, the coauthor of the script).

Attilio Bertolucci called his son's films from the 1960s "autobiographical in a symbolic sense." "We are all Catholics," he said, "Bernardo was baptized and all that. There is a contradiction in Bernardo. I think that at the same time he hates and loves his background, his life, his class. Therefore the heroes of his autobiographical films always try to break loose but fail in the end."[23] Bertolucci himself contended: "More than just being autobiographical, it was a way to exorcise my own fears. Because to be like that character is almost a destiny for all bourgeois young Europeans." When asked about the origins of his Marxist sympathies, Bertolucci said: "I was always like that. Marxism in Italy is very common."[24]

While the more immediate *Grim Reaper* has retained most of its original freshness, the impact of *Before the Revolution* has gradually weakened with the passage of time because so many of its stylistic elements are characteristic of the 1960s search for a new language. This reflective first-person film testimony is, in a way, an anthology of the efforts by 1960s filmmakers to renovate film narrative by, among other things, basing it on present-tense stream of consciousness. Bertolucci's restless camera uses many components cherished by various New Waves, which, in retrospect, appear outdated: high-angle shots culminating in frozen compositions, repetitions of the same shot from a slightly different perspective, freeze frames, unexpected and unmotivated changing of distance between camera and object, subjective tracking shots and pans, etc. Bertolucci's style is based on insistent, extremely seductive takes reminiscent of the language of Romantic poetry with its highly personal sets of signs.

In its time, *Before the Revolution* was hailed as a major achievement of the New Italian Cinema, equaled only by *Fists in the Pocket*. The film amassed many awards and strengthened Bertolucci's image as a prodigy.[25] But its box-office results were rather poor, and the producers labeled Bertolucci "noncommercial." He had to wait another four years before he could embark on his next feature film, *Partner* (1968), which reconfirmed both his exceptional talent and his avowed eclecticism.[26]

Partner centers on the incapacity of European intellectuals to join the revolt of their time. Bertolucci described his film as "the story of a professor of drama who suffers from a neurosis and his own intellectual failure."[27] The protagonist, Giacomo, evolves a fantastic idea: he creates a second self. His partner is successful whenever he fails; he has a good relationship with his students, and he incites a student revolt. Loosely based on Dostoyevsky's *The Double, Partner* once again reveals the intellectuals' impotence with regard to political-revolutionary ideology. Its message, however, remains rather confused, as does its protagonist's death: following his partner, Giacomo jumps out of a window after informing us that the film is a parable about American imperialism and syphilitic marines.

Partner is a difficult and provocative film that draws on the stylistic and ideological approach of Jean-Luc Godard. But Bertolucci lacks Godard's ability to blend surreal plot with an authentic political background. The world surrounding Giacomo—anti-Vietnam demonstrations, the 1968 student revolts—loses much of its effectiveness because of Bertolucci's prevailing interest in portraying his protagonist's self-awareness. Even more than *Before the Revolution, Partner* is representative of the effort of modern cinematic narrative to use the film screen as a mirror of characters' thought processes.

In 1962 another first-person film attempted to express the social implications of Italian life: *Un uomo da bruciare* (This Man Must Die), made by the audacious and brilliant Taviani brothers (Vittorio b. 1929, Paolo b. 1931) along with the more radical Valentino Orsini (b. 1926).

VITTORIO AND PAOLO: DESPAIR AND HOPE OF REVOLUTION

In the Taviani's fourth film, *Sotto il segno dello scorpione* (Under the Sign of Scorpio, 1968), a group of young men invades a peaceful island, and one of them, Rutolo, tries to persuade his comrades to use violence against the island's inhabitants: "Let's make them cry, let's frighten them, you must exaggerate." One comrade: "Whom? Them? But why?" Rutolo: "They must leave the island with us. Immediately. We can't do without them on the continent." Another comrade: "It's in their interest, isn't it?" Another comrade: "But this will take time." Rutolo: "That's why. Exaggerate, make them cry, frighten them. . . ." In the end, Rutolo's group massacres the men and rapes the women because they have refused to join the invaders' search for a "better world" (referred to in the film as "the continent").

This short example from one of the most accomplished of the Tavianis' films sums up the uneasy choice Vittorio and Paolo try to express in their *oeuvre:* there should be a revolution, but is there a revolution without injustice, blood, and despair? In a revolution, there are neither victors nor vanquished but only victims; revolution may be a goal, but is any goal worth so much bitterness and suffering? Can there be a revolution without one group forcing another to do what it does not want to do? But if there can be no good revolution, what is left? Is it all just utopian dreaming?[28]

These are the questions asked by Salvatore Carnevale, the protagonist of *This Man Must Die* in the days preceding his death. He knows that the Mafia wants to kill him. He experiences his death in a dream in which his past comes back to him: the past of a revolutionary, a union leader who had come to Sicily to help the peasants fight their oppressors. But the peasants turned him down, and his party rejected him too. He was too radical and also too eccentric. He was a subversive— to everyone.[29] Salvatore is torn between his desire to work for the revolutionary cause and his yearning for a normal life. Now there is the revolution, his messianic mission. "If they kill me, it will be like killing Jesus Christ," he says. But he is not sure he is doing the right thing. They shoot him in the back on a dusty road. And then his casket is carried in a grandiose funeral procession with banners, flowers, and crowds of people. The death of a revolutionary. Nobody asks who killed him. And probably nobody cares.[30]

This Man Must Die is based on a real event: in 1955, in a small village near Palermo, the Mafia murdered Salvatore Carnevale, a thirty-two-year-old union leader. At first glance, the adaptation by the Tavianis and Orsini resembles a neorealist film: shot on authentic locations with unknown or nonprofessional actors, the film was referred to as "an act of love for neorealism."[31] But the directors never attempted to comply with historical truth. They created an ambiguous character whose hesitations would have been unthinkable at the time of neorealism. Everything was shaped in accordance with the directors' personal experience. The subjective interpretation of history, based on objective facts, has always been one of the main assets of the Tavianis's *oeuvre*. The other feature of their work is a cinematic form that blends perfectly with the first-person narrative. An extremely mobile camera uses different kinds of follow shots and subjective shots to scrutinize the characters' inner selves. The structure is elaborate, with frequent aerial shots and pull-back shots, but never gratuitous ones. There is a strict correspondence between the camera movements and the narrative development, resulting in a complicated time/space continuity (real events are juxtaposed with dreams and hallucinations, the past alternates with the present).

This Man Must Die

The Tavianis and Orsini had preceded their first feature film with a great deal of experience in documentary filmmaking. They directed their first documentary, in collaboration with Zavattini, in 1954. Entitled *San Miniato, July 1944*, it recounts the massacre of innocent people by the Germans in the cathedral of San Miniato (San Miniato, a township near Pisa, was the Tavianis' birthplace). This first documentary was the only one the Tavianis actually liked. And yet *San Miniato* (prohibited for a long time by the censors) was released only on a limited basis whereas their other documentaries earned profits that were eventually used to finance *This Man Must Die*. Orsini worked with them until 1964. Born into a working-class family (the Tavianis' background was bourgeois), Orsini was an early member of the Communist party, a fiery revolutionary and resistance fighter, and was influential in shaping the Tavianis' political attitudes. The last film they made together, *I fuorilegge del matrimonio* (The Outlaws of Marriage, 1963), attacked Italian family law, especially for its prohibition of divorce. Marred by rhetorical explicitness and illustrative chronicling, the film was not successful with audiences despite its topical subject matter.[32]

The Tavianis' 1967 film *Sovversivi* (Subversives) is the key film of the socially committed Italian cinema of the 1960s. When Palmiro Togliatti, the longtime leader of the Italian Communist party died in 1964, the Tavianis, along with Maselli, Zurlini, Lizzani, and Loy, were assigned by the Communist party to film the funeral. About 4 million people paid their respects to the deceased leader who had become the symbol of an epoch. The Tavianis called his death "the end of a historical moment, of a political line, of neorealism." Or, as a character in *Subversives,* a woman in her forties, writes in a letter: "Good-bye, Togliatti, good-bye our youth."

Subversives takes place during the three days preceding the funeral. The film's story is intercut with authentic material shot during the funeral. It concentrates on four characters for whom Togliatti's death represented a turning point. But, above all, *Subversives* is a polemic against the official line of the Communist party, a polemic led by people who had become disenchanted with some of its issues and who were searching for something different. Anarchists? Utopists? Subversives? Probably all of these, in line with the long tradition of Italian revolutionary anarchism, reaching far back into the nineteenth century. Emilio, the most autobiographical character of *Subversives,* is very close to anarchism. He questions his dedication to the Communist party and is dissatisfied with his comfortable existence as a well-to-do family man. He has long discussions with Ettore, a Venezuelan revolutionary wanted by the police in his country. Ettore loathes the quiet life of the majority of Italian communists. He reproaches them for their loss of ideals and acceptance of compromises. He returns to Venezuela even though deep in his heart he would like to stay in Italy with the woman he loves, perhaps even accepting the rules of the easy-going leftist establishment. And there is Giulia, the wife of a

Sovversivi

communist functionary. Disillusioned with her husband and her own life, she tries to free herself and publicly admits her lesbianism while her husband tries to keep the appearance of a normal marriage. The problems of these characters are summed up in Lodovico's yearning to escape from this world "to search for—and thereby assert—the existence of another world that would be just as it should be." The story concludes with Ettore's departure and his last attempt to communicate with those who came to say good-bye. They can no longer hear him, and he just shouts his pathetic "Ciao" into the camera.

Subversives takes its perspective from inside Italian political life and offers deep insights into a vast range of problems of the European Left. However, it leaves the uninitiated spectator confused or, at least, with a feeling of uneasiness. This feeling is intensified by the loose, aphoristic narrative, which connects the stories of the four protagonists only by means of their mutual philosophical interdependence.

Under the Sign of Scorpio provided a logical conclusion to the main idea of the Tavianis' early films, affirming that power is used only for its own ends and not for the sake of freedom. Visibly influenced by the Hungarian director Miklós Jancsó, *Under the Sign of Scorpio* is conceived almost like a ballet, based on rhythmic movements of the camera in phase with the motion of the characters, and with an obsessive musical accompaniment. It owes much of its emotional impact to the juxtaposition of a highly stylized background (the anonymous lyrical beauty of a volcanic island) with shots of the real-life characters (the leader of the islanders and his wife).[33] Thus, the cinematic space does not simply convey the content and the message: it becomes the content itself. This phenomenon is apparent, for example, in the final scene. After the men of the island have been hunted down and killed, the women rally on the shore in a frantic rite. They tie their own feet and throw themselves into the ocean, dragging with them those who do not want to die.

Under the Sign of Scorpio is the most accomplished of the Tavianis' films from the 1960s. Its final musical outcry closes a chapter in their *oeuvre* dedicated to the examination of revolutionary options. Better than any other film, *Under the Sign of Scorpio* reflects the significance of 1968, the year when it became clear "that the world as it should be" is out of reach for all subversives and will be so for a long time.

LILIANA CAVANI AND LINA WERTMÜLLER

Only two women were among the members of the new Italian film generation: Liliana Cavani (b. 1935) and Lina Wertmüller (b. 1929). From the outset, Cavani was the more interesting of the two of them especially for her attempt to introduce aspects of modern philosophy into her films and to express them through an inventive structure of inner monologue ("I think" as opposed to "He thought"). In her first documentaries, Cavani was already concentrating on controversial subjects (Nazism, Stalinism), repeatedly asking the Nietzschean question about the distinction between good and evil. Her protagonists constantly express their contempt for conventional solutions to this question as postulated primarily by the church. Her characters are opposed to the "slave morality" of Christian civilization and to all kinds of power structures. Aside from the influence of Nietzsche, Cavani's attitude

obviously had its roots in the traditions of Italian anarchism, as well as in the dissident Catholic groups that surfaced in Italy in the mid-sixties and for whom Cavani's film *Francesco d'Assisi* became a kind of manifesto.

Cavani chose St. Francis of Assisi as the subject for her first fiction film as an example of original "unspoiled" Christianity and as the prototype of a strong individual who creates his own heroic morality. *Francesco d'Assisi* (1966) is a symbolic representation of the struggle between the "new" and the "old," primarily emphasizing Cavani's contention that "only youth can see clearly." Rendering St. Francis's dilemmas, Cavani stresses his renunciation of all earthly possessions and thus questions not only the church's right to wealth but also the double morality of Italy's consumer society.

Not unlike Rossellini, Cavani structures St. Francis's story as a spontaneous chronicle, shunning all stylization, using a hand camera, and attempting a reconstruction of "the mythology of the real." *St. Francis* was one of the first films entirely funded by the Italian Television Commission, whose executives were beginning to understand the importance of backing artistically ambitious films and attracting filmmakers of the younger generation.

Cavani's next film, *Galileo* (1968), also focuses on a controversy between a free

Francesco d' Assisi

spirit and the authorities. This time Cavani uses dazzling colors to highlight her discussion about freedom: the provocative crimson of the cardinals' capes and hats is composed in exaggerated expanses that seem to devour the entire screen, evoking an overall feeling of repression. Alternating between the ecclesiastic court that passes judgment on Galileo's ideas and the prison cell where Galileo faces the choice between a "slave morality" and freedom of thought, the film concentrates on Galileo's dialogue with his accusers. The action culminates in the scene showing the church's confiscation of Galileo's book *Two Systems of the World* (published in 1632). While this work is being condemned and its author accused of heresy, the Pope looks on, biting his nails and not even trying to conceal his boredom.[34]

In *I cannibali* (The Cannibals, 1969), Cavani exposes the philosophical ambivalence of good and evil through a story set in a fictitious country, performing a spectacular tightrope walk between political science fiction and contemporary metaphor. Whereas *Galileo* concerns a dialogue with power and the failure of all attempts at communication, *The Cannibals* is based on the refusal of all dialogue. The protagonist, a Christ-like character, never speaks a word to anybody but remains locked in his self-imposed silence. Antigone, his follower, also remains silent even when threatened and tortured, and her fiancé assumes the attributes of a dog to avoid any communication with his jailors. Inspired by the myth of Antigone (Oedipus's daughter who buried her brother in defiance of the tyrant's orders), *The Cannibals* transcends this myth and reflects the 1968 revolt of the younger generation, thus showing a kinship with films like the Tavianis' *Under the Sign of Scorpio*, Pasolini's *Pigpen*, Buñuel's *Milky Way*, Truffaut's *Fahrenheit 451*, etc.[35] The television realism of *The Cannibals* undermined the film's metaphoric substance to such a degree that it creates a feeling of perplexity. Compared with *St. Francis* and *Galileo*, *The Cannibals* is on a lower level of achievement.

Lina Wertmüller's first venture into film directing, *I basilischi* (The Lizards, 1963), falls under the heading of sociocomedy. Wertmüller, who had worked for years as Fellini's assistant, drew heavily on his *I vitelloni* but offered a completely different perspective on the theme of wasted youth. Whereas Fellini takes a metaphoric view of his subject, Wertmüller adopts from the outset the patterns of comedy Italian style, transforming it into comedy New Cinema style. Around a gripping portrait of four provincial adolescents, Wertmüller unfolds dozens of tiny stories, capturing the inhabitants of a small town in their daily routine: sleep, food, sex, sleep, sex, sleep, and a kind of work. *The Lizards* remains one of Wertmüller's best films, if not the very best. Superbly photographed by Gianni Di Venanzo, it uses a very cultivated language that pares the scenes down to bare essentials. With the exception of a few sequences that lapse into caricature (the visit of a society lady who comes to the town to film a strike of the local day laborers), *The Lizards'* approach is lyrical, attaining a kind of poignancy that gives the film a haunting power.[36]

I cannibali

Wertmüller's next film, *Questa volta parliamo di uomini* (Let's Talk About Men, 1965), differed sharply from her debut work in its simplistic caricatural vision of its central problem—the battle between the sexes. *Let's Talk About Men* is a populist farce based on a showy yet tame feminism. In her later works, she further developed the style introduced by *Let's Talk About Men* rather than returning to the promises of her first film.

TWO OUTSIDERS: ERMANNO OLMI AND CARMELO BENE

While Wertmüller, Bertolucci, and Cavani were working their way up to international fame, Ermanno Olmi, the most original filmmaker among the newcomers, remained enclosed in his small world, to which few people had access. During the sixties, Olmi directed five films, all remarkable for their dispassionate lyrical objectivity. None of them has a true "plot." They are built on the slow unfolding of a single theme, of a single life philosophy: no digressions, no compromises, no yearning for fame. When, after twenty years, the fame arrived, nobody was more surprised than Olmi himself.

Olmi's characters are never successful in the usual sense of the word. Even when they achieve something, their success is only a narrative pretext used to make the viewer realize the illusory nature of "making it." At a time when the majority of Italians worshipped the liberties of the consumer society, Olmi's nostalgia for a return to nature and the simplicity of feelings could have seemed old-fashioned, even ridiculous. Later, when attitudes started changing, Olmi's modest souls and his dedication to the simple life became popular. Even Olmi's least accomplished film, *E venne un uomo* (A Man Named John, 1965), a dramatized study of the life of Pope John XXIII and an attempt to draw an official portrait of a public figure, eludes the traps of officialdom. Though referred to as "Olmi's only widely acknowledged failure," by the British film critic Gavin Millar it retains the virtue of celebrating an ordinary man "not for his ordinariness, but for his singularity."[37]

Un certo giorno (One Day, 1968) is the most telling illustration of Olmi's conviction that modern civilization has a destructive influence on man's sense of responsibility. Blending the description of an industrial concern (which he himself had come to know so well) with his own perception of the human inner self (which had always interested him), Olmi made almost physically palpable the loss of moral values. "And now everything will be normal again," says the wife of the protagonist at the end of the film. Her husband, a successful executive in an advertisement company, has been acquitted of charges of manslaughter. During the trial, nobody is interested in the victim, a worker. Everyone accepts the lawyer's argument about the "accumulated stress on the defendant," his important work, the poor driving conditions. And the manager, free of all responsibility, can go back to his "job."

As early as his second film, *Il posto* (The Job, 1961), Olmi was concerned with the alienation generated by industrialization and bureaucracy. Whereas the protagonist of *One Day* is a middle-aged man, afraid of having a heart attack, *The Job* centers on a working-class boy whose mother one morning dresses him up in his best suit and ships him to Milan to apply for a job. *One Day* and *The Job* are based on the same

The Job

polarity, the tension between man's natural inclinations and the forces of alienation in the working world. Olmi's monochromatic style, related to neorealism, also remains unchanged: he includes in his stories all the miniscule details and shows no interest in anything other than a rigorously linear approach. Yet whereas in *The Job* Olmi asks his recurrent questions with a feeling for the tragicomic essence of life, eight years later in *One Day* his tone is charged with an angry melancholy.

The Job's strongest impact results, on one hand, from its sympathetic depiction of Domenico's determination to succeed in his first job and, on the other, from its detached rendering of the bureaucratic routine. The film's purposely subdued and dedramatized style is most successful in suggesting that the life of this simple boy will follow the same patterns as that of his older colleagues, who have been deprived of their identity and sense of values by the daily routine. The sequence that most reveals the consistency of Olmi's vision shows a New Year's Eve party that the company throws for its employees. The setting is a grand ballroom, but the occasion turns out to be desperately sad and boring, pervaded by a tragicomic lack of communication.

In Olmi's next film, *I fidanzati* (The Fiancés, 1963), the essential features are again concentrated in a ballroom sequence. The principal characters are two lovers, both holding ill-paid jobs, who because of their poverty are unable to get married. They go to a dance where they find themselves surrounded by well-meaning but basically indifferent people. The realization that none of these people, or anyone else, will be able to help increases their solitude, which eventually becomes the film's main theme. The man accepts a better job in Sicily, the woman remains alone. They exchange letters full of sorrow and helplessness. Their painful reunion is portrayed in an austere style, achieving an almost perfect analysis of two isolated human beings.

Nonnarrative, formalist cinema found its most important (and almost its only) representative in the sixties in the controversial theatrical director, actor, and writer Carmelo Bene (b. 1937). An eccentric personality reminiscent of Salvador Dali and drawing on similar sources of inspiration, Bene soon attracted attention with his narcissistic, highly provocative theatrical interpretation of Camus's *Caligula,* as well as by his theatrical personalization, rather than interpretation, of characters such as Hamlet, Ubu, Pinocchio, and Faust. After the "succès de scandale" of his *Salome* at the Spoleto Festival in 1964, he published his first novel *Nostra Signora dei Turchi* (Our Lady of the Turks, 1965), which in 1968 he made into a film of the same name.

Beginning from the ossuary at Otranto, which holds the skulls and bones of 800 victims of the fifteenth-century Turkish massacre, the film departs on a fantastic voyage, mixing mysticism and farce, provocation and sentimentality. It is an outburst of eclectic, visual, operatic, and literary imagination, demanding complete submission from its viewers.

Bene's next film *Capricci* (Caprices, 1969), full of hyperbolic egocentrism, draws its inspiration from the Elizabethan horror drama *Arden of Feversham* but is equally indebted to Roland Barthes and Giacomo Puccini. Of all those who have ever dealt with the myth, his film *Don Giovanni* (1970) probably expresses its significance best.

Un Amleto di meno

Exploring his own dreams of sexuality, Bene seems to control his personal fantasies better than in his other films. Freddy Buache once observed that Bene's films resemble "a show orchestrated by a great fashion designer who is infatuated with literature."[38] On the other hand, Alberto Moravia referred to Bene's work as "desecration by dissociation, pushed beyond the point of schizophrenic delirium" and to the overall effect of *Caprices* as that of a grotesque, delirious lynching.[39]

Bene continued his surrealist experiments well into the seventies (*Salome*, 1972; *Un Amleto di meno* [One Hamlet Less], 1973; etc.). "Bene's films are visual, lyrical, and auditory cataclysms whose lavalike outpourings are of unequalled hallucinatory perversity. Their visual density and creative exuberance defy description."[40]

THE MONSTERS OF MARCO FERRERI

Marco Ferreri (b. 1928) remained an outsider during his entire career. He had left Italy during the "difficult years," unable to find backing for his controversial projects, and came back in 1961. He joined the young Italian filmmakers in their attacks against moral conventions, surpassing most of them with his biting sarcasm and an uncompromising hatred of all dogmas. Ferreri's entire life has been marked by his refusal to fit into any artistic, social, or political pattern, which made him into one of the most difficult characters of the Italian cinema.[41]

Regina, the protagonist of his first Italian feature, *Una storia moderna* (Conjugal Bed, 1963), writes on her night gown, "I am not doing it for my pleasure but for the pleasure of God." And she means it. For her, the man is just a means of obtaining the status of a married woman and later a tool for acquiring a child. The very day she finds out that she is pregnant, she discards him like a queen bee.[42] The man (Ugo Tognazzi), who has suffered a heart attack as a result of the fertilization procedure, is cast aside into a tiny room and left there to die. At his funeral, Regina does not shed a single tear. She stands there with her child in her arms, more beautiful than ever, wearing the same victorious smile we saw on her face on her wedding day. She has fulfilled her duty in life, just as her family, her priests, and her teachers had taught her. Her desire "to possess a man" was a holy one, and she has successfully passed through all the stages of the life of an Italian woman: a model daughter, a wife-mistress, and a mother.

Conjugal Bed was Marco Ferreri's first fierce attack against the family and the Italian concept of a couple. Fascinated with the bizarre and the grotesque and possessed with a Buñuelesque tendency to view the world through its distorted aspects, Ferreri created a freakish black comedy, which, in a way, had its roots in Spain in the patterns coined by the Spanish directors Juan Antonio Bardem and Garcia Berlanga.[43]

The influence of the grotesque aspect of Spanish art became still more apparent in Ferreri's second Italian film *La donna scimmia* (The Ape Woman, 1964), the bizarre story of a bearded and hairy woman (Annie Girardot), whom her husband (Ugo Tognazzi) exhibits in the streets and at country fairs. The anomaly of their relationship is brought to a conclusion when the woman dies in childbirth and the man continues to make money by showing the two corpses—hers and the child's—

Conjugal Bed

to the greedy crowds. The intention to shock, to provoke, and to offend is one of the main elements of Ferreri's aesthetics. He seeks systematically to unveil the hypocrisy of such established values as purity, civility, and heroism. Using surreal metaphors and symbolic images of object-fetishes, Ferreri attempts to demonstrate the destructive effects of false values on any human relationship. Ferreri anticipated the emergence of two of the main phenomena of the seventies: the vulnerability of the traditional couple and the male's attempt to recapture his dominant position in sexual relationships. Ferreri's grotesque portrayals of women seem to show his awareness of the fact that it is the male-dominated society that makes these women the way he shows them. Ferreri would ultimately agree that his female monsters are products of the rules invented by his male monsters, but he would not venture beyond this concession. The only conclusion he draws is that the mutual destruction of the sexes is inevitable.

"With Ferreri one gets the impression of intellectual confusion, compounded by an inability to embody his ideas in terms of film," says Richard Roud.[44] This contention seems to apply to some of Ferreri's films (e.g., *Marcia nuziale* [The Wedding March, 1961] and *L'Harem* [The Harem, 1967]). Other films he made in the second half of the sixties—*Dillinger è morto* (Dillinger Is Dead, 1969) and *Il seme dell'uomo* (Man's Semen, 1969)—present their outlandish subjects with utmost clarity and stylistic coherence.[45]

By deforming his characters to the point of burlesque absurdity, Ferreri ties in

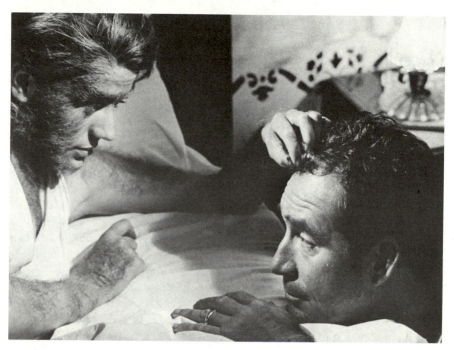

The Ape Woman

with the patterns of the theater of the absurd, represented in the sixties by Eugene Ionesco, Samuel Beckett, Fernando Arrabal, and others. Like the theater of the absurd, Ferreri makes no attempt to explore psychological motivations or to create logical relationships among the actions of his characters. However, Ferreri's freakish caricatures remain in the realm of the real world, making their perversity even more horrifying than that of the incomprehensible universe of the theater of the absurd. Ferreri's visual composition is based on the obsessive presence of objects with erotic symbolism. The objects eventually suffocate human beings, confining them in metaphorical prisons. The isolation of Ferreri's characters inevitably leads either to death or to an illusory escape. In *Dillinger Is Dead* (often considered Ferreri's masterpiece) the setting—and the "prison"—is a house equipped with every possible gadget and luxury item. The protagonist (an engineer in charge of the production of protective masks that enable one to breathe in an unbreathable environment) spends the night in a series of meaningless actions, including the preparation of an elaborate dinner and the cleaning of an old gun. Then, having viewed some 8mm films, gone through old clippings featuring the assassination of the gangster John Dillinger, and made love to the maid, he shoots his sleeping wife in the head, swims out to a sailing ship bound for Tahiti and hires himself on as a cook. The Italian film historian Paolo Bertetto concluded: "The escape to Tahiti means a total closure of all horizons, the paralysis of all possibilities; we are brought down to zero, stripped of all perspectives, and restored to the original nothingness."[46]

The isolation that results from surrounding oneself with objects becomes still more nonsensical in *Man's Semen*. The story is set on an enormous white beach in a house filled with objects that have been saved after a world catastrophe. There are electric gadgets but no electricity, toys but no children, a car but no gas. A man and a woman, survivors of the catastrophe, live in the house. The man gradually turns it into a museum of a dead civilization. His work is useless, his actions are useless, but he persists in the eternal male urge to save the world even if the world no longer exists. The woman provides food for both of them. When another woman appears on the beach and seduces the man, she kills her, chops her into pieces, cooks the meat, and feeds it to the man. The man wants to experience the ultimate manifestation of virility, to father children. He wants to do it, as Ferreri pointed out, "for society, for the world," so that his sons will perpetuate the now nonexistent human race. He repeats the same mistakes that destroyed humanity: "He will never learn anything, never overcome his immaturity and inertia."[47] The woman refuses to conceive a child. She does not care about the human race. He rapes her in her sleep and then dances naked on the deserted beach: "I have sown!" he shouts until another explosion brings to an end all the myths he has been trying to revive.

The form of *Man's Semen* is as impressive as its story. The precise and detailed narration is based on a rhythmic alternation between long views of the waterfront and close shots of the characters. The precisely timed montage creates the feeling of a vicious circle, a feeling emphasized by the rigid structure of the sequences. Their distinct beginnings and endings make more believable the potential finality of all actions: death is a possible conclusion to each of them.

TWO BELATED DEBUTS

Unlike the films of the French New Wave, which generally were preoccupied with highly stylized ways of presenting human relationships, the New Italian Cinema focused primarily on broader and more socially relevant problems. Some patterns of neorealism reappeared in these films, enriched by new visual elements and moral attitudes. The neorealist heritage was clearly apparent in *Banditi a Orgosolo* (Bandits of Orgosolo, 1961), the belated debut of Vittorio De Seta (b. 1923), already known for his excellent documentaries.

Orgosolo is a small township in central Sardinia, with stone houses built along steep narrow streets that fade out high up in the mountains. It was the ill-famed center of Sardinian gangsterism, kept alive for centuries by poverty and the silence of the people. The villagers never speak to a stranger, never reveal anything to the "carabinieri." As a matter of fact, they talk very little even to one another, and their sharply chiseled faces hardly ever reveal any emotion. Unlike the Italians, whom they consider foreigners, the Sardinians rarely smile. Sardinia is a tough country, and so is the life of its people.

De Seta structured the aesthetics of his first feature film in accordance with the characteristics of the island. He rendered the austere exoticism of the menacingly beautiful countryside with an almost motionless yet not impassive camera, favoring slow movements and few changes of angle in order to evoke an impression of

Banditi a Orgosolo

perpetual continuity. The images repeat themselves, the objects captured by the camera are changeless, and so are the expressions on the shepherds' faces. *Bandits of Orgosolo,* the story of a shepherd who has sheltered some bandits and is suspected of being their accomplice, is rooted in this static countryside. De Seta composes his images in order to make the shepherd, Michele, inseparable from the Sardinian hills and plains, his cottage, and his flock of sheep. There is nothing else in Michele's life and there never will be. When the sheep die of thirst during the flight from the "carabinieri," Michele's little brother continues to drag the sheep's drinking trough: there is no life without the sheep. Michele ends up by stealing a flock from another shepherd who is just as poor as he is. "Why do you want to ruin me?" the victim shouts after him. "They have ruined me too," replies Michele, disappearing into the mountains.

De Seta's second film, *L'uomo a metà* (Almost a Man, 1965), influenced by Antonioni, is motivated by different intentions. It attempts to visualize the inner fears of a man approaching the mid-life crisis, but it is marred by rather perfunctory characterizations. Not until the seventies, when he became one of Italy's most noteworthy directors of television films, did De Seta return to the documentarylike approach of his earlier work. His first film remains an isolated masterpiece, as untouched by the passage of time as the village of Orgosolo.

Elio Petri's *L'assassino* (The Murderer) was another belated debut of the year 1961. Since the war, Petri (1929–1982) had spent years working as a journalist, as

L' uomo a metà

a scriptwriter, and as De Santis's assistant before bringing to the screen his first independent work, a story about the alienation and the basic weaknesses of his contemporaries. Petri (in the early fifties an uncompromising, zealous critic for the Communist party press) "progresses in his films from the analysis of neurosis to the study of schizophrenia, making us aware of the fact that capitalist society generates collective traumas that affect the individual in the most serious ways."[48] To Petri's acknowledged sources of inspiration, such as Marx, Freud, and Wilhelm Reich, one would be tempted to add the name of Dashiell Hammett. Like Hammett, Petri uses the mystery genre to reveal certain features of the functioning of capitalist society. However, Petri is less successful in avoiding the traps of the stories "à thèse." In *The Murderer,* he draws a portrait of an opportunistic weakling who uses everyone, including his rich mistress, to attain his goal: a place in high society. Unfortunately, Petri's films lack visual imagination. They rarely go beyond the limits of well-narrated plots with the characters moving on a circumscribed checkerboard. Their emotional impact is weakened by the director's hesitations about what he really wants to do—mysteries, psychological studies, or political films— and this uncertainty results in a lack of style.

Among Petri's films *I giorni contati* (Numbered Days, 1963) stands out for its sensitive rendering of the final period in the life of a worker. The protagonist, Cesare, quits his job after a visit to the doctor's office: his illness has left him only a few months to live. His wandering through the streets, his longing for human intimacy, and his alienation from his wife and friends form the nucleus of the story, which is set in one of Rome's sordid working-class neighborhoods. Life has left Cesare empty-handed. The most essential thing for him has always been his work, and that is where he eventually returns: to his job repairing toilets. He dies alone, in the midst of an indifferent crowd, crouched on the seat of a tram.[49]

In the overall context of Italian cinema, Petri represented the solid middle road between cinematic art and purely commercial production. Similarly, Damiano Damiani (b. 1922)—though less ambitious and less politically committed than Petri—has from the beginning belonged to the ranks of highly regarded filmmakers who turn out good cultural products. His first two films, *Il rossetto* (Lipstick, 1960) and *Il sicario* (The Hired Assassin, 1962), are detective stories that transcend their plots through critical depiction of broader social issues. Related to the neorealist tradition (both films were coscripted by Zavattini), *Lipstick* and *The Hired Assassin* are conceived as chronicles growing out of Damiani's observation of the consumer society. Throughout the sixties and seventies, Damiani continued to direct an average of one film per year without ever attaching his name to the kind of abysmal flops that we can find in the filmography of almost any filmmaker of his status.

I giorni contati

Unlike his peers who insisted on settling their accounts with society, Florestano Vancini challenged his own generation in *Le stagioni del nostro amore* (The Seasons of Our Love, 1966). At the heart of the film is the crisis of values characteristic of a certain part of the Italian Left, which had gone through the experience of the antifascist resistance and post–World War II period and had become disillusioned with communist politics after the disclosure of Stalin's crimes and the 1956 Soviet invasion of Hungary. Vancini mixes politics with autobiography, drawing a telling portrait of an intellectual who has reached a dead end in his life. Flashbacks to the protagonist's past capture his obsession with his childhood and his early political militancy. As his youth fades away, everything that had been clear becomes unclear, obscured by doubts and uncertainty; his personal life collapses too. This story, common to all generations, gains new interest through its political references and its attempts to mix social realism with a type of psychological introspection influenced by Antonioni. The film's main asset is its relentless exposure of two dogmas—the Catholic and the communist—that affect and encircle the lives of Italians, thus constituting the basic polarity of any intellectual dichotomy.

FRANCESCO ROSI'S "TEATRUM MUNDI"

Few great personalities emerged out of the New Italian Cinema: the Tavianis, Olmi, to a lesser degree Bertolucci and Ferreri. Wertmüller and Cavani attempted a compromise between socially relevant themes and the commercial production, something that only rarely fully succeeds. Others, such as Bellocchio, Petri, Damiani, De Seta, Vancini, became well-known directors who were remembered mainly for their first or second films. Fellini, Antonioni, Rossellini, and Visconti—the four directors of international impact who came into view after the end of the neorealist period—continued their personal quest for artistic lucidity, hardly influenced by the atmosphere of the sixties. They were joined by Pier Paolo Pasolini and Francesco Rosi, who both attained remarkable achievements during this decade.

Unlike Bertolucci, the Tavianis, Ferreri, or Bellocchio, Francesco Rosi was not a rebel. When he started working on *Salvatore Giuliano,* he was almost forty years old; he had been involved in twelve films, usually as assistant director, and had made two feature films of his own. Rosi is a straightforward man, anything but a complex intellectual; his style was labeled "American" because of its approach to narrative through articulate often violent action. A native of southern Italy where the struggle for influence constitutes a substantial component of daily life, Rosi had developed a sharp eye for the structures of the world of power. His own experience made him a solid supporter of the Italian Left, but he was not an ideological man and was not interested in using film to express the intricacies of leftist politics. He knew that politics is a power game, a matter of life and death, and he was fascinated by this particular "teatrum mundi" in its postwar Italian version, as Shakespeare had been in Elizabethan England.

Was it his early apprenticeship with Visconti, his fascination with the theater, or his fling with journalism that made Rosi so aware of the fact that the politics of our time also provides its King Richards and Macbeths? Whatever his inspiration, when the overall expansion of Italian production in the sixties made room for more costly and artistically ambitious projects, Rosi used the opportunity to direct a film about Salvatore Guiliano, the famous Sicilian bandit who cast a shadow on Italian political life long after his death in 1950. Giuliano, who terrorized the Mediterranean island for seven years beginning in 1943, is only indirectly the protagonist of Rosi's film, *Salvatore Giuliano* (1961), inspired by his life. We first see his corpse, lying in a yard in Castelvetrano, and later, as Rosi centers the plot around the investigation of his death, we catch an occasional glimpse of him. From the beginning, Giuliano is a mythical figure, and as such he is powerful enough to make the investigation of the myth a thrilling dramatic experience. Rosi's interest focuses on a power struggle in which the "criminal hero" was hardly more than a pawn. Giuliano was first used by the Sicilian separatists, then by the Allies, the anticommunists, the Mafia, and by various sections of the state apparatus, even the judiciary. The evidence of this manipulation started coming together only at the trial of some of his accomplices, long after Giuliano had been murdered. But the truth remained obscure: Rosi does not pretend to have any answers to the questions surrounding the Giuliano myth. His camera, sometimes emotional, sometimes objective, reveals the drama of life and death as it had been performed in Sicily for centuries, with piles of corpses and no catharsis. Rosi's drama has no plot, no heroes. It is a drama of the discovery of patterns (though only external) in the Sicilian "way of all flesh." Rosi is not interested in *cinéma vérité* (as a matter of fact,

Salvatore Giuliano

he does not believe in it), and he has never made a real documentary. Rather, he is obsessed with the dramatic possibilities of reality, with the kind of "theatrical authenticity" of a Shakespearean play.

The approach that Rosi used in *Salvatore Giuliano* has since been imitated many times, but almost none of its imitators achieved the same kind of poetic force, a force that revealed Rosi as one of the major figures of the Italian cinema and as the creator of a new genre, the cinematic political tragedy.

Le mani sulla città (Hands over the City, 1963) earned Rosi the Golden Lion at the Venice Film Festival and the hatred of the establishment. The power structure in contemporary Italy constitutes the film's subject, its hero, and the fabric of its myth.[50] *Hands over the City* begins with a catastrophe, the collapse of an apartment house, in which many people perish. Massive corruption behind a large housing project is revealed. The city is Rosi's native Naples. Its anonymous crowds, its streets, and its social contrasts are omnipresent in the film. The central figure is the builder Nottola (Rod Steiger), a strong, ruthless man, for whom Rosi evinces a certain sympathy. But the film's true protagonist is the political machinery—and it is this protagonist that Gianni Di Venanzo's camera follows into the playhouses of the "teatrum mundi": meeting rooms, court rooms, the assembly hall, offices, bars. Its mission is to open the fourth wall on the proceedings that produce headlines in the newspapers, things that are usually revealed to us only after the fact. The trial sequence in *Salvatore Giuliano* comes to mind frequently during the film, but the drama is differently structured. The spoken word, used in the same "documentarist way" as the images of Sicily in *Salvatore*, becomes an important aesthetic component, always in tune with the authenticity of setting and the performance.

Lacking the popular myth and emotional touch of *Salvatore Giuliano, Hands over the City* does not have the same overwhelming impact. However, it confirmed the possibilities of a genre, the cinematic political drama, which has since become a permanent fixture in the Italian scene.

In 1965, Rosi went to Spain with a vague idea for a documentary and eventually returned with *Il momento della verità* (The Moment of Truth, 1965), a fiction film about bullfighting and bullfighters, about the encounter between a man and an animal—one of the essential Spanish myths. But unlike Hemingway, by whom he was admittedly inspired, Rosi blends the popular myth with an attempt to grasp the social reality behind the dreams of the impoverished masses. The film is based on the meager story of a village boy who goes to a big city (Barcelona) to escape poverty and decides to face the bull only when he realizes that all other possibilities for improving his condition are closed to him. *The Moment of Truth* contains all the features of Rosi's previous achievements except the poetic authenticity—the main resource of Rosi's aesthetic dimension. For Rosi, the southerner, Sicily had not been an impenetrable landscape (as it was, e.g., for Antonioni in *L'avventura*); nor was there any mystery in his native Naples. But in Spain he remained a tourist, a tourist with an investigative mind but still an outsider. In *The Moment of Truth*, the lack of aesthetic authenticity weakens the social argument while the myth itself does not rise above the level of an illustration.

Poetic imagination dominates still more clearly in *C'era una volta* (Cinderella

Battle of Algiers

Italian Style, 1967), a Neapolitan fairy tale that Rosi directed for Carlo Ponti with Sophia Loren and Omar Sharif in the leading roles. Rosi had intended to draw upon the surreal and grotesque aspects of the Neapolitan folklore, but his final product was a pleasant costume love story.

In 1965, Gillo Pontecorvo adopted the approach of *Salvatore Giuliano* in *La battaglia di Algeri* (The Battle of Algiers), scripted by Franco Solinas, one of *Salvatore Giuliano*'s writers. Using nonprofessional actors (with one major exception) and faithfully re-creating a historical event—the end of the French colonization of Algeria in 1954–1957—Pontecorvo did not succeed, however, in combining the imagined and the real, the fictitious and the documentary. His ideological attitude toward the material proved more radical than his cinematic form, which remained confined within conventional patterns, although producing an impressive spectacle and a strong accusation of colonialism. The film lacks cohesion as it reflects an event too overwhelming and complex to be condensed into a prevailingly didactic story, which neglects dialectical duality with its potential for an authentic tragic catharsis. *The Battle of Algiers,* in its time rightly hailed and appreciated primarily as an act of civic courage, does not stand the test of time. The one-sidedness of the ideology and the shallowness of the narration become increasingly apparent especially when compared with other films inspired by the New Left and its issues.[51]

The manicheist perspective, understandable and justifiable in the immediate postwar years, had become outdated by the sixties when a more discerning approach was required to gain an understanding of the past. Such an anachronist perspective is evident in the work of Nanni Loy (b. 1925), a good craftsman, an active filmmaker, and a devoted organizer of the film industry's unions. His two best films, *Un giorno da leoni* (One Day as a Lion, 1961), as well as *Le quattro giornate di Napoli* (Four Days in Naples, 1962), are weakened by a somewhat inarticulate narration and stereotyped characters. Preoccupied with the purity of the antifascist struggle for liberation, Loy enshrined the resistance movement in detached mythical images. Discarding the visual simplicity and candor of neorealism, he ended up with opulent Hollywood-like presentations attractive mainly for their rather monumental portrayals of Italy during the different stages of World War II.[52]

COMEDY OF MANNERS

Politics penetrated even the fifty-year-old patterns of comedy Italian style, gradually turning it into a sociocomedy of manners. In the sixties, Pietro Germi, whose appearance among the masters of the comedy came as a surprise, became the most prominent representative of this genre. In a satirical trilogy Germi tackled social inadequacies with the same pungency that had characterized his neorealist melodramas (*In the Name of the Law, The Path of Hope*). His *Divorzio all' italiana* (Divorce Italian Style, 1961) reflects the freakish absurdities of Italian society while mimicking the forces that created them. With his instinctive sense of timing, Germi structures the film so that it creates plenty of opportunities to insert gags that spot-

Divorce Italian Style

light his predilection for absurd situations arising from social insufficiencies. The story revolves around the preparations for a murder. The murderer, Ferdinando (Marcello Mastroianni), is a petty Sicilian nobleman who is in love with his cousin. In a society that forbids divorce but is indulgent to crimes of passion, Ferdinando pushes his wife into infidelity, kills her to protect his honor, and receives only a light sentence, which is applauded by his countrymen. *Divorce Italian Style* was voted one of the Twelve Best Comedy Films of All Time in an international poll of critics in 1967.

Germi's next film, *Sedotta e abbandonata* (Seduced and Abandoned, 1963), is also set in Sicily and discloses some of the most salient discrepancies in the social code through a fierce satire. In both *Divorce Italian Style* and *Seduced and Abandoned,* he succeeded in making truly popular sociopolitical films, which not only entertained spectators of all social strata but also presented serious topical problems. Germi excels in portraying Sicilian dignitaries—officials, honorable patriarchs, and voluptuous mothers. In *Seduced and Abandoned,* he added to his gallery of provincial hypocrites a shabby Don Juan who gets involved with two sisters. The seduced sister adamantly refuses to marry him and gives in only after a spectacularly staged kidnapping, which, according to unwritten Sicilian laws, provides a final and definitive reason for any marriage. In compliance with the same law, the abandoned sister has only one choice: the convent. Germi's satire is as biting as in *Divorce Italian Style,* but his overall approach is more superficial and less sophisticated.

Seduced and Abandoned

This criticism holds true still more with regard to Germi's third comedy of morals, *Signore e signori* (Ladies and Gentlemen, 1966). The ladies and gentlemen in question are the hypocritical middle class of northern Italy, and the action unfolds with a rigorous logic based on the absurd rules of provincial life. But whereas in his previous films Germi required no more than an anecdote to capture an entire social universe, in *Ladies and Gentlemen* his approach lost its consistency, and the film turned into a noncommittal recording of the provincial "sweet life."

The sixties marked a turning point in the career of Dino Risi, once an enthusiastic proponent of "pink neorealism." His films became more committed and his characters firmly rooted in a sociohistorical context. Thus, the protagonist of *Una vita difficile* (A Difficult Life, 1961) reflects some of the changes in Italian life of the previous twenty years: Silvio (Alberto Sordi) is first a partisan, then a leftist journalist, and, finally, a frightened citizen integrated into the neocapitalist system. *A Difficult Life* successfully mixes comic features with socially relevant observations, resulting in a light-hearted but accurate satire about the Italian man in the street.

Risi's analysis of contemporary manners continued in *Il sorpasso* (Speeding, 1963) where he focused on a ruthless pleasure-seeker. His stories exhibit an overall moralism, punishing deviations from certain social rules. (Bruno, the protagonist of *Speeding,* who is in love with his Lancia, is killed in a car accident.) In the years following *Speeding,* Risi continued to adapt topical problems to his own formula of

Une vita difficile

comedy of manners, eventually becoming one of the most proficient and successful Italian directors.

As other known directors turned to the genre of sociocomedy, Italian cinema was increasingly labeled *political*. This perception was undoubtedly also rooted in neorealism. Especially in the United States where from the outset the concept of cinematic art had been based on different assumptions, Italian film became a prototype of socially conscious art in the good as well as the pejorative sense of the word. The fact remains that all Italian filmmakers with any ambitions beyond the purely commercial tried to capture the problems of their time either directly or metaphorically: in dramas, melodramas, as well as in comedies and farces. These so-called political films were generally not lacking in entertainment and box-office value. On the other hand, the films that aimed purely to entertain were of such poor quality that they rarely reached the foreign market.

The commercial success of the so-called "problem films" persuaded the producers to support directors who had been labeled *difficult,* for example, Antonio Pietrangeli, who had previously been reduced to directing light comedies. In 1961, he directed *Adua e le compagne* (Adua and Her Friends), a sociocomedy inspired by the consequences of the Merlini law, the 1958 statute that closed down Italy's brothels. At that time, some of the prostitutes had tried to acquire another profession, but most of them—and this is the story of Adua—encountered social prejudices and ended up back on the streets. Skillfully mixing the serious with the spectacular, *Adua and Her Friends* was an exceptional commercial success, grossing 760 million lire in Italy alone.

One of the biggest hits of the sixties was Luigi Zampa's *Anni ruggenti* (Roaring Years, 1962), starring Nino Manfredi and inspired by Gogol's *Inspector General.* Set in 1935, the year of the fascist upsurge, Zampa's film draws a pungent portrait of a small town awakened from its somnolence by the news of an impending visit by a fascist dignitary. The narrative is structured according to the patterns of the comedy of errors, which Zampa had already mastered in the later thirties: the fascist official turns out to be a poor insurance man who loses his naïve faith in the fascist cause after being dragged through a hypocritical ceremony staged in his honor. Zampa, always at odds with any system that traps the "little man," made *Roaring Years* into a fierce satire, populating it with shrewdly observed prototypes of the period.

The Italian cinema of the sixties left a deep imprint on world patterns of filmmaking, with directors such as Antonioni, Fellini, Bertolucci, Pasolini, and Rosi influencing the film production of Europe as well as the United States. In the first half of the decade, as many as eighty directors appeared on the film scene. Few survived the pressures of the following years, but the influx of new people was stimulating for the entire industry.

The sixties ushered in a season of extremely lively polemics, which saw the return of some of the early neorealist ideas. Similar to Visconti, who as early as 1942 stressed the necessity of a human-centered cinema, the young filmmakers of the sixties called for films about people and for people who did not want to doze off in the lullaby offered by the establishment.

But the end of the sixties was disappointing with regard to the New Italian Cinema. Its decline was due to financial difficulties, to the hostility of the state, as well as to the general crisis in creativity provoked mainly by the post-1968 disillusionment. The most distressing phenomenon within the New Italian Cinema was its fragmentation, reflecting the increasing fragmentation of Italian political life and the growing dismay of a nation faced with an uncertain future. The story of neorealism seemed to repeat itself. The dream of the sixties did not survive the end of the decade, making the story of Italian cinema into a cyclic drama of rise and decline, which had repeated itself every twenty to thirty years: the first "golden age" began in 1912–1914, the second in 1941–1943, the third in 1960–1962.

IX

HIGHLIGHTS OF THE SIXTIES

FEDERICO FELLINI   *"Fellini, Fellini, what have you done with your youth? He is almost the only one who can answer without telling a lie: 'I've told everything about it.'"* [1]

At the end of Pasolini's *La ricotta,* a journalist interviewing a film director (portrayed by Orson Welles) asks his opinion of the most famous Italian director—Federico Fellini. Welles thinks for a moment and then replies: "He dances, he dances."

Fellini has danced his way through the hell and the purgatory of modern life, wearing a sadly ironic grin sometimes compared to that of Dante in *The Divine Comedy.* Dante's inspiration has also been mentioned in connection with Fellini's major films *La dolce vita* and *8½.* [2] In each we can find a Dantean guide (Marcello's friend Steiner in *La dolce vita,* the scriptwriter Daumier in *8½,* as well as Beatrice (Paola in *La dolce vita,* Claudia, the girl at the fountain in *8½*). Whereas in *La dolce vita* the journey through various stations of damnation leads to the point of no return, in *8½* a dim promise of salvation reappears in the Fellinian sky. [3]

In *Otto e mezzo* (*8½,* 1963), Fellini's own world of dreams and illusions prevails for the first time over the real world. The film's pivotal episodes take place in fantasy, and art mixes with life to a point where there is no way of telling them apart. Guido, the film director who experiences a creative and personal crisis is Fellini; and Fellini, who with *La dolce vita* had closed the book of his own youth, is Guido. Fellini attempted to exorcise his obsessions once and for all: his uncertainty with regard to religion (suggested in the scene in the steam bath where Guido asks a cardinal for advice and receives only the reply that happiness is not of this world); his relationship with women (symbolized in the "harem scene" in terms of the eternal male's search for a wife who is also a mother, a whore, and a saint at the same time); and his obsession with film (which Guido refers to as an art that "could help us, maybe, to bury all the dead things that we carry in ourselves"). In his essay "Mirror Construction in Fellini's *8½,*" the french semiologist Christian Metz wrote:

> If *8½* differs from other films that are doubled in themselves, it is not only because this "doubling" is more systematic or more central, but also, and above

221

8 ½

8 ½

all, because it functions differently. For *8½*, one should be careful to realize, is a film that is doubly doubled—and when one speaks of it as having a mirror construction, it really is a double mirror construction one should be talking about. It is not only a film about the cinema, it is a film about a film that is presumably itself about the cinema: it is not a film about a director, but a film about a director who is reflecting himself into his film.⁴

The film's content is inseparable from its reflective quality. (A successful film-maker is committed to an ambitious new production but is at a loss for ideas. He is exhausted and hounded by both his wife and his mistress. Stimulated by a famous actress, he escapes into childhood memories and sexual fantasies. He finally realizes that his artistic future lies within his own experience of life.)⁵ The cinematic build-up of Guido's crisis is achieved through a complex interplay of devices: the use of time (interdependence between the past, the present, and the future), the action (dreams are often undistinguishable from reality), and a baroque style based on an unrestricted camera and black and white shading.

8½ can be considered an anthology of Fellini's style, with jumps between shots, vertical zoom movements, aerial shots, shots against the light, and follow shots that seem to cage the protagonist within the frame. Reality is systematically subverted into dreams, and the overall illusiveness is emphasized by Nino Rota's musical accompaniment. Its theme song, a march that changes into a pensive melody, seems to express the double essence of Guido's existence. The splintered narrative, structured to unveil repressed subconsciousness, had already appeared in Fellini's previous films but never with such consistency. *8½* draws on previous cinematic attempts to capture the stream of consciousness (Resnais's *Last Year at Marienbad,* Bergman's *Wild Strawberries,* etc.) and confirms the capacity of film to express hidden features of human existence with an intensity that had previously been considered the exclusive privilege of literature. *8½* is one of the foremost achievements in the effort to make cinematic language capable of the same complexity as the traditional arts. Here, Rossellini, Antonioni, Fellini, and many of the early neorealists played a more important role than is sometimes conceded.⁶

Guido's wife Luisa, frustrated, faithful, and a hundred times betrayed, reappears as the main character in Fellini's following film *Giulietta degli spiriti* (Juliet of the Spirits, 1965). This time her name is Juliet, and she lives in a white mansion in surreal Fregene, a fashionable seashore resort. Played by Giulietta Masina, Juliet like Luisa is in love with her husband, a brilliant man whom everyone admires and who always has at least one mistress. Juliet is insecure and feels humiliated by her husband's neglect. Like all of Fellini's other films, this one too is a story of inner fears and apprehensions and of the attempt to liberate oneself from them. This time Fellini brings the fears alive in the figures of spirits, who symbolize Juliet's reminiscences, her present experiences, and her future anguishes. Sometimes amiable, sometimes repulsive, these products of Juliet's mind display the wealth of Fellini's imagination. The entire film is extremely stylized, creating a series of make-believe images with multiple meanings. The story is completely detached from reality, substituting instead fantasmagoric visions whose unnatural colors and forms suggest Juliet's instability.

But Fellini could not truly identify with the feelings of a betrayed woman. The lack of deep involvement eventually resulted in Juliet's becoming a mere reflection of the character of Guido, rehashing themes that were, in a way, a dead end. The film's extracinematic interest lies in the fact that it was intended as a gift from a husband to his estranged wife at a time when Masina's career was faltering.

In the final scene of *Juliet,* the heroine, standing at the gate of the white house, wears a smile of liberation, the same little grimace that appeared on Cabiria's face at the end of *Nights of Cabiria.* During the shooting, Fellini insisted on the perfection of this smile, having Masina do it over and over again. By this time, however, the liberation of a human mind was no longer his main preoccupation. Having reached the age of forty-five, Fellini became increasingly obsessed with the premonition of death, one of the main themes of Italian art.

In 1967, Fellini suffered a severe physical collapse. In the same year he directed one episode for the film *Histoires extraordinaires* (Tales of Mystery) based on stories by Edgar Allan Poe. Fellini's episode, entitled *Toby Dammit* (Never Bet the Devil Your Head), portrays the hallucinations and the death of an English actor (Terence Stamp) who goes to Rome to star in a film made in the Cinecittà. Charged with surrealistic visions and symbols of death, *Toby Dammit* was a preparatory exercise for Fellini's major set of variations on the theme—*Satyricon* (Fellini Satyricon,

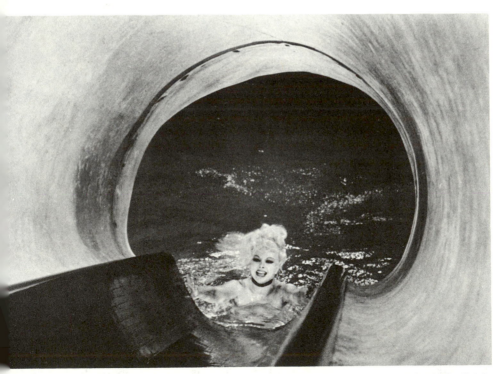

Juliet of the Spirits

1969). Inspired by stories written during Nero's reign by the Roman poet and politician Petronius (who committed suicide in the year A.D. 66), *Fellini Satyricon* is an outburst of pain provoked by man's incapacity to feel and live his own life. All of its episodes, while desperately asserting the strength of life, conclude with death. One of the most beautiful sequences (reminiscent of Steiner's death in *La dolce vita*) takes place in the "villa of suicides," where a married couple plan and accept their death not as an escape but as an act of affirmation. Another chapter shows a dinner where the host invites everyone to take part in a staged formal banquet, an advance celebration of his own death. Around these and other events, Fellini depicts life in ancient Rome, the life of a city that to "keep from dying is getting drunk on life."[7] Like *La dolce vita, Fellini Satyricon* is divided into episodes, with two young boys, Encolpius and Ascyltus, serving as guides. Fellini conceived them as predecessors of today's hippies who resemble, in his own words, "those hippies hanging around today in Piazza di Spagna, in Paris, Amsterdam, moving from adventure to adventure, even the most gruesome, without the least remorse, with all the natural innocence and splendid vitality of two young animals. Their revolt . . . is expressed in terms of utter ignorance and estrangement from the society surrounding them."[8] Fellini never pretended to be faithful to Petronius. He also drew upon other legends and myths. He "dreamed up his Petronius," as Moravia put it. Using exuberant costumes and settings (inspired not only by Pompeian art but also by African handcraft and Italian Renaissance painting), he created a tormented portrayal of a hedonistic society in the shadow of approaching destruction.

MICHELANGELO ANTONIONI

*"I wish I would not love you;
or love you in a better way."*
(Vittoria in *Eclipse*)

Fellini and Visconti reached the peak of their creativity in the early sixties (Fellini with *8½* and Visconti with *The Leopard*) and produced films of a lesser interest during the remainder of the decade. Antonioni, on the other hand, produced work of undiminishing pungency throughout this period, continuing his exploration of the decline of emotions. The four films he directed after *L'avventura* represent the gradual development of this single theme: in *La notte* (1960) the possibility of love still exists; in *L'eclisse* (Eclipse, 1962) love is eclipsed by the predominance of objects and their imagined value over human relationships; in *Deserto rosso* (Red Desert, 1964) the alienation from reality provokes a neurosis portrayed as a subconscious yearning for the return of feelings; in *Blow-Up* (1966), emotion disappears entirely and all that remains is the mystery of facts.

Lidia Pontano's walk through the streets of Milan in *La notte* has its place in any film anthology. The monumental architecture, testifying to the wealth of the city, and the noise of the hectic streets serve to underline Lidia's utter emotional confusion in her search for a love that is no more. Hoping to recapture what she once felt for her husband Giovanni (Mastroianni), Lidia (Jeanne Moreau) walks to a small hotel on the outskirts of the city where the two of them used to meet before they

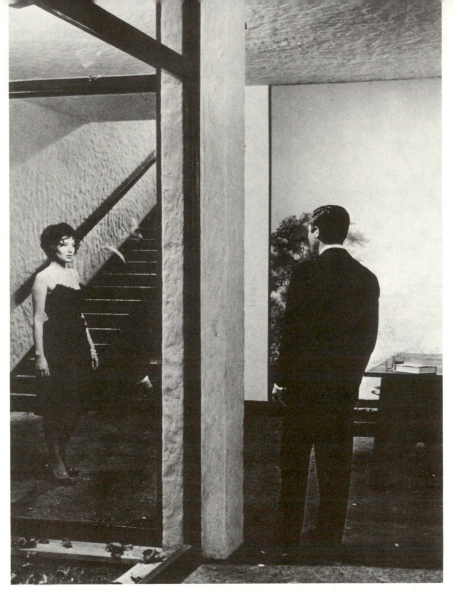

La notte

were married. But all she finds is a dilapidated neighborhood and a repulsive concierge. "I would like to die because I don't love you any more," Lidia says to Giovanni in the final sequence. They have just attended an extravagant and desperately sad party at the estate of a millionaire publisher who is trying to "buy" Giovanni, a well-known writer. It is dawn; the night is over. (The entire film takes place during one afternoon and one night.) Giovanni does not want to believe what Lidia is saying. Or he pretends not to. He pulls her down onto the grass in an attempt to recapture what used to be. As they hold each other in a tight embrace,

L'eclipse

the camera pulls back from them and then loses them, leaving in the frame only the millionaire's golf course and conveying the feeling of an utmost vacuity.

Vittoria and Piero, the protagonists of *Eclipse,* no longer pretend to love. They are aware of the fleeting essence of feelings and come to grips with what is happening to them. But the sense of solitude remains. Vittoria's walk through the streets on the outskirts of Rome at the end of *Eclipse* is a continuation of Lidia's wanderings. Vittoria has just left Piero, telling him that she will see him that evening, the following day, and the day after. He does not believe her, and she did not mean it. Vittoria passes the places where she used to meet Piero. Now, everything is empty and the streets seem to lead nowhere. Suddenly, the leading characters disappear and for seven minutes Antonioni tells his story by focusing on objects that used to have an emotional value in Vittoria's life. They pass on the screen, evoking the traumatizing realization of a loss, a void: the trees in the wind, matches in a barrel of water, the edge of the pavement, the street lamp, and so on.

The quintessential sequence of *Eclipse* takes place at the stock exchange where Vittoria meets Piero, a stockbroker. This world, where objects and their abstract values have completely disrupted human relationships, is Antonioni's hell—so different from Fellini's and yet so similar. A market recession is driving everybody to madness; the frantic atmosphere conveys the conflict between people and money. A moment of silence is observed in honor of a colleague who has died, and time seems to stop. But immediately afterwards everything returns to normal. Nobody cares about the man who died. The barriers that separate people from one another can no longer be removed. The more Vittoria talks to Piero, the less common ground they find. What ensues, according to Antonioni, is an eclipse of feelings. He once observed an eclipse of the sun, which led him to ponder the eclipse of human relationships and the silence that would follow it. ("A silence different from all other silences," he called it.)

Silence is one of the main expressive elements of *Red Desert*. Giuliana escapes into a mute neurosis whenever she can no longer come to grips with the surrounding world. In *L'avventura, La notte,* and *Eclipse,* Antonioni had used architecture to underline his characters' feelings, in accordance with his concept of "the landscape as a state of mind": the inscrutable Sicilian villages in *L'avventura,* the pompous Milanese architecture and the posh interiors of the publisher's mansion in *La notte;* the cold buildings of the modern suburban neighborhood (built in the showy style of Italian fascism) and the overwhelming space of the stock exchange in *Eclipse.* In *Red Desert,* color became Antonioni's main expressive element, endowed with a highly dramatic function. (All his previous films had been black and white.) Antonioni's "colors of sentiments" convey Giuliana's state of mind and her gradual loss of identity. The large spaces of gray and off-white emphasize her solitude just as the construction of glass and concrete underlined Lidia's dismay in *La notte.* The gray is contrasted with different shades of red, suggesting Giuliana's repressed sexuality: her bedroom is suffused in an unnatural pink; the cabin on the water, where an abortive little orgy takes place, is painted red; and in the hotel room, where Giuliana meets her lover, the red frame of the bed appears in a diagonal in several shots. Yet the basis of all the sequences is gray, the color of fog.

Antonioni deliberately changed the colors of objects and of nature to further his intention. The forest where Giuliana goes for her walks was painted white for the purpose of the film, the fruits on the street vendor's cart were painted gray, etc. Antonioni's far-reaching experiments were related to the Futurists' attempts to make colors and forms "expressive of themselves without having recourse to figurative suggestion."[9] Antonioni's visual concept in *Red Desert* was also inspired by contemporary abstract Italian painting, especially by Alberto Burri, whose canvases of the fifties and sixties were interpreted as an expression of modern man's

Deserto rosso

inability to free himself from his suffering (e.g., Burri's canvas *The Large Cello-phane* with its predominant use of white and brown on a choppy surface). On the other hand, a reciprocal influence of *Red Desert* on Italian painting cannot be ex-cluded. Burri's picture *Large White* (1968) is reminiscent of the film's color visions, especially the cracked walls against which Giuliana is repeatedly captured. (*Red Desert* was the first of Antonioni's films to be photographed by Carlo Di Palma. Beginning in 1953, all his films—except *L'avventura*—were photographed by Gianni Di Venanzo.) Antonioni is quoted as saying: "An absolute color does not exist. There is always a relation, a relation between the object and the direction of the rays that illuminate it, and between the material of the object and the psychological state of the observer; they condition one another mutually."[10]

Red Desert is set in Ravenna, the famous artistic city, and today one of Italy's most important industrial cities, where Giuliana's husband works as an engineer. He does not understand his wife's confused loneliness, which is aggravated by the ugliness of the industrial wasteland. She attempts to commit suicide, and he tries to help her with the most conventional methods. In her utter despair, she is similarly conventional: she finds herself a lover, only to run up against another wall of incomprehension. The last scene pictures Giuliana walking in a field with her little son. Vapors of unknown origin appear above the grass, dirty steaming water runs out of a faucet: yellow fumes surround the hideous chimneys of a nearby factory. "Why is the smoke so yellow?" asks the child. "Because it is poison." "So, if a bird flies over there, it will kill him?" "Yes, but the birds know it and don't fly there any more." With these words Giuliana heads out of the field and disappears from the screen.[11]

By the time he made *L'avventura,* Antonioni's style had already been fully established by his previous films, revealing its facets with the progression of the tetralogy. Since the early fifties, when he had relinquished traditional narrative, Antonioni had been increasingly concerned with capturing moments of psychological crisis rather than with telling a story, a concern that relates his work closely to contemporary literature. In 1965, with his "tetralogy of feelings" completed and his long-time relationship with Monica Vitti coming to an end, Antonioni attempted to find a new thematic framework for his recurring questions.[12] At that time, he became more and more attracted to the idea of a film set in a real desert or a jungle, places that for him represented absolute nothingness. He went in search of the most terrifying jungle and found it in the Amazon rainforest. In 1966 he wrote a script about two men looking for lost values in other civilizations who become trapped in a jungle. The producer, Carlo Ponti, rejected the final version of the script entitled "Technically Sweet" and instead offered Antonioni the opportunity to direct a film based on a short story by the Argentinian writer Julio Cortazar. Antonioni accepted when Ponti had promised to produce "Technically Sweet" immediately afterwards. Yet this next project did not materialize. (Some of its narrative elements appeared later in *The Passenger.*)

Blow-Up (1966) was shot in London, in English, with David Hemmings and Vanessa Redgrave in the starring roles. With *Red Desert* Antonioni had exhausted his subject of the failure to adjust to modern society. In *Blow-Up* the characters are integrated into modern civilization, at the price of not even attempting to understand its logic. The film uses a classic thriller plot built in cumulative episodes and sustained by the idea of the inscrutability of facts.[13] The murder in question may or may not have really occurred: no camera can ever reveal the truth of the incident — or nonincident — witnessed in a London park by a fashion photographer. He saw a young woman luring an older man into the bushes and took pictures of them. Back in the studio, he enlarged the photographs. Believing he could discern an arm with a gun aimed at the man, he returned to the park and found a corpse. He went back

Blow-Up

for the second time, and the corpse had disappeared. After a frantic inquiry into what had really happened, the photographer accepted the facts as they appeared to be, relinquishing any judgment of reality. The impossibility of distinguishing between the real and the illusory is suggested in the last scene, a tennis match with no balls, where the players pretend actually to play while the thud of the bouncing balls is heard on the soundtrack.

The puzzling tension of *Blow-Up* derives its strength from a detailed analysis of the difficulty for any human being to understand "objective reality." Antonioni adapted his style to the subject matter, replacing his characteristic slowness with fast, unexpected camera movements and lighting effects. The colors, subjective in *Red Desert,* are extremely objective in *Blow-Up,* changing just as real light does. Some critics consider *Blow-Up* one of Antonioni's most accomplished films; others, especially the British, objected to its allegedly superficial description of the English "swinging sixties," which form the background of the story. After *Red Desert,* Antonioni had moved away from words and from social scenery. London, the capital of hippies, pop art, and beatlemania, was for him a substitute for his "desert" or "jungle." *Blow-Up's* story exists in a vacuum—it could take place almost anywhere.

The original visual intensity of *Blow-Up* has not retained its traumatizing effect through the years (as have, e.g., *Girlfriends* or *L'avventura*). On the other hand, Antonioni's repetitive monologue about the mystery of intention and motive as well as his investigation of emotions have gained in strength. When we look from today's perspective at the desert in Giuliana's mind, at her loneliness in the middle of an industrialized city, or at the atrophy of human relations in *Blow-Up,* Antonioni, the most prominent representative of the phenomenological trend in film, appears almost as a prophet.

LUCHINO VISCONTI

". . . and then it will be different, but worse. We were the leopards and the lions, those who will follow us will be jackals and sheep. And all together, the lions, the leopards, the jackals, and the sheep, will always believe that they are the salt of the earth."

(Prince Salina in *The Leopard*)

His fight with the censors for the release of *Rocco* and for permission to stage Giovanni Testori's *L'Arialda* (prohibited for "obscenity") induced Visconti to leave Italy. As a matter of fact, he vowed he would never work there again. In 1961, he staged John Ford's comedy *'Tis Pity She's a Whore* for the Théâtre de Paris, with Romy Schneider and Alain Delon in the starring roles. At that time, Visconti was bound to Delon by a profound friendship, and it was primarily because of this friendship that he agreed to direct an episode for the composite film *Boccaccio '70* (1962). The lead was played by Schneider, Delon's fiancée. Visconti's episode, *Il lavoro* (The Work), inspired by a short story by Guy de Maupassant, is a small masterpiece.[14] In its protagonists—the count Ottavio and his wife Pupe—Visconti portrayed two extremely provocative types of people doomed by their origins to the bondage of money. He surrounded them with oversophisticated luxury, thus stressing the unreal essence of their relationship to the rest of the world.[15] The story of Pupe, who decides to "earn her living" by selling herself to her husband, anticipated a turning point in Visconti's *oeuvre,* which was to become increasingly concerned with the aristocracy's faded system of values. Visconti did not condemn Pupe or Ottavio. He put them in a golden cage and displayed them for all to see, not without a certain pride in their good taste and beauty.

Visconti forgot his decision never to make a feature film in Italy the very day he read the novel *Il gattopardo* (The Leopard) by Giuseppe Tomasi di Lampedusa, a Sicilian prince. Lampedusa, who had no reputation as a writer, had spent two years trying in vain to have his book published after he completed it in 1954. It was not until 1958, two years after his death, that the Feltrinelli publishing house decided to give it a try. *The Leopard*'s first modest edition of 3,000 copies sold out overnight. Within six months, the novel became a bestseller and therefore highly attractive to the film industry. But the author's widow agreed to sell the film rights only after Visconti had been signed to direct.

For Visconti, making *The Leopard* was like telling the story of his own family.

He identified with Prince Salina, *The Leopard*'s protagonist, the proud offspring of a venerable family whose coat of arms contained a dancing leopard. Visconti shared Salina's love of life and stargazing, his philosophical anticipation of death, and his acceptance of the historical changes that were disrupting his own class and his own inheritance.

Visconti's film (1963) is set in the years 1860–1862 against the backdrop of the making of modern Italy. It tells the intricate story of a Sicilian noble family caught in the turmoil of a historical transition: in 1860, Garibaldi's army landed at Marsala, ending the French occupation of Sicily; a unified Italian kingdom came into existence, and with it came the ascent of a new class—the bourgeoisie. The head of the Salina family, Don Fabrizio, is the first to understand the inevitability of the social changes. He marries off his beloved orphan nephew Tancredi to the daughter of an unscrupulous social climber, a wealthy lower-middle-class "jackal." As much as Prince Salina despises the *nouveau riche* opportunist, he recognizes that "if everything is to remain the way it is, then everything must change."[16]

The Leopard

Visconti transcends Lampedusa's novel by stressing the circumstances that led to the birth of modern Italy, particularly the betrayal of Garibaldi's revolution by the victorious middle class. This historical aspect permeates the film's last sequence, set in a palace in Palermo: princesses and duchesses dance with merchants and bankers at a magnificently staged ball, and Tancredi celebrates his engagement to Angelica, the daughter of a "jackal," while a few blocks away representatives of the new law and order execute those who wish to carry the revolution further.

For all its historical overtones, *The Leopard* is, above all, the story of Prince Salina's life and of the disintegration of an ancient family: the prince's daughter Concetta loses Tancredi, whom she loves; his sons are good for nothing; his wife, who makes the sign of the cross each time they make love, loses her authority over the family; and the old leopard himself gets increasingly tired. In the ballroom sequence, the camera follows him as he wanders among the guests. Stopping in front of Greuse's picture "Death of a Just Man," he ponders his own death, the doom of his class, and everything he has loved. The forty-five-minute-long, nonnarrative and extremely modern ballroom sequence (mercilessly massacred by the American distributor) is a foretaste of Visconti's reading of Proust, a project that he was never able to realize.

The Leopard is Visconti's most costly film, staged as a grandiose operatic spectacle: thousands of extras, superb authentic settings (an entire dilapidated mansion near Palermo was restored for the film); costumes created by Piero Tosi, the best Italian film designer; major stars in the leading roles (Burt Lancaster as Prince Salina, Claudia Cardinale as Angelica, Alain Delon as Tancredi), and authentic Italian aristocrats playing the parts of the guests at the ball. The film's original version runs for 205 minutes and is filled with exquisite images of the past. (The English version was cut by forty minutes.) The splendor and the misery of that era are re-created through a lucid analysis whose extended historical metaphor links the past to the present: to revolutions that fail, to human beings that face death in disarray, and to societies that have no place for the "leopards."

The collapse of ancient families, observed against the background of historical events, is also the topic of Visconti's subsequent films *Vaghe stelle dell'Orsa* . . . (Sandra, 1965) and *La caduta degli dei* (The Damned, 1969).[17] After seven films that had left almost no room for hope, Visconti directed these two tragedies ending with absolute damnation and excluding any possibility of a happy relationship.

In both *Sandra* and *The Damned* nobody wants to forgive or forget any longer. The past destroys them all, trapping them in a Sartrean situation with "no exit." They are all vanquished and guilty. In *Sandra*, set in contemporary Italy and loosely based on the myth of Electra, the questions of guilt are never resolved. Sandra and Gianni suspect their mother and her lover of having betrayed their Jewish father, causing his death in a fascist concentration camp. But their only proof is their own hatred, which destroys the two of them as much as it destroys those against whom it is directed. The truth of their alleged incest is never revealed either. Gianni, a stranger in the world of reason, loves his sister more than anyone else; refusing to compromise his feeling, the cherished symbol of his childhood recollections, he kills himself. Sandra remains alone, doomed to her hatred. She

The Leopard

Sandra

has destroyed Gianni's yearning for something different, and she has shattered the loving faith of Andrew, her American husband, who never understood anything of this gloomy Italian tragedy. Sandra is a typical Viscontian woman, a tragic heroine embodying the destructiveness of passions.

Visconti conceived *Sandra* as a "Kammerspiel," shot in black and white, with few actors and limited settings. He emphasized the film's claustrophobic atmosphere by locating it in Volterra, an isolated city on a rocky hill between Florence and Siena, founded by the Etruscans in the eighth century B.C. One of the film's quintessential sequences takes place in the Etruscan Museum; there, among the vases, statues, and sarcophagi, Andrew realizes that his wife, whose face bears a resemblance to the enigmatic features of the Etruscan women, may have had an incestuous relationship with her brother.

Before *The Damned*, Visconti had sometimes exempted mothers from his overall condemnation of women. In *The Damned*, the story of a family powerful enough to murder with impunity, the character of the mother joins the other Viscontian women in their damnation. The countess of Essenbeck, a modern Lady Macbeth, is raped and driven to suicide by her own son. She has committed a crime Visconti will never forgive: she persuaded her lover, a lower-middle-class "jackal," to murder the old father, the head of the von Essenbeck family.

The Damned, staged with great pomp and huge resources in Wagnerian style, takes place in Germany in 1933–1934, the first two years following Hitler's ascent to power. The rise of Nazism provides an apocalyptic background for the portrayal

The Damned

of a family of steel magnates who eliminate all their anti-Nazi relatives and end up by supporting Hitler.[18] Their self-destructive passion for power culminates at the time of the "night of the long knives," during which a thousand men who had helped Hitler in his rise to power, including the leaders of the storm troopers, were butchered on his orders. *The Damned* is one of Visconti's most impressive films where the decadence of the ruling class is dramatized to the highest pitch. Only a film-maker of Visconti's proficiency could have directed this modern version of *The Twilight of the Gods* without lapsing into caricature.

Not *Sandra*, not *The Damned*, nor even the cherished *The Leopard* absorbed Visconti's attention as much as *Lo straniero* (The Stranger, 1967), an adaptation of Camus's 1942 novel. Visconti was fascinated by its theme of lonely revolt against life and of death by one's own free choice. In the mid-sixties, when the film rights finally became available after Camus's death, no other subject attracted him more. Mersault, like Visconti's Spaniard (*Ossessione*) and Franz Mahler (*Senso*), rebelled against his surroundings; and like Gianni, Sandra's brother, saw death as an alternative to the failure of his own life.

Visconti intended to set the screen version of *The Stranger* during the Algerian war, which ended with the proclamation of Algerian independence in 1959 (the novel is set in Algiers in 1938). But Camus's widow insisted on absolute fidelity to the novel, line by line. Thus, for the first time, Visconti found himself directing a film that strictly followed someone else's visions and words. He meticulously reconstructed the old city of Algiers, where Mersault worked as a clerk in a small

The Stranger

French company; he carefully chose the beach, where Mersault casually murders an Arab, and the courtroom, where Mersault ridicules the court, defies society, and is sentenced to death.

Visconti's responsibility to the text undoubtedly weighed heavy, and the forced replacement of Delon by Mastroianni for the title role at the last minute only added to the problems. The sequences that come closest to Camus in spirit are the opening of the film, which refers to Mersault's early life through a detached, off-screen narration, and the sequence showing the murder on the beach. The courtroom sequence, closely following Camus's text, remains one of Visconti's strongest moments of social criticism. On the whole, however, the film is more a realistic illustration of the plot than an attempt to find a cinematic equivalent for Camus's approach to the problems of modern narrative.

PIER PAOLO PASOLINI   *"Either I'll kill the world or the world will kill me."*   (Vittorio in *Accattone*)

Pier Paolo Pasolini directed his first feature film, *Accattone*, in 1961. At that time he was already established as one of Italy's leading writers, probably the most important living Italian poet, a prolific scriptwriter, as well as a constant subject of scandals and trials for his homosexuality, his leftist radicalism, and his provocations of reigning taboos.[19] In the late fifties, Fellini created a production company, the Federiz, with the proclaimed goal of helping young directors. When Pasolini,

Fellini's good friend since their collaboration on *Nights of Cabiria*, decided to
direct his own scripts, Fellini immediately offered his help. Dissatisfied, though,
with Pasolini's screen tests, he dropped the project.[20] It was Mauro Bolognini who
eventually found him his first producer, Alfredo Bini, who produced all of Pasolini's films until 1969.

Pasolini's first visual exploration of the world of the "borgate" (shanty towns)
stunned the critics and the audience. Its realism was crude and brutal, distant from
the humanism of the neorealists. It had as many flaws as a first film can possibly
show, but it left no one indifferent. *Accattone* was attacked left and right: for its
ideology or its lack of it, for its style and for the absence of a style. Only those with
foresight recognized that a filmmaker had been born and a film created that would
become a constant reference in understanding the changing patterns of film language.[21] The film's central figure, Vittorio—nicknamed Accattone (beggar)—belongs to the gallery of subproletarian characters whose existence and lifestyle
occupied most of Pasolini's attention. Vittorio leaves his wife and child and goes to
live with Maddalena, a prostitute, as her pimp. He meets the innocent Stella, falls
in love for the first time in his life, and finds in her someone who loves him. He even
starts working, finding, however, no reward in the effort. He tries instead to sell
Stella into prostitution and is denounced by a vengeful Maddalena. Trying to escape on a motorscooter, Accattone runs into a car and is killed. There is no moral
judgment in the story, simply a noncommittal album of pictures of people who are
unable to cope with society as much as society is unable to cope with them.

In the mid-sixties, Pasolini published a series of theoretical articles where he
analyzed his concept of the shot as a cinematic finality. Thus, it appeared gradually

Accattone

that what might have looked like inexperience in *Accattone* was the beginning of a style. Moravia was right when he wrote, after having seen *Accattone*, that Italian literature might have lost its greatest talent to the cinema.

In 1961, Pasolini was thirty-nine years old and his ideas about film and its language were more lucid than many critics of *Accattone* thought. In his second feature, *Mamma Roma* (1962), however, he followed some of the ill advice poured on him after his debut. *Accattone*'s mythological narrative, structured by successive long shots in all their expressive possibilities, was replaced by a more dramatic plot, centered on the great actress of the Italian theater and film, Anna Magnani. This represented a radical change from just filming authentic subproletarians: Magnani, in spite of her marvelous performance, was not one of them. *Mamma Roma* is smoother and more polished, the story of a mother—a Roman prostitute, who attempts to lift her son into a higher class and fails—is told with more respect for conventional storytelling. In 1970 Pasolini said: "*Mamma Roma* is a work in which, for the first time in my life, I repeat myself. I committed this error out of sheer innocence. An innocent attitude is necessary in life, but unforgivable in the realm of aesthetics."[22]

The duality of Pasolini's philosophical and poetic world in *Mamma Roma* reappeared. His Marxist attitude with a sharp awareness of social injustice—this time as a form of protest—and his Christian poetic references used not only for the mother-son relationship but also visually were symbolized in the sequence of the son's death on a prison torture bed (directly inspired by Mantegna's painting *Cristo morto*). Vivaldi's music, used as accompaniment, generates the same inspirational power as the music of Bach, which followed Accattone to his tragic destiny.

Any remaining doubts about Pasolini's competence as a film director in his own right were dispelled after the ironic short fiction film *La ricotta* (1963), which used the crucifixion as its metaphor. The story is simple and the metaphor obvious. Stracci, a poor unemployed worker, earns a few cents as a stand-in in a trite commercial picture about Christ's life. He portrays the "good thief." During the shooting, he uses every free minute to take the food that he receives to his family. He himself overindulges on ricotta and, in fact, dies on the cross. His death is discovered at the moment when the producer visits the location with a party of upper-class guests and entertains them with a luxurious banquet.

The narrative is just part of the film's poetic message, expressed mainly through its changing style—the "true hero" of the film. Pasolini blends clichés along with the cant of the film being made (in color) with elements of slapstick, describing Stracci's character (in black and white); with a satirical observation of the film director (Orson Welles), the stars, the press, and the producer's guests; and with an almost mythical portrayal of the Roman poor. A sophisticated use of music—from the Gregorian *Dies Irae* to Scarlatti and the twist—helps to hold together this outcry against the betrayal of religion, the consumer society, social injustice, and cynicism.

La ricotta was Pasolini's contribution to a composite film by four directors, entitled *Rogopag* (the remaining three episodes were directed by Rossellini, Godard, and Gregoretti), and it immediately unleashed a scandal. (*Mamma Roma* had already been seized by the local police during the Venice Film Festival, and neo-

La ricotta

fascist youths assaulted Pasolini, Laura Betti, and others after the film's Roman premiere). Pasolini was brought to trial and given a suspended four-month jail sentence. The court based its verdict on a law from the fascist era concerning "the defamation of the state religion."[23]

Yet Pasolini soon proved that he was anything but a militant atheist interested in attacking religious myths and feelings.[24] In 1960—a few years after the publication of his collection of poetry *The Nightingale of the Catholic Church*, Pasolini visited with his friends the "Pro Civitate Cristiana," an ecumenical lay Catholic community in Assisi. This was the peak moment of John XXIII's pontificate, which helped to change the image of the church and deeply influenced Italian life. At the "Pro Civitate Cristiana," Pasolini reread St. Matthew's Gospel after many years. Soliciting the help of the "Pro Civitate Cristiana," Pasolini then wrote to Lucio S. Caruso, its film consultant:

> I read it at that time as you read a novel, in one stretch. Exalted as I was about this experience. . . . I got the idea of a film. . . . I do not believe that Christ is the son of God because I am not a believer—at least not a conscious one. But I believe that Christ is divine. I believe that humanity, which is in him, is so high, so rigorous, and so ideal that it can attain the common human goals. For that reason I speak about "poetry"—the irrational instrument capable of expressing this irrational feeling of mine about Christ.[25]

From the outset, *Il vangelo secondo Matteo* (The Gospel According to St. Matthew, 1964) was conceived as a re-creation of a myth, not as its demystification, "as the image of Christ's life plus two thousand years of tales about Christ's life."[26] The film follows closely the loose narrative and the text, which Pasolini considered the

The Gospel According to St. Matthew

most socially critical of the four Gospels. The nonprofessional cast, the landscape of the Italian south, and the expressions on people's faces suggest the predominance of the neorealist impulse, which was always Pasolini's main aesthetic reference.[27] The other experience, equally important, results from the mythology, as it has been created and re-created through all kinds of poetic languages. Piero della Francesca, Masaccio, and Duccio are among Pasolini's aesthetic models here. (Musically, the film uses Bach, Weber, Mozart, Prokofiev, a Creole mass, and Negro spirituals.) "I want to create a purely poetic work," Pasolini wrote to his producer, Alfredo Bini, "even at the risk of lapsing into aestheticism."[28] The result—an astonishingly coherent stylistic mixture of mythology and neorealism—catapulted Pasolini to world fame overnight.[29] Jean-Louis Bory, the late French film critic, wrote:

In front of this admirable film, one is eventually unable to resist thinking of Caravaggio. He too dramatized the holy story through the mere force of his glance, which first saw reality and then staged it through an interplay of light. He too provoked a scandal because his Matthew, of all people, had dirty feet and because Joseph, fleeing to Egypt, took along with him a flask of wine corked with a piece of paper; and because he took for models gigolos (the same reproach was made of Pasolini). All that, thank God, did not prevent Caravaggio from painting. And it will not prevent Pasolini from making films.[30]

In the mid-sixties, Pasolini summed up his film experience in a series of articles.[31] It is difficult to tell whether he did it to further develop his work or to answer some of the leftist critics who concentrated, to a large extent, on the subjects of his films. It is also beyond the scope of this book to discuss Pasolini's forays into the field of structuralist linguistics. But a few things must be said concerning his conclusions, which profoundly marked his later work.

The shot, uninterpreted and sacred, was for Pasolini the beginning of all things. "There is nothing more sacred than a slow panoramic shot, mainly in the hands of a novice," he proclaimed.[32] Yet already in *The Gospel According to St. Matthew*, Pasolini transcended this concept of "technical sacrality," replacing it, to some degree, with his concept of "cinema as poetry," based on a highly personalized system of signs. In an essay with that title, Pasolini affirmed the primacy of linguistics over aesthetics and of aesthetics over ideology.[33] He contended: "While the activity of a writer consists of aesthetic discoveries, the activity of a filmmaker is, above all, linguistic, and only then aesthetic. . . . Film is, above all, an artistic nonphilosophical language." He stated his belief in "personal films," in the function of the poet who rediscovers the myth and the technical awareness of form. Answering critics of his "theory of the sacred shot," he remarked about montage: "Death transforms life into a blazing montage. . . . Montage processes the film material in the same way as death processes life."[34]

Pasolini remained faithful to his concept of image/sign, which makes the spectator enter an uncertain relationship with reality. His "cinema of image" preferred the long shot, keeping the spectator always at a distance and leaving the choices open. Later, Pasolini operated the same way, even when his paradigm included different kinds of myths and cultural references, as, for example, in his subsequent film *Uccellacci e uccellini* (The Hawks and the Sparrows, 1966).

At the beginning of their picaresque journey, Totò and Ninetto (Pasolini's last subproletarian protagonists) meet a raven who comes from the Country of Ideology and lives on Karl Marx Street.[35] The journey takes them through a neorealistic, poeticized poverty, through an ironic re-creation of the evangelization of birds by St. Francis and to a metaphoric participation at the funeral of the communist leader Palmiro Togliatti (newsreel shots). At the end, they eat the raven and continue their wandering. Most of the time, the raven had been talking like an old and spent Marxist ideologist. Did Totò and Ninetto eat the bird because "this is the end of the era of Brecht and Rossellini," because "ideologies are no longer fashionable, and here is one who talks and talks not knowing what he is talking about"? Or did they eat him because Marxism can remain alive only if it integrates "the shame of the Third World, the Chinese, and, mainly, the immense history of mankind and the end of the world—including religious feeling"? Or, because, eventually, "a professor is a good professor only if he eats up another professor"?[36]

The Hawks and the Sparrows

The Hawks and the Sparrows (considered by Pasolini his purest film and by many his masterpiece) was filmed in a style reminiscent of neorealism with stylized elements such as Totò's acting, the talking raven, and different visually mediated philosophical, historical, and political references. The film is Pasolini's farewell to the world of the subproletariat as well as to the first part of his *oeuvre*.

In 1966 and 1967, Pasolini directed two short films: a little gem entitled *La terra vista dalla luna* (The Earth Seen from the Moon) and *Che cosa sono le nuvole* (What Are the Clouds). Both were originally intended as episodes for a composite film conceived as Pasolini's "homage" to Totò. After Totò's death, they were included in two composite films—*Le streghe* (The Witches) and *Capriccio all'italiana* (The Italian Capriccio).

After exhausting one source of his experience and elevating reality to the heights of myth, Pasolini turned to classical myth. It is not surprising that the first one he chose was that of Oedipus. *Edipo Re* (Oedipus Rex, 1967) is probably Pasolini's most suggestive film. There his concept of poetic cinema finds its most comprehensive and finished expression. The myth itself—the story of the son of the king of Thebes who, in spite of everyone's efforts to counter it, follows step by step the prophecy that he will kill his father and marry his mother—is surrounded by two episodes, both shot in the locales of Pasolini's own childhood. In the first episode, set in a country house in Lombardy, we see an Italian officer hanging his baby son by the feet to punish him for stealing his wife's affection. In the second, a kind of epilogue to the film, the blinded Oedipus, led by a young messenger, wanders throught the streets of Bologna ("the city where I started writing poetry and where, most naturally, I found myself integrated into bourgeois society").[37] Oedipus sings to the workers and finally returns to his native house to die there. The actual story of Oedipus was filmed in Morocco where, according to Pasolini, things and nature have few essential colors.[38] The first part, which ends with the killing of Laius and Oedipus's return to Thebes, is a true masterpiece, confirming Pasolini as one of Italy's leading filmmakers. Unlike the retelling of the myth of Christ, the myth of Oedipus was approached from an entirely subjective point of view. ("I tell the story of my Oedipus complex. I narrate my life—mythified, of course—made epic by the legend of Oedipus.")[39] The avowedly didactic ending expresses Pasolini's belief that man must face his fate, live with it, and attempt to transcend it. Eventually, even this subjectivity is sublimated. As Marc Gervais put it: "The film is nothing less than an outcry of the universal man who, in pain and disarray, faces the mystery of life."[40]

The myth in *Teorema* (1968) is entirely Pasolini's own.[41] He wrote it as a play and as a novel before he turned it into a filmscript.[42] Shot in Milan, the film begins with a newsreellike sequence (in black and white) showing an industrialist abandoning his factory to his workers. We meet his family—cultivated and rather sympathetic people—well established in its bourgeois comfort, with two grown-up children and a peasant woman as maid. This almost perfect order is disrupted by the unexpected visit of a handsome unknown young man. He lives with the family for a while, seduces all the members of the household, revealing to them their hidden sexuality, and leaves. Their world has been destroyed beyond repair. The daughter is subject to fits and has to be confined in an institution; the son becomes an action painter denying the meaning in art; the maid turns into a levitating saint and is eventually buried alive in her village; the mother grows into a nymphomaniac; and the father, after relinquishing his property, sheds his clothes at the Milan Central Railway station, and—the last we see of him—walks into a desert.

The paradox of the title resides in the fact that this theorem's logic rests entirely within the realm of the irrational, that is, of sex and religion. Thus, *Teorema*'s parable of contemporary capitalist society and its shaky values concerns itself

Teorema

again with Pasolini's main theme of the "sacred."[43] His language here tries to do justice to the orderly, elegant, and reassuring world of the bourgeois family, sheltered from everything disagreeable and unpleasant. Its brutal disruption by an uncontrollable force is expressed through an aesthetic collision between the preordained reassuring geometry of the image and the cataclysm occurring within the people who live in that world. This aesthetic concept is ideological, and the question was immediately raised whether the undramatic structure did not make it difficult for Pasolini's work to be understood by audiences.

Teorema was seized for obscenity at the Venice Film Festival. Pasolini won the trial that followed. The conflict split even the Catholic hierarchy.[44] In retrospect, *Teorema* remains an important, challenging film, whose ambiguity and complexity confirms Pasolini's success in using the cinema to deal with some of the mysteries of human existence.

In *Porcile* (Pigpen, 1969), the ideological poetic metaphor is carried further, along with a visual rendition of an essentially didactic literary parable. "My imagination has become less realistic," Pasolini told Gian Piero Brunetta, referring to *Pigpen* and *Teorema*.

I have to make believable and acceptable things that are everything but that, and I have to do it through a tightly woven narrative. Therefore, I must use a different technique. I began by using a technique that would grasp and devour reality. Now I use the camera to create a kind of rational mosaic to make a completely crazy story acceptable. My technique must bring to the surface the spiritual aspects of objects and not my inner self. This technique is a method of stylization and a reduction of various elements to their essentials."[45]

Divided into two fables, *Pigpen* is a metaphor about human society striving for order and conformity throughout the centuries and rejecting, punishing, and destroying those who do not live by its rules. In an uncertain, distant century, a young man climbs the slopes of Mount Etna, slowing dying of hunger. Finally, he chooses the road of cannibalism—the ultimate gesture of anarchy—and becomes a global rebel. He is thrown to the dogs as punishment. In the other fable, a son of a powerful German industrialist is devoured by the pigs with whom he liked to have sex; he refuses the help of a young rebel woman and integration into the world of the alliance between the old and the new capitalism. The style of the two parts is extremely different. The first episode is dynamic, barbaric, almost without words (with the exception of the protagonist's last utterance before his death: "I killed my father, I have eaten human flesh, and I tremble with joy"). The second part is static, visually reassuring, wordy, Brechtian. The film expresses Pasolini's own anarchic and pessimistic comment on the revolt of the young generation that swept Europe in 1968. To some extent, its aesthetic strategy is close to that of *The Hawks and the Sparrows*, and the concept of the cinema of poetry is brought here to its extreme.[46]

Between 1968 and 1969, Pasolini traveled to India and Africa. Whereas his *Appunti per un film sull'India* (Notes for a Film on India, 1968) is limited to his

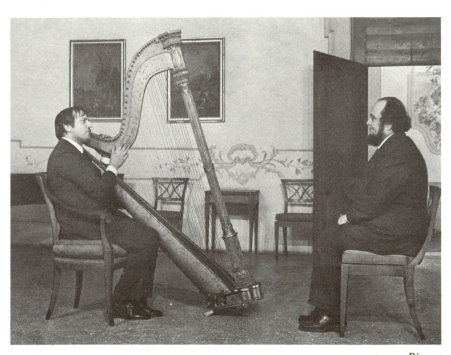

Pigpen

reaction to the subcontinent, *Appunti per una Orestiade africana* (Notes for an African Orestes, 1969) represents a revealing part of his life. Always attracted to ancient myths, Pasolini intended to make a film situated in Africa, a continent that he thought had reached the same historical turning point in our century as did Argos at the time of Orestes.[47] In the splendid documentary *Notes for an African Orestes*, Pasolini looked at Africa through the prism of Aeschylus, adopting a visually eloquent style. (The sequence that best translates his powerful imagination is that of the furies, the goddesses of vengeance, represented as trees tossed by the wind.)

Orestes, however, did not become the protagonist of Pasolini's other confrontation with the sacred world of antiquity. It was instead *Medea*, filmed in 1969. Medea's tragedy is the tragedy of a woman, powerful in her natural context but deprived of her powers when she exchanges the sacred horrors of her own barbaric world for the profanity of Western civilization, visualized in the film in the juxtaposition of prehistoric Asia and late-medieval Italy. She eventually regains her power but only to carry out her terrible revenge. Pasolini, once again, used the myth to further his own poetic metaphor, this time less personal: he centered on the conflict between the Western world and the Third World and on the changes in human attitudes that occur after nature has ceased to be sacred and has become "just natural."

As in *Oedipus Rex*, the re-creation of the barbaric world of the original myth belongs among Pasolini's most striking cinematic achievements. Again, he used elements and props from different epochs and civilizations with the results attaining a power of imagery rarely before seen in the history of Italian filmmaking. In the second part of *Medea*, when the action moves from its Turkish location to the splendors of the castle of Pisa and to a monumental Syrian castle, aestheticism prevails over immediacy. Pasolini's complex metaphor is blurred, and the impact of his most polished film weakens. The casting of Maria Callas in the title role also raised questions whether Pasolini was not already deliberately using some of the tools of commercial cinema.[48]

Between 1961 and 1971, Pasolini established himself as one of the most interesting and original filmmakers. He was firmly persuaded that cinema can express the same range of problems and emotions as traditional art forms and that a film is essentially authored by one creative mind. As Geoffrey Nowell-Smith said:

> If we examine the cinematic work of Pasolini, . . . we can see that he was an "auteur." He started as a writer; he became a film director; his work acquired a bunch of themes that can be objectively defined; and beginning with *Oedipus Rex*, he enters a process of autodescription through the discourse of his films — even as obviously, as through his presence as an actor and as a voice off. . . . But he is not an auteur like Bergman, Fellini, Antonioni, Hitchcock, or Welles, or even Ivens. He does not resemble any of them. He is an auteur like Pasolini. He is, or this is Pasolini.[49]

X

THE CHANGING IMAGE OF THE
MOVIES (1970–1982)

"And after that everything will be different, but worse," Prince Salina, *The Leopard's* protagonist, liked to say during his philosophical moments. The melancholic resignation of the "old leopard" seems to be echoed in many Italian film reviews and books dealing with the 1960s and 1970s.

The sixties actually died in 1968. Lorenzo Quaglietti gave an account of the 1968 events that wrecked almost all the Italian film institutions and agencies.[1] In March 1968, a group of filmmakers and film technicians left the National Association of Italian Filmmakers (ANAC) in protest against its increasing political involvement and created their own organization (AACI).[2] In September of the same year, the International Venice Film Festival (founded in 1932) closed its doors in the wake of severe criticism from spectators, journalists, and filmmakers.[3] One resignation followed another. Demonstrators occupied the Institute LUCE and the Centro Sperimentale di Cinematografia. At the Centro, students succeeded in forcing the appointment of Roberto Rossellini as the school's president. The struggle for better working conditions and greater artistic freedom lasted well into the seventies, becoming part of a broader political discussion about the future of Italy in general and the feasibility of Italy's independent road to socialism in particular. Then everything, or almost everything, returned to normal, to the way it had been. Apart from innumerable printed pages, only a few films were left to preserve the memory of the spirit of 1968 and of its sudden death.

Were the seventies really as bad as the general consensus seems to indicate? They were definitely different from the years before 1968. Too many hopes had been crushed, not only in Italy but also on the barricades in Paris and in the streets of Prague, and the inevitable result was disillusionment and a loss of enthusiasm. The late sixties saw not only a decline in the Italian cinema but also the end of the New Waves in filmmaking in the United States, France, England, and Czechoslovakia. In Italy, the libertarianism of the sixties and the political radicalism of the end of the decade resulted in new attempts to stabilize the society around its political center: this time with the help of the radical Left, which had been forced by the

Soviet occupation of Czechoslovakia and the Chilean experience to reassess the situation. The "children of 1968," on the other hand, continued to try to unsettle this kind of deal, eventually turning to different leftist and rightist radical organizations. This new polarization generated widespread conformism on the part of a new majority, drawn from a broad range of the political spectrum.

The seventies still managed to begin with a number of interesting films, such as Bertolucci's *The Conformist,* Maselli's *An Open Letter to an Evening Paper,* Bellocchio's *In the Name of the Father*, Ferreri's *The Audience*, Antonioni's *Chung Kuo*, the Tavianis' *St. Michael Had a Rooster*, Petri's *Investigation of a Citizen Above Suspicion,* etc. Despite the end of the "easy dollars" of the 1960s with the departure of the American film producers (hastened by Italy's growing inflation and by the decline of the dollar on the European market), the Italian film industry continued for some time to do better than many of its European counterparts. In Italy, attendance figures and the number of films produced started diminishing drastically only in the mid-seventies. The Italian love for going out would not disappear overnight. Yet changing lifestyles, together with inflation and growing violence in the streets, eventually led even the Italians to put on their slippers and to stay home to watch television. (Women in the northern cities were the first to desert movie houses whereas the most faithful moviegoers proved to be older men in the south.) By 1974, 80 percent of Italians owned a television, and approximately half of them watched television every day. Toward the end of the decade, the attendance figures shrank by another 38 percent, and the annual production of feature films fell correspondingly from 198 to 120.

Then the "old leopards" began to die—De Sica and Germi in 1974, Pasolini in 1975, Visconti in 1976, Rossellini in 1977—and the two who remained, Antonioni and Fellini, seemed to be past the peak of their creativity. The void was immeasurable, and none of the new talents seemed adequate to fill it. Among the young directors, there was a marked swing toward television, which was capable of providing more money and more stable work. Only three directors of the 1960s generation lived up to the promise of their early films, Olmi and the Tavianis. The crisis in the film industry, which the Italian critics had been forecasting for some time, suddenly became very real.

In 1972, the first terrorist bombs exploded in Italian cities and the first assassinations of establishment figures by terrorists took place. Along with Germany and Japan, the other two countries defeated in World War II, Italy began experiencing "a series of sinister absurdities punctuated by moments of sheer horror."[4]

Some of the dilemmas of the post-1968 period are reflected in Francesco Maselli's *Lettera aperta a un giornale della sera* (An Open Letter to an Evening Paper, 1970), which challenged the growing conformism of the Italian Left. The film's protagonists—all of whom belong to the communist intelligentsia—sign petitions and draw up declarations but avoid any actions that could jeopardize their personal comfort. When they send an open letter to a newspaper offering to enlist as volunteers for the Vietcong, none of them takes this pledge seriously. But their letter arouses a national and international response, and they are forced to face the con-

Lettera aperta a un giornale della sera

sequences. It is finally the Communist party that decides against their expedition, leaving them with mixed feelings of rage and relief.

An Open Letter, conceived as a series of situations and shot mostly with a hand-held camera, is one of Maselli's most successful films. The plot develops through discussions in the group, party meetings, etc., edited to music and relying on changes of rhythm. Multiple layers of metaphor emerge out of the maze of ideas, characters, and events, suggesting a complex sociopolitical background and transcending the film's immediate topicality. Like Godard or Straub—though his approach is quite different—Maselli succeeded in graphically portraying political and ideological problems, which his camera rendered as existentially important, like those dealt with, in a similar way, by Antonioni or Bergman.

In the light of Maselli's achievements, one cannot help regretting his long periods of silence. He spent the years before and after *An Open Letter* mostly in organizational activity for the ANAC and the Italian Communist party (in the mid-seventies it almost matched the strength of the ruling Christian Democrats). Maselli's next film, *Il sospetto* (The Suspect, 1974), again deals successfully with politics and recent history, this time in terms of mystery and myth. The year is 1934, the fascists control Italy, and the antifascists—in this case the communists—are operating underground and from abroad. The communists are pursued not only by Mussolini's special squads, the OVRA, but also by their own comrades, who carry out the policies of the Komintern to the letter. Only at the completion of a refined mosaic encompassing past and present—memories and immediate experience— is the truth fully revealed. Maselli's protagonist, a "professional revolutionary"

Il sospetto

dispatched from France to expose a traitor among four members of an underground group, was himself politically suspect. The party has sent him to his own death, at the same time leading the fascist police to the other four. The "hero," the primary victim, does not have to be told. He knows. His only ironic victory is to claim to his fascist jailors that he was aware of the frame-up from the outset.

Like Maselli, Gianni Toti (b. 1924) went beyond the narrative level in using film to express philosophical and moral concepts. His first film, . . . *e di Shaul e dei sicari sulla via da Damasco* (On the Road from Damascus, 1974), is an archetypical example of this notion of the medium. Toti, a poet, a journalist, and the author of several novels, used film as a vehicle for his lifelong discussion of the world's fundamental injustices. *On the Road from Damascus* is a meditation about the values of primitive Christianity as compared to the original values of Marxism. It unfolds through the story of Saul (Paul), who in the year A.D. 33 was sent to Damascus to suppress the Christians and instead became one of them. Picking up a theme abandoned by Pasolini, Toti creates a penetrating parable about a prophet and revolutionary, criticized, tortured, and misunderstood by everyone, even his own people. *On the Road from Damascus* is an avant-garde visual poem, evoking complex parallels with the present. It is filled with suggestive images of Middle Eastern life, its poverty, never-ending suffering, and the hopeless desert within and without.

Whereas the release of Maselli's and Toti's innovative films remained quite limited, Elio Petri, another exponent of "political cinema," enjoyed considerable box-office success. In his films, politics was not a subject but an object, approached on the level of narrative and entertainment. His *Indagine su un cittadino al di sopra di ogni sospetto* (Investigation of a Citizen Above Suspicion) was one of the biggest

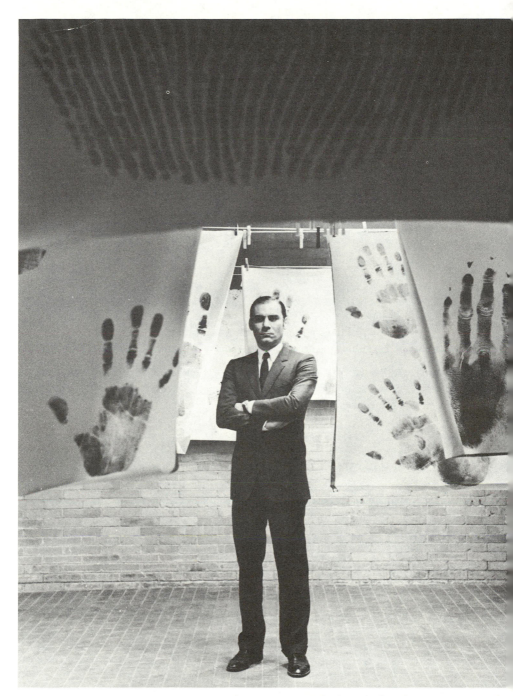
Investigation of a Citizen Above Suspicion

hits of 1970. In a country where everyone loves to hear and talk about government corruption, Petri's story about a police officer (involved in the suppression of young radicals) who murders his mistress and with the help of his superiors remains "above suspicion" found an enormous public response.[5]

Petri's transcription of Leonardo Sciascia's well-known novel *Todo modo* (1976) also received widespread, though controversial, attention.[6] Petri shifted the milieu from the high clergy to the political arena, endowing his protagonist (a high-ranking priest in Sciascia's novel) with the features and attitudes of the Christian Democratic leader Aldo Moro.[7] The plot centers around a fictitious annual gathering of the key members of the ruling class in the "Center for Spiritual Exercise": over a hundred bankers, company presidents, and members of the government meet to discuss their strategy for the future. Before the convention is over, they all mysteriously die, one after another, in spite of a massive police investigation. The destruction that the establishment generates has turned into self-destruction.

Todo modo embodies Sciascia's conviction that all systems of government are self-corrupting. Comparing the Italian political system to a "beheaded serpent," Sciascia pointed out:

> It is a system of lies: a huge machine that gulps down all the truths and spits out lies. The state will end up identifying with this machine, if this has not already happened. It will have nothing in common with the people, with the notion of human beings in which we still believe and which still exists in literature.[8]

Todo modo, like all Petri's better achievements, reveals the surface of social phenomena rather than observing their effects through the prism of individual fates. In Petri's weaker films, such as *La classe operaia va in paradiso* (The Working Class Goes to Heaven, 1971), his lack of interest in tackling the interaction of social problems with personal drama becomes a definite liability. *The Working Class Goes to Heaven* is a rather heavy-handed parable about the workers' social and political situation. Its protagonist, a young factory worker, who is gradually destroyed by the routine of work and by the inconsistency of his "class consciousness," is neither a character with whom one can identify nor a part of a stylized "Brechtian" concept. "The poor are doomed, there is no heaven for them" is the plaintive message of Elio Petri and Ugo Pirro, his longtime scriptwriter. But their protest is stifled by the film's confused metaphor and the authors' own uncertainty about their stylistic mode.

At the end of the seventies, Petri relinquished his straightforward commentary on the flaws of public life and turned toward more private topics. In *Buone notizie* (Good News, 1980) he attempted, unsuccessfully, to present personal introspection in the guise of a thriller. Petri's prevailing attitude was always moralistic, and *Good News* turned into a somewhat naïve treatise about sexual obsessions and the fear of death. Throughout his career, Petri enjoyed constant critical support, seemingly a prerogative in Europe for directors who question the assumptions of bourgeois life. Polemical consistency remained Petri's main merit, and he had a remarkable ability to turn out a successful topical product whenever there was a call for it.

The Working Class Goes to Heaven

Like Petri, Florestano Vancini vacillated between profound insight and contrived, plot-dominated scripts. In 1973, he directed *Il delitto Matteotti* (The Assassination of Matteotti), based on the 1924 assassination of the antifascist Giacomo Matteotti.[9] The subject is handled with verve, but the overall value of the film is somewhat questionable. Vancini limits himself strictly to narrative without attempting to explore the shift of the balance between the fascists and their opponents before and after Matteotti's murder. *The Assassination of Matteotti* remains a reconstruction of a fateful event, carried out with meticulous accuracy.

In the early seventies, with the death of several leading fascist figures, the walls of silence concerning Italy's fascist past were broken down still further. In the resulting atmosphere of introspection, a whole series of films dealing with fascism was produced. Marco Leto's (b. 1931) *La villeggiatura* (Holiday Making, 1973), set on a tiny island off the Sicilian coast to which the fascists exiled some of their enemies, gained immediate critical recognition. Some saw in it a successful bridge with the neorealist past in terms of both technique and artistic mode. Like the neorealists, Leto did not merely "reconstruct." He created an image, a feeling of the past, with his eyes turned toward the present. *Holiday Making's* protagonist, a liberal university professor, continues to enjoy many privileges of his social status in his exile and almost succumbs to the temptation to take a "moral vacation." Only gradually is his conscience reawakened to the fact that while his wardens—particularly the commander of the island—may be perfectly capable of sustaining an intelligent conversation of an evening, they are killers and torturers during their working hours.[10]

Among the directors of explicit political films, Francesco Rosi has been the most consistent and has received the most recognition internationally. His *Uomini contro* (Just Another War, 1970), based on famous eyewitness memoirs, went much further than Monicelli's *The Great War* in directly attacking military glory and the blind obedience required by military discipline.[11] The film is also a commentary on at least two of its well-known precursors—Kubrick's *Paths of Glory* and Losey's *For King and Country*. In contrast to their essential pacifism, Rosi offered a more concrete condemnation of the Great War, deploring the senseless deaths of masses of illiterate peasants who were sacrificed in the name of a nationalism that meant almost nothing to them. Philosophical viewpoints toward the war are counterposed in a conflict between a stupid, conceited general who sees his men only as tools in his own quest for medals and two idealistic young officers—one a socialist, the other a bourgeois idealist. But unlike early Soviet films that shared a similar perspective, *Just Another War* ends tragically: the young socialist officer dies a senseless death, and the idealistic lieutenant is sent before a firing squad to pay for his lack of military virtues.

Rosi shot most of the film in Yugoslavia, the coproducing country. *Just Another War* was the first large-scale color production dealing with World War I, and Rosi skillfully explored the diverse possibilities offered by the medium. It is the color, however, that is probably largely responsible for a certain coolness and decorative quality of the film.

In *Il caso Mattei* (The Mattei Affair, 1972) and *Lucky Luciano* (1973), Rosi continued his exploration of the avenues of power. He again used the format of criminal investigation, which had been his trademark since *Salvatore Giuliano.* Enrico Mattei was probably the first great self-made industrial mogul of international stature in post-World War II Italy. As the head of the state-owned ENI, Italy's largest petrochemical concern, he successfully defied the national and international authorities until he died in a mysterious plane crash in 1962. An official investigation concluded that the crash was an accident though many believed it was sabotage. In any case, Mattei's death was not Rosi's primary interest—he was interested rather in elucidating the relationships "between the oil-producing countries, the oil-consuming countries, and the companies that actually look for the oil, dig it out, and sell it."[12] The inquiry into Mattei's death provides Rosi with a dramatic situation, which he approaches—very successfully—from a detached perspective. Some hailed the film as a masterpiece (it was awarded the Grand Prix at Cannes in 1972) while others felt that Rosi had failed to realize his original intention.

This same criticism can more accurately be applied to *Lucky Luciano.* The subject matter is again power, this time with the accent on the mediocrity of those who wield it. Rosi uses Lucky Luciano, a famous figure of organized crime, as the vehicle for an inquiry into the methods of the Mafia. In the United States the film was literally ruined by being presented (after extended cuts) as a gangster movie, which it definitely is not. Neither is it a film where the puzzle becomes a drama itself. Rosi saw traditional narrative forms as a dead end for the contemporary

Uomini contro

artist and believed that only a blend of fiction and nonfiction could provide a way out. He applied all his usual skill to the task, but in *Lucky Luciano* he did not succeed in finding the appropriate mixture.

In 1975, with *Cadaveri eccellenti* (Exquisite Corpses, 1975), Rosi turned to fiction for his inspiration. Leonardo Sciascia's short novel *The Context* provided Rosi with refreshing poetic freedom, liberating him from the constraints of the

The Mattei Affair

semi-factual investigative format. The novel, set in an unnamed country, concerns a series of assassinations of judges, designed to destabilize the power structure and pave the way for a coup. As in *Salvatore Giuliano,* Rosi found a poetic myth, and around it he created a mythical country called Italy, which served primarily as a recognizable backdrop for the metaphoric plot. One can criticize *Exquisite Corpses* for a certain degree of literariness, but as Rosi always plays his game fairly consistently, this eventually becomes an asset. At the end of the film, however, Rosi steps out of literature: the investigator meets secretly with a representative of the opposition (the secretary of the Communist party in the film) to reveal to him what he has found out. An assassin kills both of them; but the official version of events— which the party also finds preferable—reports that the investigator killed the party secretary and then committed suicide. We are again in the middle of Italian political reality, and this time Rosi's recipe for mixing fiction with nonfiction is a success, making *Exquisite Corpses* his best film since *Hands Above the City.*

Rosi was less lucky with the legendary book of Italian antifascist literature, Carlo Levi's almost perfect blend of fiction and nonfiction *Cristo si è fermato a Eboli* (Christ Stopped at Eboli, 1979). The film fell victim to the attempt to square the circle: to serve the aesthetic requirements both of a television series and of a wide-screen film. The use of color has always been one of the major deficiencies of Rosi's films. In *Christ Stopped at Eboli,* Lucania, one of the poorest parts of Italy, photographed by Pasqualino De Santis, comes out looking like a vacation resort.

Freddy Buache called *Christ Stopped at Eboli* "an excellent exercise by a first-class technician, but not a return to *Salvatore Giuliano,* which Levi's book might have made possible."[13]

In the more intimate *Tre fratelli* (Three Brothers, 1981), Rosi used the framework of a novella by the Russian twentieth-century writer Andrei Platonov about the homecoming of three brothers for the funeral of their mother. Through the brothers' stories, dreams, and obsessions, he once again presented some of Italy's poignant problems, such as terrorism and juvenile delinquency. Despite some good performances and an excellent beginning, the film remained literary and contrived, only rarely attaining the emotional impact of Rosi's best movies.

WHERE HAVE ALL THE PRODUCERS GONE?

The expansion of the Italian cinema in the sixties was facilitated by a handful of producers who were not afraid to undertake ambitious projects. People such as Franco Cristaldi (the man behind Rosi, Maselli, Germi, Bellocchio, and others), Alfredo Bini (who produced all Pasolini's films from *Accattone* to *Oedipus Rex*), and Giuliani G. De Negri, producer of all the Taviani films, played important roles in the overall artistic rise of Italian cinema. Dino De Laurentiis and Carlo Ponti were primarily responsible for furthering its international impact. In the seventies, the producer began increasingly to play the role of a mere intermediary between the moneylenders and the exhibitors, and the element of speculation became stronger. The film critic Otello Angeli analyzed the changing role of the producers in *Cinemasessanta:*

> The producer has become an executor of the demands of the industrial complex and the financial powers. He has lost a large part of his autonomy, a fact that influences the entire production of a film, as well as the creative process as such. The division of the producer's role between financing and distribution—typical of the recent oligarchic evolution of capitalism—brought to an end the dialectical relationship that used to exist between different stages of production. The rigidity of today's film market has resulted in the absorption of the figure of the producer and the transformation of his role into a managerial and bureaucratic function.[14]

During this period, Titanus (one of the biggest Italian production companies) fell under the control of FIAT, De Laurentiis moved his office to the United States, and Carlo Ponti became more and more involved in extracinematic transactions. The era of billionlire productions such as *The Leopard, La dolce vita,* and the historical blockbusters was definitely over. Small companies were disappearing and with them went the ordinary entertainment films.

There was nothing to equal the quality of the "spaghetti westerns," and the level of the 1970s popular entertainment genres hit rock bottom. Exploiting the 1974 success of Cavani's *The Night Porter,* so-called Nazi-porno films were turned out by the dozen: *Long Nights of the Gestapo, Camp of Love, The Last Days of the Storm Troopers, The Last Orgy of the Third Reich, A Private House for Storm Troopers, Women's Hell, Women of the Special Station,* etc. Similarly, the good box-office results of Pasolini's *The Decameron* and *The Canterbury Tales* helped to pave the way for pure pornography: *Decameron Number 2, The Prohibited Decameron, The Last Decameron, Decameroticus, Hot Nights of Decameron, The Other Canterbury Tales, Canterbury Number 2,* etc.

In 1972, the state, under pressure from all sides to counter the decline of the film industry, launched a program to subsidize new directors' first feature films. Through Italnoleggio—a state agency created in the sixties to distribute films with limited release possibilities—the government cofunded over a dozen first fiction films between 1973 and 1977 (among them *Holiday Making, On the Road from Damascus, Irene, Irene,* and *Just for One Night*). Subsidies were also available for films by established directors, such as Maselli's *The Suspect,* Cavani's *Beyond Good and Evil,* the Tavianis' *St. Michael Had a Rooster,* Bellocchio's *In the Name of the Father,* Olmi's *The Circumstance* and *The Tree of the Wooden Clogs,* and Zurlini's *The Tartar Desert.* Such ambitious, mostly low-budget films would otherwise have been unable to obtain financial credit and investment money in the face of competition from American blockbusters, which were invading the European market with increasing aggressiveness. Without public funding, the image of the Italian cinema of the seventies would have been even grimmer. In addition to Italnoleggio, the government supported films through the state Television Commission. Whereas in the sixties, the commission had funded mostly television plays and television documentaries, in the seventies it began cofinancing the production of films intended for theatrical release, such as Bertolucci's *The Spider's Stratagem,* Gagliardo's *Maternale,* the Tavianis' *Padre Padrone,* Rosi's *Christ Stopped at Eboli,* Cavani's *Milarepa,* etc.

Three of the government financed "first films" stand out as attempts to break away from the prevailing narrative patterns, and all three show the influence of Michelangelo Antonioni in this regard. Whereas Visconti founded a true "school" (including, among others, Cavani and Rosi) and Rossellini influenced practically everybody, Antonioni's antinarrative modus seemed too "non-Italian" to have more than a few followers. Peter Del Monte's *Irene, Irene* (1975), Giovanna Gagliardo's *La maternale* (1976), and Carlo Di Carlo's *Per questa notte* (Just for One Night, 1977) sought to avoid plot in the traditional sense and to present instead certain significant—often seemingly dissociated—symptoms of deeper emotional structures and changes.

Gagliardo (b. 1941) was successful with this technique, capturing the relationship between a mother and daughter by examining small details of daily life in a middle-class northern Italian family.[15] "My film's characters do nothing but eat, prepare meals, remember a good cake that was served with tea and music by Chopin while another tea party was being recalled," said Gagliardo.[16] *La maternale* is a string of "forgotten memories," as she put it, whose disclosure eventually expresses the essence of a complex interdependence: the mother and the daughter are viewed as mutual victims and oppressors.

In the same way, *Irene, Irene* exposes hidden aspects of human relationships by concentrating on the visible effects of situations that no longer exist. In a style

La maternale

showing also the influence of Bergman, Del Monte tells of a marriage that has ended by the wife's unexplained departure. Through conversations with other people, the husband, a wealthy magistrate, tries to understand more of his own past, only to be faced with still more inscrutable aspects of life. The failure of his search and eventually the lonely solitude of his death stand in contradiction to everything he once thought he had achieved.[17]

Carlo Di Carlo (b. 1938), in *Just for One Night,* also concerns himself with states of mind that are often at odds with the facts of the narrative. Di Carlo—a critic, television director, documentarist, and Antonioni's longtime collaborator— blended a story of persecution and betrayal with images of violence and revolutionary struggle. The narrative follows the journey of a man—a revolutionary hunted by the police—into physical and moral destruction against the backdrop of a failed revolution and the mechanisms of repression. The man spends one night in hiding, betrays his friend, and is killed just when freedom seems within reach. Di Carlo relies primarily on visual means to maintain the tension in his loosely structured story, exploring existential problems through meticulously assembled imagery.

Of the first-time directors only the American-born Peter Del Monte remained in the spotlight. Gianni Toti returned to journalism, Marco Leto, Giovanna Gagliardo, and Carlo Di Carlo to television. But Del Monte also saw his career rocket and plummet as, since the second half of the seventies, producers refused to take risks on unknown filmmakers. It was not until 1981 that Del Monte directed another film, *Piso pisello* (Sweet Pea), where a genuinely new tone and voice were

Per questa notte

undeniable. His subsequent film, *Invitation au voyage* (Invitation to a Journey, 1982), shot for a French company, was linked to his previous movies by its interest in characters who exist on the borderline between rebellion and madness. The gratuitously split structure of the story emphasized the absurd plot (a young boy assumes the identity and looks of his tragically deceased twin sister-mistress), which is marked by distinct Del Monte imprints: characters set against an eerie atmosphere and blurred distinctions between dream and ordinary reality.

Almost all the directors of the younger generation attempted to define the boundaries of individual freedom, an issue that gained increasing attention after 1968. They felt alienated from the determinism of their precursors and asserted that human will and responsibility were unlimited. Liliana Cavani in particular continued her argument against the concept of good and evil. After *Milarepa* (1973), another of her tales about young people unable to integrate into society, Cavani directed her most successful film, *Il portiere di notte* (The Night Porter, 1974). Unlike *Milarepa* (an intricate attempt to link the mystical experience of an eleventh-century Tibetan monk with our time), *The Night Porter* was an immediate box-office success. The story concerns a sado-masochistic relationship between a young Jewish prisoner in a Nazi concentration camp and her jailor, a high-ranking SS officer. It provoked a scandal wherever it was shown. Cavani attempted to uncover the most equivoqual and unforeseeable aspects of human character as they may appear in certain extreme situations. Thus, Lucia (Charlotte Rampling), deported at the age of fifteen to a concentration camp, becomes physically and emotionally dependent on her torturer (Dirk Bogarde), who has initiated her into sadistic pleasures. When the two of them meet some fifteen years later— he is working as a night porter, she is the wife of a famous conductor—she leaves her husband and follows her first lover into insanity and death.[18]

The story is handled with considerable insight and is based on research among survivors of the Nazi camps. Cavani pointed out: "One of the survivors, a woman, told me: 'Not all victims are innocents because a victim too is a human being.' This survivor had known cruelty, horror, human experiments. But she could not forgive her jailors for showing her the ambiguity of the human character."[19] The thematic courage and intellectual lucidity of *The Night Porter* are weakened by the rather heavy-handed direction of the actors and the high-pitched drama of the final scenes. Callisto Cosulich, comparing *The Night Porter* to Munk's *The Passenger* and Lumet's *The Pawnbroker*, summed up the film's pros and cons in his review in *Paese Sera:*

The Night Porter

Thanks to her youth and her proverbial thirst for knowledge, Cavani has both the necessary detachment and the genuine coldness to be able to lay bare the relationship between Lucia and Max and to prove that such a relationship could be created only in a camp situation. She failed not because of a lack of courage but because she allowed herself to be carried away by the mechanisms of her own story, which eventually adopts the patterns of an action film.[20]

In 1977, Cavani dealt with the life of Friedrich Nietzsche in a film whose title is inspired by one of his works—*Al di là del bene e del male* (Beyond Good and Evil). Focusing on Nietzsche's friendship with Lou Salome, his libertarian disciple and lover, Cavani once again defied the taboos concerning sexual relationships. But the film does not mark any advance in her achievement. Nietzsche's descent into madness is captured through naturalistically descriptive narrative, which cannot stand up to the intensity of Cavani's purpose. The characterization of Lou Salome is likewise weak, being too sketchy to support Cavani's intention to portray her as one of the first truly liberated women. Cavani's "teatrum mundi," propelled, like Visconti's, by destructive and maddening passions, is successful in conveying the desired image of the dimensions of insanity. But it lacks some "madness" of its own.

This discrepancy is particularly evident in her 1980 adaptation of Curzio Malaparte's controversial book *La pelle* (The Skin, written in 1949), which captures the atmosphere of Naples in 1943, a city invaded by victorious troops from all over the world. Malaparte wrote a collection of naturalistic cynical vignettes exposing the bitterness of victory where both the victors and the vanquished continued "to offend the only flag one can truly offend in the catastrophe of war—the human skin." Cavani concentrated mainly on the sensational aspects (the prostitution of a virgin girl, scenes in brothels, carnal violence, and humiliation). On the screen, Malaparte's sophisticated variations on the persecutor-victim relationship became so shrill and ostentatious that all the latent perversities came to the surface in a torrent of inconclusive clichés, heavy with labored attempts to build suspense and with no artistic perspective.

FROM PASOLINI TO COMEDY ITALIAN STYLE AND LA RIVISTA

Sergio Citti (b. 1934) and Nanni Moretti (b. 1955) were the only directors of the seventies who were able to continue beyond their first films without giving up too many of their original ambitions. Of the two Citti brothers, both faithful followers and friends of Pier Paolo Pasolini, Sergio was always the more intellectual, and he succeeded in combining his intellectual curiosity with the ingenuousness of a "ragazzo di vita"—one of the Roman subproletarian youth whose way of life was such a strong influence in Pasolini's *oeuvre*.

Citti's first feature film, *Ostia* (1970), was scripted by Pasolini and was profoundly indebted to Pasolini's poetics. But Citti never shared Pasolini's tragic sense of life nor his later attitude of resignation to circumstances. From the outset, Citti combined melodramatic features with comical and slightly farcical perspectives.

Ostia is a declaration of love to his brother Franco. Its protagonists are two brothers (one played by Franco Citti), the poor and naïve children of an anarchist. One night, they push their father out of the window and, without shedding a tear, continue their life together—sleeping in the same bed, making love to each other, sharing the same desires and the same pleasures. When a girl befriends them, one brother kills the other and then sits next to his body on the seashore at Ostia, which had always been their favorite place. At dusk, he takes the body out onto the ocean and lowers it into the waves. The story, pervaded by an intense atmosphere of lingering sadness, takes place in a Rome consisting of poor neighborhoods and dirty river banks, observed with a touch of both true authenticity and sheer fantasy.

Citti's ability to effect transitions of mood and atmosphere shaped his subsequent film *Storie scellerate* (Infamous Stories, 1974), set in nineteenth-century Rome. Love, sex, violence, and farce are mingled in an intriguing narrative in the style of Boccaccio and Pasolini. After Pasolini's death, his influence on Citti waned, but Boccaccio remained, and Citti's irony was gradually stifled with overtones of the comedy Italian style. The films *Casotto* (Beach House, 1978), *Due pezzi di pane* (Two Pieces of Bread, 1979) and *Il minestrone* (1980) secured Citti's position among the established directors of comedy. All three films are delightfully personal views of life, bathed in a sympathetic warmth. Their concern with realism

Ecce Bombo

and a tasteful sense of humor prevent them from lapsing into vulgarity, but none of them fully escapes the clichés of the farce.

Despite their differences in background and overall creative modus, Nanni Moretti shares with Citti an awareness of tragicomic human weaknesses and an intense consciousness of existential sorrows. Moretti, the only "enfant terrible" of the Italian cinema of the seventies, became a kind of spokesman for his generation. He has much in common with Jean-Luc Godard and Milos Forman, who had represented the attitudes of the young people of the sixties. In both thematic and stylistic terms his work often seems more a product of the previous decade. The two films he made in the seventies, *Io sono un autarchico* (I am an Autarchic, 1976, shot in super 8mm) and *Ecce Bombo* (1978), portray the "vitelloni" and the "lizards" of his generation, as frustrated and confused as those of Fellini and Wertmüller. But unlike the original "vitelloni" and "lizards," Moretti's protagonists do not try to escape the monotony of their lives. They indulge in their own stereotypes (movies, pizzeria, dancing) with a precocious indifference to everything and everybody. Moretti's sketches of these Roman youngsters follow the patterns of a personalized "rivista" with the narrative fragmented into "numbers" and connected by the figure of the main protagonist (played by Moretti himself in both films). Moretti calls his films "stories of dream, utopia, and illusions, which shatter on contact with real life; stories of young people who fail their exams and dismally adhere to the politics of the extreme Left."[21] *Ecce Bombo* was a great success among young audiences, who identified with the reluctance of its characters to integrate into society.

Moretti was the only one of the new generation to start a "trend." The end of the seventies saw the emergence of three filmmakers who shared Moretti's attitudes and further developed his style: Massimo Troisi (b. 1954), Carlo Verdone (b. 1946), and Maurizio Nichetti (b. 1945). Less involved in political and social issues than their predecessors, they adopted a highly critical and slightly sarcastic approach toward society. Some believe that their aggressiveness, on the one hand, and their attitude of indifference, on the other, may well be a cover for shyness and vulnerability. Moretti's generation is less cinematically sophisticated than those who began their careers in the sixties, using less elusive forms and relying more on the rivista style and on the heritage of Chaplin and Keaton. They are all "auteurs": they write their films, direct them, and appear in them.

Massimo Troisi seems the most gifted. Shaped by his work with the Neapolitan theater group La Smorfia, Troisi returned to Neapolitan sentimental comedy, renewing its past glory. His film *Ricomincio da tre* (Starting from Three, 1980) is an extremely sensitive grotesque comedy, in which the topical satire of the sixties is replaced by a less political and possibly more profound view of the individual's relationship to society. *Starting from Three* is spoken in pure, almost incomprehensible dialect and thus in effect can be considered by many a silent movie.[22]

Carlo Verdone also adopted the rivista style in *Un sacco bello* (Life Is Beautiful, 1979), intertwining three sketches of contemporary youth, somewhat neurotic, somewhat frustrated, filled with far-fetched dreams (all three characters are played by Verdone himself).

Similarly, Maurizio Nichetti's *Ratataplan* (1979) examines the marginal existence of its protagonists, who bear many similarities to Moretti's *Ecce Bombo*. A newly graduated engineer is turned down by a large multinational company and goes back to his usual way of life, his usual state of seclusion. Longing for true relationships, for "something different," he always seems to find himself back at zero. Young people identified with Nichetti's resigned protagonist just as they had with *Ecce Bombo*, viewing his self-imposed anonymity as the best alternative to the hell one has to go through for money. Like *Starting from Three*, *Ratataplan* can be considered virtually a silent movie, in this case not because of the language used but because the film has almost no dialogue at all.

Moretti himself summed up some of the issues of his generation in his 1981 *I sogni d'oro* (Golden Dreams), a kind of *8½* of the seventies, which uses the language of the post-1968 generation while mocking its concepts. The protagonist, a young film director who makes a film entitled *Freud's Mama*, tries to come to grips with his professional and personal problems and has as little success as the characters of Troisi's, Verdone's, and Nichetti's films. The direct, detached style of Moretti and his "followers" may represent the beginning of a new cycle, a successor to the one that started with neorealism and ended, in a way, with the metaphors of directors such as Fellini, the Tavianis, Ferreri, and Bellocchio.

CHANGING PATTERNS OF FILMMAKING: SCOLA, BRUSATI, RISI

Just as Italian films had continued to utilize neorealist formulas well into the 1950s, so did the films of the seventies absorb and adapt many of the linguistic and thematic innovations of the sixties. The mixture of new patterns and previous inspirations brought about a cinematic language that differed substantially from what had preceded it: less subjective than the films of the sixties, less emotional, less "romantic," relying more on dialogue or situations than on the flow of images. Influenced by television, the filmmakers of the seventies generally used a less assertive camera, and the shots lost some of their intensity. The 1960s aestheticizing camera, closely watching the characters and in a way guiding the viewer through the events, was abandoned in favor of a more aloof approach. Aerial shots, freeze frames, jump shots, and close-ups, cherished by Bertolucci's generation, now became outdated as did the "abandonment of figures in space," characteristic of Fellini and Antonioni.

On the other hand, the overall style of the 1960s, with its substantially enlarged grammar (as compared with the fifties), served to enrich many general features of the new movies. The dialogue became less contrived, and the overall approach to the subject matter increased in ambiguity, even in the more commercially oriented pictures. A new kind of stylized narration prevailed, often consciously avoiding any identification with the viewpoint of a particular character and adopting the aesthetics of long shots.

The sixties had altered the attitude toward film in Europe, and it was now accorded the definitive status of an art form in its own right. Under the influence of this prevailing position, some filmmakers attempted to raise the level of their work, abandoning pure entertainment in favor of more ambitious projects. In this connection, two names in particular emerge: Ettore Scola (b. 1931) and Franco Brusati (b. 1922).

Franco Brusati had been a prolific scriptwriter and director since 1950. In 1974, he made *Pane e cioccolata* (Bread and Chocolate), a mature sociocomedy, and in 1978 *Dimenticare Venezia* (To Forget Venice), an accomplished comedy of manners. Ettore Scola had scripted more than fifty comedies and directed nine films, all of only marginal interest. But in the seventies he became one of the most widely discussed Italian directors, successfully adapting the formula of the comedy Italian style to a wide range of subjects. *C'eravamo tanto amati* (We All Loved Each Other So Much, 1974) and *La terrazza* (The Penthouse, 1979) examine the existential problems of the director's peers in different periods of their lives. *We All Loved Each Other So Much*, which is reminiscent of Vancini's *Seasons of Our Love*, follows the progress of several friends who twenty-five years earlier were all members of the same antifascist group. Their stories form a cross-section of their generation: some made it, some did not, most of their ideals are dead, their expectations are giving way to disillusionment. Scola's film is extremely self-referential, allowing

To Forget Venice

spectators from all walks of life to identify with its atmosphere of retrospection and middle-age crisis.

In *The Penthouse*, the characters of *We All Loved Each Other So Much* (some played by the same actors) are eight years older, more established in society, more cynical, more resigned. They meet at fashionable parties in the posh baroque penthouse of an aristocratic lady, a setting typical of a certain strata of Roman society. The revolution that they once dreamed of has been forgotten, and disillusionment has taken over entirely. A journalist, an actor, a film producer, a famous scriptwriter . . . Scola shapes their self-derision, their manias, and their exhibitionism with a feeling for clear-cut situations and characters, but one is continually worried by the tendency to move into caricature.

In both *We All Loved Each Other So Much* and *The Penthouse* Scola dealt with problems that he knew well. In *Brutti, sporchi e cattivi* (Dirty, Mean, and Nasty, 1975), he moved onto less familiar ground—the milieu of the Roman subproletariat. Lacking Pasolini's and Citti's direct relationship with the marginal elements of the society, he did not really attempt to understand the tragicomic character of their lot and instead pictured them as a herd of strange animals trapped in a boorish

We All Loved Each Other So Much

subculture. *Dirty, Mean, and Nasty* thus became a mediocre comedy Italian style, exploiting some of the drastic contradictions of Italian society to show "how strange we are."

Una giornata particolare (A Special Day, 1977) also centers on social discrepancies. Yet this time Scola used a very condensed style, carefully respecting the unity of the narrative. The entire story takes place in a single day—May 6, 1938, the day Hitler came to Rome to sign the treaty of alliance between Italy and Germany. While everybody else is out in the festively decorated streets, two people remain inside their apartments: a woman, a good "fascist" mother of six (Sophia Loren), and a homosexual (Marcello Mastroianni). They meet, talk, discover their common anguishes, they even make love. Then the special day is over, and the man, accused of homosexuality, is taken away by the police.[23]

Like Bellocchio, Rosi, and some others, Scola became increasingly interested in psychological dramas and beautiful images, relating, in a sense, to the aesthetic tradition of Italian Calligraphism. His *Passione d'amore* (Passion of Love, 1981), based on a late nineteenth-century novel, meticulously suggests the atmosphere of the period, unfolding a strange love story between an unattractive provincial spin-

A Special Day

ster and a handsome, womanizing officer. The film's main concern, however, is the confrontation between "beautiful" and "ugly," reminiscent of fantastic stories by romantics like E. T. A. Hoffmann.

In his best films, Scola makes good use of his two primary skills: his writing ability, which enables him to endow his characters with psychological credibility, and his ability to create a believable sociohistorical background. A similar talent for combining writing and directing has also been the strength of Franco Brusati. Brusati's *Bread and Chocolate* and *To Forget Venice* go beyond formulas of Italian-style comedy, relying instead on a system of motifs with symbolic overtones. *Bread and Chocolate*, set in Switzerland, chronicles the vain efforts of an Italian emigrant worker to adapt to a foreign way of life. *To Forget Venice*, paraphrasing Bergman, Chekhov, and Mann, attempts to elucidate the relationships among the members of a family by depicting a series of events that occur in the space of several days: the older sister, who has been the head of the family, dies, and the family home loses its appeal as a refuge. In an elegant, polished style Brusati evokes the twilight of an old bourgeois milieu in a manner reminiscent of Chekhov's plays. Yet the end brings neither Bergmanian self-castigation nor Chekhovian sadness over "a life that has slipped by, and one would say it had hardly begun." Instead, the film's protagonist ponders the future over a cold meal and a bottle of wine, ready to forget the family trips to Venice and, along with them, the past.

But it was neither Scola nor Brusati who authored the greatest box-office hits of the 1970s Italian comedy of manners. That distinction again went to Dino Risi and Mario Monicelli, with Risi's *Profumo di donna* (Sweet Smell of Woman, 1975) and Monicelli's *Un borghese piccolo piccolo* (That Little Man, 1976), grossing over 1 billion lire in Italy in their respective years of production. Both films are exceptions in their directors' *oeuvres* in that they are based on novels. *Sweet Smell of Woman* transcribes Giovanni Arpino's successful novel *Obscurity and Honey*, and *That Little Man* is an adaptation of the bestseller of the same title by Vincenzo Cerami.[24]

The appeal of Monicelli's *That Little Man* lay mainly in its subject matter, which struck a responsive chord with many Italians: when the son of a petty clerk is killed during a hold-up, the father sets out to find the murderer and takes justice into his own hands, becoming a killer himself. In the role of the father, Alberto Sordi personified to perfection the average Italian, stressing his basic mistrust of all government authority and his obsession with the idea that he is a helpless victim in some far-reaching political frame-up.

Vittorio Gassman, who played the leading role in *Sweet Smell of Woman*, embodies the opposite of Sordi's "little man." In this and other roles, Gassman personifies the Italian yearning for grandeur and concern with "savoir vivre." The protagonist of *Sweet Smell of Woman* is a blind middle-aged man, endowed with great serenity, common sense and an epicurean knowledge of the pleasures of life. Lonely and exploited by his young boy friend, he undertakes a journey whose destination is unknown: death or love, solitude or the sweet smell of woman.

Risi charges his films with a strong touch of real life, guided by an unerring instinct for the significant topics of the moment. Thus, in 1979, when terrorism in

Sweet Smell of Woman

Italy (often the work of the children of the establishment) was reaching its peak, he wrote and directed *Caro papà* (Dear Daddy), again with Gassman in the starring role. This time Gassman plays a successful industrialist who is "kneecapped" (shot in the legs) by his own son, a member of a radical leftist group. The incident leaves the father crippled for life but ultimately seems to improve his relationship with his son.[25]

THE RUSH FOR LITERATURE

One of the symptoms of the 1970s crisis in the Italian cinema was a lack of original scripts, resulting from the producers' fear of backing unproven subjects. In the seventies, as in the early forties, the use of literary adaptations tended to encourage a calligraphic approach to filmmaking. Its most prominent representative remained Mauro Bolognini.

Bolognini's *Metello* (1970), based on a 1955 novel by Vasco Pratolini, and his *L'eredità Ferramonti* (Heritage, 1976), based on a late nineteenth-century novel by Gaetano Chelli, are representative of Bolognini's efforts. He approaches his subjects on the level of a sophisticated style, stressing beautiful photography and the re-creation of a milieu. The meticulousness with which Bolognini arranges his settings represents the main asset of his films, but his detached perspective occasionally proves to be a liability. *Metello* portrays the environment of the working class in

Florence between 1875 and 1902. In 1902, the Italian workers staged a decisive strike, which ended with the building industry capitulating to the demands of the masons. Metello is the main organizer of the strike, and it is his personal story that forms the core of the film, integrated into—but never dominated by—Bolognini's description of the social context. *Metello* is Bolognini's best film, pervaded by a warmth and a personal involvement, atypical in light of Bolognini's detached approach.[26]

In *Heritage*, set in Rome at the turn of the century, Bolognini became involved with the central character, a beautiful ruthless woman who is determined to win the struggle over the estate of a wealthy family. Bolognini does not always succeed in imposing a satisfactory shape on literary material, and his theatrical manner of composition is open to question. His *oeuvre*, which contains no truly brilliant successes but also no spectacular flops, sums up the merits as well as the flaws of Italian film's venture with literature.

Unlike Bolognini, Valerio Zurlini was concerned primarily with the re-creation of a symbolic atmosphere woven from obsessions and dreams. His fascination with supressed emotions undoubtedly influenced his decision to film one of the most discomforting Italian novels, *Il deserto dei Tartari* (The Tartar Desert, 1976), written in 1940 by Dino Buzzati. Buzzati's interests are largely metaphysical, centering on the basic human fear of the unknown. In *The Tartar Desert*, this fear is symbolized by a forbidding desert on the border of some unspecified country. A fortress

Heritage

Il deserto dei Tartari

towers over the desert, and its garrison is expected to stop any attack that might be launched by some unknown enemy. For years, the members of the garrison come and go, come and die, come and grow old, waiting for an enemy who never appears. When the invasion finally occurs, the story's protagonist, who had come to the fortress as a young officer, is sick, aging, and too weak to fight. He dies without ever having the chance to give meaning to his life.

In his transcription of Buzzati's novel, Zurlini does justice to its Kafkaesque vision by means of an intense style characterized by repetitiveness, stylized acting, and unnatural colors. Yet Zurlini—like most cinematic adapters of surreal literature—apparently did not understand that artists such as Kafka, Buzzati, and Buñuel are so compelling precisely because of the overwhelmingly suggestive realism of all the details of their work.

The Italian cinema seldom attempted to transcribe literature that was not essentially narrative in character. The novels that were chosen had more or less clearly delineated plots, and the so-called traditional novelists (e.g., Alberto Moravia, Vasco Pratolini, Elio Vittorini, Vitaliano Brancati) were favored over those who questioned certain established components of the narrative, such as the representative or mimetic quality of language (Carlo Emilio Gadda, Italo Calvino, Luigi Malerba, etc.). Thus, when Bernardo Bertolucci set out to make a film that would be more successful at the box office than his personal films of the sixties, he turned to an established author. And it was his transcription of Moravia's novel *The Conformist* that catapulted him to world fame and thus enabled him to direct another personal film—*Last Tango in Paris*.

BERTOLUCCI'S SEARCH FOR FAME

In his adaptations of literature, Bertolucci has always maintained his own autonomy. In *Il conformista* (The Conformist, 1971), he pursues his own themes, stressing the impotence of intellectuals and the necessity of breaking free from one's "spiritual fathers," this time against a background of politics and sex. Moravia's novel, set during the fascist period, is a meditation on the motives behind human conformism. Its protagonist, Marcello Clerici, a bright young man from a wealthy family, goes along with fascism "in order to conceal his own unconfessed abnormality; he is a fascist because he hopes to hide his own disorder in the fascist collective myth and its apparent order; in the name of fascism, he kills, attempting to wipe out his previous crime by another criminal action, which is this time, so to speak, legalized."[27]

Bertolucci's *The Conformist* follows a clear-cut narrative sustained by a meticulous montage (previously, Bertolucci had considered montage the least important element in the entire creative process). The dramatic highpoints are emphasized through flamboyant direction marked by an often extravagant rendering of Moravia's more discreet eroticism. Elegant, brilliant, violent, decadent, making the utmost use of the visual hallmarks of the late twenties (the architecture of the fascist era, the Parisian "touch," the atmosphere of decadence), *The Conformist* offers a full display of Bertolucci's cinematic talent with all its tics and gestures. It is, in a sense, a perfect transitional film between the sixties and seventies.

Marcello's murder of his former professor, the exiled antifascist philosopher Quadri, represents Bertolucci's symbolic assassination of Jean-Luc Godard, who had influenced Bertolucci's films of the sixties, especially *Partner*.[28] At the time of *The Conformist*, Bertolucci was undergoing extensive psychoanalytic treatment.[29] Devastated by the failures of his previous films, he attempted to alter his narrative modus as well as his attitude toward the role and meaning of film. Yearning for the recognition of a "popular director," he gradually changed his way of filmmaking, adopting the patterns of the melodrama with "operettic" overtones.[30]

The switch in Bertolucci's "modus creandi" was already apparent in the film that preceded *The Conformist, Strategia del ragno* (The Spider's Stratagem, 1970), inspired by a short story by Jorge Luis Borges. In the film, a young man returns to his native town to investigate the circumstances of his father's murder by the fascists. But the truth he finds is far different from what he had expected: his father, a man with an honorable reputation, had in fact denounced his antifascist friends to the police. His friends then arranged to preserve his image by sending him to death and never revealing his betrayal. Bertolucci's own dilemmas continue to fill the film's texture. The destruction of the father-myth this time encompasses the entire generation that grew out of the antifascist resistance and witnessed the crumbling

The Conformist

of its ideals; and the dual aspect of human nature is symbolized through the equivocal father-son relationship. Stylistically, *The Spider's Stratagem* marks the passage
from Bertolucci's "cinema as poetry" to "cinema as spectacle" in that it accommo-
dates personalized camera movements and a multilevel narrative to the demands of
a television drama (the film was funded by the Italian Television Commission).
Thus, "the most immediate parameters of this work are essentially naturalistic,
even if the narrative process is structured around an alternation of fantasy and
reality, of impressionism and surrealism to spill over into an oneiric dimension."[31]
This combination provides for an ambivalence in most of the shots and creates an
atmosphere of imminent mystery, which is the film's main asset.

"The tango is a pantomime coitus for the camera," Marinetti wrote in 1914.
"The tango is a way of walking through life," Bertolucci asserted, quoting Borges.
Acclaimed as "a landmark in movie history"[32] by some and denounced as pornography by others, *Ultimo tango a Parigi* (Last Tango in Paris, 1972) combines

these two disparate definitions. Paul, a forty-five-year-old American living in Paris, meets Jeanne, a French woman of twenty, in an empty apartment, which they both want to rent. They make love and return during the following days, acting out their sexual fantasies. No names are mentioned, no strings attached. When Jeanne decides not to come again, Paul realizes he loves her and follows her home to her apartment. Putting on her dead father's cap, he tries to provoke her, and she shoots him with her father's gun, mumbling as if in recrimination: "I don't know him, he tried to rape me, I don't even know his name."

As for the alleged pornography, the film is charged with four-letter words, masturbation, fellatio, sodomy, masochism, etc. Then there is Paul's story, which unfolds between the meetings in the decaying apartment at the Pont Mirabeau. He owns a seedy hotel, his life is in a shambles, and his wife has committed suicide on the day he met Jeanne. The most impressive sequence captures him walking aimlessly in the streets after he has spent the night with his wife's dead body and cried out his childlike dismay in a desperate monologue.[33] Here is Bertolucci at his best, creating a stifling atmosphere of crumbled hopes, with no way out of the maze. He returns to the subjective camera of his early films, to the insistent takes, to figures lost in vast spaces, to shadows on wet pavements and the grayish colors of the early morning hours. For Jean-Louis Bory, *Last Tango* was a "romantic refusal turned into a sexual dizziness accompanied by a nihilistic grin and a destructive provocation."[34] Jean de Baroncelli contended: "The film is immersed in a delirious pessimism and self-destruction. One cannot escape its sadness and its almost metaphysical despair."[35]

The Spider's Strategem

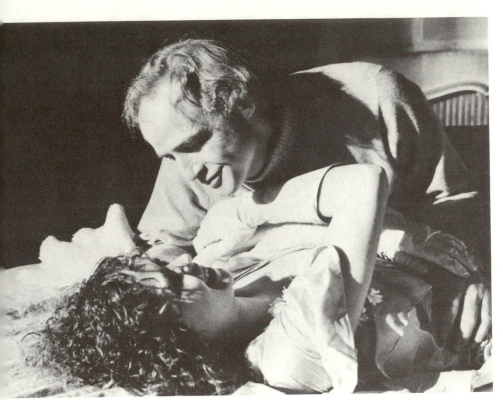

Last Tango in Paris

Pages and pages have been written about *Last Tango* and about Marlon Brando (Paul), who improvised the entire monologue about his childhood in front of the camera and "put forty years of his own experience into the film: his relations with his father, his mother, children, lovers, friends—all come out in his performance of Paul."[36] Some liked this kind of improvisation; others (such as Norman Mailer) saw it as the downfall of the film.

In retrospect, there is no doubt that in its time the sexual explicitness of *Last Tango* had a certain "liberating impact" (as Pauline Kael put it). But in fact the erotic scenes in the Paris apartment did not age as well as the depiction of "the way of walking" of an American in Paris. *Last Tango* hardly was "the most stimulating film of the decade." It was, and it remains, one of Bertolucci's most interesting films and, along with *The Conformist*, one of the two best films he made in the seventies.

After *Tango*'s fabulous worldwide financial success, Bertolucci was free to pursue whatever projects he wanted. All the producers courted him. In 1973, he embarked on the five-hour-and-forty-five-minute-long *Novecento* (1900), which he did not complete until 1976.[37] The script, written by Bertolucci and his younger brother Giuseppe, is a monumental melodramatic saga staged as a political epic.[38]

1900, paid for by American capitalists, supports the politics of the Italian communists and manages to avoid any in-depth analysis of the fascist era (which forms the setting for a significant portion of the film). Shot near Bertolucci's native Parma, *1900* mixes together everything that a film "à thèse" can encompass: the lyricism of Dovzhenko with the naturalism of Vidor, Marx with Freud and Mao, Zhdanovist socialist realism with eclectic modernism, revolutionary bathos with anarchistic nihilism, sexual perversion with true love, big-name stars with nonprofessional extras. A German critic described it accurately: "*1900* is Bertolucci's most personal and most helpless film. Trying to achieve a harmonious relationship between Marx and Freud, Bertolucci got stuck in hopeless confusion."[39]

The story begins in 1900 with the birth of two children: Olmo (Gérard Depardieu), son of a poor peasant, and Alfredo (Robert De Niro), son of a rich landowner. Against the background of peasant strikes, the rise and fall of fascism, the 1945 victory of the antifascist forces, and the first visions of a communist future, the film follows the destinies of the two men, who remain friends in spite of vast

1900

political and philosophical differences. Olmo becomes an ardent revolutionary, is jailed by the fascists, enjoys a perfect marriage with a school teacher who shares his political beliefs, and in 1945 joins the Communist party. Alfredo manages the family property, collaborates with the fascists, suffers through an unhappy marriage (his wife Ada goes mad), in 1945 is condemned for his past deeds by a "people's tribunal," and is set free only through Olmo's intervention.

1900 is an extremely uneven film with masterly scenes as well as awkward moments. Bertolucci is most at ease portraying the upper-class milieu of the thirties (Ada's story) or capturing moments of high-pitched personal emotions (the suicide of the old landowner).[40] On the other hand, the story of the revolutionary struggle with Olmo in its center is contrived and unconvincing, despite the director's tenacious effort to establish it as the film's leitmotif.

In *La luna* (1979), Bertolucci abandoned his eclecticism in favor of a straightforward "operettic" approach. Picking up one of the cherished themes of the Italian family melodrama—that of children without a father—he concocted a story about an American opera singer (played by Jill Clayburgh) who after fifteen years is reunited with the father of her son. Describing his filmmaking technique in 1973, Bertolucci contended: "I mix Hollywood studio with the technique of *cinéma vérité*. This permits the best possible conditions for improvisation and gives the public a continuous sense of risk and danger." This technique worked perfectly in *Last Tango* but marred the original impulse of *1900* and was ultimately responsible for the failure of *La luna*, turning it into a "posh product, an exercise in style, made by an exceptionally talented director, who is betrayed by his own, very personal, inspiration."[41]

THE CASE OF LINA WERTMÜLLER

Probably no other Italian director has been the object of more disparate reactions than Lina Wertmüller. Idolized in the United States, almost ignored in Europe, and little appreciated in Italy, she held the spotlight for six years. Her rise to fame, which began in 1972 with *Mimì metallurgico ferito nell'onore* (The Seduction of Mimi), was as unexpected as her fall was precipitous. In retrospect, Lino Miccichè was probably right when he wrote in his 1974 review of *Travolti da un insolito destino nell'azzurro mare d'agosto* (Swept Away): "We have to grant one merit to Lina Wertmüller: she is consistent. Her films get worse and worse, there is a gradual progression from film to film. It would be admirable if it were not so deplorable."[42] Yet while Italian critics were deriding Wertmüller, on the other side of the Atlantic Warner Brothers was offering her a contract to make four English-language films.[43] And in 1978, New York critic John Simon, expressing sentiments shared by many of his colleagues, wrote:

> She goes from strength to strength and is already becoming a myth—even on Long Island. There, not long ago, on the marquee of a movie theater you could read "Lina Wertmüller's *8½*." How Fellini's ephemeral assistant will blush when she reads this: her revered master's work being ascribed to her, her reputation eclipsing his. Eclipsing, no; but, in due time, equaling? I can't see why not.[44]

Wertmüller's cinematic craftsmanship consists mainly in her ability to mingle sex with politics, which she conceives as a game, expressing political issues through generally accepted commonplaces. She is also sometimes successful in capturing characteristic features of Italian society, such as the strategy for survival and the myth of virility. Wertmüller's avowed aim has always been to create popular entertainment, and she has never attempted to achieve more. That she has become "a case" probably surprised her as much as anyone.

Wertmüller has a sarcastic view of human relationships, which plays a part in shaping the type of presentation she has developed. Her most coherent film of the seventies is *Film d'amore e d'anarchia* (Love and Anarchy, 1973), in which her outrageously ironic style counterbalances an equally provocative story. It features a young provincial anarchist who comes to Rome to kill Mussolini, becomes involved in a peculiar love affair with two whores, and ends in an erotico-political trap.

Love and Anarchy

Politics provides an effective background for a sentimental plot with sardonic overtones in a setting that approximates the real world and shows a wide-ranging appreciation of the bizarre.

In *Love and Anarchy*, all the subplots are linked to one point (the plan to assassi-
nate Mussolini). In *The Seduction of Mimi* (1972), however, Wertmüller orches-
trates her story by accumulating jokes, puns, and grotesque situations, which her
protagonist is supposed to reconcile. Wertmüller attempts to draw an analogy/
opposition between the dilemmas of the main character: his infatuation with a girl
who is a communist activist, his own ambivalence toward his political beliefs and
the imperatives of society, his faith in the myth of macho honor, etc. But the will-
fulness of her conjunction between the dreamlike and the matter-of-fact fails to
provide a sound basis for the film's apparent intention to demonstrate the impossibility of combining survival with integrity.

Wertmüller's American success was triggered by *Swept Away* (1974). The film's
strong point is its explicitness, through which Wertmüller captures the relationship
between a man and a woman, a servant and his master, who find themselves on a
deserted island and gradually reverse their roles: the woman, a high-society lady,
becomes a slave to her own servant, relishing her total submissiveness and eventually falling in love with her "master."

Swept Away

All Wertmüller's films are parodies: parodies of the styles, narrative patterns, and cinematic routines of filmmakers such as Pietro Germi, Mario Monicelli, Elio Petri, etc. Parody can often generate a style, which then must be used for some original purpose or it degenerates. This is what happened when Wertmüller turned for inspiration to Cavani (*The Night Porter*), Pasolini's *Salò* and the Nazi-porno films of the seventies. In *Pasqualino Settebellezze* (Seven Beauties, 1976), the parody was diluted by Wertmüller's lack of her own inspiration, and it could not support her attempt to create a more profound metaphor (the protagonist, a pimp interned in a Nazi concentration camp, is forced to make love to the camp's monstrous woman commander in order to survive). In the United States, the film found a good reception. One of the reasons for Wertmüller's American success was probably the similarity between the traditions of American vaudeville and those of the Italian variety shows, the rivista. In addition, some American critics mistakenly attributed to Wertmüller's originality qualities that actually stemmed from the intelligence of the artifacts she parodied.[45]

By 1982, Wertmüller had shot only two of her originally contracted four American films. *La fine del mondo nel nostro solito letto in una notte piena di pioggia* (The End of the World in Our Usual Bed in a Night Full of Rain, 1977) contains some interesting points (it depicts the marriage of a macho Italian and a "liberated" American woman against the background of the changing social patterns of the seventies). In her subsequent film *Fatto di sangue fra due uomini per causa di una vedova* (A Bloody Feud Between Two Men Because of a Widow, 1978), she again adopts some of the most boorish clichés of the dialect farce. Gianni Rondolino contended:

> In a geographically improbable Sicily, against the background of the birth of fascism (improbable, too), three improbable characters meet, love each other, hate each other, and then go their separate ways: a woman, a socialist, and an Italo-American gangster are symbolically reunited in death. All this is interspersed with picture-postcard landscapes, dialogues spoken in an incomprehensible dialect, and with key scenes reminiscent of the worst family melodramas and soap operas.[46]

FERRERI'S FAREWELL TO THE MALE

Marco Ferreri's films have remained little known outside Europe despite topical subjects vaguely reminiscent of those of Lina Wertmüller. But Ferreri never tried to be a popular entertainer, and not everyone could come to grips with his provocative challenge of established myths. *La grande abbuffata* (The Grande Bouffe, 1973), his most successful film of the seventies, made some spectators feel sick and/or walk out.

Like Ferreri's earlier films, *The Grande Bouffe* deals with the equivocal character of the consumer society. The oppressively asphyxiating objects of *Man's Semen* and *Dillinger Is Dead* are this time replaced by food, the most exquisite dishes in abundant quantities. The four male protagonists—successful establishment figures—kill themselves by overeating, watched by a woman who eats as much as

The Last Woman

they do and still manages to survive. With their deaths, the men in the film reject the ready-made freedom guaranteed them by their social status and choose their own freedom: the freedom not to participate any longer and to select their own way to live or die.

In his best films, Ferreri brings into play a highly metaphorical narrative staged with strict realism. Every element in his absurd world is real; nothing is suggested; everything is spelled out in vivid colors and in great detail. Ferreri's representation of fantasies and dreams is not amenable to standard psychological interpretation but rather is aimed at particular social structures. His black humor has various degrees of effectiveness, but it usually succeeds in transmitting Ferreri's message concerning the demise of the traditional male referred to by Umberto Eco as: "This banner, this symbol that has lost all value; the only thing that was left to him (his sex) must be destroyed. Only then can the male again become a human being."[47]

Thus, Ferreri's film *L'ultima donna* (The Last Woman, 1976)—which Umberto Eco calls "the story of a man and his penis"[48]—ends in a self-castration performed with an electric carving knife. Gérard, who has always worshipped his penis, is unable to reconcile himself to the idea that man's virility (and sex as such) has become a common thing in women's lives, something that is no longer admired. Unable to offer Valerie the tenderness and understanding she craves, he offers her his penis, which for him represents the expression of absolute love. "Once again man attributes to his penis an exaggerated importance, which the penis does not and should not have."[49]

In *The Last Woman*, the male still takes care of his child, finding it much easier to communicate with an infant than with an adult. In *Ciao, maschio* (Bye-bye, Male, 1978) and *Chiedo asilo* (No Child's Land, 1980), the man refuses to take on the responsibility of having a child and instead chooses to address his affection (and communication) to a monkey (*Bye-bye, Male*) or a mute boy (*No Child's Land*).[50]

In some of his films of the seventies, Ferreri seems to relinquish the Spanish tradition of the absurd, which inspired his early works, in favor of a rather contrived, Kafkaesque approach. Whereas in his best films Ferreri never left the realm of the "normal" and the real, in *Udienza* (The Audience, 1971), he tried a more literary kind of surrealism. Inspired by Kafka's *Castle*, *The Audience* tells the tale of a devout young Catholic's frustrated quest for a private audience with the Pope. Like Ferreri's previous films, it is structured on the interplay between the surface of everyday life and the frightening realities that lie beneath it. Yet this concept—perfectly suitable for stories such as *Conjugal Bed*, *The Man with the Balloons*, or *Dillinger Is Dead*—is out of place in an abstract parable. *The Audience*'s incoherent blend of the naturalistic (its rendering of the Vatican) and the fantastic turns the central character into a caricature and weakens the film's philosophical impact. *Bye-bye, Male* and *No Child's Land* also leave the ground of absurd "normality" for purely imaginary milieus. The social criticism becomes less biting, and the narrative is diluted by elements of science fiction. In a way, Ferreri's discourse about the fragility of existing values culminates with the scene of Gérard's emasculation when "Gérard presses his bleeding sex into Valerie's hands and faints. Valerie, holding his penis, looks at him as if he were an apparition and screams: "NO . . . " (end of film).[51]

BELLOCCHIO'S FAREWELL TO PARENTS

Throughout the seventies, Marco Bellocchio, the angry man of the sixties, continued to question the role of the family and of social institutions. In 1980, he closed this chapter of his *oeuvre* with *Salto nel vuoto* (Leap into the Void), which is somewhat thematically related to *Fists in the Pocket*. Like Bertolucci, Bellocchio tolls the bell for parents (both the real ones and their substitutes—educators, spiritual fathers, and older brothers). The results are uneven, ranging from accomplished works (*Nel nome del padre* [In the Name of the Father], 1971) to films of only limited interest (*Leap into the Void*). During the seventies, Bellocchio turned his attention to the theater and television in an attempt to break free from the stylistic paths of his early, and best, films. He eventually adopted a more conventional style sustained by a traditional psychological approach (*Marcia trionfale* [Victory March], 1976). He turned from loose antipsychological metaphors to structured narratives, through which he sought to reach wider audiences and, at the same time, to exorcise his own political frustration. Bellocchio, in the sixties and early seventies a fervent supporter of a pro-Chinese leftist movement, proclaimed in 1980:

> At the time of the Union of the Marxist Leninist communists, the conjecture was that in order to change, the bourgeois intellectuals should serve the people, live among the people, for the people have the correct ideas, etc. But actually the

people in question did not exist, were nowhere to be found. It was a myth, an abstraction, and all that came to nothing. Once again a desire was frustrated.[52]

With *In the Name of the Father*, "the film's message is suggested exclusively through style: a cold, objective, explicit style that reveals an ironic approach detached from the seductive plot. The spectators cannot fall prey to any ambiguity and are led into a constructive disapproval in agreement with the author."[53] Bellocchio leads the viewers through what he sees as the hell of a Catholic boarding school, making them accept his own hatred of its cool rigidity and his own rejection of any parental authority. At the opening of the film (set in 1958), Angelo is accompanied by his father and the family's chauffeur to the boarding school. The father reacts to one of Angelo's remarks by slapping his face. "Angelo immediately hits him back. The father kicks him and Angelo kicks back, with more violence and more precision. Now his father takes him by surprise. Angelo starts hitting him from all sides. The father runs away. The chauffeur, carrying the suitcases, does not interfere."[54]

This scene, staged with an outrageously low-key casualness, is complemented by the "mother theme," expressed in an equally detached way: Angelo comes home to discuss with his friends a play that they want to stage at the school. When his

In the Name of the Father

mother keeps disturbing them, one of Angelo's friends asks: "Why don't you kill her?" Angelo aims his gun at his mother and then fires several shots at a mirror that reflects her image.

In the Name of the Father is an intricate parable whose themes range from rebellion against traditional authorities to class conflicts (the revolt of the school servants). Bellocchio succeeds in blending his parallel themes into a clear and measured flow of imagery, creating—as he did in *Fists in the Pocket*—an unusual mixture of intellectual lucidity and poetic diction.

The character of the insecure and high-strung Angelo, whose drawers are full of all kinds of pills, reappears in *Victory March* as the oversensitive Paolo, trapped in the routine of military life. A brutal, sadistic officer succeeds in turning him into an obedient soul, subordinating him to a kind of fascist demagoguery and fostering a father-son relationship with homosexual overtones between the two of them. *Victory March* points up the special susceptibility of an unstable mentality to demagoguery and arbitrary acts. Yet it lacks the pungent originality of Bellocchio's previous films, and it comes dangerously close to moralizing.

The change in Bellocchio's creative modus is still more apparent in *Leap into the Void*, which shows thematic ties both to *Fists in the Pocket* on one side (a sado-masochistic brother-sister relationship) and to the semi-documentary *Matti da slegare* (Fit to Be Untied, 1975). *Fit to Be Untied* had exposed the ineffectiveness of society's institutions for dealing with madness; *Leap into the Void* presents a fictional account of people destroyed by insanity. In place of the documentary's external analysis, *Leap into the Void* attempts to explain aberrant behavior through a psychoanalytic approach. The plot concerns a man who tries to get rid of his insane sister and goes mad himself when she frees herself from him and is cured. The excellent acting and the skillful depiction of the relationship between the two protagonists are indisputable assets, which make the film a success despite its lesser originality. Bellocchio's switch to a different kind of narrative (motivated in part by his own experience with psychoanalysis) resulted in the loss of some of his provocative sensitivity. A pattern of visually beautiful literariness with psychological overtones became increasingly pronounced in his movies and throughout the Italian cinema as well.

The overall situation of the cinema at the end of the seventies (when the question arose whether film would survive as an independent art or whether its release possibilities would merge with those of other communication media, such as cable television and video cassettes) made the evolution of a coherent trend still more problematic than in the sixties.[55] With the exception of a few leading personalities, many Italian directors found it increasingly difficult to maintain a certain consistency even within their own *oeuvres*. Cavani, Wertmüller, Scola, and Petri seemed to conform to the trends of the international film market, to direct what they were offered, leaving less pronounced personal imprints on their films than in the previous years. More than any other art, film was subdued to a precise marketing policy, characterized, as Peter Cowie put it, "by a nostalgia for what was essentially superb trash."[56] Since the second half of the seventies, the Italian film industry had nothing but indications of a catastrophic condition: "diminishing attendance, reduced gross profit in the home market, a decrease in film production, and investment with a consequent reduction in employment among industry workers."[57] In this situation, worsened by the general economic crisis of the Western world, the Italian cinema only painfully maintained the image it had created in past decades: that of a cinema whose artistic evolution is fully dependent on the creative force of a handful of personalities. But this state of affairs was, alas, shared with the other major film industries of the world.

XI

THE DUSK OF THE LEOPARDS

The mid-seventies were marked by the passing of De Sica, Pasolini, Visconti, and Rossellini. Some claim that after their deaths the Italian film was never the same again, that the void has never been filled. All of them worked until the last minutes of their turbulent lives, leaving many unfinished projects.

De Sica, one of neorealism's three founding fathers, went first, carried away by cancer. His last film, *Il viaggio* (The Voyage, 1974), was released the year of his death. It is a woeful love story set in Sicily at the beginning of the century, with Sophia Loren and Richard Burton playing the leading roles. The script is based on a story by Luigi Pirandello, but it captures little of Pirandello's emotional subtlety or his precise observations of provincial life. This uneven result bears witness to De Sica's vacillations between a more profound artistic commitment and the imperatives of the film business. Since his first film produced by Carlo Ponti in 1954, De Sica had centered much of his creative force on the personality of Ponti's wife, Sophia Loren.[1] *The Voyage*, whose greatest weakness is Loren's poor performance, proves the futility of De Sica's efforts to make Loren into a true actress. The films involving De Sica, Ponti, and Loren bring to mind De Sica's words from the early forties: "I do not like the person who gave me wealth. I am his slave. But I am considering a revolt. I was betrayed by the easy clowning and a ready smile. Calmly, implacably, and definitely, and I will now betray them."[2]

Toward the end of his life, De Sica attempted several times to revive his early artistic ambitions. In 1971, he directed *Il giardino dei Finzi-Contini* (The Garden of the Finzi-Continis), based on one of Giorgio Bassani's best novels, and in 1973 he returned to the neorealistic inspiration in *Una breve vacanza* (A Brief Vacation). *The Garden of the Finzi-Continis* fails to capture the dreamlike atmosphere of Bassani's story as it seldom goes beyond mere illustration of the plot—the emotional ripening of a young boy from a wealthy Jewish family in a period overshadowed by the approaching war and anti-Semitic laws. *A Brief Vacation*, on the other hand, is one of De Sica's best films and bears touching testimony to his lifelong interest in the "simple hearts and simple dreams" of the Italian underprivileged. The protagonist, a working-class woman, whose stay in a sanatorium represents the only vacation she has ever had, is reminiscent of the little maid in *Umberto D.*, De Sica's most cherished film.

Pasolini's films of the seventies differ as much from those he made in the previous decade as the two decades differ from one another. After the idolization of the subproletariat and the ideological metaphors of his 1960s films, Pasolini turned to populism. As if acknowledging the futility of his fight against the bourgeoisie, he began to play along, to a certain extent, with their game. In Boccaccio, Chaucer, and the *Arabian Nights*, he hoped to rediscover the pleasure of eroticism and sex, which were being commercialized all around him.[3]

The Decameron (1971) is an adaptation of eight episodes from Boccaccio, using mostly nonprofessional actors.[4] The opening sequence suggests a poetic approach to the subject matter comparable to the evocation of ancient myths in Pasolini's previous films. In the rest of the film, Pasolini progressively falls victim to the shortcomings of his models. His deliberate populism leads him to imitate commercial cinema with some of its worst clichés: the rusticity turns into vulgarity and the preindustrial world of the peasantry becomes a caricature. Boccaccio is shortchanged, and Pasolini's own distinction between eros, eroticism, and pornography appears blurred. "Eros is something wonderful, one of the marvelous things in our lives. Eroticism is the social, aesthetic, and ideological way of expressing Eros. Pornography, on the other hand, is the vulgar social exploitation of Eros."[5]

I racconti di Canterbury (The Canterbury Tales, 1972), shot in England, follows the same aesthetic principles as *The Decameron*. But while *The Decameron* was redeemed, in the eyes of some critics, by its charming Italianate quality, *The Canterbury Tales* lacked even this asset—Pasolini's imagination alone could not recreate an adequate Chaucerian world. Only a couple of episodes (particularly the one intended as an homage to Chaplin), permeated with a strangely fascinating morbid lugubriousness (foreshadowing *Salò*), and a superbly directed Franco Citti serve to remind us that the film was made by the same great artist.

Il fiore delle Mille e una notte (Arabian Nights, 1974) is the most successful part of the "trilogy of life." Though Pasolini did not succeed in finding the poetic measure of the eroticism of the original tales, he did manage to convey some of their magic spell. This accomplishment seems to be due mostly to his own fascination with the vanishing world of Oriental architecture, whose eerie character he rendered with the poetic simplicity that was always characteristic of his camera work. The film is also successful because of Pasolini's strong identification with the subject matter. "I know the Arabs better than I know the 'Milanese,'" he liked to say. This paradox is inherent in all Pasolini's best films and is essential for the understanding of his work: like so many modern artists, he never really felt "at home" in his own country.

By the time he finished the "trilogy of life," Pasolini himself recognized its flaws and even renounced it, although not without self-mockery. His poetic approach and his originality had fallen victim to the modes of commercial cinema, which he had hoped to use to get his message across to larger audiences. In an article called "Abjuration of the Trilogy of Life," Pasolini maintained that "the reality of innocent bodies has now also been stained, manipulated, and destroyed by the power of the consumer society" and that he hated "the bodies and the sexual organs [of the young Italian boys and girls]."[6]

This change of perspective seems to be fundamental to Pasolini's last film, *Salò o le 120 giornate di Sodoma* (Pasolini's 120 Days of Sodom, 1975). Not only had Pasolini arrived at the conclusion that making sex the centerpiece of cinematic populism brings one closer to exploitation than to liberation, but he was also reacting to the exploitation of sex in the Nazi-porno films that were flooding the Italian market at that time. In *Salò*, the substitution of the Italian fascist establishment for the Nazi-porno caricatures of German war criminals became an important part of Pasolini's cultural commentary.

The other source of inspiration for *Salò* include the Marquis de Sade (in whom Pasolini had a lifelong interest), Nietzsche, Bataille, and Klosowski. In one way or another, all are referred to in the film. The action of *Salò* is adapted from Sade's *120 Days of Sodom* (written in a prison cell prior to the 1789 French Revolution and first published in 1904), with the setting transferred to the Italian Social Republic of 1944. The protagonists of the film—an Italian government minister, a duke, a president, and a bishop—order scores of young women and men to be rounded up in the neighboring villages and incarcerated in a mansion. There the victims are

Salò

exposed to the abuses, atrocities, and humiliations of several circles of hell—resembling Dante's as much as Sade's. As the macabre ritual unfolds, three old "madames" relate the worst perversities they have witnessed and performed, with a fourth "madame" accompanying them on the piano.

The motivation behind this deliberately scandalous film is multifold, comprising many of Pasolini's favorite themes. And as Richard Roud observed, there is Pasolini's longstanding idea that "it is also the victim's look that suggests the violence which will be done to him or to her." Given the bizarre circumstances of Pasolini's death just after the film was finished, *Salò* is a "frighteningly prophetic work,"[7] which left the critics perplexed. Their opinions ranged from unconditional admiration to unconditional rejection. Initially, not too many Italians had a chance to see the film as it was immediately seized by the censors, the same censors who had not objected to the pornography of the Nazi-erotic genre. Roland Barthes probably made the best characterization of *Salò* (in *Le Monde*, June 16, 1976):

> Pasolini's literal approach exerts a strange and surprising effect. One might think that literality serves the cause of truth or reality. Not at all: the letter distorts matters of conscience on which we are obliged to take a stand. By remaining faithful to the letter of the scenes in Sade, Pasolini managed to distort Sade as a matter-of-conscience and fascism as a matter-of-conscience. . . . His film misses on two counts: everything that renders fascism *unreal* is bad, and everything that renders Sade *real* is wrong. And still . . . Pasolini's film has a value of hazy recognition of something in each of us, poorly mastered but definitely embarrassing: it embarrasses us all, thanks to Pasolini's own naïveté; it prevents us from redeeming ourselves. This is why I wonder if, as the outcome of a long string of errors, Pasolini's *Salò* is not—when all is said and done—a peculiarly "Sadian" object: absolutely irreclaimable. Nobody, in fact, seems to be able to.[8]

One morning in 1975, Pasolini's mutilated body was found on a filthy vacant lot near the beaches of Ostia. A young "ragazzo di vita," whom Pasolini had picked up the previous night near the Central Station, in Rome, confessed to the crime. Some claimed that Pasolini, having reached the lowest depths of pessimism, had subconsciously been looking for a murderer. But most believed otherwise. Bernardo Bertolucci said: "I do not know his murderer. Nor do I know his motive, but the fact is that by killing him, they gagged him. As if someone had decided to shut him up forever."[9]

Thus, the voice of Pier Paolo Pasolini was silenced. He was only fifty-three at the time of his death. His enemies were many and powerful. But so were his friends and admirers. "Pasolini marked a great period in the intellectual history of our country," said Italo Calvino. And Alberto Moravia contended, in the foreword to the first posthumous edition of *Children of Life*, that Pasolini was a "central figure of our culture, a poet, and a narrator who left his mark on an entire period, a filmmaker of genius and an inexhaustible essayist."[10]

In 1977, shortly before his death, Roberto Rossellini said in Cannes: "For the last fifteen or sixteen years, I have been totally out of touch with the production of fiction films, yet each year I have produced a big work—none of which has been a big enough success to make me really popular. But my purpose is to illustrate moments of thoughts, moments of renaissance. Throughout history, anyone who has come up with a new idea has been treated with cruelty. In terms of fear, this is a part of our nature. Desire and fear are the two passions in human beings. Desire leads to adventure: fear stops us. So the world is a conflict between conservatives and revolutionaries. Both are necessary for the world to advance."[11]

In the early sixties, Rossellini made his last fiction films—*Viva l'Italia* (Long Live Italy, 1960) and *Vanina Vanini* (1962). In *Long Live Italy*, he attempted to account for the events surrounding the expedition of Garibaldi's "1000," which led to the proclamation of Italian unity in 1861. His aim was not a dramatization of the events but a historical newsreel shot partly on authentic locations. But Rossellini failed to establish a style appropriate to his reconstruction of facts. His "facts" look contrived, and his "pure history," deprived of any subjective insight, is bland and uninteresting.

The romantic story of *Vanina Vanini*—based on Stendhal's account of a love affair between a revolutionary and a princess in his *Chroniques italiennes*— was also approached as a "news item" (un fatto di cronaca). Rossellini intended to create a "historical documentary" about life in papal Rome at the beginning of the nineteenth century. But as in *Long Live Italy*, the result instead resembled a series of populist picture-postcards, and the deliberate absence of a romantic style marred the potential of the romantic tale.

As became clear later, at that time Rossellini's interest was no longer with any kind of fiction film. In 1964, he wrote, produced, and supervised a television film in five episodes, *L'età del ferro* (The Iron Age), directed by his son Renzo. The result was rather mediocre. More important were Rossellini's programatic statements accompanying the production of the film, as well as his overall activity in the television field.

For the last fifteen years of his life, two major problems occupied Rossellini: the general situation of film and television all over the world and the question of how to use the modern media to enlighten the average citizen about his historical roots and the progress of human knowledge (which, for Rossellini, represented the only progress of mankind). Rossellini became increasingly attracted by the idea of "didactic" cinema and eventually devoted himself entirely to it. At the same time, he tried to alert public opinion to the importance of high quality television programs and to facilitate a better understanding between film and television.

One result of Rossellini's preoccupations was a small masterpiece produced by the French television network. *La prise du pouvoir par Louis XIV* (The Rise to Power of Louis XIV, 1966) is a documentary reconstruction of the birth of absolute monarchy in France in the early seventeenth century. First we see the prolonged death of Cardinal Mazarin, who bequests the financier Colbert to the young king. Then, with the court still in mourning, the young king tells the council of the realm: "It is about time that I should rule alone." The takeover by the short, unattractive king is portrayed as a cold ritual, without elaborate speeches or spectacular demonstrations. (The spectacle follows later when Louis XIV displays his power and creates the sumptuous ceremonies whose grandeur came to be symbolized by Versailles.) Rossellini's own experience with a detached rendition of human relationships enabled him to create an impressive portrayal of the young king and his relationships with his relatives, friends, and courtesans. Rossellini had always been one of the most consistent proponents of the sequence shot, which made his transition to the techniques of television particularly smooth. His distance from the material, as well as his almost ideal mixture of the unique and the general, anticipated some of the features of the "new cinema of the seventies." In 1971, Rossellini briefly summed up his approach:

> I came to understand film as a means of confronting real life, as getting, in a way, close to authentic things. Neorealism was for me a moral attitude and a precise effort to learn. Nothing else. Later I realized that films are too suggestive, and because this suggestiveness is so easy to attain, there is a lot of theorizing about the product, ultimately creating a mythical aura about it. I tried to rationalize my feeling and eventually achieved a transition between the two approaches to filmmaking.[12]

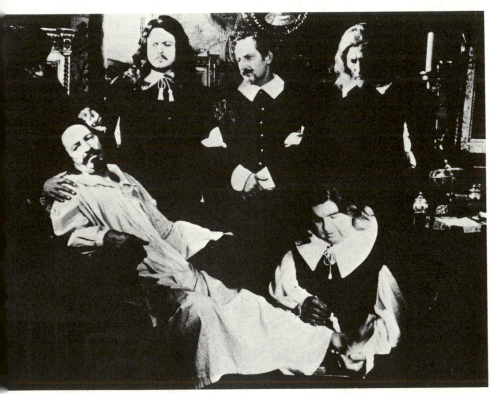

The Rise to Power of Louis XIV

Between 1967 and 1975, Rossellini coauthored and directed seven television programs about people who, in his eyes, had been instrumental in creating the foundations of our civilization: *Atti degli apostoli* (The Acts of the Apostles, 1968), *Socrate* (Socrates, 1970), *Blaise Pascal* (1971), *Agostino d'Ippona* (Augustine of Hippo, 1972), *L'età di Cosimo* (The Age of the Medici, 1973), *Cartesius* (Descartes, 1974), and *The Messiah* (1975). With the exception of *The Messiah* (backed by the American Family Theater), all the programs were produced by the Italian television network, sometimes in collaboration with other networks, most often the French national network. All seven productions were conceived specifically for television, and it is a disservice to Rossellini to release them as large-screen films. None of them matches the cinematic qualities of *The Rise to Power of Louis XIV*, but these qualities were not Rossellini's primary concern.

His ambition was to reach the largest possible television audiences ("the Sardinian shepherds") by depicting the everyday life of people who had changed the face of the world. Rossellini presented each historical figure in the context of the civilization into which he was born. His main success rests in the way in which (in his best programs—*Blaise Pascal* and *Augustine of Hippo*) he managed to avoid the boredom of a purely didactical approach. He never lectured or preached but always strove simply to inform. In 1966, he pointed out:

> It is not important to educate. One should undergo a certain education, but out of his free will, after he had access to an enormous amount of information. Instead, we tend to reduce the part played by information in the process of instruction in order to act with more power and efficiency. At the same time, we tend to transform art into a means of escape, into a sign of decadence. Where has all the thinking gone? There is no greater joy than that provided by thinking. Unfortunately, we live in a society that does everything to make people as superficial as possible. I would even say as shallow as possible. . . . As I live a rather isolated life, I am always amazed to discover that people circulate not only received ideas but also received phrases. It is as if people have acquired them at a supermarket, the same way you buy things made out of plastic.[13]

Similarly, Rossellini was preoccupied with the future of the art of film, which, he envisioned, would entail close cooperation with television. Toward the end of his life, he wrote:

> If we managed to establish a collaboration between the two media, the chances for the development of creativity would be enhanced. Film would profit from a larger and relatively more secure market. If television became associated with movie production, it would receive a part of the films' profits and could become less dependent on commercials.[14]

In May 1977, Rossellini accepted the chairmanship of the jury of the International Film Festival in Cannes. He used his position to conduct an international colloquium on the crisis of the world and the corresponding crisis in the film industry. The jury's decision to award the Grand Prize to *Padre Padrone* by Vittorio and Paolo Taviani, a small-budget 16mm film made for Italian television, provoked a scandal. The pressures on Rossellini to reconsider the decision were enormous, but he held firm. Eventually, he appeared alone on the stage to present the award, as the festival's president had decided to demonstrate his disapproval by his absence. This was the first incidence of such open conflict in the festival's long history. Rossellini died of a heart attack a week later.

At the time of his death, Rossellini was preparing another television production. It was a biography of the young Karl Marx, covering the years before the publication of the *Communist Manifesto*. As this project was not destined to be completed, *The Messiah* remains Rossellini's last work. In his 1976 review the French critic Claude Beylie paid tribute to the filmmaker: "You have to love film madly, you have to reach the outermost limits of its possibilities, you have to refuse all its deceptive temptations and vain artifice to arrive at such sublime austerity as was achieved by the man called Roberto Rossellini."[15]

The two disparate concepts of art, which had dominated the Italian cultural scene since the nineteenth century (a direct approach to reality on the one hand and an emphasis on the imagination on the other) were gradually fused into a single aesthetic combining the neorealist tradition with the authentic Italian joy of fantasizing. The mixture of Zavattini's unconditional acceptance of "life as it is" and Della Volpe's "cinematic poetry" became the hallmark of the best Italian films (Antonioni, Visconti, Pasolini, the Tavianis, Bertolucci, Bellocchio, Olmi, and

The Messiah

Ferreri). After years of concentrating on the quest for reality, the Italian cinema achieved a Pavesian blend of realistic experience with the symbolic metamorphosis of reality, in short, a "reality Italian style."

One filmmaker in particular seems to exemplify this entire process of synthesis, the creation of a new artistic vision. Federico Fellini adopted not only the Pavesian "profound meaning of symbolism" but also Pirandello's vision of life as illusion and Calderón's dreamed-up world. Yet Fellini's symbols, illusions, and dreams always remained those of a neorealist who maintains a certain historical context and re-creates an unmistakable atmosphere.[16]

In 1967, while convalescing from a serious illness, Fellini wrote a collection of reminiscences entitled *My Rimini*. It begins with his awakening in a hospital bed and then goes back to his first dreams, to his childhood, and to the people who were part of it. In the early seventies, after exorcising his fear of death in *Satyricon*, Fellini returned to this book of recollections and directed three avowedly autobiographical films: *The Clowns* (1971), *Fellini Roma* (1972), and *Amarcord* (1973). Some consider this period of Fellini's career an involution (which may be so) or a degeneration of his original ambitions (which is doubtful).

The development of Fellini's *oeuvre* into a type of visual remembrance seems virtually inevitable.[17] But Fellini is not Proust, who evoked his childhood through the prism of the experience of a sophisticated French intellectual. Fellini is an Italian country boy who "remained a boy too long," and, above all, he is a master of ceremonies.[18]

The Clowns, Roma, and *Amarcord* transform Fellini's private world into a spectacle that can go on forever or, as Fellini put it, "as long as the money lasts." As in *Juliet of the Spirits,* Fellini again evokes spirits and apparitions—which this time assume real proportions and belong to his own world—and as in *8½,* he assembles them into parades and processions, marching to Nino Rota's obsessive music. The play of memory, characteristic of all Fellini's films, becomes the center of his chronicles, which juxtapose recollections, images, stories, impressions, and dreams. There is no plot, there are no protagonists, even the picaresque quality of Fellini's previous films gives way to a loose mixture of real and unreal, of the possible and the fantastic.

The Clowns, made for television and originally intended as a documentary about the last great clowns, turned into a documentary about Fellini's infatuation with the circus and about Rimini where his childhood dreams were born. Fellini himself assumes the role of a Dantean guide, leading us in person through the entire film, pondering the manifold aspect of the phenomenon referred to as clownishness. Fellini divides all humanity into white clowns and augustes.

> The elegance, grace, lucidity, and intelligence that the white clowns represent symbolize ideal and unique situations and an uncontested divinity. . . . Auguste, a baby who soils its pants, rebels against such perfectionism, gets drunk, rolls over, embodying eternal defiance. . . . Moravia is an auguste who wanted to be a white clown. Pasolini is a beautiful and self-assertive clown. Antonioni is one of those silent, sad, and nice augustes. Picasso? A triumphant, impudent auguste, free of complexes, who knows everything. Einstein: a dreaming, charming

auguste who never says a word but at the last moment pulls out of his costume the solution of the puzzle posed by the cunning white clown. Hitler: white clown. Mussolini: auguste. Freud: white clown. Jung: auguste.[19]

After *The Clowns,* Fellini turned to Rome, that city that he had adopted and where he "eventually" grew up. In 1972, he directed *Roma,* which provoked controversial reactions. Most Romans, and probably most Italians, do not like *Roma.* Its exaggerations offend them, and its concept of a "city as a state of mind" seems remote from Rome's chaotic order. Yet for Fellini, exaggeration has always served to emphasize a nucleus of meanings linked to the formative process of his own personality. He never pretended, never intended, to see his Rome as Rome. The voluptuous women with enormous buttocks and breasts, the fashion show of clerical attire, the open mouths gulping down incredible amounts of spaghetti, the traffic jam at the entrance to Armageddon, "the merry-go-round of images that takes us from the grotesque to the supernatural, from emotions to hilarity and that has enraptured me, moved me, and excited me," as Jean de Baroncelli put it,[20]—all this belongs to Fellini's own personal theater, so far away from Visconti's "teatrum mundi." In the terminology of Umberto Eco, *Roma* is an "open work," like an "oriented invitation (neither coercive nor univocal) to the rather free integration of the interpreter inside a world which remains controlled by the author."[21]

Like *Roma, Amarcord* is a stream of apparitions from Fellini's life, connected by meager narrative links and embodied in flamboyant images.[22] Fellini roams freely in his reminiscences, and along with them he presents their historical context of fascism, which is staged as the world's greatest circus. Fascist parades with enormous portraits of Mussolini, inane music, and bombastic speeches fit perfectly into the Fellinian world where monsters have always held a special place.

In *Amarcord,* the protagonist Moraldo/Fellini returns from Rome to Rimini, from his mid-life crisis to childhood innocence. He brings back to life all the people he used to be fond of, creating a portrait of a period, in which nothing is authentic but its spirit. The parade of apparitions includes Fellini himself as the little Titta, his parents, his "vitelloni" friends yawning in the outdoor cafés, a crazy uncle, fascist jailors and their prisoners—and the women: women of all ages, sizes, and reputations led by Gradisca, a whore with a red beret and a heart of gold.

Long before *Amarcord,* and even *Satyricon,* Fellini had wanted to make a film "about women only," loosely based on the novel by Mario Tobino *The Free Women of Magliano.* Tobino's story, which takes place in a women's hostel, might have provided a perfect springboard for Fellini's repetitive tales of women-mothers-wives-whores. But in 1980, Fellini finally wrote his women film himself, centering it around an aging Moraldo (Marcello Mastroianni) and his quest for the ideal woman. *La città delle donne* (The City of Women) is a *Reader's Digest* of Fellini's myths. Their repetitiveness, though rightly admired by Ugo Casiraghi in *Amarcord* ("It is because it repeats recurrent motifs that Fellini's fantasy appears unsurpassed") here loses all forward impetus, and the necessary link to reality is lacking. *The City of Women* repeats the same questions that Moraldo had been asking twenty years earlier—"Where am I? Where am I going?" Now though the answers hold little interest.[23]

Amarcord

Actually, at the time of *The City of Women,* Fellini had already made a "women film." His 1976 *Casanova* tells the story of a man's journey through life with women waiting at each of its stations and deciding its further course. At the end of his wanderings, the man fulfills his lifelong quest for the ideal woman by falling desperately in love with a dancing doll who does everything he desires. And it is with her that he waltzes on a frozen Venetian lagoon in his last dream before his death.

Casanova, the film that Fellini was reluctant to direct ("His memoirs are boring like a phone book; it is anticinema," he claimed), became his most ambitious film of the seventies. In his vision of the eighteenth-century "dolce vita" with Casanova as a humpbacked, perspiring satyr at its center, Fellini created a mirror of contemporary anxieties and their dependence on the power structures. The producer's insistence that the film be in English (a major reason for Fellini's aversion to the project) eventually helped Fellini attain a higher degree of visual abstraction. Deprived of his usual verbal contact with the actors, Fellini re-created Casanova's *Memoirs* through sheer personal fantasy and supreme stylization, thus finding what was probably the best possible approach to the book's meticulous sexual chronicling. Casanova's journey through women's bodies is re-created as a mythical trip leading to self-annihilation and expressing a pathological yearning for self-pity. In *Casanova's* picaresque chain of split stories (memory sequences), Fellini relinquished the flow of images characteristic of *8½* and *Amarcord* in favor of abrupt transitions from scene to scene, reminiscent of *La dolce vita.* The imagery bursts with a baroque opulence, lavish colors, far-fetched fancies, and unexpected whims and is charged with erotic symbolism. The sexual symbolism and voyeurism became the focal point for many critical evaluations of the film with only a few critics recognizing the protagonist's existential quest as the main theme.

Still more controversy greeted Fellini's television film *Prova d'orchestra* (Orchestra Rehearsal, 1979). Some rejected it as "reactionary and nihilistic"; others emphasized the pertinence of its parable. *Orchestra Rehearsal* is a seventy-minute satirical television sketch about an orchestra whose members, for different reasons, refuse to follow the conductor. Order is restored only after the rehearsal hall has fallen to pieces and one of the musicians has been injured. The parable this time is neither abstract nor far-fetched. The deconsecrated chapel where the rehearsal takes place is Fellini's Italy, paralyzed by strikes, protest movements, and terrorism, a country of an exorbitant individualism where a return to dictatorship can never be excluded.

Shot in four weeks and cast with nonprofessionals (except for the conductor), *Orchestra Rehearsal* is yet another outpouring of Fellini's imaginativeness, blending realistic observation (the musicians' faces, gestures, and stories) with a fantasmagoric vision of a world in disarray. "To interpret it clumsily is to be in danger of dismantling it forever," Vincent Canby warned.[24] The danger of overinterpretation applies to all of Fellini's *oeuvre*: the *oeuvre* of a minstrel and a street singer ("cantastorie," as he always calls himself), of a brilliant auguste roaring with laughter and crying with despair. "My job is to draw music out of silence, to turn wine into blood and bread into flesh," says the conductor in *Orchestra Rehearsal*. Or is it rather Fellini who is speaking?

Antonioni was thirty-eight years old when his first feature film, *Chronicle of a Love*, was released. When he finished *Red Desert*, he had just turned fifty-three. In fifteen years he had made nine fiction films and had created a style that placed him among the exceptional artists referred to by Penelope Houston when she wrote: "Some filmmakers change the way we see things; a few more change some of the things we see."[25]

His intimate knowledge and understanding of Italy enabled Antonioni to reach the high degree of phenomenological abstraction that became his trademark. But in the mid-sixties, his way of "changing some of the things we see" gradually became emancipated from its original source. At one time Antonioni had even contended that as a northerner he could not make a film in southern Italy. Then he made *L'avventura*, and with this film his style and vision became independent of the concrete context for the first time. The story of a group of Romans cruising along the shores of Sicily provided Antonioni with an unfamiliar landscape that could be observed but not explained or understood. Subsequently, he went on to find similarly unscrutable backgrounds in the cities of Milan and Ravenna.

There was no particular reason why Antonioni's exploration of Italy should not have continued. But he had begun considering the possibility of filming in a completely alien environment, such as a desert or a jungle. For the next fifteen years he did all his work outside Italy, going to England, to the United States, then to China, Spain, and the African desert.

All the films that follow *Red Desert* share one recurrent theme. Their real concern is not "swinging London" (*Blow-Up*), or California's "flower children" (*Zabriskie Point*), or Mao's China (*Chung Kuo*), or European and African merchants of death (*The Passenger*). Their single message is man's failure to grasp anything that reaches beyond immediate reality.

Antonioni got the idea for *Zabriskie Point* (1970) when he stopped in the American West on the way home from Japan. Its story was written quickly, and the film was shot without any major problems. Its protagonist, Mark, unjustly suspected of being involved in the killing of a policeman during a university campus riot, takes off for the desert in a "borrowed" small airplane. At Zabriskie Point, at the bottom of Death Valley, he meets Daria, another social outlaw. They fall in love, as if the original paradise still existed. Intoxicated with happiness, Mark flies back to return what he has "borrowed" and is shot down by the police. In her rage and despair, Daria imagines blowing up her boss's house, which to her symbolizes the vapidity and power of the business establishment.

Despite Antonioni's poignant observations and his ideal perspective as a complete outsider, the metaphor of *Zabriskie Point* does not work. Unlike Antonioni's Italian films or even *Blow-Up, Zabriskie Point* is not an existential metaphor rooted in a concrete milieu but only an idea for a metaphor. Its failure testifies to the impossibility of attaining poetic abstraction through equally abstract presuppositions.

The metaphor in *Chung Kuo* (China, 1972) is more concrete. "I presented China through a series of images of China, not through the idea that the Chinese would like me to have about China," Antonioni told Aldo Tassone. "Their social structures are abstract realities that require a different kind of visual discourse, more didactic than the extemporaneous and instinctive discourse to which I was accustomed."[26]

Invited to China by Chou En-lai, Antonioni shot nine hours of footage there (of which he ultimately used about a fourth). He traveled from Peking to Nanking but was not allowed to visit all the places he wanted to. He never established any contact with individuals. "There are no gestures analogous to ours," he said. "There are no similar syllables and intonations." Thus, he filmed what he saw: different gestures, syllables, and intonations. "Do not look for anything else but my own vision of China. I am a spectator and my camera is my notebook." There is much more to the film than this, though. The masses of people captured by his camera—in the streets, at a market, at a funeral—speak a language that for us is the equivalent of silence. And yet it suggests something, and we almost have the feeling we can understand. "They all speak, addressing each other, asking each other questions, looking at us, and finally they generate a crisis in our own silence."[27]

Chung Kuo is an extremely impressive film, probably the best ever made about contemporary China. Antonioni used the same detached, seemingly indifferent approach in his following film, *Professione: Reporter* (The Passenger, 1975), set in the African desert. A reporter, Locke, switches passports with a stranger named David Robertson, who has just died in a sleazy African hotel. Along with Robertson's passport, he inherits his mistress and his career as an idealistic gun runner. But there is only one path he can take: from the first death in a hotel room to another death in another hotel room.

The Passenger's structure is very straightforward, allowing the metaphor to emerge with all the complexity and ambiguity Antonioni had been seeking. It suggests the existential situation of a man who has lived just as a witness to the events around him and who suddenly finds himself participating in things he has tried to avoid. Juxtaposing the main narrative with images from England and Barcelona, Antonioni leads the protagonist to his second death. This final sequence, which lasts seven minutes, epitomizes Antonioni's "quest for reality." Locke is resting on his hotel bed. His mistress has just left the hotel and is standing outside. In the stifling hot little square, two children are playing, and an old man is sitting nearby observing them. A car arrives. A black man gets out and walks toward the hotel, his white driver asks David's girlfriend something, the black man returns, and the car speeds off. Almost immediately afterwards, a police car arrives, followed by another car with David's wife and with men in business suits. They enter the hotel and go to David's/Locke's room. His body lies stretched out on the bed. One of the men pronounces him dead. David's wife declares that she does not know him while his girlfriend identifies him as David Robertson. The final image is a shot of the orderly, expressionless façade of the hotel. Antonioni explains, quoting the Austrian philosopher Ludwig Wittgenstein: "One should keep silent about things one cannot speak of."

After *The Passenger*, Antonioni did not make another film for five years. In 1980, he shot in video *Il mistero di Oberwald*, a teleplay based on Jean Cocteau's play *The Two-Headed Eagle*. Except for an Antonionian use of colors and the casting of Monica Vitti in the main role, the film has little in common with Antonioni's vision. Some thought that Antonioni might follow Rossellini's example and find in television a new medium for himself. But Antonioni did not feel at ease with the television camera, which, according to him, "rapes reality."[28]

With *Identificazione di una donna* (Identification of a Woman, 1982), after five films made abroad, the seventy-year old Antonioni returned to his homeland, to his "roots," as he put it, to his lifelong, intense, and uneasy relationship to women. *Identification of a Woman*, set in Rome and Venice, can be read as a "hommage" to women made by someone who has tried to understand them all his life, to grasp their feelings by all means, even by dissecting their reactions like those of some strange animals. But the enigma—the post-neorealist "enigma of facts"—remained. Both the heroines of the very autobiographical *Identification of a Woman* elude the protagonist, a film director, who is painfully coping with a private and professional crisis. "You are too lucid," he says to them at different moments, confessing his dismay and his acceptance of nonunderstanding. At the end of his career, Antonioni, like many great artists, has the guts to say that the "reality of life" has evaded him.

Identification of a Woman sums up Antonioni's themes and imagery in a perfectly balanced but slightly academic way. It may represent his thematic return to Italy but not to the roots of his art. For the first time in Antonioni's career, the characters are detached from their background, lacking historical specificity. For the first time, their symbolic message stifles their interdependence with the outside world, the determining element of Antonioni's analysis of the human psychological

Identification of a Woman

machinery. The metaphor prevailed in its "irrational, romantic, and gratuitous way," as Galvano Della Volpe might have put it.

The "night of the long knives" in *The Damned* was Visconti's last spectacular action sequence. After suffering a stroke in 1971, he had to renounce the kind of filmmaking that requires major physical effort—directing crowds and organizing large sets—such as the ball in *The Leopard* or the battle at Custoza.

His last films—*Morte a Venezia* (Death in Venice, 1971), *Ludwig* (1973), *Gruppo di famiglia in un interno* (Conversation Piece, 1974), and *L'innocente* (The Innocent, 1976)—concentrated more on the protagonists' inner conflicts than on conflicts among the characters. Their plots centered around the evocation of a Sartrean "loss of self," on a progressive blurring of the distinction between the characters and their environment. The portrayal of the relationship between the characters and the environment, which had been one of the hallmarks of Visconti's *oeuvre*, became less effective whereas the Viscontian dilemma between passion and reason became increasingly agonizing and was tainted with a Proustian despair.

In 1971, unable to find funding for a long-planned adaptation of Proust's *Remembrance of Things Past*, Visconti turned to Thomas Mann's novella *Death in Venice*. Since 1945, he had had in mind a film set in early twentieth-century Venice, which for him symbolized the paradise lost of a certain segment of the European aristocracy.

Because his other project to bring to the screen "The Trial of Maria Tarnowska," the story of a notorious Venetian adventuress, also never materialized, it was eventually Mann's work that became his vehicle for portraying the decadence of "belle époque" Europe.[29] Visconti changed the profession of the main character, Gustav von Aschenbach, from writer to composer, imbuing him with many resemblances to Gustav Mahler.[30] But the essence of the story remained unchanged. Both Mann and Visconti merge the aging man's passion for a fourteen-year-old Polish boy with his lifelong quest for ultimate beauty, observing his growing isolation and his lonely death through the prism of his yearning for the sublime. Visconti's re-creation of the other face of Venice—not the city of travel brochures, but a cold, gray, and hostile place—conveys the feeling of time passing, of historical eras ended, of loves abandoned and passions spent. A chain of memories is developed into a series of flashbacks showing Aschenbach's married life and artistic endeavors in a structure that enhances Mann's parallel between creation and death. As in *Senso*, Visconti uses color to provide the final touch in most scenes, be it the flamboyance of Tadzio's mother's dresses or the ash-paleness of a city stricken by the plague.

Death in Venice is Visconti's last great film. *Ludwig* (1973), which depicts the descent into madness of the notorious nineteenth-century Bavarian king, suffers from numerous weaknesses. Visconti again displayed his decorative and operatic talents as well as his unique knowledge of a certain European cultural atmosphere, but the ornate portrayal of a "personalité intime," which formed the core of the

Death in Venice

script, failed to come to life on the screen. The film was further damaged by drastic cuts by the producer and the distributors and is rarely seen in its entirety.[31]

In 1972, a second stroke left Visconti partly paralyzed. Now his films had to be reduced to "Kammerspiele" confined to interiors and using few actors. *Conversation Piece* and *The Innocent* were the products of this last attempt to continue working against all odds.[32] *Conversation Piece*—a success in Europe, a failure in the United States—is a portrait of a man facing his death and a requiem for the society he once represented. In a dilapidated Roman palace, whose secret rooms and sinuous staircases bring to mind the Leopard's wondrous Sicilian villa, an old professor, set in his ways, confronts the dreams and vices of the young generation of the early seventies. The clash of two cultures is revealed when this lonely man rather unwittingly decides to rent part of his house to a nouveau riche family and becomes a reluctant, yet curious, witness to their "scenes from a marriage," scenes from a revolution, and scenes of violent death.

Conversation Piece is a rigorously directed film that achieves its strength by establishing a connection between the claustrophobic spaces of the palace and the limitations imposed by human mortality. But Visconti's judgment has lost its dialectical dimension, which was his strong point in *Senso* and *Rocco*. The portrait of the protagonist is drawn with persuasive authority, but the characters of the young tenants are weakened by overgeneralization, and they do not fit into coherent relationships.

The Innocent

Visconti's shift into a private world was accomplished with impressive grace and style in *The Innocent* where the subject was more concise and the subplots more dramatically compressed. For these qualities the film is indebted to Gabriele D'Annunzio's 1892 novel. It is a story of lives wrecked by passion and an ever-increasing tension that provided Visconti with the opportunity to indulge in the evocation of the isolated splendor of a decadent aristocratic world at the turn of the century and to reveal its ambiguous morality with the knowledge of a true connoisseur. As in *Senso*, the film's decorative richness enhances the haunting atmosphere where fantasy is presented as fact and fact as fiction. The protagonist, a sophisticated, cultured man, is overcome by jealousy when his estranged wife has a child by another man. In an effort to rid himself of his emotion, the first unambiguous feeling he has experienced in his life, he kills the child. "Love it or leave it, it is quintessentially Visconti," David Sterrit wrote in 1979.[33]

On March 17, 1976, Visconti listened several times to Brahms's Second Symphony and then said to his sister Uberta: "Adesso basta!" (Enough now!). Minutes later he was dead, leaving the final editing of *The Innocent* to others.

XII

UNDER THE SIGN OF VIOLENCE

Question: "In a way, you have something in common with Ferreri
and Bellocchio. You were all born under the sign of
violence."
Vittorio Taviani: "Yes, under the sign of our time."[1]

In the seventies, a new quest for reality—that unattainable holy grail of the Italian cinema—was manifest in the films of the Tavianis and Ermanno Olmi. Departing from both Zavattini's demand for unvarnished realism and Rossellini's subjective authenticity, the Italian cinema gradually adopted more metaphoric visions. The direct relationship to real life, however, which has always guided the vision of Italian filmmakers, was never abandoned and remained their hallmark. The best films of the seventies were characterized by the fusion of a metaphoric language with the neorealist insistence on complete continuity between life and the screen.

A metaphoric approach to reality also signifies the directors' rejection of existing political structures and their conviction that the traditional aesthetic values had become increasingly associated with the reigning order. In the postfascist era, the neorealists' attitude toward their society had been predominantly positive, in fact optimistic. They did not consciously attempt to create distorted visions of reality, nor were they alienated from society. They themselves invented the form of their films, and this form had not yet been integrated into the traditional cinematic structures, nor was it being used by the political establishment for its own needs.

The cinematic avant-garde of the seventies, on the other hand, was in profound disagreement with the Italian regime and, unlike the neorealists, could not see any immediate possibility for effecting political modifications, let alone substantial social change.[2] Their narrative became increasingly metaphoric, elusive, and elaborate whereas their form was frequently linked to ideology. The search for a style often was an intrinsic part of the ideological search, suggesting the authors' alienation from official moral values. In this sense, the disruption of traditional forms, tainted with rebellion and defiance, is reminiscent of the time of *Ossessione*. In the early seventies, Bruno Torri contended:

The true heirs of neorealism, if it serves any purpose to search for them, are not those directors who are imprisoned in the naturalistic tradition and in the general concept of commitment, but rather the filmmakers whose films, including some very elusive and strange ones, have laid bare the basic contradictions of Italian reality. It is clear that these contradictions reach beyond national boundaries: many of their characteristics merge to a large degree with elements of broader and even more revolting reality, such as Western neocapitalism.[3]

An intricate metaphorical dimension pervaded the entire fabric of the Tavianis' films *San Michele aveva un gallo* (St. Michael Had a Rooster, 1971) and *Allonsanfan* (1973), which can also be read as contributions to an internal debate within the Italian Left after 1968. Both films, while set in the past, are conceived as parallels to the post-1960s situation with various leftist factions suggesting radical strategies for destabilizing the Italian regime through the introduction of so-called "propaganda through action." Some leftist leaders read these two films as attacks on their politics. Such a reading betrayed a misinterpretation of their dialectical approach as well as their understanding of radical options. Guido Aristarco, member of the Leftist party Democrazia proletaria, pointed out: "The assumption that the Tavianis are against the New Left is not correct. They are critical only of some extraparliamentary (spontaneous) groups. Their critical attitude must be understood in the context of human sympathy." Aristarco documents the Tavianis' objective portrayal of characters who bear a resemblance to members of contemporary radical groups. This objectivity often contrasts with the prevailingly subjective form, subjective camera, music, colors.[4]

St. Michael Had a Rooster, often considered the Tavianis' best film, is loosely inspired by Tolstoy's story "The Divine and the Human." Set in 1870, its theme is again revolutionary utopia, which survives against all odds and which represents— for the Tavianis as well as a part of the Italian Left—the "moment of truth" (even a crushed or abortive revolution is a step toward future change). Expressed in an allegorical key, the film's narrative develops a convincing case against the possibility of establishing permanence through revolution: each revolution denies the previous one and attempts to negate its achievements. Like all the Tavianis' films, *St. Michael* centers around the conflict between the political and the human (collectivity versus individuality). These forces are perceived as two absolutes that require, but hardly ever reach, a reciprocal accord to achieve mutual realization. As the Tavianis have always preferred Shakespeare to Schiller, they do not present their protagonists as symbols of spokesmen for an epoch but rather concentrate on their human features.

St. Michael is above all the story of a personal tragedy reminiscent of *This Man Must Die*. Giulio Manieri, leader of an international anarchistic revolutionary movement, organizes a symbolic expedition to a small Italian village. He demolishes the grain warehouse and distributes the grain to the peasants. But the peasants react with fear and indifference. Abandoned by his comrades, he is imprisoned. In his cell, he creates an entire imaginary world for himself. In this world he lives as if he were free, talking to his comrades and eating sumptuous imaginary

St. Michael Had a Rooster

meals. Released after ten years, he realizes that the new generation of revolutionaries rejects the ideas for which he was persecuted. The young radicals reproach him "for having delayed the birth of the workers' movement for at least fifteen years." Manieri, set in his romantic, idealistic way, and unable to come to grips with the new scientific socialism, kills himself. Had he not died, the Tavianis seem to suggest, he would have ended by betraying his cause, like Fulvio, the protagonist of *Allonsanfan*. The Tavianis contended: "Those who reject their own social class to dedicate themselves to revolution set out on a road of no return. If they do return, they have already betrayed their goal. One cannot betray one's social class and also the revolutionary option and not pay the price of a fundamental renunciation of all human dignity."[5]

Beginning with the early seventies, the issues raised in *St. Michael* and other Taviani films are typical of the discussions between the traditional Left and the New Left. Manieri (like the Scorpionists or the Sublime Brethren in *Allonsanfan*) represents certain radical groups who were attempting to achieve social changes immediately and at any cost while his adversaries advocate a philosophy typical of the parliamentary Left, especially the Communist party. (These conflicts appear also in *Subversives*, in the discussions between the Venezuelan revolutionary Ettore and his Italian counterparts.)[6]

St. Michael's theme of revolution is further developed in *Allonsanfan*. Its original script begins with a historical introduction: "1816. In Italy, as in the whole of Europe, which has been ravaged by twenty years of war, dethroned monarchs return to power. The last achievements of the French Revolution are annulled, the last revolutionaries scattered throughout the world." Fulvio (Marcello Mastroianni), an aristocrat who had sided with the revolution for twenty years, tries to set himself free from his revolutionary commitment and return to his previous life. Yet his successive attempts to get rid of his comrades only drag him into deeper involvement, culminating with his participation in what amounts to a collective suicide.[7]

In *Allonsanfan*, commitment to the revolution is seen as an irreversible choice. There is no escape, not even through betrayal. The film's structure underlines the conflict between the ideal of historical necessity (the alliance with the peasants as postulated by Fulvio's comrades) and the impossibility of its practical realization. Some scenes are shot with a subjective camera (from Fulvio's point of view); others are rendered objectively. The Sublime Brethren, a secret revolutionary sect, are seen through Fulvio's eyes as a group of fanatic madmen, incarnating the mystical faith in a cause. On the other hand, Allonsanfan, the youngest and the most rational member of the sect, is portrayed with an objective camera as the only one who realizes the real possibilities of a revolution. The Brethren set out for the south, decided to liberate the peasants, and believe the poor will join them. But Fulvio betrays the Brethren and

they are butchered by those they came to liberate. At that moment, the camera changes from Fulvio's ironic, even hateful, view of the Brethren to an objective approach that registers not only the massacre but also Allonsanfan's vision of unity between the revolutionaries (intellectuals) and the oppressed (workers).

The color structure follows the same interlaced subjective-objective schema. The Tavianis reject the notion of "color-symbol" (white standing for good, black for evil). They adopt instead Eisenstein's theory of changing values of colors, along with Goethe's psychology of colors: green, the color of hope, may become the color of despair in certain circumstances. Each character has an inner tonality of color that governs the color changes that occur according to the immediate relationships between characters. The moral symbolism of the colors complements their social symbolism.

In *St. Michael* and *Allonsanfan*, sound is a vital element in the final shape of the narrative. In the first film the tune of a children's song about "St. Michael, who had a white, red, green, and yellow rooster" opens the story and keeps coming back in crucial moments. The song lends a subjective perspective—it is relevant only for the protagonist, and only he seems to hear it. In *Allonsanfan*, the obsessive ditty "Dirin din din," which Fulvio's sister used to sing when they were children, has the same subjective dramatic function. In contrast, the Neapolitan saltarello that accompanies the appearance of the Brethren is used objectively. The Tavianis, both talented musicians, consider music to be the closest art form to filmmaking. Relinquishing all coded significance in sound, they never use music as a mere accompaniment. "We structure our films according to musical rhythms. When we first start contemplating a new film, when we shoot, edit, create the soundtrack—we are always led by the rhythm of music. Literature influences us only in a distant and indirect way. A written page and a cinematic page follow two different rhythms."

Padre Padrone (1977) is the second of the Tavianis' films to be inspired by a work of literature, but as in *St. Michael*, the literary impulse is rather vague and thoroughly restructured in the mode of the cinematic language. In *Padre Padrone*, the Tavianian utopia assumes a concrete dimension for the first time.[8] Its protagonist, an illiterate Sardinian shepherd, reaches a seemingly unattainable goal: he goes back to school and earns a degree in linguistics. Having spent his youth in the mountains with a flock of sheep and tyrannized by his "father-master," he rebels and succeeds in his "revolution." The narrative is carried forward by a dialectical interplay between silence and communication, dialect and language, tribal traditions and modern laws, and also by the ambivalence of the father-son relationship. The form is less allusive and decorative than in the Tavianis' previous work, this time closer to Rossellini than to Visconti. Some critics referred to *Padre Padrone* as a "return to neorealism," substantiating this contention partly by the fact that the literary original, a novel by Gavino Ledda, was based on a true story, Ledda's own life.[9] But one could hardly speak of a return to something that had never entirely disappeared from either the Tavianis' work in particular or from the best Italian cinema in general.

Padre Padrone, a small-budget film shot in 16mm and funded by the Italian state television, was the Tavianis' first commercial success. It was awarded the

Padre Padrone

Grand Prix at the 1977 Cannes Festival, following the dramatic events that led to
Roberto Rossellini's death.[10]

The Tavianis' following film, *Il prato* (The Meadow, 1979), does not digress
from the goal that the Tavianis set for themselves at the very beginning of their
career: to act out the radical options of the present in various formal and historical
settings. *The Meadow*, again funded by the Italian state television, maintains the
Tavianis' characteristic impact in its imagery and the dialectical layer of interlaced
problems. But it does not attain the level of the Tavianis' previous films. The directors do not seem to be at ease with the deepened Brechtian approach or with the
detached form à la Jean-Marie Straub that reveals the story line (more accurately
the problem line) through spoken dialogue or literary commentary. The plot of *The
Meadow* is shaped by discussions among the protagonists, who happen to meet in a
small town in Tuscany where the peasants are engaged in a struggle to acquire
some untilled land (the meadows). The main characters are Giovanni, a romantic
idealist, who dreams of becoming a film director; Enzo, a militant radical; Eugenia,
a teacher, who is emotionally involved with both of them; and Giovani's father, who
represents the disillusionment of the older generation.[11] The driving force of the

film is the attempt to dramatize the anguish of the contemporary world at a time when, according to the Tavianis, the generation gap is not as pronounced as it is during the times of revolution. (Giovanni's father shares the sorrows of today's generation in contrast to the animosity that existed between the Islanders and the Scorpionists or between Giulio Manieri and the new radicals.) The four protagonists consider utopia to be not only the revolution but also happiness, a life free from the schizophrenic split between desire and necessity. Yet the absence of happiness does not mean that happiness does not exist, the Tavianis argue. Nor does Giovanni's suicide negate the revolutionary goals. On the contrary, it confirms the need for a life free of social constraint, having the same positive meaning as Manieri's death, the butchering of the Sublime Brethren, or the desperate journey of the Scorpionists as they head for an unknown "continent."

La notte di San Lorenzo (The Night of the Shooting Stars, 1982) represents not only the romantic highpoint in the Tavianis' *oeuvre* but also the culmination of the attempts of the Italian cinema at a synthesis of its long-time trends—the metaphorico-poetic and the historico-realistic. *The Night of the Shooting Stars* has the effect of a realistic fairy tale set in everyday life. The escape of a group of Italian peasants from the Germans in 1944 and their nonsensical search for the

Il prato

American army are again re-created as an eternal quest for something that may or may not exist. On the one hand, the film is rooted in the reality of the Tavianis' childhood reminiscences (re-created earlier in their documentary *San Miniato, July 1944*); on the other hand, it freely roams in the unlimited spaces of fantasy and poetic imagery. Out of these two alternatives, an extremely solid, well-structured narrative emerges—quite different from the loose associations of the previous Taviani films—which makes *The Night of the Shooting Stars* into a poetic epic of overwhelming terror and beauty. Mino Argentieri summed up the Tavianis' approach: "The Tavianis keep reminding us that thinking is necessary and that it forces us to make choices. This is an important reminder at a time when we are repeatedly asked to not look under the surface of the reigning order and to misapprehend everything so that nothing changes."[12]

Mino Argentieri's words could apply also to the work of Ermanno Olmi, who has concerned himself from the outset with the alienation of contemporary man from the work process, stating man's need not to disregard the simple essentials. His films (e.g., *The Job, One Day, Durante l'estate* [During the Summer, 1971], *La circostanza* [The Circumstance, 1973]) are distinguished by an awesome Kafkaesque and Gogolian perception of the oppressive milieu of bureaucracy, which deprives people of their sense of responsibility.

In 1978, following five years of self-imposed silence, Olmi returned to the film scene with his magnum opus, a three-hour-long film, *L'albero dei zoccoli* (The Tree of the Wooden Clogs), in which the realistic vision is extended into metaphoric dimensions, thus bringing to fulfillment some of the most ambitious aesthetic concepts of Italian film theory.

"I see neorealism as the beginning of the evolution of the Italian cinema as art," Visconti said at the 1953 conference on neorealism at Parma. In a way, *The Tree of the Wooden Clogs* closes the circle begun thirty years earlier by such films as *Paisan* and *Bicycle Thief*. Olmi's picture of nineteenth-century peasant life—a picture seemingly preoccupied simply with a precise registration of facts—could also be considered an example of the "documentary cinematic poetry," which Galvano Della Volpe postulated as a logical continuation of the neorealistic "style of crude reality" as early as 1948. *The Tree of the Wooden Clogs* achieves a synthesis of goals set forth by Zavattini, Della Volpe, and Pasolini (the cinema of poetry), to name only three theoreticians prominent in the "reality versus imagination dilemma." Olmi's film is a faithful portrayal of actual people—Zavattini's ideal—while at the same time it reaches into the symbolic dimension of Della Volpe and also functions on the contemplative level sought by Pasolini.

The year is 1897–1898, the place a Lombard farmstead, the protagonists landless peasants who work the farm and return two-thirds of their harvest to the landlord. Olmi follows several families in their struggle for survival, telling the stories of their humble lives as they were once told to him by just such a peasant, his grandmother. The impulse behind the film is a return to the roots of Italian civilization, which—unlike the French or the English—originated in a rural culture.[13] Along with Pasolini, Olmi considers the loss of traditions to be one of the principal reasons for the alienation and dismay of contemporary man. With *The Tree of the*

The Night of the Shooting Stars

Wooden Clogs he created his own "remembrance of things past," bringing back to life the Rossellinian "things and tears" of a former epoch. He shot the film in an authentic abandoned farmstead; he dressed modern-day peasants in the attire of their ancestors and let them speak in their own dialect, imposing on them only the main lines of a loosely shaped script. The film was distributed in two versions: one version was dubbed into Italian, the other was spoken in the Lombard dialect and subtitled in Italian. The shooting lasted two years. Olmi scripted, directed, photographed, and edited the film and was paid a lump sum of 30 million lire (approximately $27,000). The film became an immediate success worldwide, winning the Grand Prix at the 1978 Cannes Festival, and a popular triumph in Italy.

The episodes follow one another in an uninterrupted flow of narration in accordance with the slow rhythm of peasant daily life and the changing of the seasons. The film introduces the peasants as they prepare for the winter, cleaning the stables and the farm implements. The landlord comes to weigh the corn, and Finard hides a few stones in his barrow. Batisti's wife makes a bag for Minek, one of the few children who goes to school. Before the first snow comes, the corn is taken to the mill. Fifteen-year-old Peppino starts working in the mill to help support his widowed mother and his five brothers and sisters. When it gets cold, the peasants

The Tree of the Wooden Clogs

spend their evenings in the stables. The women work, the men smoke and talk. But above all, they love to tell stories from the past. Old Anselmo gets up secretly at night to spread manure on his tomatoes because his family thinks he is crazy to do that in the winter. A few days before the feast of St. Mary, Trili arrives with his cart full of scarves, ribbons, and fabrics. Maddalena's mother buys some beautiful fabric for her daughter who is going to get married. In the spring, Finard finds a gold coin at the county fair and hides it under the shoe of his horse. Batisti's wife gives birth to another baby. Minek breaks one of his clogs, so at night Batisti secretly cuts down a tree near the brook and makes him new clogs. Finard, unable to find his coin, beats his horse, calling him a thief. The horse retaliates by nearly killing him. Maddalena gets married and goes to Milan with her husband. In the city, for the first time in their lives, the newlyweds are confronted with the facts of politics: a peasants' revolt has been suppressed and they see the villagers being taken away by the police, tied together like cattle. The couple spend the night at a cloister, visiting Maddalena's aunt. In the morning, they receive their wedding gift—a twelve-month-old foundling for whose upbringing the church will give them support payments for the next fourteen years. Anselmo's tomatoes have ripened, and he sells them at the town market. The landlord finds out about the stolen tree and evicts

Batisti from the farmstead. Batisti loads his cart with his family and few belongings, not knowing where to go. Only when the cart has left the courtyard do the peasants come out of the farmstead and stand silently looking after it.

Olmi tells his disconnected anecdotal stories in an extremely elaborate language, using an almost calligraphic, mobile camera and a broad range of colors to follow the changes of the natural light (daylight or the light of the kerosene lamps). His camera (according to Pasolini's definition of the cinema of poetry) "moves from an association of three or four images to an association of twenty images, mutually connected through syntactical webs: from one movement to another, from a freeze-frame to a moving shot, from a close-up to a long shot."[14] Thus, a second dimension is created and transforms the film's basic observation of real life into a metaphor for life remembered, for its unfolding and for the bonds between its various seasons.

Olmi, son of Italian peasants who has spent his life far from the city crowd, commented on the reasons that induced him to make *The Tree of the Wooden Clogs:*

> I returned to the peasant roots of our culture because I am forty-six years old and I feel profoundly disoriented in my present situation. Many people find it impossible to make plans for the future because they have lost all their connections with the past. However, the past is not dead, filed away forever. The main problem of rural society was survival. The contemporary consumer society has resolved this problem but has gotten caught in the tangle of other essential issues. We recognize only two entities: the individual and the crowd. We have lost the sense of "relationship," of the couple, the group, the community, the larger human society. A person approaching the crowd enters into a relationship with strangers. The sense of graduated relationship, which is necessary if we want to get to know the others, has disappeared.[15]

Olmi, the Tavianis, Bellocchio, Ferreri, and all their cinematic fathers and brothers, seem to have achieved new ways of interrogating the social reality that has always been the challenge and the inspiration of Italian cinema. That cinema, having achieved so much that warrants preservation on the shelf of history along with the other arts, can now begin to contemplate some of the grand human themes, starting with Unamuno's "tragic sense of life." The circle leading from reality to metaphor, which all art has to follow over and over again, has been closed once more. A new circle is about to begin, involving another generation, in a changing Italy, in a different world.

Notes

FIRST ENCOUNTERS (BEFORE 1942)

1. Quoted in Alberto Farassino, *Giuseppe De Santis* (Milan: Moizzi, 1978), p. 10. See also Gianni Puccini, "I tempi di cinema," in Orio Caldiron, ed., *Il lungo viaggio del cinema italiano* (Padua: Marsilio, 1965), p. 82.

2. Cesare Pavese, *The Burning Brand: Diaries, 1935–1950* (New York: Walker, 1961), p. 320.

3. Antonio Gramsci, *L'ordine nuovo* (Turin: Einaudi, 1967), pp. 167–68.

4. Interview published in *Nuovi materiali sul cinema italiano, 1929–1943,* 2 vols. (Rome: Mostra Internazionale del Nuovo Cinema, 1976), 2:109.

5. Ibid., p. 125.

6. Ibid., p. 108.

7. The anniversary of Mussolini's march on Rome.

8. *Nuovi materiali,* 2:117.

9. Ibid., p. 138.

10. Ibid., 1:88.

11. Quoted in Robert Dombroski, "Brancati and Fascism: A Profile," *Italian Quarterly,* no. 49, 1969, p. 42.

12. According to Francesco Savio, *Ma l'amore no: Realismo, formalismo, propaganda e telefoni bianchi nel cinema italiano di regime, 1930–1943* (Milan: Sonzogno, 1975), p. xxiv. Other publications give different numbers: 707 according to *Annuario del cinema italiano* (Rome: Garzanti, 1959), 666 films according to *Materiali sul cinema italiano* (Rome: Mostra Internazionale del Nuovo Cinema, 1975), p. 238.

13. *Istituto nazionale LUCE: Origini, organizzazione, e l'attività dell'Istituto nazionale LUCE* (Rome: Istituto Poligrafico dello Stato, 1934), introduction.

The corporative state was based on the fascist conception of government, that is to say, the conception of a monolithic state controlling and directing every activity, ostensibly in the interest of the nation at large. . . . The various corporations, representing every branch of production and every profession, were created by decree of the minister of corporations, who also appointed their executive officers. Their functions included the arrangement of collective contracts, the organization of labor exchanges, the settlement of labor disputes, vocational training, and social welfare in the widest sense. In all these matters, the government acted as umpire and final arbiter. . . . Mussolini has swept away all obstacles to the exercise of dictatorial power. (Ivonne Kirkpatrick, *Mussolini: A Study in Power* [New York: Avon Books, 1964], pp. 241–42)

14. "Why would a cinema inspired by the great fascist revolution not be born along with the cinema inspired by the communist revolution?" G. V. Sampieri asked in *Rivista Italiana di Cinetecnica,* no. 4, May 1930, p. 5.

15. Corrado Pavolini, "Dare all'Italia una coscienza cinematografica"; quoted in *Nuovi materiali,* 1:72.

16. Ibid., p. 119.

17. It is interesting to note that the Centro was funded by the annual revenue of the Venice casino, which was making huge profits during the Venice International Film Festival.

18. Reacting against this reorganization, the four major American companies (MGM, Twentieth Century-Fox, Paramount, and Warner Brothers) severed all contacts with Italy.

19. After the capitulation of Italy in 1943, the greatest part of Cinecittà equipment was taken by the Germans to Germany. Only some of it was saved by Freddi and transferred to Venice.

20. Luigi Freddi, quoted in Fabio Carpi, *Il cinema italiano del dopoguerra* (Milan: Schwarz, 1958), p. 87.

21. In 1937, the ratio of moviegoers per seat in an Italian movie theater was 29.7 as compared with 7.10 in the United States, 15.3 in England, and 19.1 in France.

22. Pierre Leprohon, *The Italian Cinema* (London: Secker & Warburg, 1972), p. 7.

23. According to Luigi Barzini, the fascist upright salute came from this version of *Quo Vadis?*; see Barzini, "The Bad Tooth," *New York Review of Books,* June 15, 1978, p. 24.

24. At the time of *Cabiria,* D'Annunzio lived in Paris, leading a sumptuous life and disposing of a monthly allowance given to him by one of his mistresses. He was in constant need of money, obsessed, among other things, with the fear of dying in poverty.

25. *Corriere della Sera* (Milan), February 28, 1914; quoted in Gian Piero Brunetta, ed., *Letteratura e cinema* (Bologna: Zanichelli, 1976), p. 15.

26. Jakob Burckhardt, *The Civilization of the Renaissance in Italy* (New York: Harper and Brothers, 1958), p. 42.

27. *La Rassegna del Teatro e del Cinematografo* (Milan), February 2, 1926, reads: "The opening images (of *The Last Days*), which show the men and women of Pompeii in the bath, and many others, may be artistic. . . . However, they are, first of all, the most lax exhibition of nudity" (quoted in Aldo Bernardini and Vittorio Martinelli, eds., *Il cinema italiano degli anni venti* [Rome: La Cineteca Nazionale, 1979], p. 78).

28. Burckhardt, *Civilization,* p. 163.

29. Both films were frequently shown in Umberto Barbaro's legendary courses at the prewar Centro Sperimentale di Cinematografia, attended by many who later comprised the neorealist generation.

30. Vladimir Petric, ed., *The Language of the Silent Film* (New York: Museum of Modern Art and Vladimir Petric, 1975), p. 9.

31. According to Ugo Casiraghi's testimony, the negative was stolen by the Germans during the war. After the war, Casiraghi and Francesco Pasinetti followed its traces across Germany, but the negative was never recovered. See also "Sperduti nel buio," *Cinema Nuovo,* no. 10, 1953, p. 263.

32. Francesco Casetti, Alberto Farassino, Aldo Grasso, and Tatti Sanguinetti, "Neorealismo e cinema italiano degli anni '30," in Lino Miccichè, ed., *Il neorealismo cinematografico italiano* (Venice: Marsilio, 1974), p. 336. According to them, the retrospective was organized to prove the primacy of the Italian film in some fields and was inspired by the fascist nationalistic policy. Today, we can assume that the majority of historians who praise the merits of Martoglio's film have never seen it.

33. "Un film italiano di 25 anni fa," *Scenario* (Rome), November 1935; reprinted in

Umberto Barbaro, *Servitù e grandezza del cinema* (Rome: Editori Riuniti, 1961), p. 147. The article was reprinted in different publications in several modified versions.

34. Leprohon, *Italian Cinema*, p. 41.

35. Antonio Pietrangeli, "Analisi spettrale del film realista," *Cinema*, no. 146, 1942, pp. 393–94.

36. Petric, ed., *Language of the Silent Film*, p. 10.

37. The critics of the time did not like the social backdrop of Notari's films, condemning it with words similar to those used years later by the adversaries of neorealism. "This is not the real Naples," said the review of *E piccerella* in *La Rivista Cinematografica*. "It is true, in Naples, like everywhere, acts of violence happen, but to reproduce in a film the most vulgar and disgusting part of the manners and feelings of a city is something that does not deserve applause" (Florence, April 1924; reprinted in Bernardini and Martinelli, eds., *Il cinema italiano*, p. 53).

38. The majority of Notari's films disappeared in the 1930s, but some were reconstructed and made public in the late 1970s.

39. A typical "mamma film" was, e.g., *Miss Dorothy*, made in 1921 by the veteran director Giulio Antamoro (1877–1945). Its heroine, an irretrievable femme fatale, loves the same man as her daughter, who, in turn, does not know who her mother is. (Italian film abounds with stories about illegitimate children, foundlings, or just children of nobody.) The man loves the mother, but she gives him up to the daughter, blesses their union, and immediately dies of a heart attack, leaving her daughter to wonder who this unhappy woman was.

40. Neapolitan films were instrumental in shaping Italian realistic cinema. The directors adopted the realistic perspective for production reasons (because of scarcity of means and the possibility of using free natural resources) or because the realistic approach was in keeping with their own ideological and cultural choices. Neapolitan productions were popular among the lower strata of the population, but they only partly adopted the point of view of the class they were addressing. Although the Neapolitan cinema centered on dramas structured around traditional patterns of guilt and punishment, it was not motivated by didactic intentions as were the productions of Turin and Rome. In their hearts, the directors of Neapolitan movies were close to their protagonists' situations, feeling and understanding their motivations. The moral judgment, which often concluded their stories, was more an obligatory toll paid to the reigning morality and the censors than a demand originating in the narrative. (Gian Piero Brunetta, *Storia del cinema italiano, 1895–1945* [Rome: Editori Riuniti, 1979], p. 163)

41. Brunetta, ed., *Letteratura e cinema*, p. 10.

42. Quoted in Edward R. Tannenbaum, *The Fascist Experience* (New York: Basic Books, 1972), p. 260.

43. See Aldo Santini, "Futurismo non fa più rima con fascismo," *Europeo*, December 1978, p. 71.

44. James Joll, *Antonio Gramsci* (New York: Penguin Books, 1977), p. 31.

45. Enrico Prampolini, in *Gazzetta Ferrarese*, August 20, 1913; quoted in Umbro Apollonio, *Futurist Manifestos* (New York: Viking Press, 1973), p. 118.

46. Apollonio, in the introduction to *Futurist Manifestos*, p. 16.

47. F. T. Marinetti et al., "Primo manifesto per la cinematografia futurista"; reprinted in Brunetta, ed., *Letteratura e cinema*, pp. 11–14.

48. Apollonio, *Futurist Manifestos*, p. 27.

49. Marinetti, "Manifesto tecnico della letteratura futurista"; reprinted in Mario Ver-

done, ed., *Cinema e letteratura del futurismo* (Rome: Centro Sperimentale di Cinematografia, 1968), p. 147.

50. *L'Impero* (Rome) dedicated a large space to cinema, publishing reviews by such men as Umberto Barbaro and Alessandro Blasetti.

51. "Art in Cinema," a symposium on avant-garde film, San Francisco Museum of Modern Art (New York: Arno Press, 1968).

52. Apollonio, *Futurist Manifestos*, p. 219.

53. Flame is a typical D'Annunziesque symbol of passion. In 1915, Giovanni Pastrone shot *Fuoco* (Fire), often considered quintessentially D'Annunziesque. It abounds in intertitles such as: "Your love is like a lantern. Its light is dim, and it lasts all night, watch your flame, your passion, rising toward the sky, Burn me! Burn my soul."

54. Nino Frank, quoted in Leprohon, *Italian Cinema*, p. 35.

55. Some Italian critics limit "fascism" in Italian film of this period only to undisguised propaganda, leaving aside almost completely films permeated with the spirit of fascism in its multiple manifestations. According to the article by Riccardo Redi, "E stato fascista il cinema italiano?" (Was Italian Film Fascist?), the number of "fascist" films made in 1929–1943 varies from zero to fourteen, depending upon the assessment of different critics (*Cinema 70*, no. 121, May–June 1978, p. 38). This contention is disputed by Brunetta, who writes in his *Storia del cinema italiano*:

> During the entire postwar period, efforts were made, from the historical point of view, to regard the phenomenon of fascist cinema as marginal and episodic and to identify as genuinely fascist only films dealing directly with fascism or the fascists. The part of the film industry that collaborated with fascism, accepted all its directives, or attempted to conform to the climate created by the regime was not taken into consideration. The prevailing contention that only about a dozen propagandistic films were made is only partly true. The truth is that the film industry did not miss any of the regime's identification with great moments of history, that it followed and registered all the ideological changes at the top as well as the basic choices of the regime's cultural policy, thus reflecting, even in films that were seemingly not directly propagandistic, the fundamental fascist directives. (p. 381)

56. There were almost no white telephones in Italian films, as is often asserted. The nickname probably originated because of the presence of white telephones in American movies, which became the symbol of upper-class affluence in Italy.

57. Some Italian historians, referring to an "uninterrupted spectacular tradition," consider these films the continuation of the so-called "scripted songs" (canzoni sceneggiate). The "scripted songs" were silent films with their entire plot centered on a popular Neapolitan song, which was sung by one or two singers behind the screen during the projection. The most famous "sceneggiate" of the twenties were *Reginella, Lucia Lucì, Si me vulisse bene* (If You Loved Me), and *Fenesta ca lucive* (The Glaring Window). This last film was conceived as a monumental spectacle, intended to surpass the famous *Cabiria*.

58. *Everybody's Lady* was made mainly to counter the stagnation in the exportation of Italian films and to make Isa Miranda into a star who could compete with her American counterparts. Ophüls was invited to Italy by Angelo Rizzoli, the successful Italian publisher, who was trying to create a film company as a branch of his publishing house.

59. After the success of the film at the Venice Film Festival, the story was bought by Twentieth Century-Fox and made in Hollywood under the same title by Walter Lang in 1938.

60. *Cinema*, August 25, 1941; quoted in Savio, *Ma l'amore no*, p. 32.

61. Thanks to Visconti and his *Bellissima* made in 1951, we have a telling portrait of Blasetti. Visconti had Blasetti play the role of a film director, who selects his future star among hundreds of applicants, and accompanied his appearances with the motif of a quack from Donizetti's opera *Elisir d' amore.*

62. "Giovanni Gentile pointed out in an article published in *Critica Sociale* in 1929: 'Fascism is the child of risorgimento.' Following his declaration, all of fascist historiography moved in this direction. The Garibaldian trend of the time played a preparatory role, helping to demonstrate the historical continuity between the red and the black shirts" (Brunetta, *Storia del cinema italiano,* p. 235).

63. After the war, this ending disappeared from the prints distributed in Italy.

64. Carlo Lizzani, *Storia del cinema italiano* (Florence: Parenti, 1961), p. 58. In no case, however, should the antifascist element of *1860* be overestimated. The film's main idea remains the continuity between the national revolution and the fascist "revolution."

65. *L'Impero* (Rome), October 26, 1929; reprinted in Bernardini and Martinelli, eds., *Il cinema italiano,* p. 88.

66. *Corriere della Sera* (Milan) wrote on January 16, 1935: "This is a true fascist film. It penetrates so deeply into the human and popular origins of the fascist faith, unveiling fascism's most intimate roots in the heart of the masses, that it becomes a moral catharsis" (quoted in Savio, *Ma l' amore no,* pp. 386–87).

67. Gramsci quoted in Joll, *Antonio Gramsci,* p. 78.

68. A print of *The Eagle's Cry* was found only in the late seventies.

69. Quoted in Savio, *Ma l' amore no,* p. 30.

70. Antonioni in *Cinema,* September 25, 1940; quoted ibid., p. 52.

71. Visconti staged it in 1953 in Milan.

72. Giuseppe De Santis, "Film di questi giorni," *Cinema,* December 25, 1942, p. 752.

73. Alfonso Gatto later called it a "necessary reaction against the clarity of fascism and its meretricious rhetorics"; quoted in Tannenbaum, *Fascist Experience,* p. 265.

74. Antonioni in *Cinema,* September 25, 1940; quoted in Ernesto Laura and Orio Caldiron, eds., *Cinema italiano degli anni quaranta* (Rome: Centro Sperimentale di Cinematografia, 1978), p. 24.

75. *Problemi del film* (with Barbaro, 1940); *Cinque capitoli sul film* (1941); *La regia* (1946); *Il film nella battaglia delle idee* (1954), etc.

76. In 1945, when Chiarini was compromised by his fascist past, Barbaro replaced him as director of the Centro and editor of the journal *Bianco e Nero.*

77. Both films were coscripted by the versatile playwright and scriptwriter Aldo De Benedetti, a Jew, who, thanks to people like Poggioli, Blasetti, and De Sica, continued to work even after the 1938 anti-Semitic laws were enacted. Recently, some Italian writers attempted to establish a link between Poggioli's homosexuality and his attitude toward fascism, which never tolerated "different" people. Thus, nonconformist by nature, homosexuals tended toward the nonconformist side of society. In the seventies, this theme surfaced in Italian film and literature, e.g., Ettore Scola's *A Special Day.*

78. Giovanni Verga, whose work became probably the most important literary inspiration of the neorealist movement, considered Capuana as one of his teachers.

79. Mino Doletti, in *Film,* January 16, 1943, p. 7.

80. Only recently, in the seventies, was Soldati's work properly assessed, especially during the 1974 Mostra Internazionale del Nuovo Cinema in Pesaro, dedicated to Italian neorealism.

81. De Santis wrote: "For the first time in the history of our cinema, we saw a landscape that was neither rarified nor picturesque, but which corresponded to the humanity of the

characters either as an emotive element or as a clue to their feelings" ("Per un paesaggio italiano," *Cinema,* no. 116, April 25, 1941; reprinted in *Sul neorealismo: Testi e documenti* [Rome: Mostra Internazionale del Nuovo Cinema, 1974], p. 12).

82. Quoted in Orio Caldiron, ed., *Letterato al cinema: Mario Soldati anni '40* (Rome: Centro Sperimentale di Cinematografia, 1979), p. 58.

83. Ibid., p. 70.

84. De Santis, in *Cinema,* no. 158, 1943, p. 60.

85. Soldati quoted in Caldiron, ed. *Letterato al cinema,* pp. 8–10.

86. In 1979, Soldati, at that time author of some thirty books (novels, short stories, essays), published his *Addio, diletta Amelia* (Good-Bye, Beloved Amelia), capturing his trips to the United States (Milan: Mondadori, 1979).

87. Emilio Cecchi, in his book *America amara* (1939) (Bitter America), rejected Steinbecks's novel *Of Mice and Men* (1937) as "pathologic." Pavese idolized Steinbeck and translated *Of Mice and Men,* referring to it as "a creation of a new legend." Talino, one of the main characters in his first novel *Paesi tuoi* (1941) (*Harvesters,* 1961), who falls in love with his sister and later kills her, could be Lennie's younger brother.

88. One of the best descriptions of the American dream was provided by Carlo Levi in his book *Cristo si è fermato a Eboli* (Christ Stopped at Eboli, [New York: Farrar, Straus and Giroux, 1973], pp. 120–32).

89. Dominique Fernandez, *Il mito dell'America negli intellettuali italiani del 1930– 1950* (Rome and Caltanissetta: Salvatore Sciascia, 1969), pp. 105–06. In 1945, Pavese wrote: "Over there, we were searching for ourselves and we found ourselves. The American culture enabled us to see our own drama as on an enormous screen" (ibid.).

90. Giaime Pintor, *Il sangue d'Europa* (Turin: Einaudi, 1950), p. 159.

91. Quoted in Sergio Pacifici, *A Guide to Contemporary Italian Literature* (Cleveland and New York: Meridian Books, 1962), p. 306.

92. The writer Vasco Pratolini, in a letter to Donald Heiney, described the effect of Hemingway in Italy: "The reading of Hemingway is like a childhood disease. Whoever has not gone through it remains a child. Hemingway, for a number of writers of my generation, was our Stendhal" (quoted in Nicolas A. Demara, "Pathway to Calvino," *Italian Quarterly,* no. 55, 1971, p. 33).

93. Eugenio Montale won the Nobel Prize in literature in 1975.

94. Shortly before the outbreak of the war, Jean Renoir gave lectures at the Centro Sperimentale di Cinematografia and became an object of cult admiration among his students.

95. Antonioni, quoted in Miccichè, *Il neorealismo cinematografico italiano,* p. 392.

96. *Nuovi materiali,* 2:277.

97. These groups (GUF) existed in all major cities. Their film sections produced films, organized local film festivals, and promoted film criticism. Some of the most important Italian filmmakers and critics started their careers in the GUFs.

98. De Narzi, in *Il Bo* (Padua), January 27, 1935; quoted in *Nuovi materiali,* 1:308. At the first Venice International Festival in 1932, the Soviet film *Toward Life* was hailed by the critics and press. In a public referendum, Nikolay Ekk received the greatest number of votes as the most popular director. Umberto Barbaro attributed a decisive influence on Italian film to the Soviet cinema. This was an exaggerated attitude shared by some of the Italian Marxist critics in the late forties and early fifties. Barbaro's article "Influssi del cinema sovietico" (Influences of Soviet Film) paid a heavy tribute to the time, the years of Stalinism. It was first published in Czechoslovakia where Barbaro lived in the early fifties, then reprinted in *Cinema Nuovo,* July 1, 1953. This critical evaluation was contested, e.g., by Giuseppe De Santis, who was Barbaro's student at the Centro during the fascist years. In an

interview published in Paris in *Cinema 59* (no. 35, 1959), De Santis said: "It is possible that at the time I rediscovered the tone of the Soviet films, but this is no doubt because I had the same things to say. In no case did I consciously undergo this influence" (p. 48).

99. Having written his letter, Pintor got on his bicycle and headed for the closest area held by the partisans. He was shot to death by the Germans while attempting to cross the lines to get there.

I OBSESSION (1942–1944)

1. Quoted in Giansiro Ferrata, ed., *La voce: Antologia* (Rome: Luciano Landi, 1961), pp. 586–87.

2. Jan Kott in the preface to Jerzy Andrzejewski's *Appeal* (New York: Bobbs-Merrill, 1971), p. viii. The Polish historian Jan Kott wrote about the necessity of "seeing the truth and emerging from insanity" in connection with his own generation emerging from the years of Stalinism in the sixties.

3. Alberto Moravia, in *La Nuova Europa,* December 10, 1944; quoted in David Overbey, ed., *Springtime in Italy: A Reader on Neorealism* (London: Talisman Books, 1978), p. 35.

4. Croce's last public appearance was connected with the editing of an antigovernmental manifesto in 1925. After the murder of Matteotti, deputy of the Socialist party and Mussolini's fierce opponent, Croce drafted a manifesto that was signed by a large number of leading personalities. His manifesto was intended as a response to the "Manifesto of Intellectuals on Fascism" conceived by another prominent Italian philosopher, Giovanni Gentile (born in 1875 and executed by partisans in 1944), who supported fascism from the start and, in 1926, became minister of education. The purpose of Gentile's manifesto was to isolate the antifascists. It stated among other things: "Today in Italy, people are finding themselves in two opposing camps: on one side the fascists, on the other their adversaries, democrats of all tendencies. These two words exclude one another." Condemning Gentile's attack on democracy, Croce's manifesto reasserted the value of free institutions and took a stand against fascism as a "religion of force and violence" (in Edward R. Tannenbaum, *The Fascist Experience* [New York: Basic Books, 1972], pp. 282, 284).

5. Ibid., p. 282.

6. Gramsci, the closest friend of Palmiro Togliatti, the postwar leader of the Italian Communist party, traveled repeatedly to Moscow in the five years preceding his arrest. In 1926, he was jailed and two years later sentenced to twenty years in prison. Mussolini is said to have demanded that "this brain be prevented from functioning for twenty years," and this demand was repeated by the prosecutor during the trial. His brain never stopped functioning, but Gramsci died in prison just as the order of his provisional release on the ground of ill health was signed. The British Marxist historian E. J. Hobsbawm wrote in 1974 that "by a pleasing irony of history, Gramsci was saved from Stalin because Mussolini put him behind bars" (James Joll, *Antonio Gramsci* [New York: Penguin Books, 1977], pp. 23).

7. The title was paraphrasing Macchiavelli's sixteenth-century political essay *The Prince,* which was inspired by the necessity of a unified Italian state and the memory of ancient Rome.

8. Antonio Gramsci, *The Modern Prince and Other Writings* (New York: International Publishers, 1972), p. 137.

9. E.g., Ugo Casiraghi and Glauco Viazzi, "Presentazione postuma di un classico," *Bianco e Nero,* no. 4, 1942; reprinted in *Nuovi materiali sul cinema italiano, 1929–1943,* 2 vols. (Rome: Mostra Internazionale del Nuovo Cinema, 1976), 2:98–100.

10. After 1945, De Robertis shot eleven fiction films of limited interest.

11. Gianni Rondolino, *Roberto Rossellini* (Florence: La Nuova Italia, 1974), p. 2.

12. The brother of Gianni Puccini.

13. April 25, 1942. "Vittorio Mussollini was a nice boy (bravo ragazzo)," Rossellini said in 1971. "He was surrounded by the whole movement of the journal *Cinema*, to which he was rather distant" (Rondolino, *Rossellini*, p. 3).

14. The film was coscripted by Asvero Gravelli, editor-in-chief of the journals *Gioventù fascista* (Fascist Youth) and *Antieuropa*.

15. Rossellini, interviewed by Mario Verdone, in "Colloquio sul neorealismo," *Bianco e Nero,* no. 2, 1952, p. 9.

The plot [of *Man with the Cross*] leads us to understanding the ways in which men of very different views can leave a mark on each other: the chaplain of the invading army and the Russian POWs taken by the Italians. The structure of *Open City* is based on the same idea. This theme of two opposing extremes anticipates the subject that will dominate Rossellini's postfascist films: the effort to overcome the barriers and obstacles on the road leading toward a profound human communion. (Mino Argentieri, "Storia e spiritualismo nel Rossellini degli anni quaranta," *Cinema 70,* no. 95, 1974, p. 33)

16. Orio Caldiron, ed., *Vittorio De Sica, Bianco e Nero* (special issue), nos. 9–12, 1975, p. 173.

17. In the fifties, there were several pretenders to the "first actor place" left empty by De Sica. Yet it was only Alberto Sordi who, without having his good looks, approached De Sica's equivalent in the sixties.

18. Tito Ranieri, "De Sica neorealista," in Lino Miccichè, ed., *Il neorealismo cinematografico italiano* (Venice: Marsilio, 1974), p. 300.

19. Vittorio De Sica, "Il mio sorriso non basta a dir le mie virtù," *Scenario* (Rome), May 5, 1940; reprinted in Caldiron, ed., *De Sica,* p. 253.

20. Jean Gili, "La naissance d'un cinéaste," in Caldiron, ed., *De Sica,* p. 54.

21. At the time of his first collaboration with De Sica, Zavattini was already speculating about another type of cinema, anticipating the neorealist method. In 1940 he wrote:

The cinema free of any commercial subordination might find its expression in a story about a person who sleeps or has an argument, without montage and, I dare to say, without any subject. . . . To be able to return to Man as to an entirely spectacular being. . . . Film footage might be obtained with the help of a camera placed in the middle of a street, or a room . . . to watch with a never satisfied curiosity, to educate us in the contemplation of the most elementary acts of our neighbor. ("I sogni migliori," *Cinema,* no. 92, April 25, 1940, p. 259)

22. One of the most pertinent observations of the woman's condition in Italy was made by Cesare Pavese in his poem "Ancestors," published in 1936:

In our family women don't count
What I mean is, our women stay home
and have children, like me, and keep their mouths shut.
They just don't matter, and we don't remember them.
Every woman adds something to our blood,
but they kill themselves off with work. We
just get stronger and stronger, so it's the men who last.
Oh, we've got our faults, and whims, and skeletons,
we, the men, the fathers, and one of us even killed himself!

But there is one disgrace we've never known:
we've never been women, we've never been nobodies.

>   (*Hard Labor*, trans. William Arrowsmith
>   [New York: Viking Press, 1976], p. 6)

23. *Segnalazioni cinematografiche, 1944–1945* (Rome: Centro Cattolico Cinematografico, 1946), p. 54.

24. The fascist attitude toward suicide is mentioned, e.g., in Giorgio Bassani's masterly novella *The Gold-Rimmed Eyeglasses* set during fascism. Its protagonist learns about his friend's suicide from the newspapers. Later he remembers:

> I began reading the half-column beneath the headline, which said nothing about suicide, of course, but following the style of the time, spoke only of an accident. No one was allowed to do away with himself in those years: not even disgraced old men with no further reason to stay in the world. (Giorgio Bassani, *The Gold-Rimmed Eyeglasses,* published in the collection of Bassani's writings, *The Smell of Hay* [New York and London: Harcourt Brace Jovanovich, 1975], p. 193)

25. Giuseppe De Santis, in *Cinema*, January 18, 1943; quoted in Francesco Savio, *Ma l'amore no: Realismo, formalismo, propaganda e telefoni bianchi nel cinema italiano di regime, 1930–1943* (Milan: Sonzogno, 1975), p. 286.

26. In 1975, these letters were used in a documentary film *Lettere dal fronte* (Letters from the Front).

27. Alberto Lattuada, in the foreward to *Occhio quadrato* (Milan: Corrente, 1941), pp. xiii–xv.

28. Giovanni Verga, in the preface to his short story "Gramigna's Mistress"; translation quoted from Sergio Pacifici, *From Verismo to Experimentalism* (Bloomington: Indiana University Press, 1969), p. 12.

29. Luchino Visconti, "Cadaveri," *Cinema*, no. 119, 1941, p. 336.

30. He was not his assistant, as is sometimes erroneously stated, nor did he design the sets. He was just one of Renoir's free collaborators.

31. Quoted in Alberto Farassino, *Giuseppe De Santis* (Milan: Moizzi, 1976), p. 12.

32. "The whole operation was deliberate," Ingrao wrote in 1976.

> We must not forget that when in 1941 Alicata and De Santis asked in *Cinema* for a "revolutionary art inspired by the sufferings and hopes of humanity," they did not have in mind an abstract revolution. . . . The path they were trying to follow in *Ossessione* was the one of a culture redefining itself in relationship to a new historical subject matter. This understanding was the fruit of a long-term political and intellectual labor that began in the second half of the thirties. "Humanity that suffers and hopes" was the coded name alluding to the working class. These contributors to the *Cinema* journal were themselves one aspect of the struggle that culminated in political conspiracy. (Pietro Ingrao, "Luchino Visconti: L'antifascismo e il cinema," *Rinascita*, no. 13, 1976.)

33. Lino Miccichè, "Per una rilettura di 'Ossessione,'" in Adelio Ferrero, ed., *Visconti e il cinema* (Modena: Ufficio Cinema del Commune di Modena, 1977), p. 152. Miccichè's essay provides a meticulous analysis of the resemblances between the film and the novel.

34. The story was filmed in Hollywood in 1946 by Tay Garnett with John Garfield and Lana Turner, and in 1981 by Bob Rafelson with Jack Nicholson and Jessica Lange.

35. The extant prints of *Ossessione* are made from a duplicate negative that was in Visconti's possession. According to his testimony, they are incomplete even if very close to the original. The original negative was taken in 1943 by the fascists to Venice where a new

film city was to be created. There, it was cut and distributed in a forty-minute version. The original negative was never found, and Visconti assumed that it was destroyed. Because Visconti had never acquired the rights to the Cain novel, *Ossessione* was not released in the United States until the early seventies.

36. The fact of Spagnolo's homosexuality remained for at least twenty years unmentioned by Italian critics and film historians. The task would have been difficult, and the word "different" took care of it. Otherwise, how could one explain to people that the fighter for a better world and the symbol of the Spanish war was a homosexual and an informer? "This censorial suppression contains a lot of the Latin repressive phallocracy," writes Miccichè. "And in the first place a complete lack of understanding of the real antifascism" ("Per una rilettura di 'Ossessione,'" p. 169).

37. The book was written in 1938 and published in a limited edition in 1941, then republished in 1942 and seized. However, for years copies of the novel circulated underground (translation quoted from Elio Vittorini, *A Vittorini Omnibus* [New York: New Directions, 1973], p. 98).

38. In the train scene of Vittorini's *In Sicily*, people in the compartment comment on the presence of two policemen in plain clothes standing in the corridor: "Don't you notice the smell?" "The smell? What smell?" "What? You don't notice it? I mean the smell out there."

39. Luchino Visconti, "Cinema antropomorfico," *Cinema*, nos. 173–175, 1943, pp. 108–09.

40. Calamai's fame was short-lived. Her next-to-last role was the nostalgic character of a prostitute in Visconti's *The White Nights* (1957). In 1979, Girotti said: "My relationship to Visconti was fundamental, not only for my career, but in the first place for my life. It was a fundamental experience, on the professional and personal level" (*La città del cinema* [Rome: Napoleone, 1979], p. 179).

41. *L'Avvenire d'Italia* (Bologna), June 15, 1943; quoted in Massimo Mida Puccini, "A proposito di Ossessione," *Cinema*, no. 169, 1943, p. 19.

42. Ingrao, "Luchino Visconti."

43. Caldiron, ed., *De Sica*, p. 65.

44. Pagliero played the role of the communist Manfredi in Rossellini's *Open City* and in 1946 worked with him on *Paisan*.

45. *Ossessione* became Rossellini's obsession. He had chosen Clara Calamai for the role of Pina in *Open City*, but when he could not get along with her, he asked Anna Magnani, ironically Visconti's choice for the role of Giovanna (at that time Magnani was pregnant).

II LACRIMAE RERUM (1944–1948)

1. Quoted in Gianni Rondolino, ed., *Catalogo Bolaffi del cinema italiano, 1945–1965*, 2 vols. (Turin: Giulio Bolaffi, 1967), vol. 1, introduction.

2. Lorenzo Quaglietti, *Il cinema italiano del dopoguerra* (Rome: Mostra Internazionale del Nuovo Cinema, 1974), p. 5.

3. Antonioni completed his film in 1947.

4. In April 1944, Visconti was sentenced to death for his underground activities. He was saved by his famous name and by the arrival of the allied armies.

5. Caterina D'Amico de Carvalho, ed., *Album Visconti* (Milan: Sonzogno, 1978), p. 7.

6. Parts of the war material were reconstructed. The filmmakers wanted to show partisan actions in Italy. The partisan units, however, had only poor film equipment and no real film service. Nevertheless, the film comprises authentic scenes showing the partisans resting, transfers of units, and meetings.

7. Pietro Koch was the head of the notorious prison Pensione Jaccarino where Visconti was held during his arrest. Visconti was a witness for the prosecution during Koch's trial.

8. The influence of this film is still evident in the elaborate courtroom sequences of films made fifteen to twenty years later by Francesco Rosi, Visconti's former assistant.

9. The political purges in the film industry were very mild. In July 1944, a special commission was appointed with Alfredo Guarini, Umberto Barbaro, Mario Camerini, Mario Chiari, Mario Soldati, and Luchino Visconti as members. The commission sent a list of all filmmakers who collaborated with the fascists to the High Commission for Purges. Eventually, only three directors, Goffredo Alessandrini, Carmine Gallone, and Augusto Genina, were punished. The sentence was a six-month interdiction of work. The producers protested against the temporary exclusion of three directors whose names were considered the most secure guarantee for a film. Soon after that, the decision of the commission was revoked, and the film purges were over and closed.

10. In 1945, Visconti staged the following plays in the two most prestigious Roman theaters, Eliseo and Quirino: *Les parents terribles* by Jean Cocteau, *The Fifth Column* by Ernest Hemingway, *La machine à écrire* by Cocteau, *Antigone* by Jean Anouilh, *No Exit* by Jean-Paul Sartre, *Adam* by Marcel Achard, and *Tobacco Road* by John Kirkland based on Erskine Caldwell's novel.

11. Rossellini referred to the critical response as "sincerely and unanimously unfavorable," which is an overstatement.

12. The film was sold to the United States for a ridiculously small sum, something between $3,000 and $8,000, according to various sources, and grossed between $1 million to $3 million. There are many stories regarding the financing of *Open City*. The scriptwriter, Sergio Amidei, recalls:

> We did not have a penny, and we were shooting by borrowing it from a certain Venturini, a dealer in textiles. When the film was completed, the photographer Ubaldo Arata talked Minerva, the distribution company, into buying it. The production costs were 11 million lire, and the distributor offered 13 million. Poor Venturini could not believe his eyes. When he died of a heart attack twenty years later, he was living in a bare room furnished with only a plank bed. The Internal Revenue [*la finanza*] had seized all of his possessions, refusing to believe that he sold the film for only 13 million. (*La città del cinema* [Rome: Napoleone, 1979], p. 78)

During just the first few months, until the end of 1945, *Open City* grossed 61 million lire in Italy.

13. Georges Sadoul, *Dictionary of Films* (Berkeley and Los Angeles: University of California Press, 1972), p. 317.

14. The most famous scene of the film (Anna Magnani runs screaming after a German truck and is cut down by gunfire) was originally conceived quite differently: in Prati, Pina was to approach a group of Germans and be killed after having slapped one of them in the face. "We had no money to shoot the scene as it was written," recalls Sergio Amidei.

> We had found a vicar, sort of a bastard, who allowed us to shoot at night at Trastevere behind the police barracks. It so happened that Anna Magnani had a row with Massimo Serato. I did not want to get involved, so I remained outside and I saw Serato running out of the house, jumping into a pick-up truck, and telling Todini (a lawyer and De Laurentiis's associate) to take him downtown. The car started to move, and at that moment, la Magnani came running out on her shaky crooked legs, mad as hell, and screaming, "You bastard! You son of a bitch! You mother-fucker!" That's how the idea of the climactic scene of the film was born. (*La città del cinema*, p. 78)

15. In the preface to the scripts of his war trilogy, Rossellini remarked:

I believe there is no substantial difference between these films (*Open City, Paisan,* and *Germany, Year Zero*) and the didactic television documentary, such as *The Rise of Louis XIV,* or *Man's Struggle for Survival. Open City* and *Paisan* were also didactic, and even *Germany, Year Zero* was didactic because I was making an effort to understand events that had involved me personally and that had overwhelmed me. They were an exploitation of historical facts, but more particularly of attitudes and types of behavior determined by a particular historical climate or situation. (Rossellini, *The War Trilogy* [New York: Grossman Publishers, 1973], pp. xv–xvi)

16. "The realism and simplicity of *Rome, Open City* was heart-shocking. No one looked like an actor and no one talked like an actor. There was darkness and shadows, and sometimes you couldn't hear, and sometimes you couldn't even see it. But that's the way it is in life . . . you can always see and hear, but you know that something almost beyond your understanding is going on. It was as if they'd removed the walls from the houses and rooms, and you could see inside them. And it was more than that. It was as if you were *there,* involved in what was going on, and you wept and bled for them." (Ingrid Bergman, *My Story* [New York: Delacorte Press, 1980], p. 2)

17. Alberto Farassino, *Giuseppe De Santis* (Milan: Moizzi, 1978), p. 17.

18. In June 1944, 80,000 partisans were fighting against the Germans on Italian soil. In 1945, there were 150,000 of them. Forty-six thousand died in action.

19. In his 1943 film *Quelli della montagna* (Those from the Mountains), Vergano had already used nonprofessional actors and real-life settings. The result was hampered by a contrived story set against the backdrop of the war. After 1945, Vergano directed six films, none of them of particular interest (except *I fuorilegge* [The Outlaws, 1950] dealing with the phenomenon of gangsterism).

20. Quoted in Sadoul, *Dictionary of Films,* p. 271.

21. The title derives from the G.I.'s slang term for an Italian.

22. According to some Italian historians, the myth of Rossellini's unpopularity and critical failures was later created mainly by Rossellini himself. See Lino Miccichè, "Per una verifica del neorealismo," in Lino Miccichè, ed., *Il neorealismo cinematografico italiano* (Venice: Marsilio, 1975), p. 21.

23. Quoted in Pierre Leprohon, *The Italian Cinema* (London: Secker & Warburg, 1972), p. 98.

24. Roberto Rossellini, quoted in Edoardo Bruno, ed., *Teorie e prassi del cinema in Italia, 1950–1970* (Milan: Gabriele Mazzotta, 1972), p. 42.

25. Ibid.

26. The other two were Wolfgang Staudte's *Die Mörder sind unter uns* (The Murderers Are Among Us, 1946), produced in East Berlin, and Helmut Käutner's *In jenen Tagen* (In Those Days, 1947), made in West Germany. Both films draw heavily on the traditions of pre-Nazi German Expressionism and Symbolism. Nevertheless, they are often referred to as the only German efforts that parallel the neorealist search for authenticity. Unlike German literature, the German cinema was quite hesitant in dealing with the past and its consequences.

27. Ulrich Gregor and Enno Patalas, *Geschichte des modernen Films* (Gütersloh: Sigbert Mohn Verlag, 1965), p. 24.

28. Siegfried Kracauer, *Theory of Film: The Redemption of Physical Reality* (New York: Oxford University Press, 1960), p. 248.

29. In *Open city,* the German Gestapoman Bergmann was a homosexual and Ingrid, his aide, was a lesbian. Enning, Edmund's teacher, was also a homosexual.

30. The French Rossellini cult started with a series of articles in *Cahiers du Cinéma*. In its issue of April 1955, Jacques Rivette, one of the leading directors of the French New Wave, published an article entitled "Le cinéaste le plus moderne" (The Most Modern Filmmaker), followed by articles by Eric Rohmer and especially by Jean-Luc Godard, who, in an interview, called Rossellini "the only filmmaker who had the right total vision of things" ("Jean-Luc Godard," *Cahiers du Cinéma*, no. 138, 1962, p. 27). Rohmer's interview with Rossellini was published in *Cahiers du Cinéma*, no. 145, 1963, pp. 2–13.

31. In 1947, Vasco Pratolini published his novel *Chronicle of Poor Lovers*, fictionalizing the events in 1925–1926, which were marked by the transformation of fascism into dictatorship. When Visconti tried to film Pratolini's novel, he could not find a producer. Some exhibitors even refused to program *Paisan*, pretending that such films "divide the nation." The film producers considered many subjects too "antifascist," invoking the well-known argument that film is much more influential than books.

32. The word *marò* refers to the fascist movement; quoted in Vasco Pratolini, *A Hero of Our Time* (Englewood Cliffs, N.J.: Prentice-Hall, 1951), p. 183.

33. Elio Vittorini, quoted in Miccichè, ed., *Il neorealismo cinematografico italiano,* p. 303.

34. Dominique Fernandez, *Il romanzo italiano e la crisi della coscienza moderna* (Milan: Lerici, 1960), p. 173.

35. The Italian title, *Sciuscià,* in postwar slang referred to poor, mostly homeless, young boys who made their living by shining the shoes of the Allied soldiers in exchange for cigarettes and food.

36. De Sica always claimed that the two books that had influenced him most were the masterpieces of Italian and French sentimental realism: *The Heart,* a collection of stories by Edmondo De Amicis, and "The Simple Heart," a story by Gustave Flaubert. Throughout his career, De Sica hoped to film "The Simple Heart." At one point, he planned to have Sophia Loren play the role of the housemaid whose dedication to her masters continues even after their death.

37. Pavese's remark appears in almost all pieces on De Sica. In context, its meaning is more ambiguous. In a radio interview Pavese was asked about his literary predilections. After having named Plato, Herodotus, and the Italian philosopher Giambattista Vico, he said: "And now those who are alive. But why should I make enemies out of my interesting friends! It is better to avoid the trap and say, according to the truth, that for Pavese the greatest contemporary narrator is Thomas Mann and among the Italians Vittorio De Sica" (quoted in Orio Caldiron, ed., *Vittorio De Sica, Bianco e Nero* [special issue], nos. 9–12, 1975, p. 137).

38. Bartolini's well-written but rather mediocre book provided the film with just the title and basic plot. When the film was completed, Bartolini, at that time a fashionable writer, made some angry statements about it.

39. Vittorio De Sica, in *La Fiera Letteraria,* February 6, 1948; quoted in David Overbey, ed., *Springtime in Italy: A Reader on Neo-realism* (London: Talisman Books, 1978, p. 88).

40. Cesare Zavattini, *Umberto D.* (Rome and Milan: Fratelli Bocca, 1953), p. 8.

41. Quoted in Overbey, ed., *Springtime in Italy,* p. 70.

42. André Bazin, *What Is Cinema?* 2 vols. (Berkeley and Los Angeles: University of California Press, 1972), 2:60.

43. The production costs on the neorealist films (except for the very first ones) were usually as high as those of films shot in the studios. The legend of the low-budget films is only partly true. Shooting time was usually longer and transportation costs higher. On the other hand, the neorealists expended less money on scriptwriters and actors.

44. American funding became unavailable when De Sica refused to have Cary Grant play the role of the unemployed Roman worker.

45. Bazin, *What Is Cinema?* 2:50.

46. By 1947, it was becoming increasingly difficult to release an independent film on the Italian market, which was flooded by American movies. *Tragic Hunt* was produced by the National Association of Italian Partisans (who had financed *The Sun Rises Again*) and was released almost exclusively through the channels of the Italian Communist party in third-class theaters. Among the 393 movies released in Italy in 1947, 274 were American, 46 Italian, 23 French, and 28 British. In 1948, the number of American pictures rose to 301, in 1949 to 332. (See Quaglietti, *Il cinema italiano del dopoguerra*, pp. 63–66.)

47. Giuseppe De Santis, "Per un paesaggio italiano," *Cinema*, no. 116, April 25, 1941; translation quoted from Overbey, ed., *Springtime in Italy*, p. 126.

48. In September 1947, 600,000 peasants and day laborers went on strike in the Po valley. At the same time, a campaign was started for the Agrarian Constituency for land reform.

49. According to a certain neorealist typage, Daniela's lesbianism symbolizes her fascist past.

50. The overall postwar atmosphere involved a tendency toward the simplification of present events and those of the immediate past. In this context, *Tragic Hunt* was not understood by some, who accused it of unnecessary complexity. (Daniela, e.g., is not the usual fascist beast but a complex character who remains unbroken even in defeat. Scripted by Antonioni, Daniela anticipated his later antiheroes and their emotional ambiguity.)

51. It has become a habit not to translate the titles of the early Visconti's films: *Ossessione, La terra trema, Bellissima,* and *Senso.*

52. In 1960, Visconti wrote:

I have a profound interest in all the things that excite, unsettle, and horrify Italy. This is why the problem of the south was always one of the sources of my inspiration. To be exact, it was literature that brought it to my attention, that made me discover it: the novels by Giovanni Verga, that is. This happened in the years 1940–1941 while I was preparing *Ossessione.* I felt strongly that the novels by Verga, *Mastro Don Gesualdo, The House by the Medlar Tree,* were the only ones among my college readings with which I was able to reestablish any relationship while getting ready to tackle, within the limits given by fascism, the problems of contemporary life. The war followed, and with it the Resistance. Within this context, all the problems of Italy began to appear as problems of social structure, of cultural, spiritual, and moral orientation. ("Da Verga a Gramsci," *Vie Nuove*, no. 42, 1960)

53. Verismo, represented mainly by Verga and Luigi Capuana, reached its climax in the decade 1875–1885. The works representative of verismo focus on the dark side of life, whose evils are seen as resulting from historical and social circumstances. They emphasize facts and reject the unusual. The veristic method provoked violent polemics on the Italian literary scene. The verists were attacked for having a simplified vision of the world, for forging an unfavorable image of Italy, etc. (The neorealists were to face the same arguments seventy years later.) Among those who praised the veristic endeavors highly was Benedetto Croce, who understood their importance for future literary development. However, verismo found little favor with the influential literary historian Francesco De Sanctis, who saw in it a restrictive artistic one-sidedness. The veristic movement produced several works that appear in retrospect as uncontested masterpieces. In addition to Verga's well-known novels *The House by the Medlar Tree* and *Mastro Don Gesualdo* (the latter translated into English

by D. H. Lawrence) and his short story "Cavalleria rusticana" (which provided the libretto for Pietro Mascagni's opera), there are dozens of other outstanding stories by Verga, Capuana, Virgilio Titone, and others that are still capable of surprising us with their profound depiction of the human condition and human relationships.

54. Mario Alicata and Giuseppe De Santis, "Verità e poesia: Verga e il cinema italiano," *Cinema*, no. 127, 1941, p. 219.

55. This event brings to mind the little known masterly story by Verga, "Liberty," which describes the slaughter of the aristocrats by the Sicilian peasants in 1863. According to the original concept, Visconti intended to shoot *La terra trema* as a trilogy. The first part, the only one that he completed (entitled "Episode of the Sea") was to be followed by a film dealing with the situation of the miners in the sulphur mines and their revolt; eventually the third part would have captured the peasants' fight against the landowners.

56. Visconti was never a member of any political party. He did not believe in binding political affiliations for anyone who wanted to preserve artistic freedom. This is why he disapproved of some of De Santis's later activities. He accepted many of the values of his class and voted communist.

57. Some historians speak of the influence of Flaherty's *Man of Aran*. This seems to be a misunderstanding of two quite different approaches and purposes.

58. Bazin, *What Is Cinema?* 2:44–45.

59. The original version, which runs for three hours, was preserved only in film archives. In the sixties, it was released in some art theaters. The version supervised by Visconti was further slashed to ninety minutes, this time without Visconti's approval.

60. O. Del Buono, "La terra trema, ieri e oggi," *Cinema Nuovo*, no. 134, 1958; reprinted in *Premier Plan*, no. 17, 1961, p. 87.

61. Ugo Casiraghi, the influential Italian critic, hinted that Germi had to submit the script to the Mafia and make several concessions. "The film offers an idealized version of the Mafia," he contended. "The Mafiosi, and in particular their leader, are portrayed as knights of honor" (*Ecran Français,* June 1949; quoted in Leprohon, *Italian Cinema,* p. 119).

III NEOREALISM, ACT II (1948–1953)

1. In 1948, movie production in Italy fell to forty-eight feature films a year, compared with sixty-five in 1946 and sixty-four in 1947.

2. Following the referendum of June 2, 1946, Italy was proclaimed a republic (by 12,717,923 votes against 10,719,284 cast in favor of the monarchy). In the 1946 elections, the Christian Democrats won with 35.2 percent of the vote, the Socialists had 20.7 percent, and the Communists 19 percent. Two years later, at the beginning of the Cold War, the Christian Democrats swept 48.5 percent while a coalition of Socialists and Communists lagged far behind with 31 percent.

3. In 1948, 864 films were imported from the United States; 578,872 tickets were sold, for a gross return of 42.7 billion lire: only 13 percent of this amount went to the Italian industry whereas the Americans received 77 percent. In 1950, 24 percent of the returns went to Italian films and 67 percent to American producers.

4. In 1953, producer Carlo Ponti stated:

Today, everyone, intending to produce a film has to cross a minefield of compromise, intimidation, and all risks of pressure. . . . If a producer is brave enough, he can take a risk, but only once. The second time, he prefers to invest his money into films of pure entertainment, from which he is sure to get a return and which invariably bring him a subvention for exceptional quality. (Pierre Leprohon, *The Italian Cinema* [London: Secker & Warburg, 1972], p. 127)

5. This number varies from source to source and from country to country. According to some classifications, as many as sixty-two neorealist films were made (*Ecran,* no. 37, 1972, p. 42).

6. On August 7, 1952, the journal *Araldo dello Spettacolo* (Rome) published a note concerning the film *Case aperte* (Houses of Ill-Fame), which was to be directed by De Santis. The note stated: "The film will not be made. The 'Ministry' read the script and prohibited its filming after it found out that the director was to be De Santis. Until then, they had no objections" (quoted in Lorenzo Quaglietti, *Storia economico-politica del cinema italiano, 1945–1980* [Rome: Editori Riuniti, 1980], p. 82).

7. The full text of Andreotti's letter is reprinted in Lorenzo Quaglietti, *Il cinema italiano del dopoguerra* (Rome: Mostra Internazionale del Nuovo Cinema, 1974), p. 37.

8. Alberto Moravia, in *Europeo,* December 10, 1950. In Moravia's novel *Ghost at Noon* (New York: Farrar, Straus & Cudahy, 1955), set in the film world, Moravia lets one of his main characters, the corrupted producer Battista, express his high-class opinion about neo-realism (in a discussion with the novel's protagonist, a writer who sold himself to Battista for big money while profoundly despising him).

> Battista . . . now went on to explain: "When I say the neo-realist film is not healthy, I mean that it is not a film that inspires people with courage to live, that increases their confidence in life. The neo-realistic film is depressing, pessimistic, gloomy. Apart from the fact that it represents Italy as a country of ragamuffins, to the great joy of foreigners who have every sort of interest in believing that our country really is a country of ragamuffins, apart from this fact, which, after all, is of considerable importance, it insists too much on the negative sides of life, on all that is ugliest, dirtiest, most abnormal in human existence. It is, in short, a pessimistic, unhealthy type of film, a film which reminds people of their difficulties instead of helping them to overcome them." I looked at Battista and once again I remained uncertain as to whether he really believed the things he was saying or only pretended to believe them. There was a sincerity of a kind in what he said; perhaps it was only the sincerity of a man who easily convinces himself of the things that are useful to him. (pp. 80–81)

9. Pietro Germi, in *Rinascita,* March 3, 1949. In the same issue appeared articles signed by Blasetti, De Santis, Germi, De Sica, Lattuada, and Visconti; the scriptwriters Sergio Amidei, Piero Tellini, and Zavattini; and the actor Gino Cervi.

10. A. A. Zhdanov, probably the most powerful member of the Soviet leadership under Stalin in the period just after the war, was closely associated with Soviet cultural policy. It was he who presented the party's views to the First Congress of Soviet Writers in 1934, where the method of "socialist realism" was canonized. In the post-World War II period, Zhdanov launched a brutal campaign against Soviet intellectuals, condemning all deviations from official doctrine (socialist realism) and attacking the so-called "bourgeois and cosmo-politan" (read: Jewish) influence in Soviet cultural and scientific life. Zhdanov's speeches became a kind of manual for dealing with cultural problems throughout the entire communist movement. (In Italy, they were published under the title *Politica e ideologia* in 1949.)

11. Sereni, quoted in Ugo Finetti, "Cenni sulla critica marxista e il neorealismo," in Lino Miccichè, ed., *Il neorealismo cinematografico italiano* (Venice: Marsilio, 1975), p. 264.

12. The polemic between De Santis and *L'Unità* is summed up in Alberto Farassino, *Giuseppe De Santis* (Milan: Moizzi, 1978), pp. 25–26.

13. As though anticipating Andreotti's previously mentioned letter to De Sica, Pudovkin declared: "To what avail is the poisoning of the youth through the exhibition of unpunished cruelty? One of the main tasks of the cinema is to bring to the screen the characters of positive people and to show them an example to follow. This is what Soviet films do" (quoted in Finetti, "Cenni sulla critica marxista," p. 268).

14. The speeches delivered at the Perugia congress are reprinted in *Sul neorealismo: Testi e documenti* (Rome: Mostra Internazionale del Nuovo Cinema, 1974), pp. 105–26.

15. Renzo Renzi, "Una tendenza sedentaria contro gli impegni del realismo," *Cinema Nuovo,* no. 1, 1952, pp. 9–11, 30.

16. Pavese issued a first warning as early as 1946 when he wrote:

> We are told that we have a duty toward our readers and that we should produce a kind of objective, realistic literature, accessible to these new audiences; that we should follow the example of the Soviet writers who invented socialist realism. I would rather postpone my judgment on socialist realism until I can judge it by its texts. At this moment, it is not my problem, but the problem of the Soviet writers. (quoted in Finetti, "Cenni sulla critica marxista," p. 271)

17. Elio Vittorini, "Politica e cultura: Lettera a Togliatti," *Politecnico,* no. 35, 1947; quoted in David Overbey, ed., *Springtime in Italy: A Reader on Neo-realism* (London: Talisman Books, 1978), p. 63.

18. In Rossellini's and De Sica's films, death often took the form of a fall, usually a suicide (a code taken up by Lattuada and Antonioni). There was Silvana's fall into emptiness in *Bitter Rice,* Edmund's jump from the top of a bombed-out house in *Germany, Year Zero,* Jerry's fall into the ocean in *Without Pity,* the suicide of Irene's son in *Europe 51* (a jump from the top of a staircase), and that of Paola in *Desire* (a leap from a bridge). And finally there was the grandiose collapse of a staircase, accompanied by the fall of dozens of women in *Rome, 11 O'Clock.*

19. *Umberto D.* and *Miracle in Milan* triggered a discussion in the prestigious journal *Cinema Nuovo* about the reasons for the so-called "negativism" of Italian films. Given the tense political and ideological climate in Italy at the time, it is not surprising that the most meaningful answers to the questions came from abroad. In an interview published in *Cinema Nuovo,* Jean-Paul Sartre took the part of the Italian filmmakers whom the critics had labeled as pessimistic. He maintained:

> The kind of pessimism that results from the awareness of a common evil and that, denouncing the evil, suggests the necessary means to remove it, is an active and extremely human feeling. It is immersed in the kind of life that admits the existence of hope, which may not be generally accepted and is connected with certain political regimes. Such a pessimism reflects the conditions of the real Europe. Hence the extraordinary strength of persuasion of the films of the Italian school. (*Cinema Nuovo,* September 1, 1954, p. 428).

20. Umberto Domenico was the name of De Sica's father, to whom the film is dedicated.

21. The translation of the title reads "Attention, Bandits." This warning was posted by the Germans wherever partisans were in action.

22. In his book *Storia del cinema italiano,* published in 1953 (revised and updated in the sixties and seventies), Lizzani traced the history of the Italian cinema alongside the evolution of social and historical structures, explaining the neorealist trend through the common denominator of resistance and the postwar struggle for a new society.

23. In his *Patterns of Realism,* Roy Armes writes: "The principles of socialist realism, the adoption of the viewpoint of the working class and the belief in the intrinsic superiority of the socialist state (whatever its imperfections) over the capitalist system, have exercised an enormous influence on the Italian postwar cinema, for a number of key figures are Marxists, including Visconti, Lizzani, and Antonioni" ([London: Tantivy Press, 1971], p. 19).

24. Raf Vallone, who debuted in *Bitter Rice* and later became one of the most famous Italian actors, originally worked on the staff of the Turin edition of *L'Unità.* Another member of the staff was Cesare Pavese, at that time engaged to Constance Dowling. Constance's sister Doris Dowling (who appeared in Wilder's *Lost Weekend*) played the role of Francesca, Silvana's good counterpart in *Bitter Rice.* Silvana Mangano herself won the Miss Italia contest and from there found her way to *Bitter Rice,* which made her internationally famous. In 1947, the same title was won by Lucia Bosè, who then made her debut in *No Peace Under the Olives.* The method of selecting actresses continued, especially with the "pink neorealism," whose most famous stars, Gina Lollobrigida and Sophia Loren, had participated in several beauty contests (but never won).

25. *Anna* was the first Italian film that grossed over 1 billion lire.

26. Much of the sequence that takes place at the Roman police station had to be cut, which made the subsequent plot difficult to understand.

27. Rossellini, interviewed by Mario Verdone; translation quoted from Christopher Williams, ed., *Realism and Cinema* (London: Routledge & Kegan Paul, 1980), p. 32.

28. Carlo Salinari, *Preludio e fine del realismo in Italia* (Naples: Morano, 1967), p. 47.

IV WHAT IS REALITY?

1. Quoted in *Sul neorealismo: Testi e documenti* (Rome: Mostra Internazionale del Nuovo Cinema, 1974), p. 205.

2. Galvano Della Volpe (1895–1967), the most important Italian Marxist philosopher of the postwar era. His work is seminal in the evolution of modern cinematic language.

3. Quoted in *Sul neorealismo,* p. 119.

4. Siegfried Kracauer, *Theory of Film: The Redemption of Physical Reality* (New York: Oxford University Press, 1960), p. 194.

5. Ibid., p. 245.

6. These were the basic watchwords of Vertov's group: The film-drama is the opium of the people. Down with the immortal kings and queens of the screen. Long live ordinary, mortal people, captured in the midst of life going about their daily tasks. Down with bourgeois fairy-tale scenarios. Long live life as it is. Down with the scripting of life: film us unawares, just as we are. In 1953, Zavattini wrote:

The cinema should never turn back. It should accept, unconditionally, what is contemporary. Today, today, today. It must tell reality as if it were a story; there must be no gap between life and what is on the screen. I am bored to death with heroes more or less imaginary. I want to meet real protagonists of everyday life. I want to see how he is made, if he has a moustache or not, if he is tall or short. I want to see his eyes, and I want to speak to him. . . . Neorealism has perceived that the most irreplaceable experience comes from things happening under our own eyes from natural necessity. I am against exceptional personages. The time has come to tell the audience that they are the true protagonists of life. The result will be a constant appeal to the responsibility and dignity of every human being. Otherwise the frequent habit of identifying oneself with fictional characters will become very dangerous. We must identify ourselves with what we are. The world is composed of millions of people thinking of myths. (quoted in Christopher Williams, ed., *Realism and Cinema* [London: Routledge & Kegan Paul, 1980], pp. 25, 29, 30)

7. Constructivism was a Russian artistic movement related to Futurism. Founded in 1913, it sought to achieve an artistic synthesis by decomposing and recomposing objects and ideas.

8. Translation quoted from David Overbey, ed., *Springtime in Italy: A Reader on Neorealism* (London: Talisman Books, 1978), p. 75.

9. At the Constituent Assembly of the Association of Filmmakers held in Rome in 1944, Zavattini was the first and only one to deliver a self-critical speech (on his work during the fascist period), and he asked the others to do the same. Nobody ever followed his challenge.

10. In Paris, Zavattini declared that the films of René Clair, once his master and his model, were useless. "The house is on fire," he said, "even if Clair has never noticed it" (Lino Miccichè, ed., *Il neorealismo cinematografico italiano*, [Venice: Marsilio, 1975], p. 220.

11. *Sul neorealismo*, p. 105.

12. In the seventies, at the time of the reevaluation of neorealism, many denied the importance of Zavattini's theory. Lorenzo Quaglietti wrote:

Zavattini is everything but a theoretician, at least in my eyes. His antinomy Lumière-Méliès is acceptable as a poetic choice but cannot be sustained as aesthetics. He denied it himself when he made *Miracle in Milan*, which is closer to realism without the "neo" than *Bicycle Thief* and *Umberto D*. His idea of making a film by "following a person" [pedinamento] cannot be considered on any theoretical level either. ("Il realismo non è più attuale," *Cinema 70*, no. 116, 1977, p. 50)

13. Bruno Torri, *Cinema italiano: Dalla realtà alle metafore* (Palermo: Palumbo, 1973), p. 32; by the "previous period" Torri means the years 1945–1948.

14. *Il neorealismo e la critica: Materiali per una bibliografia* (Rome: Mostra Internazionale del Nuovo Cinema, 1974), p. 16. Already in 1972, a similar evaluation was voiced by Edoardo Bruno, editor-in-chief of the journal *Filmcritica*. He wrote:

In the 1950s, the official film critics did not elaborate a theory. Their most important argument remained the defense of subject matter that challenged the bourgeois ideology. The critics did not understand that without theoretical support the neorealist film would turn into a flat and uninteresting reproduction, approaching populist parameters. (*Teorie e prassi del cinema in Italia, 1950–1970* [Milan: Gabriele Mazzotta, 1972], p. iii)

15. In the fifties, the phenomenological approach started prevailing in a segment of European literature. It represented a reaction against some principles of postwar existentialism brought into being by events that had also given shape to neorealism: the experience with fascism, the war, and the postwar struggle for social change. Both movements shared some characteristics: a concern with immediate political commitment, attempts to interpret the world, hostility toward authority, etc. The phenomenologists, on the other hand, refused to concern themselves with any questions, to look for any solutions. They showed things and people "as such" without attempting any interpretation of what they saw.

16. "A Talk with Michelangelo Antonioni on His Work," *Film Culture*, no. 24, 1962, p. 46; translation from *Bianco e Nero*, nos. 2–3, 1961.

17. Rossellini's film was not completed until 1951.

18. Della Volpe illustrates his contention with the scene in *Battleship Potemkin* "where the shots of a stone lion are edited with the shots of the revolt on the battleship so as to make

the sleeping lion open his eyes and roar." According to Della Volpe, this movement expresses the idea of revolution. Eisenstein's use of the moving lion represents

> the moment of transition from naturalism, which is, to a certain degree, the foundation of the cinema, to a metaphoric interpretation free of the demands of an elementary probability, or, to put it differently, it represents the transition from imitation to verisimilitude. This verisimilitude does not concern reality (that means any real situation). It concerns the inner coherence of relationships and situations. ("Il verosimile filmico," in Galvano Della Volpe, *Verosimile filmico e altri scritti di estetica* [Rome: Edizioni Filmcritica, 1954]; reprinted in Bruno, ed., *Teorie e prassi del cinema in Italia*, p. 15)

19. Ibid., p. 19.

20. Ibid., p. v.

21. *The Miracle* was the first of two episodes of the film *L'amore* (The Love). The second episode, *La voce umana* (The Human Voice), based on Jean Cocteau's one-act play, captures the telephone conversation between a woman and her lover who is marrying someone else. The camera remains focused on the woman' face, trying to capture the slightest changes in her state of mind. Anna Magnani, who shared Rossellini's life at that time, starred in both episodes. *The Human Voice* was an ambitious experiment based on having the camera scrutinize a human face with the same intensity it employed in examining the landscape around Nannina.

22. The subject of madness as a consequence of our time became the main concern of the French psychologist and philosopher Michel Foucault. According to him, the contemporary madness is bred by the world of machines and the disappearance of feelings between human beings. In his book *Histoire de la folie à l'age classique: Folie et déraison* (Paris: Plon, 1961), Foucault analyzes the reasons for the growing interest of contemporary artists in schizophrenia that is generated by alienation. In Italian literature, rational metaphors, which use the abnormality of the characters to convey a general feeling about a special situation, abound. To name just a few: Elio Vittorini's *In Sicily*, most of Pavese's work, most of Giorgio Bassani's work, and Moravia's *Empty Canvas*. In film, after Rossellini, Fellini, and Antonioni, Marco Bellocchio became the most prominent representative of this approach.

23. Rossellini, quoted in Pio Baldelli, *Roberto Rossellini* (Rome: Samonà e Savelli, 1972), pp. 95–96.

24. In 1949, Ingrid Bergman went to Italy to shoot a film with Rossellini. Shortly afterwards she left her husband and daughter, provoking a scandal, mainly in the United States. She married Rossellini and had three children by him. They divorced in 1957.

25. Stromboli is one of the Aeolian islands off the Sicilian coast; it is dominated by an active volcano.

26. In 1948, Rossellini wrote in a letter to Ingrid Bergman:

> I tried to imagine the life of the Latvian girl, so tall, so fair, in this island of fire and ashes, amidst the fishermen, small and swarthy, among the women with the glowing eyes, pale and deformed by childbirth, with no means to communicate with these people of Phoenician habits, who speak a rough dialect, all mixed up with Greek words, and no means to communicate with him, with the man she got hold of at the camp of Farfa. . . . Suddenly the woman understands the value of the eternal truth that rules human lives; she understands the mighty power of he who possesses nothing, this extraordinary strength that procures complete freedom. In reality she becomes another St. Francis. An intense feeling of joy springs from her heart, an immense joy of living. (Ingrid Bergman, *My Story* [New York: Delacorte Press, 1980], p. 9)

27. Gianni Rondolino, *Roberto Rossellini* (Florence: La Nuova Italia, 1974), p. 85.

28. Comic strips with narratives illustrated by photographs of actual people.

29. *Variety Lights* is the "½" in Fellini's autobiographical movie *8½*. Lattuada never stopped contesting the assessment that Fellini's part in directing *Variety Lights* was more important than his.

30. Masina was Fellini's wife (they married in 1943), and Del Poggio was married to Lattuada. The pathetic character of Checco was portrayed by Peppino De Filippo, a member of the famous De Filippo theatrical family. Peppino was one of the most popular, and best, Italian actors.

31. John Kitzmiller was a pathetic figure on the Italian film scene. Born in the United States, he went to Italy with the army and in 1947 was picked up by Luigi Zampa for the role of a black G. I. in *To Live in Peace*. He never went back home but tried to establish himself as an actor in Rome where he died in 1967. His best part was Jerry in Lattuada's *Without Pity*. He was awarded a prize as best actor at the 1957 Cannes Festival for his role in France Stiglic's *Valley of Peace* (made in Yugoslavia).

32. The title does not translate into English. Fellini explained it as follows:

The *vitelloni* are the unemployed of the middle class, the mamma's boys. Why don't they do anything all day long? They themselves don't know. Each of them has someone to support him: a father, a mother, a sister, an aunt. They eat at home, sleep at home, get their clothes there, and still manage to extort some money for cigarettes and movies. None of them knows what he wants to do. They have studied a little, but have no special interest. They are always waiting for a letter, an offer for something that will take them to Rome or to Milan, where they will be entrusted with an important, vague, and lucrative assignment. Going on thirty, they spend their days with sophomoric jokes and small talk. (Franco Pecori, *Federico Fellini* [Florence: La Nuova Italia, 1974], p. 42)

33. Federico Fellini, "Moraldo in città," *Cinema*, no. 139, August 1954; portions reprinted in Pecori, *Fellini*; quote is from p. 62.

34. In 1943, Cesare Pavese wrote in his diaries:

Italian poets like great constructions made up of very short chapters, brief savory passages, the fruit of the tree (Dante's short cantos, Boccaccio's short stories, Macchiavelli's brief chapters in his great works, Vico's aphorisms in *Scienza nuova*, not to mention the sonnet). This is why Italian literature seldom concerns itself with narrative, which requires a long, extended outpouring of effort as in Russian or French novels but is instead intellectual and argumentative. (*The Burning Brand: Diaries, 1935–1950* [New York: Walker, 1961], p. 230)

35. Pecori, *Fellini*, p. 62.

36. From a letter to Davide Lajolo published in Lajolo, *Il vizio assurdo: Storia di Cesare Pavese* (Milan: Mondadori, 1972), p. 310. Fitzgerald was one of Pavese's favorite writers, and Pavese translated several of his books into Italian. Fitzgerald's novel *Tender Is the Night* is among the books left behind by Anna, the young woman who disappears in Antonioni's 1959 film *L'avventura*.

37. Pavese, *Burning Brand*, p. 162.

38. Lajolo, *Vizio assurdo*, p. 333. All five pictures that Antonioni directed in the years 1950–1956 met with mixed success with both critics and audiences. In 1957, the negative reaction to *Il grido* was so strong that Antonioni seriously considered giving up filmmaking. At the first showing of *L'avventura*, at the 1959 Cannes International Film Festival, the film was applauded by the critics in the morning and booed by the audience at the evening gala performance.

39. Pavese, *Burning Brand*, p. 161.

40. Quoted in Giorgio Tinazzi, *Michelangelo Antonioni* (Florence: La Nuova Italia, 1976), pp. 4–5.

41. From the script of *Chronicle of a Love* (Bologna: Cappelli, 1973), p. 105. Some writers, considering only the basic plot of *Chronicle of a Love* (a woman and her lover decide to murder her rich husband and collect the insurance), suggest the resemblance to *Ossessione*. Such a perspective, however, contradicts the very essence of *Chronicle*'s intentions and meaning.

42. Antonioni's approach was referred to as "inner neorealism." He himself pointed out: "The only way to renew neorealism is to interiorize it" (quoted in the preface by Carlo Di Carlo to *Il primo Antonioni* [Bologna: Cappelli, 1973], p. 18).

43. *La dame aux camélias* (The Lady with Camelias), Alexandre Dumas's famous theatrical melodrama (known in English as *Camille*), has been filmed several times, including a 1936 version by George Cukor with Greta Garbo.

44. The extant print of *People of the River Po* was edited from about 30 percent of the original material, the rest having been accidently destroyed in the laboratories. Even these remaining nine minutes convey a sense of a dense atmosphere and contain some extraordinary images attesting to Antonioni's visual preoccupations (the visual component of the film anticipated Antonioni's 1956 *Il grido*).

45. Michelangelo Antonioni, "La signora senza camelie non offende il cinema italiano," *Cinema Nuovo*, no. 6, 1953, p. 146.

46. Antonioni always insisted that he had been present at the birth of neorealism. In 1959 he pointed out: "When I was making my first documentary at the end of 1942, Visconti was shooting *Ossessione*. *People of the River Po* was a documentary about fishing, boats, and fishermen, that is, about people, things, and place. Without being aware of it, I was following the same line as Visconti. I remember well my distress at not being able to develop my subject on a narrative basis, to make a fiction film" (quoted in Tinazzi, *Antonioni*, p. 11).

47. Quoted in Ian Cameron and Robin Wood, *Antonioni* (London: Studio Vista, 1968), p. 48.

48. Antonioni was the first of the many filmmakers to deal with the problems of juvenile delinquency, which was viewed as a consequence of the war and the postwar situation. In the mid-fifties, such films abounded. In Poland, Aleksander Ford shot *The Five Boys from Barska Street*; in France, Marcel Carné stirred controversy with *Les tricheurs*; in West Germany, Georg Tressler made *The Wolfpack* (Die Halbstarken); in the United States, Richard Brooks directed *The Blackboard Jungle*; etc.

49. The original treatment dealt with a group of neofascist youngsters who perpetrate an unsuccessful terrorist act. Antonioni had to remove all references to neofascism and reduce the plot to the story of a rich boy who smuggles cigarettes and kills a man.

50. Francesco De Sanctis, *Storia della letteratura italiana*, 2 vols. (Bari: Laterza, 1964), 2:423–24.

51. Luchino Visconti, in the editorial "Opinione degli assenti," *Cinema Nuovo*, no. 26, 1953, p. 399.

52. Francesco De Sanctis, *Saggio critico sul Petrarca* (Turin: Einaudi, 1964), p. 32.

53. *Rosalinda*, blending ballet scenes with Shakespeare's plot, is among Visconti's most remarkable achievements. The sets were designed by Salvador Dali, with Franco Zeffirelli as art director. Franco Interlenghi, discovered by De Sica for *Shoeshine*, appeared opposite such Visconti regulars as Paolo Stoppa, Rina Morelli, Vivi Gioi, and Vittorio Gassman; and the twenty-five-year-old Marcello Mastroianni made his theatrical debut in *Rosalinda*.

54. Luchino Visconti, "Sul modo di mettere in scena una commedia di Shakespeare," *Rinascita*, no. 12, December 1948.

55. In the years 1954–1957, Visconti directed Callas in her first appearances at La Scala (*La Vestale, La Sonnambula, La Traviata, Anna Boleyna,* and *Iphigénie en Tauride*).

56. Originally, Visconti had planned to direct Magnani in a film version of Prosper Mérimée's *The Coach of the Golden Sacrament,* a coproduction with France, which was to be Visconti's first color film. At the last moment, the producers decreed that the director had to be French. In 1952, the film was made by Renoir.

57. The cooperation between Visconti and Zavattini was a difficult one. Zavattini profoundly disliked the film. Even for Visconti, *Bellissima* was just an interlude, something to fill the void between *La terra trema* and his next major film. (Several of his scripts were vetoed by the censors; "The Wedding March," depicting the story of a marriage ending with the wife's suicide, was one whose rejection he most regretted. The treatment of "La marcia nuziale" was published in *Cinema Nuovo,* nos. 10, 12, and 13, 1953.) Blasetti, who played the role of the film director, was also offended by the end result and wrote Visconti an angry letter. In his answer, Visconti pointed out: "We're all charlatans, we directors. We put illusions into the heads of mothers and little girls. . . . We are selling a love potion that isn't really a magic elixir. It is simply a glass of Bordeaux, the same as in an opera. I'd apply this 'Charlatan's air' quite as much to myself as to you" (quoted in Monica Sterling, *A Screen of Time* [New York and London: Harcourt Brace Jovanovich, 1979], p. 86).

58. Lino Miccichè, *Il cinema italiano degli anni '60* (Venice: Marsilio, 1975), pp. 15–16. Miccichè points out that because of the nonexistence of a homogenous cinematic trend, "a historiography of the Italian cinema and a more profound critical evaluation are extremely difficult." He concludes: "For these reasons nobody has so far tried to write a comprehensive critical evaluation of the film trends linked to the 1950–1960 period" (ibid.).

V NEOREALISM IS LIKE . . .

1. Quoted in an interview with Victoria Schultz, *Film Culture,* no. 52, Spring 1971, p. 3.

2. Peter Graham, ed., *Dictionary of Cinema* (London: Tantivy Press, 1968), p. 76.

3. Lino Miccichè, ed., *Il neorealismo cinematografico italiano* (Venice: Marsilio, 1975), p. 27.

4. In this respect it is interesting to mention Calvino's contention in the preface to his novel *The Path to the Nest of Spiders* that neorealism in literature represented the only major effort to translate the Italian spoken language into a written form. "For the neorealists, the musical score is more important than the libretto," he noted (Italo Calvino, *The Path to the Nest of Spiders* [New York: Ecco Press, 1976] p. vii). See also Ben Lawton, "Italian Neorealism: A Mirror Construction of Reality," in Luciana Bohne, ed., *Italian Neorealism,* special issue of *Film Criticism,* no. 2, 1979, pp. 8–22.

5. Miccichè, ed. *Il neorealismo cinematografico italiano,* p. 27.

6. Basil Wright, *The Long View* (New York, Knopf, 1974), pp. 221–22.

7. James Monaco, *How to Read a Film* (New York: Oxford University Press, 1977), p. 251.

8. Roger Manvell, ed. *The International Encyclopedia of Film* (New York: Crown, 1972), p. 287.

9. Louis Marcorelles, *Living Cinema* (London: Allen & Unwin, 1973), p. 38. Proponents of the direct cinema inspired by neorealism included Robert Drew, Richard Leacock, Jean Rouch, D. A. Pennebaker, Pierre Perault, etc.

10. Stephen Member, *Cinéma Vérité in America* (Cambridge, Mass: MIT Press, 1974), p. 17.

11. Louis D. Giannetti, *Godard and Others* (Rutherford, N.J.: Farleigh Dickinson University Press, 1975), p. 150.

12. Analogous trends appeared at the same time in China, as is described in Ugo Casiraghi's book on Chinese cinema *Il cinema cinese, questo sconosciuto* (in the chapter entitled "Neorealismo sotto il Kuomintang"). The film *Crossroads,* written and directed by Chen Hsi-ling in 1936, is especially referred to as a precursor of Italian neorealism (Turin: Centrofilm, *Quaderni di documentazione cinematografica,* nos. 11–12, 1960, pp. 10–28).

13. Quoted in Mira Liehm and Antonin Liehm, *The Most Important Art* (Berkeley and Los Angeles: University of California Press, 1977), p. 203.

14. Quoted in "L'avventura polacca del neorealismo," in *Il neorealismo e la critica: Materiali per una bibliografia* (Rome: Mostra Internazionele del Nuovo Cinema, 1974), p. 149.

15. Ibid.

16. Quoted in Hadelin Trinon, *Andrzej Wajda* (Paris: Seghers, 1964), p. 112.

17. The situation changed in the sixties, mainly in Hungary and Czechoslovakia (in Poland, the distribution of Western films has always been less restricted). But in the fifties, the mood was as reflected in the Soviet film journal *Iskustvo Kino* where L. Kogan contended:

> When traveling across Italy, we felt that neorealist films did not show the entire truth. How could they not have seen the revolutionary struggle of the Italian people led by the Communist party? Neorealist films lack beautiful strong people like Gorky's heroes. Art needs exceptional characters who are not special because they elevate themselves above the people but because they serve the people with an exceptional passion. Lenin taught us that human knowledge moves from the "first essential" to the "second essential" and then to the third. Despite its great success, neorealism practically has not transcended the limits of the first essential. (no. 9, 1958)

18. *Films et Documents,* no. 5, 1952; quoted in Marcel Martin, "Le néoréalisme vu par la critique française," *Ecran,* no. 37, 1975, p. 34.

19. *La Revue du Cinéma,* no. 4, 1947, p. 21.

20. Giuseppe Ferrara, "Il neorealismo italiano," in Adelio Ferrero, ed., *Momenti di storia del cinema* (Florence: Centro Studi del Consorzio Toscano Attività Cinematografiche, 1965), p. 106.

21. Umberto Barbaro, in *Film,* June 5, 1943, p. 20. Here, Barbaro used the term *neorealism* for the first time, yet he did not apply it to the Italian cinema, as many have since believed, but to the French cinema of the thirties. He pointed out: "We can affirm, justly and truthfully, that the films of French neorealism represented an outcry of alarm." There are many hypotheses as to who used the word *neorealism* for the first time. (There are many candidates, such as Libero Solaroli, the outstanding Italian economist, Mario Serandrei, the editor of *Ossessione,* the critic Antonio Pietrangeli, etc.) Antonioni said in 1958: "No one talked of neorealism during the war, nor in the immediate postwar period. The passionate reality of the time gave birth to a movement that the critics baptized *neorealism* only much later" (Antonioni, "Crisi e neorealismo," *Bianco e Nero,* no. 9, 1958, pp. 2–3).

22. Jurij Lotman, *Semiotics of Cinema* (Ann Arbor: University of Michigan Press, 1976), p. 21.

23. Neorealism in literature adopted a more radical stand, condemning the literature of fascism as "calligraphy without art." The reasons were evident. In the thirties, Italian literature was totally paralyzed by the censors and by self-imposed restrictions whereas the cinema blossomed. After the war, neorealism in literature picked up some of the most radical cinematic methods (life caught unawares) and fused them with the influence of American

realism. Neorealism proclaimed an absolute predominance of the chronicle over the narration. However, such attitudes soon wore out. Pavese was the first to transcend it, followed by Italo Calvino, Pratolini, and others. In 1959, *Italian Quarterly* published an article by Dante Della Terza, in which the author claimed:

> In Italy, it is not possible as it is in France, for a writer to turn his back on tradition and, by ignoring it or attacking it, simply liquidate it. The Italian writer must realize that for him the description of the human condition is possible only in a specific historical context and that it changes as the reality it describes changes. Questions about literature and the life of the nation, popular language and literary language, imitation of reality and mythical transformation of it, the relationship between the spoken and the written word, between the language and the dialect, are asked again and again as Italian society reacts to the crisis of the modern world. ("Italian Fiction from Pavese to Pratolini," no. 11, 1959, pp. 29–30)

24. Amedée Ayfre, "Du premier au second néoréalisme," in *Le néoréalisme italien: Bilan de la critique, Etudes Cinématographiques* (Paris) (special issue), nos. 32–33, 1964, pp. 59–60.

25. André Bazin, *What Is Cinema?* 2 vols. (Berkeley and Los Angeles: University of California Press, 1972), 2:21.

26. Quoted in Patrick H. Hovald, *Le néoréalisme italien et ses créateurs* (Paris: Du Cerf, 1959), p. 205.

27. Bazin, *What Is Cinema?* pp. 89–90.

28. Luigi Chiarini, *Il film nella battaglia delle idee* (Milan and Rome: Fratelli Bocca, 1954), pp. 131–32.

29. Mario Gromo, *Cinema italiano, 1903–1953* (Milan: Mondadori, 1954), p. 97.

30. Brunello Rondi, *Il neorealismo italiano* (Parma: Guanda, 1956), pp. 19–20.

31. Gerald Mast, *A Short History of the Movies* (New York: Pegasus, 1971), p. 340.

32. Peter Bondarella, in Bohne, ed., *Italian Neorealism*, p. 24.

33. Georges Sadoul, *Histoire générale du cinéma* (Paris: Denoël, 1971), p. 340.

34. Umberto Barbaro, "Importanza del realismo," *Filmcritica*, no. 4, 1951, p. 114.

35. Raymond Borde and André Buissy, *Le Néoréalisme italien* (Lausanne: La Cinémathèque Suisse, 1960), p. 11.

36. Ulrich Gregor and Enno Patalas, *Geschichte des modernen Films* (Gütersloh: Sigbert Mohn Verlag, 1965), p. 21.

37. Siegfried Kracauer, *Theory of Film: The Redemption of Physical Reality* (New York: Oxford University Press, 1960), pp. 98–99.

38. *Cinema Nuovo*, August 1955; quoted in Bazin, *What Is Cinema?* pp. 95–101.

39. Rossellini, quoted in Christopher Williams, ed., *Realism and Cinema* (London: Routledge & Kegan Paul, 1980), p. 31.

VI DIFFICULT YEARS (1953–1959)

1. S. Zambetti, in Adelio Ferrero, ed., *Storia di cinema*, 5 vols. (Venice: Marsilio, 1978), 3:58. In the late forties in several European countries, the overall effort to prevent a social change from becoming a consequence of the war cataclysm brought into power centrist governments with distinct right-wing characteristics. In Italy, after the 1946 amnesty, this kind of centrism was pulled further right by the appearance of the profascist party Movimento Sociale Italiano (M.S.I.), which integrated many former fascists and led a strong campaign against political pluralism and individual freedom. This period in Italy, with its

intolerant nationalism and militant anticommunism, corresponded to the McCarthyism in the United States and to the worst moments of Stalinism in the USSR and the countries of Eastern Europe.

2. Georges Sadoul, *Histoire du cinéma mondial* (Paris: Flammarion, 1974), p. 334.

3. Also De Santis's personal life was in shambles. Forgotten by everyone, even by some of his friends, he tried to make ends meet by doing all kind of work, mainly for television. At the age of fifty, he suffered a severe stroke.

4. In 1953, the poet Franco Fortini, one of the most important Italian essayists and literary critics, wrote:

> The core of Italian and European reality, with its tensions and conflicts, lies in the life of the middle class. In the literary field, this means that "realism" is Balzac, Tolstoy, Mann, and also Proust and Kafka, not the "social novel." The bridge that both the Italian cinema and Italian novel have to cross leads to the representation of middle-class culture. It is there that the mystery is hidden, together with a less simplifiable reality that cannot be prearranged according to certain formulas. (*Cinema Nuovo*, June 15, 1953; reprinted in Gian Piero Brunetta, ed., *Letteratura e cinema* [Bologna: Zanichelli, 1976, 1976], p. 86)

5. The Neapolitan production of the 1950s came into life as a reaction against American films, which had little success in Naples. Neither Marilyn Monroe, nor Kim Novak, nor Jerry Lewis attracted Neapolitan audiences, who stormed movie houses playing traditional Neapolitan comedies and melodramas. Thus, in Naples, *Totò, Peppino, e la malafemmina* (Totò, Peppino, and the Bad Woman), a B picture, grossed 10 million lire while at the same time *Bus Stop* made only 6 million.

6. In 1959, Soldati ended his film career with *Policarpo, ufficiale di scrittura* (Policarpo, the Writing Officer), a free transposition of a well-known nineteenth-century story. *Policarpo* was marked by the same stylistic urgency as Soldati's calligraphist films of the early forties.

7. Carlo Salinari, *Preludio e fine del realismo in Italia* (Naples: Morano, 1967), p. 49.

8. During fascism, Comencini, along with Alberto Lattuada, collected old film prints, thereby laying the foundations for the future National Film Archives in Milan.

9. Quoted in Aldo Vigano, *Dino Risi* (Milan: Moizzi, 1977), p. 11.

10. The first television transmission in Italy took place in 1954. In 1959, there were 1,572,000 television sets and 10 million viewers. By 1956, the number of film spectators declined by 29 million.

11. Mario Monicelli, in *La città del cinema* (Rome: Napoleone, 1979), p. 217.

12. The direct reference is Jules Dassin's *Du rififi chez les hommes.*

13. Vittorio Spinazzola, *Cinema e pubblico: Lo spettacolo filmico in Italia, 1945–1965* (Milan: Bompiani, 1974), p. 209.

14. In 1979, the Italian film historian and critic Mino Argentieri pointed out:

> The years 1945–1955 were filled with passionate conflicts. Politics became a great drama, a theater; the streets were turned into a stage with the masses as protagonists. In the postwar period, politics became a type of social life, a ritual, a place that brought people together. For us, politics is a play. We enjoy ourselves by getting involved in politics. That's how the Italian "homo ludens" is. Politics consists of stories, encounters, and the pleasure of storytelling. A politician is an actor, his personality and his character play probably a greater role than they would anywhere else. Politics is like sport; it breaks up boredom, the monotony of life and work. And there is the Italian infatuation with oration, with the spoken word. (personal interview with Argentieri)

15. Matarazzo, quoted in Spinazzola, *Cinema e pubblico,* p. 71.

16. Amedeo Nazzari, who was one of Italy's foremost romantic actors for over twenty years, played the lead in most of Matarazzo's films. Between 1949 and 1954, Nazzari starred in twenty-eight films, which altogether grossed over 11 billion lire. In 1957, he portrayed himself in the opening episode of Fellini's *Nights of Cabiria.*

17. Bruno Torri, *Il cinema italiano: Dalla realtà alle metafore* (Palermo: Palumbo, 1973), p. 54.

18. Aristarco, *Cinema Nuovo,* no. 52, February 10, 1955; reprinted in Brunetta, ed., *Letteratura e cinema,* p. 88.

19. The actors, Alida Valli and Farley Granger, were Visconti's second choices. Originally, he had offered the parts to Ingrid Bergman and Marlon Brando, both of whom refused.

20. Georges Sadoul, in *Les Lettres Françaises* (Paris), February 9, 1956.

21. The text of the deleted scenes was published in *Cinema Nuovo,* no. 24, 1953, pp. 334–36.

22. In this connection it is relevant to quote Gramsci: "In our popular culture, music has, in a way, taken the place of the popular novel, in as much as Italian artistic 'democracy' has expressed itself through music and not literature" (quoted in Brunetta, ed., *Letteratura e cinema,* p. 96).

23. Geoffrey Nowell-Smith pointed out: "After *The White Nights,* Visconti entered in a period of involution, doubling back on himself and recapitulating themes and motifs first developed earlier in his career" (Nowell-Smith, *Visconti* [Garden City, N.Y.: Doubleday, 1968], p. 120.

24. Torri, *Il cinema italiano,* p. 52.

25. Geneviève Agel, who wrote one of the best books on Fellini, calls it "the abandonment in space" (*Les chemins de Fellini* [Paris: Du Cerf, 1956], p. 72).

26. Ian Cameron and Robin Wood wrote about one sequence of *The Girlfriends:* "Even the most detailed study on the moviola reveals no mistakes and no manipulation in the cutting" (*Antonioni* [London: Studio Vista, 1968], p. 51).

27. Quoted in Giorgio Tinazzi, *Michelangelo Antonioni* (Florence: La Nuova Italia, 1974), p. 37.

28. Ibid., p. 14.

29. Federico Fellini, *Il contemporaneo* (Rome), April 9, 1955; reprinted in Salinari, *Preludio,* pp. 50–51.

VII **THE RIFT** (1959–1960)

1. This was only the second time since the first postwar Venice festival in 1947 that an Italian film had won the highest award. None of the neorealist masterpieces was ever awarded the Golden Lion, and many were not even chosen to represent Italy in competition. In 1948, the jury preferred Laurence Olivier's *Hamlet* to *La terra trema.* All these facts can be explained by the low esteem accorded to the masterpieces of neorealism by the governmental institutions sponsoring the festival. In 1954, Castellani won the Golden Lion with his rather unimaginative *Romeo and Juliet,* eliminating its competitors *Senso* and *La strada.*

2. Morando Morandini, "The Year of Dolce Vita," *Sight and Sound,* no. 3, 1960, p. 124.

3. Sandro Zambetti, in Adelio Ferrero, ed., *Storia di cinema* 5 vols. (Venice: Marsilio, 1978), 3:59.

4. Describing the situation in France of the New Wave, Eric Rhode writes:

The producers were impressed by the need to employ young directors to capture the teenage market. Youngsters who could not bear to stay at home in the evenings loathed all that their parents admired and hungered for a less conventional kind of movie. In one sense, this feeling of dissent was bound up with the adolescent condition; in another sense, its long-lasting intensity implied the existence of genuine social grievances. It was no accident that the French New Wave and its imitators in other countries have followed the Beat movement in the United States and that later it should have some connection with the university revolts of 1968. (Eric Rhode, *A History of Cinema from Its Origins to 1970* [London: Allen Lane, 1976], p. 569)

5. Interview with Jean Gili, in his book of interviews *Le cinéma italien* (Paris: Union Générale d'Edition, 1978), pp. 182–83.

6. The story of *The Violent Summer* bears a striking resemblance to the 1971 Robert Mulligan film *The Summer of '42.*

7. "I wrote the script for *The Challenge* in Rome," Rosi explained.

Then I went to Naples to check what I had written and to find some locations for shooting. The shock of this encounter was so strong that I had to start again from scratch. *Dry Goods Dealers* suffers from the lack of such continuous checking. . . . In both films my interest focused exclusively on the social aspect. Only in *Salvatore Giuliano* did I really discover the true relationship between the political and the ideological aspect. (Michel Ciment, *Le dossier Rosi* [Paris: Stock, 1976], pp. 84–85)

8. Gian Piero Brunetta, "Literature and Cinema in the Works of Mauro Bolognini," in *Bolognini* (Rome: Ministero degli Affari Esteri, 1977), p. 121

9. After Pasolini's death, Bolognini told Jean Gili: "For me, working with Pasolini was very important. He would come to the editing room and say: 'Why don't you splice it this way?' I would answer: 'But, Pier Paolo, you are mad. It just cannot be done. There must be a minimum of cinematic grammar.' He would be silent and then say: 'But why?' Actually, he was invariably right" (Jean A. Gili, "Talking with Mauro Bolognini," in *Bolognini*, pp. 30–31).

10. Guido Aristarco, *Cinema italiano 1960: Romanzo e antiromanzo* (Milan: Il Saggiatore, 1961), pp. 90–91. The neorealist refusal of the traditional plot, mentioned by Aristarco, was one of the main sources of the dedramatization, referred to as the most important feature of modern cinema. Also the neorealist asymmetrical off-center framing, typical mainly of De Sica's work (*Bicycle Thief*) became a distinguishing element of the dedramatized plot.

11. The crudeness of *Rocco*'s style provoked the retribution of the Italian establishment. After harassment by the Milanese authorities during the shooting, the film was seized and Visconti was asked to delete four scenes (Nadia's rape and murder). Visconti obtained vindication only in 1966 with a verdict proclaiming *Rocco* to be a work of art "to which the incriminated scenes add a degree of profound and universal emotionality" (see Monica Sterling, *A Screen of Time* [New York and London: Harcourt Brace Jovanovich, 1979], pp. 151–53).

12. Anna Kael and Christian Strich, eds., *Fellini on Fellini* (London: Eyre Methuen, 1976), p. 69.

13. "To my scared provincial eyes it wasn't even Rome, it was a fairy-tale vision, Monte Carlo or Baghdad. In the screenplay of *La strada*, there was a sequence which expressed this highly personal view of Via Veneto. Zampano's motor-bike arriving from the Pincio swoops

down the slope of Via Veneto, sputtering and popping; from inside, behind half-open swaying curtains, Gelsomina looks out, wide-eyed, at the lights, the illuminated signs, the palm trees and cafés. Then she goes to sleep again and wakes up the next morning in a dreary field, the gypsies' Rome, with the cupolas in the background" (ibid.).

14. Ibid., p. 79.

15. Federico Fellini, "Deux questions d'Alain Resnais," *L'Arc,* no. 45, 1971, p. 26.

16. *L'Espresso,* October 31, 1963; quoted in Franco Pecori, *Federico Fellini* (Florence: La Nuova Italia, 1974), p. 86.

17. Fellini, "Deux questions," p. 79.

18. Appalled by the hostile reaction to *L'avventura* at Cannes, Rossellini and thirty–five other filmmakers, producers, distributors, and critics joined in publishing the following statement in "Le Bulletin du Festival" on May 16, 1960: "Aware of the exceptional importance of Michelangelo Antonioni's film *L'avventura* and appalled by displays of hostility it has aroused, the undersigned critics and members of the profession are anxious to express their admiration for the maker and this film."

19. "We must attempt to substitute the world of 'significances' with a more stable, more immediate world. The objects and gestures must assert themselves through their presence, excluding all attempts at explanation and all systems of references" (Alain Robbe-Grillet, *Il nouveau roman* [Milan: Feltrinelli, 1961], p. 13).

20. Quoted in Ian Cameron and Robin Wood, *Antonioni* (London: Studio Vista, 1968), pp. 25–26.

21. Richard Roud, ed., *Cinema: A Critical Dictionary,* 2 vols. (London: Secker & Warburg, 1980), 1:86.

22. Quoted in Cameron and Wood, *Antonioni,* p. 9.

VIII THE GLORIOUS SIXTIES (1961–1969)

1. In 1960, Italy produced 168 fiction films (eighty-seven in coproduction). In 1961, the volume rose to 213 films (ninety-seven in coproduction); in 1963 to 245 films (113 in coproduction). There was also an increase in exported films: in 1953, there were only 1,716 sales as compared with 3,897 in 1962 and 3,953 in 1963. The number of Italian films imported by the United States increased from forty-three in 1953 to 106 in 1963. Similarly, in France the box office of Italian films increased by 160 percent between 1957 and 1961; and in 1962 Italian works ranked second among the foreign films released in France. In January 1962, *Variety* referred to 1961 as "the great year of the Italian cinema," acknowledging the success of *La dolce vita, Rocco and His Brothers,* and *Two Women* in the United States as another "symptom of power." In the second half of the sixties, the volume of Italian production fell to 250 films per year. Symptoms of an economic crisis reappeared, but its impact became manifest only at the end of the decade. Despite the growing influence of television, the number of filmgoers remained relatively stable during the first half of the sixties. Whereas in England the annual number of spectators declined from a billion and a half in the fifties to 500 million in 1961, and in Germany during the same period from 800 million to 600 million, Italian statistics were less depressing; the annual average of 800 million spectators for the fifties sank to 741 million in 1961, to 728 million in 1962, to 697 million in 1963, and to 663 million in 1965.

2. Serge Bernstein and Paul Milza, *L'Italie contemporaine des nationalistes aux européens* (Paris: Armand Collin, 1973), pp. 375–76.

3. "Americans spend half of their money on organization to make sure that everything will work as planned. They take into consideration all possible circumstances, except rain and an actress who has eaten too many beans. No Italian producer has ever spent a penny to make sure that everything would run smoothly, as in Italy things change all the time. With the beginning of coproductions, incredible things started happening, making us roar with laughter.

"Each of us was used to taking care of everything: when there was no electrician, then the cameraman gladly took his place. With the Americans we quickly understood that only one person is allowed to move the chairs on the set. The foreign crew immediately stopped working whenever somebody did something that he was not supposed to do. The unions were dividing the tasks more and more. Finally, we adopted some of these rules, which are not inherently bad. To know that there is somebody who will take care of certain things just means that these things will get done." (production manager Clemente Fracassi, in *La città del cinema* [Rome: Napoleone, 1979], p. 168)

4. To name just a few of the mythological films: *The Vengeance of Hercules, The Love of Hercules, Hercules Challenges Samson, The Challenge of the Giants, The Triumph of Maciste, Maciste in Hell, Maciste Against the Vampires, Maciste Against the Monsters, The Titans Are Coming, Samson Against the Pirates, The Heroes of Babylon, Goliath and the Rebellious Slave*, etc.

5. Lino Miccichè, *Il cinema italiano degli anni '60* (Venice: Marsilio, 1975), p. 160.

6. Vittorio Spinazzola, *Cinema e pubblico: Lo spettacolo filmico in Italia, 1945–1965* (Milan: Bompiani, 1974), p. 334.

7. Robertson means "the son of Roberto Roberti." Roberti, Leone's father, was a prominent director of the silent era. He directed, e.g., *The Serpent* (1919) starring Francesca Bertini.

8. Quoted in Gianni Rondolino, ed., *Catalogo Bolaffi del cinema italiano, 1945–1965*, 2 vols. (Turin: Giulio Bolaffi, 1967), vol. 2.

9. The authors of *Yojimbo* accused Leone of plagiarism and eventually obtained 15 percent of the film's world profits.

10. "Why are James Bond's adventures so successful? Simply because at least fifty scenes out of sixty hold the audience in suspense. Americans have always represented the West in an extremely romantic form: the horse always arrived on command" (Sergio Leone, quoted in Oreste De Fornari, *Sergio Leone* [Milan: Moizzi, 1977], p. 12).

11. Miccichè, *Il cinema italiano degli anni '60*, p. 116.

12. "Postwar Italy is one of the most puritanic countries in the world. The idolization of the family, strongly embedded in the overall provincial way of life, seems a secure rampart against any spiritual turmoil" (Jean-François Revel, *Pour l'Italie* [Paris: Julliard, 1958], p. 45).

13. Miccichè, *Il cinema italiano degli anni '60*, p. 112.

14. Edgar Morin, "Mai mais, mais mai," *Le Monde*, June 1, 1978, p. 15.

15. Quoted in Carlo Salinari, *Preludio e fine del realismo in Italia* (Naples: Morano, 1967), p. 173.

16. Guido Oldrini, *Problemi di teoria e storia del cinema* (Naples: Guida, 1976), p. 326.

17. Quoted in Miccichè, *Il cinema italiano degli anni '60*, p. 180.

18. Laura Betti did not appear in a film by Bertolucci until 1976. In his *Novecento* (*1900*) she was the vicious wife of a fascist satrap.

19. Pasolini dedicated to Bertolucci a poem called "For a Boy," in which he addressed him as "shy, ardently quiet, attentive to the ironies and passions of others." Bertolucci re-

plied in his own volume of poetry *In Search of Mystery*, mentioning "the timidity and emotions" that he experienced in Pasolini's presence.

20. Pasolini is quoted as saying about *Last Tango*: "In my opinion it is a product of subculture. It is supposed to portray something new, but it does not. What's new about sadism?" (Kent E. Carrol, ed., *Last Tango in Paris* [New York: Grove Press, 1973], p. 22).

21. Enzo Siciliano, *Vita di Pasolini* (Milan: Rizzoli, 1979), p. 241.

22. Mel Gussow, "Bertolucci Talks About Sex, Revolution, and *Last Tango*," *New York Times*, February 2, 1973, p. 20.

23. *Last Tango in Paris*, p. 19.

24. Joseph Gelmis, *The Film Director as Superstar* (Garden City, N.Y.: Doubleday, 1970), pp. 115–16.

25. Pauline Kael called her review of *Before the Revolution* "Starburst by a Gifted 22-Year-Old," in *Life* Magazine, August 13, 1965.

26. In the years 1964–1965, Bertolucci made a television documentary in three installments and one short film, and he coauthored the script for Sergio Leone's film *Once Upon a Time in the West*.

27. *Aspekte des italienischen Films* (Bad Ems: Verband der deutschen Filmclubs, 1969), p. 136.

28. "'For me utopia represents the moment of truth,' says Ettore, the protagonist of *Subversives*. These words might also have been uttered by Salvatore or Giulio or the 'Scorpionists,' all of whom are looking for a new world, about which they know nothing and which may very well not exist at all" (Marco De Poli, *Paolo e Vittorio Taviani* [Milan: Moizzi, 1977], p. 81).

29. The Tavianis contended: "In our situation in Europe, all subversive changes lie in the distant future. The revolutionary leap appears as a fable, a utopia. We say utopia, not an escape: the necessity to oppose a desired imaginary future to a present that such a distant prospect might otherwise reduce to shapelessness" (quoted in ibid.).

30. Salvatore was the first important role of Gian Maria Volontè, one of the finest Italian actors.

31. In 1959–1960, the Tavianis were in Sicily shooting the third episode for Joris Ivens's documentary *L'Italia non è un paese povero* (Italy Is Not a Poor Country). When they mailed the footage to Ivens in Rome, he responded: "The material is excellent, but it is suitable for a fiction film." That's how *This Man Must Die* came into being.

32. In 1968, Orsini directed a semifictional film *I dannati della terra* (The Doomed of the Earth), a complex subjective portrait of a middle-aged intellectual who is confronted with political and personal crisis, responsibilities, and guilt. The result was unconvincing, despite an interesting admixture of cinematic material from the Third World as well as from Italy, in combination with staged sequences of the protagonist, his family, and work. Later, Orsini worked mainly for television. In 1980 he adapted Vittorini's novel *Uomini o no* (Men and Others) for the screen.

33. They are portrayed by Gian Maria Volontè and Lucia Bosè, who made her comeback to Italian cinema after a long absence.

34. *Galileo* was made in coproduction with the Bulgarian State Film Organization, which provided magnificent settings, lavish costumes, and studio facilities. Bulgarian authorities interpreted Cavani's film solely as an attack on the Catholic church, though the structure of the trial, ending with Galileo's self-criticism and abjuration of his beliefs, brings to mind the methods and victims of the communist regimes.

35. In 1972, Cavani, who identified completely with the film's young protagonists, contended: "The cannibals are people who want to regain their true human nature and the

religious sense of life, refusing to be conditioned by the so-called civilized society. Searching for a genuine purity and for a forgotten sincerity, they are rejected as 'cannibals' because they disturb the often inhuman external order of law" (quoted in Ciriaco Tiso, *Liliana Cavani* [Florence: La Nuova Italia, 1975], p. 82).

36. *The Lizards* was produced by an independent company, "22 Dicembre," founded by Olmi, the film critic Tullio Kezich, and others in 1961. This company produced also Olmi's *The Fiancés*.

37. Gavin Millar, in Richard Roud, ed., *Cinema: A Critical Dictionary*, 2 vols. (London: Secker & Warburg, 1980), 1:725.

38. Freddy Buache, *Le cinéma italien, 1945–1979* (Lausanne: L'Age d'Homme, 1979), p. 325.

39. Quoted in Amos Vogel, *Film as a Subversive Art* (New York: Random House, 1975), p. 56.

40. Ibid.

41. Ferreri started working in film in the early fifties when he collaborated on the *Documento mensile* (Monthly Bulletin), a kind of neorealist newsreel that lasted for only three editions. (Its main promoter was Zavattini, and among his collaborators were Visconti, De Sica, Antonioni, and Fellini.) In 1956, Ferreri went to Spain to sell Totalscope anamorphic lenses. There in 1958, he shot his first fiction film *El pisito* (The Apartment), based on the subject by the Spanish writer Rafael Ascona. Ascona wrote the scripts for his most important films, including *Conjugal Bed*. *The Apartment* tells the story of a young man who marries an eighty-year-old woman just to get her apartment. Ferreri's second film, *Los chicos* (The Boys, 1959), permeated with a sophisticated cruelty reminiscent of Buñuel's *Los olvidados*, portrayed a group of loafers living at the margins of society. It was *El cochechito* (The Wheelchair, 1960) that projected Ferreri to international fame. Ascona and Ferreri again used human deformity to express their idea of the impossibility of any valid relationship within the family nucleus. In 1961, Ferreri returned to Italy.

42. The film's original title was *L'ape regina* (The Queen Bee). Ferreri changed it, after the film had been held up by the censor for six months, into *Una storia moderna, l'ape regina*.

·43. Although he denies it, Ferreri's films are antifeminist. "I am considered a misogynist. But it is our culture that is misogynist, the relationship between the society and women is" (quoted in Jean A. Gili, *Le cinéma italien* [Paris: Union Générale d'Edition, 1978], p. 165).

44. Roud, ed., *Cinema: A Critical Dictionary*, 1:348.

45. One of Ferreri's most ambitious films was *L'uomo dei cinque palloni* (The Man with the Balloons, 1965; the film is sometimes shown under the title *Break-Up*). The producer, Carlo Ponti, cut the original version from a feature length to a featurette and included it in the composite film *Ieri, oggi, domani* (*Yesterday, Today, and Tomorrow*) against the director's will. Ferreri later restored the film to its original form. The story of a man who tries to find out how much air can be blown into a balloon without bursting it and who kills himself when he does not succeed is a telling example of Ferreri's personal philosophy.

46. Paolo Bertetto, *Il cinema dell'utopia* (Salerno: Runna, 1970), p. 153.

47. Jacques Aumont, Eduardo de Gregorio, and Sylvie Pierre, "Trois entretiens avec Marco Ferreri," *Cahiers du Cinéma*, no. 217, 1969, pp. 31–32.

48. Jean A. Gili, *Elio Petri* (Nice: Faculté des Lettres et Sciences Humaines, 1974), p. 8.

49. The film was inspired by the life of Petri's father.

50. The Austrian philosopher Ernst Fischer's definition of Rosi's approach to politics is: "In the modern myth, destiny is just politics, in the broader sense of the term. In other

words: destiny is the man's fight to preserve or to modify the whole system of administrative, economic, and social relations that man himself had created and whose total alienation wears a mask borrowed from antique destiny" (in Michel Ciment, *Le dossier Rosi* [Paris: Stock, 1976], p. 18).

51. The subject of the Algerian revolution was for many years taboo in French cinema and, to a certain degree, in the rest of Western Europe. Despite official protests of the French delegation, Pontecorvo's film was awarded the Golden Lion at the 1966 Venice Festival.

52. Possibly the best film dealing with the fascist era was made in 1961 by the documentarists Lino Del Fra and Cecilia Mangini, joined by the film critic Lino Miccichè. *All' armi siam fascisti!* (At Arms, We Are Fascists!), the first documentary of its kind, used archival material and historical footage to recapture half a century of Italian history, from 1911 to 1961.

IX HIGHLIGHTS OF THE SIXTIES

1. Lo Duca, in the foreword to *Amarcord* (Paris: Seghers, 1974), p. 7.

2. Barbara K. Lewalski, "Federico Fellini's Purgatorio," in Peter Bondanella, ed., *Federico Fellini: Essays in Criticism* (New York: Oxford University Press, 1978), p. 113.

3. The film is entitled *8½* because prior to then Fellini had made seven feature films and two episodes for composite films. The *½* stands for *Variety Lights*, which he codirected with Lattuada.

4. Christian Metz, *Film Language: A Semiotics of the Cinema* (New York: Oxford University Press, 1974), p. 229.

5. Georges Sadoul, *Dictionary of Films* (Berkeley and Los Angeles: University of California Press, 1972), p. 229.

6. The film was the official Italian entry at the Moscow Film Festival. It caused a sensation. Its domination of the competition was so towering that the majority of the jury resisted even the most extreme official Soviet pressure and awarded the film the Grand Prize. But the film was never released in the Soviet Union.

7. Lino Miccichè, *Il cinema italiano degli anni '70* (Venice: Marsilio, 1980), p. 39.

8. Quoted in *Fellini's Satyricon* (New York: Ballantine Books, 1970), p. 44.

9. Umberto Boccione, one of the leading Futurists, quoted in Marco Valsecchi, "Italian Painting Today," *Italian Quarterly*, nos. 7–8, 1959, p. 24.

10. Antonioni, quoted in Giorgio Tinazzi, *Michelangelo Antonioni* (Florence: La Nuova Italia, 1976), p.5.

11. Antonioni, *Il deserto rosso* (the screenplay) (Bologna: Cappelli, 1978), p. 135. In an interview with Jean-Luc Godard, Antonioni contended: "It is an oversimplification to say that I condemn the industrialized inhuman world where the individual falls apart and ends up with neurosis. My intention was to express the beauty of this world where even factories can be beautiful. But while you know well where you start, you can never tell where you will end up" (Godard, "La nuit, l'eclipse, l'aurore," *Cahiers du Cinéma*, no. 160, 1964).

12. Monica Vitti played Claudia in *L'avventura*; Valentina, the millionaire's daughter, and Giovanni's passing flirt, in *La notte*; and Giuliana in *Red Desert*. She became the representative of Antonioni's alienated protagonists, and her acting, image, and appearance have been imitated all over the world.

13. In the foreword to the book version of the script of *Blow-Up*, Antonioni wrote: "We know that under one revealed image, there is another one more faithful to reality; and under this one there is yet another one. Until we reach the true, absolute, and mysterious reality,

which nobody will ever see. Or maybe we'll reach the decomposition of all images, of all reality. In this perspective, abstract films have their reason to exist" (Tinazzi, *Antonioni*, p. 4).

14. The remaining episodes of *Boccaccio '70* were directed by Monicelli (*Renzo e Luciana*, a story of poor lovers, which attempts to relate to some of the neorealist themes), by De Sica (*La riffa* [The Lottery,] with Sophia Loren as the film's main asset), and by Fellini (*Le tentazioni del dottor Antonio* [The Temptations of Doctor Antonio], a rather undistinguished satire on the advertising world).

15. During the shooting, Visconti drove everybody mad with his insistence on the authenticity of every detail in Ottavio's palatial home. The collection of art objects came from Visconti's own house, and two marble busts sculpted by Sarah Bernhardt were lent by Sophia Loren. The eighteenth-century French bookcases were equally rare, as were the carpets and Ottavio's Afghan hounds. Visconti asked Coco Chanel (the Parisian fashion designer and his lifelong friend) to take Romy Schneider in hand and teach her elegance. With the help of the designer Mario Carbuglia everything worked out as planned. And, thanks to her performance in the film, Schneider was launched as an international star.

16. The film follows only the first six chapters of the novel, which goes on to cover twenty more years, including the prince's death and the family's decline.

17. The original title of *Sandra* translates "Bright Stars of the Ursa," which is a quotation from Leopardi's (1789–1837) collection of poems *Le ricordanze* evoking the poet's youth. The original title of *The Damned* translates "The Fall of the Gods" and is taken from Wagner.

18. Visconti was later accused of having portrayed the von Krupps, the most powerful German family of armament tycoons.

19. The list of Pasolini's appearances in court between 1947 and 1961 fills three printed pages. Those between 1961 and his death in 1975 fill another eleven pages (Laura Betti, ed., *Pasolini: Chronique judiciaire, persécution, exécution* [Paris: Seghers, 1977], pp. 213–27).

20. "Federiz, that spaceship destined to explore new horizons, failed at its first trial trip and never flew again" (Enzo Siciliano, *Vita di Pasolini* (Milan: Rizzoli, 1979), p. 229.

21. "Today, these shanty cottages were thrown into our faces. We can no longer be justified just by imagining their existence and feeling sorry. We enter them and we feel creepy" (Ugo Casiraghi, "Accattone," *L'Unità*, November 1, 1961; quoted in Marc Gervais, *Pier Paolo Pasolini* [Paris: Seghers, 1973], p. 150).

22. Jean Duflot, *Entretiens avec P. P. Pasolini* (Paris: P. Belfond, 1970), p. 104.

23. Pasolini appealed and won, and the sentence finally came under amnesty. The film's career, however, was irreparably damaged, and it remains little known today.

24. After *La ricotta*, Pasolini attempted to express his preoccupation as a critic and essayist through the film medium. Thus, three films of documentary character and of lesser importance came out of this: *La rabbia* (The Rage, 1963), a rather confused montage of film footage commenting on political issues of postwar Europe; *Soppraluoghi in Palestina per Il vangelo secondo Matteo* (Looking in Palestine for Locations to the Gospel According to St. Matthew, 1963–1964); and *Comizi d'amore*, the most interesting of the three, consisting of interviews with Italians of all classes about their attitudes toward love and sex.

25. P. P. Pasolini, quoted in Siciliano, *Vita di Pasolini*, p. 269. The head of "Pro Civitate Cristiana," Don Giovanni Rossi, became one of the religious consultants on *The Gospel According to St. Matthew*.

26. Oswald Stack, *Pasolini on Pasolini* (London: Thames & Hudson, 1969), p. 83.

27. Many of the cast were Pasolini's friends, with his own mother as the Virgin Mary.

28. Siciliano, *Vita di Pasolini*, p. 272.

29. Pasolini was a talented painter. After his death, his friend Giuseppe Zigaina, a prominent Italian painter, organized expositions of his work in several Italian cities. The first exposition was held in a small town in Friuli where both Pasolini and Zigaina were born.

30. Jean-Louis Bory, *Arts* (Paris), March 10, 1965; reprinted in Gervais, *Pasolini*, p. 153.

31. Later assembled in Pasolini, *Empirismo eretico* (Milan: Garzanti, 1972).

32. Gervais, *Pasolini*, p. 25.

33. "Cinema di poesia" was originally a paper read by Pasolini at the seminar "Critica e il Nuovo Cinema" at the Mostra Internazionale del Nuovo Cinema (Pesaro, 1965). Later, it was reprinted in many journals in many countries. In 1972, it was published in his *Empirismo eretico* (also in Pier Paolo Pasolini, *L'expérience hérétique* [Paris: Payot, 1976], pp. 136–55).

34. P. P. Pasolini, quoted in Sandro Petraglia, *Pier Paolo Pasolini* (Florence: La Nuova Italia, 1974), pp. 77–78.

35. Ninetto was portrayed by Ninetto Davoli, a nonprofessional actor and Pasolini's closest friend who appeared in several of Pasolini's films.

36. Quoted from the screenplay *Uccellacci e uccellini* (Milan: Garzanti, 1966).

37. Duflot, *Entretiens avec P. P. Pasolini*, p. 108.

38. "Pasolinian realism . . . serves the purpose of imposing the presence of mythology through the mediation of a brutal reality, the corporality of bodies, arms, clothes, and nature as such" (Christian Zimmer, "Le système," *Les Temps Modernes*, no. 282, January 1970, p. 1132).

39. Jean Narboni, "Rencontre avec Pier Paolo Pasolini," *Cahiers du Cinéma*, no. 192, 1967, p. 31.

40. Gervais, *Pasolini*, p. 79.

41. The word *theorem*, in mathematics and logic, is a statement in words or symbols that can be established by means of deductive logic.

42. In 1968, the novel was in competition for the coveted Italian literary award Premio Strega and created a scandal that divided the Italian literary scene.

43. "The sacred is true; it is the only essential reality that preoccupies me. All my work focuses on the relations of human beings with the sacred and on the presence of the sacred in daily life. The capitalist bourgeois society tries by all means to repress it, but it surfaces again and again" (Pasolini, in Gervais, *Pasolini*, p. 87).

44. The film received the Catholic Film Office's award, which triggered an angry denunciation of *Teorema* by the Vatican. The award was later revoked, and Pasolini returned it along with the one he received for *The Gospel According to St. Matthew*.

45. Gian Piero Brunetta, *Cahiers du Cinéma*, May 1969; quoted in Gervais, *Pasolini*, p. 147.

46. As Pasolini told Oswald Stack, the first part of the film, *Orgia* (Orgy), was originally written to complement (for release purposes) Buñuel's *Simon of the Desert*, which Pasolini considered Buñuel's best film (Stack, *Pasolini on Pasolini*, p. 141).

47. In 1960, Pasolini translated Aeschylus's tragedy *Orestes* for the theater. When he was shooting in Africa, he also had in mind a film about St. Paul, in which the road from Damascus would have led through the contemporary American world.

48. Cherubini's *Medea* was one of Callas's most famous roles. Before and during the shooting of the film, Callas and Pasolini became very close (this was just after her separation from Onassis). This "amorous friendship" lasted for several years (see Siciliano, *Vita di Pasolini*, pp. 329–33).

49. *Pasolini: Séminaire dirigé par M. A. Macciocchi* (Paris: Grasset, 1980), p. 91.

X   THE CHANGING IMAGE OF THE MOVIES   (1970–1982)

1. Lorenzo Quaglietti, *Storia economico-politica del cinema italiano, 1945–1980* (Rome: Editori Riuniti, 1980), pp. 195–204.

2. "Until 1968, the main problem had been to organize in order to support the Italian film industry as a whole in its struggle against Americanization. The year 1968 became our moment of truth. We felt that we could no longer speak of the great family of the Italian cinema united in one combat line (as had been the official policy of the Communist party). The document written to this effect by the film section of the Communist party split our organization in two. ANAC (Zavattini, Maselli, Bellocchio, Ferreri, etc.) argued that we had to concern ourselves with our working conditions, along with the methods of production and distribution, and that we had to enact laws that would curtail the power of the industry and foster movies motivated by other than purely mercenary motives. AACI (Age, Germi, Monicelli, Loy, Scarpelli, Scola, etc.), on the other hand, stood for the defense of unity and for professional interests. For three years we went separate ways; then the two bodies were reunited again." (Francesco Maselli in an unpublished personal interview)

3. Unlike the Cannes Festival, Venice did not survive the 1968 tempest and ceased to exist as an international competition. In 1969, it reemerged with its structure fundamentally changed: no jury and no awards but with a format of thematic surveys of new directions and retrospectives of previous trends. Only in 1979, with Carlo Lizzani as its director, did the Venice Festival resume its former role as an international competition.

4. M. West, "Terror as Historical Inheritance," *Esquire*, April 25, 1978; quoted in *Foreign Affairs* (New York), no. 4, 1979, p. 934.

5. An Italian joke tells about two men sitting in a bar. "It's raining again," one says. "The sun is shining," contends the other. They start arguing and come to blows. At that point, a third man, who has been quietly sipping his wine in the corner, jumps to his feet: "Rain or shine, the government is a bunch of thieves."

6. The title is a quotation from Ignatius of Loyola, the founder of the Jesuit order, exhorting the Christian to "use all means in the search for the divine will" ("Todo modo para buscar la voluntad divina").

7. Aldo Moro was kidnapped and assassinated by terrorists two years later.

8. Leonardo Sciascia, "Le coeur de l'état italien n'existe pas; sa cervelle non plus," *Le Monde*, February 4–5, 1979. *Todo modo* anticipated the events that shook Italy soon after the book had been written and the film made: the assassination of Aldo Moro (five-time prime minister and candidate for the presidency) in 1978, the killing of the communist labor leader Guido Rossi and the judge Emilio Alessandrini in 1979, the massacre at the Bologna railroad station in 1980, etc. There were 2,597 terrorist attacks in Italy in 1979 (as compared with 702 in 1975) perpetrated by both the extreme Left and the extreme Right.

9. Giacomo Matteotti was a Socialist member of the Parliament and an outspoken adversary of the fascist regime. He was kidnapped and murdered on Mussolini's orders. With the opposition shorn of its leadership, divided, and weakened, the country fell under the control of Il Duce.

10. Marco Leto pointed out:

In my opinion, the true fascism is white-collar fascism, the fascism of those who pull the strings, the fascism that penetrates the mentality of certain forces and the structures of a state. The Italian state was born authoritarian and remained authoritarian under all regimes. The police officer in my film represents the continuity of the state; he is the personification of this type of mentality. It is no accident that he says to the professor: "In a few years, you will have the democracy you are fighting for: by that time I shall be retired, but I shall find myself a party to vote for." (*Il Messaggero* [Rome], May 6, 1973; reprinted in *La villeggiatura* [Rome: Italnoleggio Cinematografico, 1973], p. 3 [press-book])

11. *Just Another War* is based on memoirs by Emilio Lussu, a well-known leftist Italian politician.

12. Rosi, interviewed by Gary Crowdus and Dan Georgakas, "The Audience Should Not Be Just Passive Spectators," *Cinéaste*, no. 1, Fall 1975, p. 3.

13. Freddy Buache, *Le cinéma italien, 1945–1979* (Lausanne: L'Age d'Homme, 1979), p. 336.

14. Otello Angeli, "Anatomia di una crisi," *Cinema 70*, no. 125, 1979, p. 9.

15. Before making her film, Gagliardo coscripted Miklós Jancsó's Italian films *The Pacifist, The Technique and the Rite, Rome Wants Another Caesar*, and *Private Vices and Public Virtues*.

16. *Gesamtprogramm der Internationalen Filmwoche* (Mannheim: Internationale Filmwoche, 1978), p. 48 (pressbook).

17. Del Monte freely admitted the influence of Bergman in his 1970 graduation film at the Centro Sperimentale di Cinematografia *Fuori campo* (Off Camera). The film concerns two young people seeking a new comprehension of reality and new ways to communicate with one another.

18. "They say the film is quite good, but morally ambiguous and politically dangerous. They say its interest in re-creating the culture of the past (the fashion of the roaring thirties) leads to a horrifyingly nostalgic evocation of Nazism. They say that the passion of an ex-prisoner for her jailor provokes feelings of unbearable discomfort. They called it "Last Tango in Vienna in Nazi uniforms." They say that it is immoral to show the victim and her jailor on the same level while Hitler stands between them. They say that it generates a dangerous confusion between political perversion of Nazism and the sexual perversion of sado-masochism. They say it is an extreme case and that Lucia would have denounced Max if she had been a normal human being. . . . Whatever they say, though, the film's images reveal a very important thing: this society coerces us into complicity, and not even the craziest passion can save us." (Morando Morandini, "Un portiere troppo chiachierato," *Tempo*, August 2, 1974; reprinted in *Il portiere di notte* [Rome: Italnoleggio Cinemato-grafico, 1974], p. 71 [pressbook])

19. Quoted in Ciriaco Tiso, *Liliana Cavani* (Florence: La Nuova Italia, 1975), p. 97.

20. Callisto Cosulich, "Assassino in congedo," *Paese Sera*, April 14, 1974; reprinted in *Il portiere di notte*, p. 7.

21. Nanni Moretti, quoted in *L'Italie au XXXIe Festival de Cannes* (Rome: Anica-Unita-lia, 1978) (pressbook).

22. *Starting from Three* cost only $450,000 and became one of the highest-grossing films, surpassing American superproductions such as *The Empire Strikes Back*.

23. Scola pointed out:

Under fascism, women were officially "queens of the household": but in reality they were kept away from all decisions. Their only task was to have children because, as Mussolini pointed out, "Power lies in numbers." The only role of sex was procreation and the wor-ship of the male. Homosexuality just did not exist, not even as a concept. The word never appeared in newspapers. In a country, such as Italy, homosexuals simply could not exist, which meant that they had to be regarded as subversives and dissidents trying to disrupt the reigning order. Those who were accused indirectly had to leave their jobs and were exiled to Carbonia where they lived in confinement. (Jean A. Gili, *Le cinéma italien* [Paris: Union Générale d'Edition, 1978], p. 315)

24. Cerami was a close friend and ex-disciple of Pasolini. After his death, he became a permanent collaborator of Sergio Citti.

25. "Kneekapping" was a frequent "punishment" administered by terrorists to establishment figures in the seventies.

26. *Metello* should not be confused with the film *The Organizer*, which is the U.S. distribution title for Mario Monicelli's 1963 film *I compagni*.

27. Morando Morandini, *Cineforum*, nos. 99–100, 1971; reprinted in Francesco Casetti, *Bernardo Bertolucci* (Florence: La Nuova Italia, 1975), p. 75.

28. Dispatched by the fascist police to Paris to kill Quadri, Marcello telephones him and reminds him of the words that the professor had often repeated to his students: "The time of meditation is over; the time of action has arrived." These same words open Godard's 1960 film *The Little Soldier*.

29. "Beginning with *The Spider's Strategem*, a direct influence of my analysis became manifest. I said to my analyst: 'Your name should be in the credits of all my films'" (Bertolucci, in Gili, *Le cinéma italien*, p. 63).

30. "At the press conference following the showing of *The Conformist*, Bertolucci said that the difference between his film and Visconti's *The Damned* is that *The Damned* is operatic while his film is operettic, which is, in a way, quite right" (Vincent Canby, "Bertolucci Equates Politics with Sex," *New York Times*, September 19, 1970, p. 32).

31. Carlo Tagliabue, "The Narrow Road to a Forked Path," *Framework*, no. 3, 1976, p. 11.

32. Pauline Kael, "The Current Cinema: Tango," *New Yorker*, October 28, 1972, p. 130. Her rave review was reprinted as an advertisement on two full pages of the *New York Times*, December 24, 1972.

33. Paul's mother is played by Maria Michi, who was the drug-addicted girl in *Open City* and the prostitute in the Roman episode of *Paisan*. His wife's lover is Massimo Girotti, once the leading neorealist star. One of the crucial scenes shows Brando and Girotti in identical dressing gowns (gifts from the same woman), comparing their experiences and memories.

34. Jean-Louis Bory, "Huis clos sur un matelas," *Le Nouvel Observateur*, December 23, 1972, p. 59.

35. Jean de Baroncelli, "Bernardo Bertolucci: On s'exprime toujours par ses pensées," *Le Monde*, December 15, 1972, p. 15.

36. "Self-Portrait of an Angel and Monster," *Time*, January 22, 1973, p. 53. Like Bertolucci, Brando was undergoing psychotherapy at the time of *Last Tango*. After finishing the film, he told Bertolucci: "I would never do such a thing again. You violated my inner self" (Brando, quoted in Michel Delain, "Bertolucci passe aux aveux," *L'Express*, December 11–17, 1972, p. 52).

37. In most countries, a drastically shortened version of *1900* was shown in two parts.

38. Since *1900*, Giuseppe Bertolucci has acted as his brother's producer. He has also tried to establish himself as a film director, with mediocre success.

39. Wolfgang Limmer, "Die Verstümmelung eines Meisterwerks," *Der Spiegel*, no. 45, 1976, p. 218.

40. Burt Lancaster, looking just as he did in *The Leopard*, plays the role of the landowner, who hangs himself in a cowshed after sexually molesting a little peasant girl.

41. Jean de Baroncelli, "Luna de Bertolucci à Venise," *Le Monde*, September 5, 1979, p. 13.

42. *Avanti* (Rome), December 18, 1974; reprinted in Lino Micchichè, *Il cinema italiano degli anni ' 70* (Venice: Marsilio, 1980), p. 212.

43. The Italian film world nicknamed Wertmüller "Santa Lina di New York" (see *Corriere della Sera*, January 18, 1978, review of *The End of the World* by Giovanni Grazzini; reprinted in his *Cinema '78* [Rome and Bari: Laterza, 1979], p. 7).

44. *The Screenplays of Lina Wertmüller* (New York: Warner Books, 1978), p. xvii.

45. Diane Jacobs wrote in Peter Cowie, ed., *International Film Guide, 1977:*

Seven Beauties is Wertmüller's most interesting film. The formula is the same: a flawed man fights the System, which in turn exacts a compromise: but the counters here are much more complex. . . . Wertmüller's juggling of polemics and humor in *Seven Beauties* is her finest directorial performance to date. The key of all her earlier works can be found in the statement of a prisoner: "Man in disorder—that is the only hope." She still does not answer her perennial dilemma, but her questions are becoming increasingly compelling. ([London: Tantivy Press, 1977], pp. 61–62; parts of this article were published in *Film Comment*, March–April, 1976)

46. Gianni Rondolino, ed., *Catalogo Bolaffi del cinema italiano, 1978–1979* (Turin: Giulio Bolaffi, 1979), p. 48.

47. Marco Ferreri, "Faire de l'homme un animal social," *Ecran*, no. 47, 1976, p. 31.

48. *L'ultima donna* (screenplay) (Turin: Einaudi, 1976), p. 283.

49. Ibid., p. 289.

50. "During a serious crisis, or in periods of historical transition, a monkeylike image emerges because at such times, the eternal questions are once more raised: Who are we? Where do we come from? Thus the monkey brings a series of latent problems to the surface. The image of rats, of monkeys, etc., is not new since it lies dormant within Man and re-emerges in periods like the one in which we are now living. I believe the crux of the problem is not to reconstitute this reality but rather to exploit this phase of enormous contradictions in order to create a New Man, or at least to try to determine the course of History. Women too are faced with the problem of reaffirming their ancient identity, though they have not yet created a new one for themselves. But I feel the position of Woman is more vital than that of Man because it is more conscious and contested: while Man is cracking up, Woman is growing up" (Ferreri, in the pressbook to *Bye-Bye, Male* [Rome: Anica-Unitalia, 1978]).

51. *L'ultima donna*, p. 275.

52. Marco Bellocchio, "Le saut dans le vide," *L'Araldo*, May 15–16, 1980, p. 3.

53. Nuccio Lodato, *Marco Bellocchio* (Milan: Moizzi, 1977), p. 10.

54. Ibid., p. 7.

55. Recent statistics state that in Italy more than 500 private television stations broadcast more than 2,500 films per week.

56. Cowie, ed., *International Film Guide*, p. 19.

57. Ibid., p. 191.

XI THE DUSK OF THE LEOPARDS

1. De Sica directed ten films for Ponti, seven starring Loren.

2. See p. 47.

3. "Yes, I have lost the feeling of reality in which I had been immersed. . . . I used to consider this involvement a kind of categorical imperative, an obligation, and a moral

choice. Now reality appears to me more like a game. This has probably something to do with age, with a series of disillusionments. When you keep moving from one delusion to another, you end up viewing reality as something horrendous, something intolerable, as a perfidious game played by some God, the Creator, who resembles the Devil. Or you just accept it as a game" (Pasolini, quoted in Nabil Reda Mahaini, "Decameron: Intervista con P. P. Pasolini," *Cinema 60*, nos. 87–88, 1972, p. 70).

4. Pasolini himself appears in the film as Giotto. In *The Canterbury Tales* he plays Chaucer. Pasolini referred to *The Decameron, The Canterbury Tales*, and *Arabian Nights* as the "trilogy of life."

5. Pasolini at a press conference at the 1972 Berlin International Film Festival (Paul Willemen, ed., *Pier Paolo Pasolini* [London: British Film Institute, 1977], p. 73).

6. "Abiura dalla Trilogia della vita," in P. P. Pasolini, *Trilogia della Vita* (Bologna: Cappelli, 1975), pp. 9–19.

7. Richard Roud, ed., *Cinema: A Critical Dictionary* 2 vols. (London: Secker & Warburg, 1980), 2:771.

8. The English translation is from Willemen, ed. *Pasolini*, pp. 65–66.

9. Bertolucci, quoted in Nereo Condini, "Pasolini's Last Film: A Shocker You May Never See," *Village Voice*, March 15, 1976, p. 158.

10. Peter W. Jansen and Wolfram Schütte, eds., *Pier Paolo Pasolini* (Munich: C. Hanser Verlag, 1977), p. 12.

11. Roberto Rossellini, *Un esprit libre ne doit rien apprendre en esclave* (Paris: Fayard, 1977), p. 202.

12. Gianni Rondolino, *Roberto Rossellini* (Florence: La Nuova Italia, 1974), p. 9.

13. Quoted in ibid., pp. 35–36.

14. Rossellini, *Un esprit libre*, p. 202.

15. Claude Beylie, "Le messie," *Ecran*, no. 45, 1976, p. 59.

16. "Those who mourn the passing away of neorealism are antihistorical in their attitude, but as a spiritual state of mind neorealism must still be deemed a formative experience of inestimable value" (Fellini, quoted in Patrizio Rossi and Ben Lawton, "Reality, Fantasy, and Fellini," in Peter Bondanella, ed., *Federico Fellini: Essays in Criticism* [New York: Oxford University Press, 1978], p. 257).

17. According to Carlo Salinari, the Italian literary critic, childhood has become a significant theme of contemporary literature because it represents

the longing for a place that is free of the chaos and contradictions of contemporary society, for an oasis of original innocence that cannot be reached by echoes of the violence and ugliness of our life, in which conflict and struggle disappear, in which our problems vanish. A longing that is born of a natural desire to avoid man's slavery of things, the frenzy of industrial society, the inevitability of war, and the rule of money (*Miti e coscienza del decadentismo italiano* [Milan: Feltrinelli, 1960], p. 172; translation from Gian-Paolo Biasin, *The Smile of the Gods* [Ithaca: Cornell University Press, 1968], p. 102).

18. Pavese's poem "The Boy in Me."

19. Franco Pecori, *Federico Fellini* (Florence: La Nuova Italia, 1974), p. 121.

20. Jean de Baroncelli, "Fellini-Roma," *Le Monde*, May 15, 1971.

21. Umberto Eco, "Open Work," *Italian Quarterly*, Winter-Spring 1967, p. 30. "You can be open at the level of images, at the level of narrative, at the level of ideological response. You can establish the openness at different levels" (Eco, interviewed by William Luhr, "Semiotics and Film," *Wide Angle*, no. 4, 1977, p. 72).

22. In the dialect of the Romagna, *amarcord* means "I remember" (io mi ricordo). Other

interpretations have been suggested, e.g., a cryptic word consisting of *amare* (to love), *cuore* (the heart), *ricordare* (to remember), and *amaro* (bitter). The entire film is spoken in a nonexistent dialect similar to "romagnolo," which sometimes sounds completely surrealistic. *Amarcord* was shot in Cinecittà, and even those sets that seem absolutely authentic are made of pasteboard.

23. Nino Rota died in 1979. The absence of his music is deeply felt.

24. Vincent Canby, *New York Times*, August 17, 1979, p. C13.

25. Roud, ed., *Cinema: A Critical Dictionary* 1:83.

26. Aldo Tassone, *Parla il cinema italiano*, 2 vols. (Milan: Il Formichiere, 1979), 1:36. Tassone also discusses with Antonioni his own conversation with Joris Ivens and Marceline Loridan about their film on China. Tassone: "I remember how Loridan objected to your making a film without knowing the people. 'How can Antonioni, the director of incommunicability, understand the Chinese?' she asked." Antonioni: "It seems to me that my film gives a picture of the China of that time with a foreboding of today. Once, when Mao was still alive, I asked Marceline Loridan: 'Are there different social classes in China?' She answered: 'Of course, there are.' I should have said: 'Why don't you show them in your film?' But that would have been too naïve. China is too complex a problem" (ibid.). Umberto Eco said about the negative reception of Antonioni's film by the Chinese authorities:

> The Chinese authorities viewed the film as an offense to the Chinese people, as a fascist movie, as an attempt to show China in an unpleasant and nasty light. What happened? After the uproar I had the opportunity to discuss the movie with some Chinese. It happened that some images that, for Western spectators, acquire a positive meaning, for Chinese spectators acquire a negative meaning. The most typical example is the question of the Nanking bridge, which, according to the Chinese newspaper, was presented by Antonioni as if it were on the verge of collapse. Now, if you look at the sequence of the Nanking bridge, you will see that Antonioni shoots it in a long traveling shot from a boat which is passing under the bridge. He is shooting it in an oblique way, transversally—in the same way a Western movie would shoot a skyscraper or monument: from beneath, to try to give the impression of majesty and power; transversally to give the impression of tension and a leap towards the sky. But this is a stylistic device typical of Western movies, and of the late Western movies, and I tried to recall how the Chinese today represent, in their propaganda posters, buildings, and various other things. They are very frontal, very symmetric. Therefore, for them, Antonioni's method of shooting expressed trembling, expressed collapse, expressed an unstable situation or, at least, it was possible to take it this way (Eco, interviewed by Luhr, "Semiotics and Film," pp. 70–71).

27. Maria Antonietta Macciocchi, "Mettre en crise notre propre silence, "*Le Monde,* September 6–12, 1973, p. 11.

28. Tassone, *Parla il cinema italiano,* 1:27.

29. Maria Tarnowska was a countess who shocked Venetian society with her lifestyle and was sentenced to death for murder (though never executed) shortly before World War I.

30. In his report on Mahler's death in 1911, Mann noted: "Gustav von Aschenbach not only bears his Christian name, but the author of *Death in Venice* has given him the face of Mahler." And later, in a letter to Wolfgang Born, in whose illustrations to *Death in Venice* Aschenbach resembles Mahler, Mann pointed out: "The conception of my story was influenced in the spring of 1911 by the death of Gustav Mahler whom I had previously known in Munich and whose personality, full of such intense ardor, has impressed me beyond measure" (quoted in Monica Sterling, *A Screen of Time* [New York and London: Harcourt Brace Jovanovich, 1979], p. 208).

31. The entire version was screened at the 1980 Venice Festival and released in 1983.

32. Among Visconti's collaborators, *Conversation Piece* was referred to as a "small conspiracy of friendship." Visconti's lifelong scriptwriters, Enrico Medioli and Suso Cecchi D'Amico, helped him to devise a story that could take place in one interior, while Burt Lancaster, Silvana Mangano and Helmut Berger were refusing all other offers even before the script was finished, in order to be free the moment a producer was found.

33. David Sterrit, "Two New Italian Films, Including Visconti's Last," *Christian Science Monitor,* February 5, 1979.

XII UNDER THE SIGN OF VIOLENCE

1. Aldo Tassone, *Parla il cinema italiano,* 2 vols. (Milan: Il Formichiere, 1979), 2:364.

2. Marco Bellocchio pointed out: "Today, in 1980, we can say that the year 1968 did not succeed in creating a new society or a new culture. The veterans of 1968 had the following choices: to kill, to shoot, or to integrate into the society. Or to remain in between and be permanently unhappy and full of pathetic despair à la Woody Allen" (F. Accialini, L. Colucelli, and C. Valentinetti, "Conversazione con Marco Bellocchio," *Cinema e Cinema,* no. 22–23, 1980, p. 74).

3. B. Torri, *Il cinema italiano: Dalla realtà alle metafore* (Palermo: Palumbo, 1973), p. 180.

4. See Guido Aristarco, *Sotto il segno dello scorpione: Il cinema degli fratelli Taviani* (Messina and Florence: G. D'Anna, 1977), pp. 114–15.

5. The theme of betrayal appears in almost all the Tavianis' films; see Tassone, *Parla il cinema italiano,* 2:362–63.

6. In one of the final scenes, Ettore says: "I'm off to Venezuela, hoping that one day there will be a million people with red banners on the main square of Caracas. But you see how different and ambiguous everything is. Here, there are a million people waving red banners on the square, but they are not waving them for the revolution."

7. The title *Allonsanfan* stands for the first two words of "La Marseillaise" the way the Italians pronounce them.

8. "I do not understand utopia in the popular negative sense as an illusion, an adventure, a crazy dream, a postponement. For us, utopia means a perspective, a strategy, a final goal that has not yet been realized, but in whose name we act" (V. Taviani, in Tassone, *Parla il cinema italiano,* 2:326).

9. "The entire village, beginning with my father, thinks that I have gone beserk. For them it's madness that I am going forward with giant steps. I'm moving, while they are immobile, like the stones and like their mountains. The sun rises every morning. Years go by and the sun always finds them on the same spot" (Gavino Ledda).

10. See Chapter IX.

11. Eugenia is played by Isabella Rossellini, daughter of Ingrid Bergman and Roberto Rossellini.

12. Mino Argentieri, "Una monografia dedicata ai Taviani," *Cinema 70,* no. 116, 1977, p. 14.

13. "The peasant civilization is both our father and our mother" (Olmi, quoting Pasolini, in an interview with Tullio Kezich, *La Repubblica,* April 1, 1978; reprinted in *L'arbre aux sabots* [Rome: Italnoleggio Cinematografico, 1978], p. 27 [pressbook]).

14. P. P. Pasolini, "In calce al cinema di poesia," in Edoardo Bruno, ed., *Teorie e prassi del cinema in Italia, 1950–1970* (Milan: Gabriele Mazzotta, 1972), p. 110.

15. Olmi, in Tassone, *Parla il cinema italiano,* 2:215, 218.

Bibliography

GENERAL REFERENCES

Albrecht Carié, René. *Italy: From Napoleon to Mussolini.* New York: Columbia University Press, 1950.

Allum, P. A. *Italy: Republic Without a Government.* New York: W. W. Norton, 1973.

Annuario del cinema italiano. Rome: Garzanti, 1959.

Apollonio, Umbro. *Futurist Manifestos.* New York: Viking Press, 1973.

Argentieri, Mino. *La censura del cinema italiano.* Rome: Editori Riuniti, 1974.

Aristarco, Guido. *Cinema italiano 1960: Romanzo e antiromanzo.* Milan: Il Saggiatore, 1961.

Armes, Roy. *Patterns of Realism.* London: Tantivy Press, 1971.

Aspekte des italienischen Films. Bad Ems: Verband der deutschen Filmclubs, 1969.

Barbaro, Umberto. *Il film e il risarcimento marxista dell' arte.* Rome: Editori Riuniti, 1960.

―――. *Servitù e grandezza del cinema.* Rome: Editori Riuniti, 1961.

―――. *Neorealismo e realismo.* Rome: Editori Riuniti, 1976.

Barzini, Luigi. *The Italians.* New York: Bantam Books, 1965.

Bazin, André. *What Is Cinema?* 2 vols. Translated by Hugh Gray. Berkeley and Los Angeles: University of California Press, 1972.

Bergman, Ingrid. *My Story.* New York: Delacorte Press, 1980.

Bernardini, Aldo, and Martinelli, Vittorio, eds. *Il cinema italiano degli anni venti.* Rome: La Cineteca Nazionale, 1979.

Bernstein, Serge, and Milza, Paul. *L'Italie contemporaine des nationalistes aux européens.* Paris: Armand Collin, 1973.

Bertetto, Paolo. *Il cinema dell'utopia.* Salerno: Runna, 1970.

Bohne, Luciana, ed. *Italian Neorealism.* Special issue of *Film Criticism* (Edinboro, Pa.), no. 2, 1979.

Borde, Raymond, and Buissy, André. *Le néoréalisme italien.* Lausanne: La Cinémathèque Suisse, 1960.

Brunetta, Gian Piero. *Storia del cinema italiano, 1895–1945.* Rome: Editori Riuniti, 1979.

―――, ed. *Letteratura e cinema.* Bologna: Zanichelli, 1976.

Bruno, Edoardo, ed. *Teorie e prassi del cinema in Italia, 1950–1970.* Milan: Gabriele Mazzotta, 1972.

Buache, Freddy. *Le cinéma italien d'Antonioni à Rosi.* Paris: Maspero, 1969.

―――. *Le cinéma italien, 1945–1979.* Lausanne: L'Age d'Homme, 1979.

Burckhardt, Jakob. *The Civilization of the Renaissance in Italy.* Translated from the German by S. G. C. Middlemore. New York: Harper and Brothers, 1958.

Caldiron, Orio, ed. *Il lungo viaggio del cinema italiano.* Padua: Marsilio, 1965.

Carpi, Fabio. *Il cinema italiano del dopoguerra.* Milan: Schwarz, 1958.

Casiraghi, Ugo. *Il cinema cinese, questo sconosciuto.* Turin: Centrofilm, 1960. *Quaderni di Documentazione Cinematografica,* nos. 11–12.

Chiarini, Luigi. *Il film nella battaglia delle idee.* Rome and Milan: Fratelli Bocca, 1954.

La città del cinema. Rome: Napoleone, 1979.

Cowie, Peter, ed. *International Film Guide.* 14 editions to date. London: Tantivy Press, 1968–.

Della Volpe, Galvano. *Verosimile filmico e altri scritti di estetica.* Rome: Edizioni Filmcritica, 1954.

De Sanctis, Francesco. *Saggio critico sul Petrarca.* Turin: Einaudi, 1964.

———. *Storia della letteratura italiana.* 2 vols. Bari: Laterza, 1964.

Fernandez, Dominique. *Il romanzo italiano e la crisi della coscienza moderna.* Translated from the French by Franca Lerici. Milan: Lerici, 1960.

———. *Il mito dell' America negli intellettuali italiani del 1930–1950.* Translated from the French by Alfonso Zaccaria. Rome and Caltanissetta: Salvatore Sciascia, 1969.

Ferrara, Giuseppe. *Il nuovo cinema italiano.* Florence: Le Monnier, 1957.

———. "Il neorealismo italiano." In Adelio Ferrero, ed., *Momenti di storia del cinema.* Florence: Centro Studi del Consorzio Toscano Attività Cinematografiche, 1965.

Ferrata, Giansiro, ed. *La voce: Antologia.* Rome: Luciano Landi, 1961.

Ferrero, Adelio, ed. *Storia di cinema.* 5 vols. Venice: Marsilio, 1978.

Fortini, Francesco: *Dieci inverni, 1947–1957.* Bari: De Donato, 1973.

Foucault, Michel. *Histoire de la folie à l' age classique: Folie et déraison.* Paris: Plon, 1961.

Gelmis, Joseph. *The Film Director as Superstar.* Garden City, N.Y.: Doubleday, 1970.

Giannetti, Louis D. *Godard and Others.* Rutherford, N.J.: Farleigh Dickinson University Press, 1975.

Gili, Jean A. *Le cinéma italien.* (Interviews with M. Bellocchio, B. Bertolucci, M. Bolognini, L. Comencini, M. Ferreri, M. Monicelli, E. Petri, D. Risi, E. Scola, P. and V. Taviani, V. Zurlini.) Paris: Union Générale d'Edition, 1978.

Graham, Peter, ed. *Dictionary of Cinema.* London: Tantivy Press, 1968.

Gramsci, Antonio. *L'ordine nuovo.* Turin: Einaudi, 1967.

———. *The Modern Prince and Other Writings.* Translated by Louis Marks. New York: International Publishers, 1972.

Grazzini, Giovanni. *Gli anni sessanta in cento film.* Rome and Bari: Laterza, 1971.

———. *Cinema '78.* Rome and Bari: Laterza, 1979.

Gregor, Ulrich, and Patalas, Enno. *Geschichte des Films.* Gütersloh: Sigbert Mohn Verlag, 1962.

———. *Geschichte des modernen Films.* Gütersloh: Sigbert Mohn Verlag, 1965.

Gromo, Mario. *Cinema italiano, 1908–1953.* Milan: Mondadori, 1954.

Guidirizzi, Ernesto. *La narrativa italiana e il cinema.* Florence: Sansoni, 1973.

Hovald, Patrick H. *Le néoréalisme italien et ses créateurs.* Paris: Du Cerf, 1959.

Istituto nazionale LUCE: Origini, organizzazione e l' attività dell' Istituto nazionale LUCE. Rome: Istituto Poligrafico dello Stato, 1934.

Kirkpatrick, Ivonne. *Mussolini: A Study in Power.* New York: Avon Books, 1964.

Kracauer, Siegfried. *Theory of Film: The Redemption of Physical Reality.* New York: Oxford University Press, 1960.

Lattuada, Alberto. *Occhio quadrato.* Milan: Corrente, 1941.

Laura, Ernesto, and Caldiron, Orio, eds. *Cinema italiano degli anni quaranta.* Rome: Centro Sperimentale di Cinematografia, 1978.

Lawton, Benjamin. *Italian Cinema: Literary and Political Trends.* Los Angeles: Center for Italian Studies, UCLA, 1975.

Leprohon, Pierre. *The Italian Cinema*. Translated from the French by Roger Greaves and Oliver Stallybrass. London: Secker & Warburg, 1972.

Liehm, Mira, and Liehm, Antonin. *The Most Important Art*. Berkeley and Los Angeles: University of California Press, 1977.

Lizzani, Carlo. *Storia del cinema italiano*. Florence: Parenti, 1961.

_____.*Il cinema italiano, 1895–1979*. Rome: Editori Riuniti, 1979.

Lotman, Jurij. *Semiotics of Cinema*. Translated from the Russian by Mark E. Suino. Ann Arbor: University of Michigan Press, 1976.

Mack Smith, Denis. *Italy: A Modern History*. Ann Arbor: University of Michigan Press, 1969.

Manvell, Roger, ed. *The International Encyclopedia of Film*. New York: Crown, 1972.

Marcorelles, Louis. *Living Cinema*. Translated from the French by Isabel Quingly. London: Allen & Unwin, 1973.

Mast, Gerard. *A Short History of the Movies*. New York: Pegasus, 1971.

Materiali sul cinema italiano. Rome: Mostra Internazionale del Nuovo Cinema, 1975.

Materiali sul cinema italiano degli anni '50. 2 vols. Rome: Mostra Internazionale del Nuovo Cinema, 1978.

Member, Stephen. *Cinéma Vérité in America*. Cambridge, Mass.: MIT Press, 1974.

Metz, Christian. *Film Language: A Semiotics of the Cinema*. Translated from the French by Michael Taylor. New York: Oxford University Press, 1974.

Miccichè, Lino. *Il cinema italiano degli anni '60*. Venice: Marsilio, 1975.

_____.*Il cinema italiano degli anni '70*. Venice: Marsilio, 1980.

_____, ed. *Il neorealismo cinematografico italiano*. Venice: Marsilio, 1975.

Monaco, James. *How to Read a Film*. New York: Oxford University Press, 1977.

Il neorealismo e la critica: Materiali per una bibliografia. Rome: Mostra Internazionale del Nuovo Cinema, 1974.

Le néoréalisme italien: Bilan de la critique. Special issue of *Etudes Cinématographiques* (Paris), nos. 32–33, 1964. pp. 59–60.

Novotná, Drahomíra. *Film velkých nadejí*. Prague: Orbis, 1963.

Nuovi materiali sul cinema italiano, 1929–1943. 2 vols. Rome: Mostra Internazionale del Nuovo Cinema, 1976.

Oldrini, Guido. *Problemi di teoria e storia del cinema*. Naples: Guida, 1976.

Overbey, David, ed. *Springtime in Italy: A Reader on Neo-realism*. London: Talisman Books, 1978.

Pacifici, Sergio. *A Guide to Contemporary Italian Literature*. Cleveland and New York: Meridian Books, 1962.

_____, ed. *From Verismo to Experimentalism*. Bloomington: Indiana University Press, 1969.

Pasolini, Pier Paolo. *Empirismo eretico*. Milan: Garzanti, 1972.

_____. *Scritti corsari*. Milan: Garzanti, 1975.

_____. *L'expérience hérétique*. Translated by Anna Rocchi Pullberg. Paris: Payot, 1976.

Pavese, Cesare. *The Burning Brand: Diaries, 1935–1950*. Translated by E. A. Murch. New York: Walker and Company, 1961.

Petric, Vladimir, ed. *The Language of Silent Film*. New York: Museum of Modern Art and Vladimir Petric, 1975.

Pintor, Giaime. *Il sangue d'Europa*. Turin: Einaudi, 1950.

Politica e cultura del dopoguerra: Con una cronologia 1929–1964 e una antologia. Rome: Mostra Internazionale del Nuovo Cinema, 1974.

Procacci, Giulio. *Storia degli italiani*. 2 vols. Rome and Bari: Laterza, 1968.

Quaglietti, Lorenzo. *Il cinema italiano del dopoguerra*. Rome: Mostra Internazionale del Nuovo Cinema, 1974.

_____. *Storia economico-politica del cinema italiano, 1945–1980*. Rome: Editori Riuniti, 1980.

Revel, Jean-François. *Pour l'Italie*. Paris: Julliard, 1958.

Rhode, Eric. *A History of Cinema from Its Origins to 1970*. London: Allen Lane, 1976 .

Robbe-Grillet, Alain. *Il nouveau roman*. Milan: Feltrinelli, 1961.

Rondi, Brunello. *Il neorealismo italiano*. Parma: Guanda, 1956.

Rondolino, Gianni, ed. *Catalogo Bolaffi del cinema italiano, 1945–1965*. 2 vols. Turin: Giulio Bolaffi, 1967.

_____. *Catalogo Bolaffi del cinema italiano, 1966–1975*. Turin: Giulio Bolaffi, 1975.

_____. *Catalogo Bolaffi del cinema italiano*. Since 1975 published yearly; 8 editions to date. Turin: Giulio Bolaffi, 1975–.

_____. *Dizionario Bolaffi del cinema italiano: Registi*. Turin: Giulio Bolaffi, 1979.

Rossellini, Roberto. *Un esprit libre ne doit rien apprendre en esclave*. Translated by Paul Alexandre. Paris: Fayard, 1977.

Roud, Richard, ed. *Cinema: A Critical Dictionary*. 2 vols. London: Secker & Warburg, 1980.

Sadoul, Georges, *Histoire générale du cinéma*. Paris: Denoël, 1971.

_____. *Dictionary of Films*. Translated, edited, and updated by Peter Morris. Berkeley and Los Angeles: University of California Press, 1972.

_____. *Histoire du cinéma mondial*. Paris: Flammarion, 1974.

Salinari, Carlo. *Miti e coscienza del decadentismo italiano*. Milan: Feltrinelli, 1960.

_____. *Preludio e fine del realismo in Italia*. Naples: Morano, 1967.

Savio, Francesco. *Ma l'amore no: Realismo, formalismo, propaganda e telefoni bianchi nel cinema italiano di regime, 1930–1943*. Milan: Sonzogno, 1975.

Sciascia, Leonardo. *L'affaire Moro*. Translated by Jean-Noël Schifano. Paris: Grasset, 1978.

_____. *La Sicile comme métaphore*. Translated by Marcelle Padovani. Paris: Stock, 1979.

Segnalazioni cinematografiche, 1944–1945. Rome: Centro Cattolico Cinematografico, 1946.

Solé, Robert. *Le défi terroriste*. Paris: Seuil, 1979.

Spinazzola, Vittorio: *Cinema e pubblico: Lo spettacolo filmico in Italia, 1945–1965*. Milan: Bompiani, 1974.

Sul neorealismo: Testi e documenti. Rome: Mostra Internazionale del Nuovo Cinema, 1974.

Tannenbaum, Edward, R. *The Fascist Experience*. New York: Basic Books, 1972.

Tassone, Aldo. *Parla il cinema italiano*. 2 vols. (Vol. 1: interviews with M. Antonioni, F. Brusati, L. Comencini, A. Lattuada, M. Monicelli, G. Pontecorvo, D. Risi, F. Rosi; vol. 2: interviews with M. Bellocchio, B. Bertolucci, F. Carpi, L. Cavani, V. De Seta, E. Olmi, E. Petri, E. Scola, P. and V. Taviani, V. Zurlini.) Milan: Il Formichiere, 1979.

Torri, Bruno. *Il cinema italiano: Dalla realtà alle metafore*. Palermo: Palumbo, 1973.

Trinon, Hadelin. *Andrzej Wajda*. Paris: Seghers, 1964.

Verdone, Mario, ed. *Cinema e letteratura del futurismo*. Rome: Centro Sperimentale di Cinematografia, 1968.

Vogel, Amos. *Film as Subversive Art*. New York: Random House, 1975.

Williams, Christopher, ed. *Realism and Cinema*. London: Routledge & Kegan Paul, 1980.

Witcombe R. T. *The New Italian Cinema*. New York: Oxford University Press, 1982.

Wright, Basil. *The Long View*. New York: Knopf, 1974.

Zavattini, Cesare. *Sequences from a Cinematic Life*. Translated by William Weaver. Englewood Cliffs, N.J.: Prentice-Hall, 1970.

_____. *Diario cinematografico*. Milan: Bompiani, 1979.

_____. *Neorealismo ecc*. Milan: Bompiani, 1979.

MONOGRAPHS

MICHELANGELO ANTONIONI

Cameron, Ian, and Wood, Robin. *Antonioni*. London: Studio Vista, 1968.

Cowie, Peter. *Antonioni, Bergman, Resnais*. London: Tantivy Press, 1963.

Di Carlo, Carlo, ed. *Michelangelo Antonioni*. Rome: Centro Sperimentale di Cinematografia, 1964.

Giacomelli, A. M, and Saitta, I. *Crisi dell'uomo e della società nei film di Visconti e di Antonioni*. Alba: Paoline, 1972.

Leprohon, Pierre. *Michelangelo Antonioni*. Paris: Seghers, 1962.

Strick, Philippe. *Antonioni*. London: Motion, 1963.

Taylor, John Russel. *Michelangelo Antonioni*. London: Methuen, 1964.

Thirard, Jean-Paul, ed. *Michelangelo Antonioni*. Special issue of *Premier Plan* (Lyon), no. 15, 1960.

Tinazzi, Giorgio. *Antonioni: Il romanzo della crisi*. Lugano: Cenobio, 1961

————. *Michelangelo Antonioni*. Florence: La Nuova Italia, 1976.

BERNARDO BERTOLUCCI

Carrol, Kent E., ed. *Last Tango in Paris*. New York: Grove Press, 1973.

Casetti, Francesco. *Bernardo Bertolucci*. Florence: La Nuova Italia, 1975.

Morandini, Morando. *Bernardo Bertolucci*. Turin: AIACE, 1973.

VITTORIO DE SICA

Agel, Henri. *Vittorio De Sica*. Paris: Editions Universitaires, 1961.

Caldiron, Orio, ed. *Vittorio De Sica*. Special issue of *Bianco e Nero* (Rome), nos. 9–12, 1975.

Grisolia, Michel. *Vittorio De Sica*. Cinéastes III. Brussels: Casterman, 1974.

Leprohon, Pierre. *De Sica*. Paris: Seghers, 1973.

FEDERICO FELLINI

Agel, Geneviève. *Les chemins de Fellini*. Paris: Du Cerf, 1956.

Bondanella, Peter, ed. *Federico Fellini: Essays in Criticism*. New York: Oxford University Press, 1978.

Boyer, Deena. *The Two Hundred Days of 8½*. Translated by Ch. Lam Markman. New York: Macmillan, 1964.

Budgen, Suzanne. *Fellini*. London: British Film Institute, 1966.

Fellini. Special issue of *L'Arc* (Aix-en-Provence), no. 45, 1971.

Kael, Anna, and Strich, Christian, eds. *Fellini on Fellini*. London: Eyre Methuen, 1976.

Pecori, Franco. *Federico Fellini*. Florence: La Nuova Italia, 1974.

Perry, Ted. *Film Guide to 8½*. Bloomington: Indiana University Press, 1975.

Salachaz, Gilbert. *Federico Fellini*. Paris: Seghers, 1963.

Solmi, Angelo. *Fellini*. London: Merlin Press, 1967.

Taylor, John Russel. *Federico Fellini*. London: Eyre Methuen, 1964.

MARCO FERRERI

Grande, Maurizio. *Marco Ferreri*. Florence: La Nuova Italia, 1974.

Grizolia, Michel. *Marco Ferreri*. Cinéastes III. Brussels: Casterman, 1974.

Morandini, Morando. *Marco Ferreri*. Turin: AIACE, 1970.

PIER PAOLO PASOLINI

Betti, Laura, ed. *Pasolini: Chronique judiciaire, persécution, exécution*. Paris: Seghers, 1977.

Duflot, Jean. *Entretiens avec P. P. Pasolini*. Paris: P. Belfond, 1970.

Ferrerio, Adelo. *Il cinema di Pier Paolo Pasolini*. Milan: Mondadori, 1978.

Gervais, Marc. *Pier Paolo Pasolini*. Paris: Seghers, 1973.

Jansen, Peter W., and Schütte, Wolfram, eds. *Pier Paolo Pasolini*. Munich: C. Hanser Verlag, 1977.

Pasolini: Séminaire dirigé par M. A. Macciocchi. Paris: Grasset, 1980.

Petraglia, Sandro. *Pier Paolo Pasolini*. Florence: La Nuova Italia, 1974.

Siciliano, Enzo. *Vita di Pasolini*. Milan: Rizzoli, 1979.

Stack, Oswald. *Pasolini on Pasolini*. London: Thames & Hudson, 1969.

Willemen, Paul, ed. *Pier Paolo Pasolini*. London: British Film Institute, 1977.

FRANCESCO ROSI

Ciment, Michel. *Le dossier Rosi*. Paris: Stock, 1976.

Ferrara, Giuseppe. *Francesco Rosi*. Rome: Canesi, 1965.

Zambetti, Sandro. *Francesco Rosi*. Florence: La Nuova Italia, 1976.

ROBERTO ROSSELLINI

Baldelli, Pio. *Roberto Rossellini*. Rome: Samonà e Savelli, 1972.

Bruno, Edoardo, ed. *Roberto Rossellini*. Rome: Bulzoni, 1979.

Degener, David. *Sighting Rossellini*. Berkeley: University Art Museum, 1971.

Guarnier, José Luis. *Roberto Rossellini*. London: Praeger, 1970.

Menon, Gianni, ed. *Dibattito su Rossellini*. Rome: Partisan, 1972.

Mida, Massimo. *Roberto Rossellini*. Parma: Guanda, 1961.

Rondolino, Gianni. *Roberto Rossellini*. Florence: La Nuova Italia, 1974.

Verdone, Mario. *Roberto Rossellini*. Paris: Seghers, 1963.

LUCHINO VISCONTI

Baldelli, Pio. *I film di Luchino Visconti*. Manduria: Lacaita, 1965.

D'Amico de Carvalho, Caterina, ed. *Album Visconti*. Milan: Sonzogno, 1978.

Ferrara, Giuseppe. *Luchino Visconti*. Paris: Seghers, 1964.

Ferrero, Adelio, ed. *Visconti e il cinema*. Modena: Ufficio Cinema del Commune di Modena, 1977.

Giullaume, Yves. *Visconti*. Paris: Editions Universitaires, 1966.

Jansen, Peter W., and Schütte, Wolfram, eds. *Luchino Visconti*. Munich: C. Hanser Verlag, 1976.

Luchino Visconti. Special issue of *Premier Plan* (Lyon), no. 17, 1961.

Novotná, Drahomíra. *Luchino Visconti*. Prague: Orbis, 1969.

Nowell-Smith, Geoffrey. *Visconti*. Garden City, N.Y.: Doubleday, 1968.

Sterling, Monica. *A Screen of Time*. New York and London: Harcourt Brace Jovanovich, 1979.

OTHER DIRECTORS AND WRITERS

Marco Bellocchio

Bory, Jean-Louis. *Les poings dans les poches de Marco Bellocchio*. Cinéastes II. Brussels: Casterman, 1971.

Lodato, Nuccio. *Marco Bellocchio*. Milan: Moizzi, 1977.

Carmelo Bene
Grande, Maurizio. *Carmelo Bene: Il circuito barocco*. Special issue of *Bianco e Nero* (Rome), nos. 11–12, 1973.

Mauro Bolognini
Bolognini. Rome: Ministero degli Affari Esteri, 1977.

Anton Giulio Bragaglia
Verdone, Mario. *Anton Giulio Bragaglia*. Rome: Centro Sperimentale di cinematografia, 1965.

Liliana Cavani
Tiso, Ciriaco. *Liliana Cavani*. Florence: La Nuova Italia, 1975.

Giuseppe De Santis
Farassino, Alberto. *Giuseppe De Santis*. Milan: Moizzi, 1978.
Wagner, Jean. *Giuseppe De Santis*. Cinéastes II. Brussels: Casterman, 1971.

Carlo Di Carlo
Cosetti, Giorgio. *Carlo Di Carlo: I documentari, i film, 1961–1978*. Rome: Bulzoni, 1979.

Antonio Gramsci
Fiori, Giuseppe. *La vie de Antonio Gramsci*. Translated by Claude Ciccione. Paris: Fayard, 1970.
Joll, James. *Antonio Gransci*. New York: Penguin Books, 1977.

Alberto Lattuada
De Sanctis, Filipo. *Alberto Lattuada*. Parma: Guanda, 1961

Sergio Leone
De Fornari, Oreste. *Sergio Leone*. Milan: Moizzi, 1977.

Cesare Pavese
Biasin, Gian-Paolo. *The Smile of the Gods: A Thematic Study of Cesare Pavese's Works*. Translated by Yvonne Freccero. Ithaca: Cornell University Press, 1968.
Lajolo, Davide. *Il vizio assurdo: Storia di Cesare Pavese*. Milan: Mondadori, 1972.

Elio Petri
Gili, Jean A. *Elio Petri*. Nice: Faculté des Lettres et Sciences Humaines, 1974.

Dino Risi
Vigano, Aldo. *Dino Risi*. Milan: Moizzi, 1977.

Mario Soldati
Caldiron, Orio, ed. *Letterato al cinema: Mario Soldati anni '40*. Rome: Centro Sperimentale di Cinematografia, 1979.

Vittorio and Paolo Taviani
Aristarco, Guido. *Sotto il segno dello scorpione: Il cinema degli fratelli Taviani*. Messina and Florence: G. D'Anna, 1977.
De Poli, Marco. *Paolo e Vittorio Taviani*. Milan: Moizzi, 1977.

Cesare Zavattini
Zavattini nella città del cinema. Special issue of *Cinema e Cinema* (Venice), no. 20, 1979.

SELECTED ARTICLES

Accialini, F., Colucelli, L., and Valentinetti, C. "Conversazione con Marco Bellocchio." *Cinema e Cinema* (Venice), nos. 22–23, 1980, pp. 70–78.

Angeli, Otello. "Anatomia di una crisi." *Cinema 70* (Rome), no. 125, 1979, pp. 5–13.

Antonioni, Michelangelo. "La signora senza camelie non offende il cinema italiano." *Cinema Nuovo* (Milan), no. 6, 1953, pp. 146–47.

――――. "Crisi e neorealismo." *Bianco e Nero* (Rome), no. 9, 1958, pp. 1–3.

――――. "La malattia dei sentimenti." *Bianco e Nero* (Rome), nos. 2–3, 1961, pp. 69–95.

――――. "Making a Film Is My Way of Life." *Film Culture* (New York), no. 24, 1962, pp. 43–45.

Aprà, Adriano, and Ponzi, Maurizio. "Intervista con Bertolucci." *Filmcritica* (Rome), nos. 156–157, 1965, pp. 262–75.

Argentieri, Mino. "Storia e spiritualismo nel Rossellini degli anni quaranta." *Cinema 70* (Rome), no. 95, 1974, pp. 28–37.

――――. "Una monografia dedicata ai Taviani." *Cinema 70* (Rome), no. 116, 1977, pp. 11–14.

Aumont, Jacques, de Gregorio, Eduard, and Pierre, Sylvie. "Trois entretiens avec Marco Ferreri." *Cahiers du Cinéma* (Paris), no. 217, 1969, pp. 25–38.

Barbaro, Umberto. "Importanza del realismo." *Filmcritica* (Rome), no. 4, 1951, pp. 113–17.

Baroncelli de, Jean. "Fellini-Roma." *Le Monde* (Paris), May 15, 1971.

――――. "Bernardo Bertolucci: On s'exprime toujours par ses pensées." *Le Monde* (Paris), December 15, 1972, p. 15.

――――. "Luna de Bertolucci à Venise." *Le Monde* (Paris), September 5, 1979, p. 13.

Barzini, Luigi. "The Bad Tooth: D'Annunzio a Fiume." *New York Review of Books*, June 15, 1978, pp. 24–25.

Bellocchio, Marco: "Le saut dans le vide." *L'Araldo* (Rome), May 15–16, 1980, p. 3.

Bertolucci, Bernardo, and Comolli, Jean-Louis. "Le cinéma selon Pasolini." *Cahiers du Cinéma* (Paris), no. 169, 1965, pp. 22–25.

Bettetini, Gianfranco. "On Neorealism." *Framework* (Coventry, Great Britain), no. 2, 1975, pp. 20–21.

Beylie, Claude. "Le messie." *Ecran* (Paris), no. 45, 1976, pp. 58–60.

Bontemps, Jacques, and Marcorelles, Louis. "Entretien avec Bernardo Bertolucci." *Cahiers du Cinéma* (Paris), no. 164, 1965, pp. 30–32.

Bory, Jean-Louis. "Huis clos sur un matelas." *Le Nouvel Observateur* (Paris), December 23, 1972, p. 59.

Bragin, John. "A Conversation with Bernardo Bertolucci." *Film Quarterly* (Berkeley), no. 1, 1966, pp. 39–44.

Brigante, Louis. "Three New Italian Filmmakers: De Seta, Olmi, Pasolini." *Film Culture* (New York), no. 24, 1962, pp. 34–41.

Cameron, Ian. "Michelangelo Antonioni." *Film Quarterly* (Berkeley), no. 1, 1962, pp. 1–58.

Canby, Vincent. "Bertolucci Equates Politics with Sex." *New York Times*, September 19, 1970, p. 32.

――――. "Orchestra Rehearsal." *New York Times*, August 17, 1979, p. C13.

Cantwell, Mary. "Fellini on Men, Women, Love, Life, and His New Movie." *New York Times*, April 5, 1981, Section 2, pp. 1, 24.

"Le cinéma italien par ceux qui le font." *Cinéma 76* (Paris), no. 205, 1976, pp. 27–73.

Condini, Nereo. "Pasolini's Last Film: A Shocker You May Never See." *Village Voice* (New York), March 15, 1976, back page and p. 158.

Crowdus, Gary, and Georgakas, Dan. "The Audience Should Not Be Just Passive Spectators: An Interview with Francesco Rosi." *Cinéaste* (New York), no. 1, Fall 1975, pp. 3–8.

Delahaye, Michel, and Wagner, Jean. "Un entretien avec De Santis." *Cinéma 59* (Paris), no. 35, 1959, pp. 46–57.

Delain, Michel. "Bertolucci passe aux aveux." *L'Express* (Paris), December 11–17, 1972, p. 52.

Della Terza, Dante. "Italian Fiction from Pavese to Pratolini." *Italian Quarterly* (Berkeley), no. 11, 1959, pp. 29–41.

Demara, Nicolas A. "Pathway to Calvino." *Italian Quarterly* (Berkeley), no. 55, 1971, pp. 25–49.

De Santis, Giuseppe. "Per un paesaggio italiano." *Cinema* (Rome), no. 116, April 25, 1941.

––––––. "Film di questi giorni." *Cinema* (Rome), December 25, 1942, p. 752.

Domarchi, Jean, Douchet, Jean, and Hoveyda, Fereydoun. "Entretien avec Roberto Rossellini." *Cahiers du Cinéma* (Paris), no. 133, 1962, pp. 1–15.

Dombroski, Robert. "Brancati and Fascism: A Profile." *Italian Quarterly*, (Berkeley), no. 49, 1969, pp. 41–63.

Eco, Umberto. "Open Work." *Italian Quarterly* (Berkeley), Winter-Spring 1967, pp. 3–38.

Fellini, Federico. "La capacité d'émerveillement." *Cahiers du Cinéma* (Paris), no. 164, 1965, pp. 20–24.

Ferreri, Marco. "Faire de l'homme un animal social." *Ecran* (Paris), no. 47, 1976, pp. 31–32.

Gay, Clifford. "Casanova." *Framework* (Coventry, Great Britain), nos. 7–8, 1978, pp. 17–19.

Gervais, Marc. "P. P. Pasolini-contestatore." *Sight and Sound* (London), Winter 1968, pp. 2–6.

Gevandan, Franz. "Visconti le magnifique." *Cinéma 76* (Paris), no. 211, 1976, pp. 73–99.

Godard, Jean-Luc. "La nuit, l'eclipse, l'aurore." *Cahiers du Cinéma* (Paris), no. 160, 1964.

Grant, Jacques. "Carnet de notes pour une Orestiade africaine." *Cinéma 76* (Paris), no. 216, 1976, pp. 102–106. (On Pasolini).

Gussow, Mel. "Bertolucci Talks About Sex, Revolution, and *Last Tango*." *New York Times*, February 2, 1973, p. 20.

Hughes, John. "Recent Rossellini." *Film Comment* (New York), no. 4, 1974, pp. 16–21.

Ingrao, Pietro. "Luchino Visconti: L'antifascismo e il cinema." *Rinascita* (Rome), no. 13, 1976.

"Jean-Luc Godard." *Cahiers du Cinéma* (Paris), no. 138, 1962, pp. 21–39. (An interview).

Kael, Pauline. "The Current Cinema: Tango." *New Yorker*, October 28, 1972, p. 130.

Kast, Pierre. "Giulietta et Federico." *Cahiers du Cinéma* (Paris), no. 164, 1965, pp. 10–18.

Lane, John Francis. "The Cinema Is Life, Life Is Cinema: A Conversation with E. Olmi." *Sight and Sound* (London), no. 3, 1970, pp. 148–52.

Laura, Ernesto. "Il film nell'estetica italiana." *Bianco e Nero* (Rome), nos. 7–8, 1962.

––––––. "Vicende legislative della censura in Italia." *Bianco e Nero* (Rome), nos. 4–5, 1961, pp. 4–17.

Lawton, Ben. "Last Tango in Paris." *Italian Quarterly* (Berkeley), no. 65, 1973, pp. 83–91.

Levine, Irving. "A Conversation with Federico Fellini." *Film Comment* (New York), no. 1, 1966, pp. 77–84.

Limmer, Wolfgang. "Die Verstümmelung eines Meisterwerks." *Der Spiegel* (West Berlin), no. 45, 1976, pp. 218–21.

Luhr, William. "Semiotics and Film: An Interview with Umberto Eco." *Wide Angle* (Athens, Ohio), no. 4, 1977, pp. 65–77.

Macciocchi, Maria Antonietta. "Mettre en crise notre propre silence." *Le Monde* (Paris), section hebdomadaire, September 6–12, 1973, p. 11.

――――. "Aujourd'hui encore je dénonce." *Le Monde* (Paris), March 20, 1975, pp. 15, 17. (An interview with L. Visconti)

Mahaini, Nabil Reda. "Decameron: Intervista con P. P. Pasolini." *Cinema 70* (Rome), nos. 87–88, 1972, pp. 62–70.

Manceaux, Michèle. "An Interview with Antonioni." *Sight and Sound* (London), no. 1, 1960–1961, pp. 5–8.

Martin, Marcel. "Le néoréalisme vu par la critique française." *Ecran* (Paris), no. 37, 1975, pp. 28–36.

Masi, Stefano. "Il cinema regionale della sceneggiata." *Cineforum* (Bergamo), no. 184, 1979, pp. 266–81.

Mauriac, Claude. "Brando comme on ne l'avait jamais vu." *L'Express* (Paris), December 11–17, 1972, p. 55.

Mellen, Joan. "An Interview with Gillo Pontecorvo." *Film Quarterly* (Berkeley), no. 1, 1972, pp. 2–10.

――――. "Fascism in Contemporary Film." *Film Quarterly* (Berkeley), no. 4, 1972, pp. 2-19.

Meyers, Jeffrey. "Symbol and Structure in Leopard." *Italian Quarterly* (Berkeley), Summer-Fall 1965, pp. 51–70.

Morandini, Morando. "The Year of Dolce Vita." *Sight and Sound* (London), no. 3, 1960, pp. 123–27.

Morin, Edgar. "Mai mais, mais mai." *Le Monde* (Paris), June 1, 1978, p. 15.

Narboni, Jean. "Rencontre avec Pier Paolo Pasolini." *Cahiers du Cinéma* (Paris), no. 192, 1967, p. 31.

Overbey, David. "The Other Bertolucci." *Sight and Sound* (London), no. 4, 1979, pp. 239–41.

Paladini, Aldo. "Il neorealismo non è pessimista." *Cinema Nuovo* (Milan), no. 142, 1954, pp. 152–54. (An interview with Sartre)

Pasolini, Pier Paolo. "Cinematic and Literary Stylistic Figures." *Film Culture* (New York), no. 24, 1962, pp. 42–43.

――――. "Le cinéma de poesie." *Cahiers du Cinéma* (Paris), no. 171, 1965, pp. 55–64.

――――. "Il cinema di poesia." *Filmcritica* (Rome), nos. 156–157, 1965, pp. 275–93.

――――. "Discours sur le plan séquence." *Cahiers du Cinéma* (Paris), no. 192, 1967, pp. 27–31.

Perlmutter, Ruth. "The Cinema of the Grotesque: Fellini's Casanova." *Georgia Review*, Spring 1979, pp. 186–93.

Perry, Ted. "The Road to Neorealism." *Film Comment* (New York), no. 14, 1978, pp. 7–13.

Pietrangeli, Antonio. "Analisi spettrale del film realista." *Cinema* (Rome), no. 146, 1942, pp. 393–94.

Puccini, Gianni. "I tempi di 'Cinema.'" *Filmcritica* (Rome), no. 5, 1951, pp. 151–55.

Puccini, Massimo Mida. "A proposito di Ossessione." *Cinema* (Rome), no. 169, 1943, p. 19.

Quaglietti, Lorenzo. "Il realismo non è piu attuale." *Cinema 70* (Rome), no. 116, 1977, pp. 50–51.

Redi, Riccardo. "E stato fascista il cinema italiano?" *Cinema 70* (Rome), no. 121, May–June 1978, pp. 38–44.

Renzi, Renzo. "Una tendenza sedentaria contro gli impegni del realismo." *Cinema Nuovo* (Milan), no. 1, 1952.

Rhode, Eric. "Why Neorealism Failed." *Sight and Sound* (London), no.1, 1960–1961, pp. 27–32.

Rohmer, Eric. "Nouvel Entretien avec Roberto Rosselini." *Cahiers du Cinéma* (Paris), no. 145, 1963, pp. 2–13.

Ronchey, Alberto. "Guns and Gray Matter: Terrorism in Italy." *Foreign Affairs* (New York), no. 4, 1979, pp. 921–40.

Roud, Richard. "Bertolucci on La Luna." *Sight and Sound* (London), no. 4, 1979, pp. 236–39.

Sampieri, G. V. "Lo stile e gli indirizzi del nuovo cinema italiano." *Rivista Italiana di Cinetecnica* (Rome), no. 4, May 1930, p. 5.

Santini, Aldo. "Futurismo non fa più rima con fascismo." *Europeo* (Rome), December 1978, pp. 71–75.

Sarris, Andrew. "Rossellini Rediscovered." *Film Culture* (New York), no. 32, 1964, pp. 60–63.

Sciascia, Leonardo. "Le coeur de l'état italien n'existe pas; sa cervelle non plus." *Le Monde* (Paris), February 4–5, 1979.

Schultz, Victoria. "Interview with Roberto Rossellini." *Film Culture* (New York), no. 52, Spring 1971, pp. 1–31.

"Self-Portrait of an Angel and Monster." *Time* (New York), January 22, 1973, pp. 51–55. (Cover story on *Last Tango in Paris*)

Simsolo, Noël. "Entretien: Carmelo Bene, Capricci." *Cahiers du Cinéma* (Paris), no. 166, 1969, pp. 18–19.

Solaroli, Libero. "Da 'Rotaie' a 'Ossessione.'" *Cinema Nuovo* (Milan), nos. 2, 4, 6, 8, 10, 12, 14, 1953.

Sterrit, David. "Two New Italian Films, Including Visconti's Last." *Christian Science Monitor* (Boston), February 5, 1979.

Tagliabue, Carlo. "The Narrow Road to a Forked Path." (*The Spider's Stratagem*) *Framework* (Coventry, Great Britain), no. 3, 1976, pp. 11–13.

"A Talk with Michelangelo Antonioni on His Work." *Film Culture* (New York), no. 24, 1962, pp. 45–61.

Valsecchi, Marco. "Italian Painting Today." *Italian Quarterly* (Berkeley), nos. 7–8, 1959, pp. 19–42.

Verdone, Mario. "Colloquio sul neorealismo." *Bianco e Nero* (Rome), no. 2, 1952, pp. 8–16.

Visconti, Luchino. "Cadaveri." *Cinema* (Rome), no. 119, 1941, p. 336.

————. "Cinema antropomorfico." *Cinema* (Rome), nos. 173–174, 1943, pp. 108–109.

————. "Sul modo di mettere in scena una commedia de Shakespeare." *Rinascita* (Rome), no. 12, December 1948.

————. "Da Verga a Gramsci." *Vie Nuove* (Rome), no. 42, 1960.

West, M. "Terror as Historical Inheritance." *Esquire* (New York), April 25, 1978.

Zalaffi, Nicoletta. "Entretien avec Marco Bellocchio." *Image et Son* (Paris), no. 217, 1973, pp. 100–07.

Zavattini, Cesare. "I sogni migliori." *Cinema* (Rome), no. 92, April 25, 1940, pp. 258–59.

————. "Polemica col mio tempo." *Filmcritica* (Rome), nos. 6–7, 1951, pp. 15–17.

————. "Some Ideas on Cinema." *Sight and Sound* (London), October 1953, pp. 64–69.

Zimmer, Christian. "Le système." *Les Temps Modernes* (Paris), no. 282, January 1970, pp. 1125–45.

SCREENPLAYS

MICHELANGELO ANTONIONI

Il deserto rosso. Bologna: Cappelli, 1978.

Il primo Antonioni (shorts, *Cronaca di un amore, I vinti, La signora senza camelie, Tentato suicidio*). Bologna: Cappelli, 1973.

Screenplays (*Il grido, L'avventura, La notte, L'eclisse*). Translated by Judith Green. New York: Orion Press, 1963.

Sei film (*Le amiche, Il grido, L'avventura, La notte, L'eclisse, Il deserto rosso*). Turin: Einaudi, 1964.

Techniquement douce. Translated by Anna Buresi. Paris: Albatros, 1977.

Zabriskie Point. Bologna: Cappelli, 1970.

MARCO BELLOCCHIO

Nel nome del padre. Bologna: Cappelli, 1971.

I pugni in tasca. Milan: Garzanti, 1967.

BERNARDO BERTOLUCCI

Ultimo tango a Parigi. Turin: Einaudi, 1973.

MAURO BOLOGNINI

La viaccia. Bologna: Cappelli, 1961.

LILIANA CAVANI

Francesco D'Assisi, Galileo. Turin: Gribaudi, 1970.

Il portiere di notte. Turin: Einaudi, 1974.

VITTORIO DE SICA AND CESARE ZAVATTINI

The Bicycle Thief. Translated by Simon Hartog. New York: Simon & Schuster, 1968.

Umberto D. Rome and Milan: Fratelli Bocca, 1953.

FEDERICO FELLINI

Amarcord. Translated by Michèle Natascha Nahon. Paris: Seghers, 1974

I Clowns. Bologna: Cappelli, 1970.

La dolce vita. Bologna: Cappelli, 1959.

Early Screenplays (*Variety Lights, The White Sheik*). Translated by Judith Green. New York: Orion Press, 1961.

Fellini's Satyricon. Translated by Eugene Walters and John Matthews. New York: Ballantine Books, 1970.

Juliet of the Spirits. Translated by Howard Greenfeld. New York: Orion Press, 1965.

MARCO FERRERI

Non toccare la donna bianca. Turin: Einaudi, 1974.

L'ultima donna. Turin: Einaudi, 1976.

PIETRO GERMI

Sedotta e abbandonata. Bologna: Cappelli, 1964.

PIER PAOLO PASOLINI

Accattone. Milan: Garzanti, 1965.
Mamma Roma. Milan: Rizzoli, 1962.
Oedipus Rex. Translated by John Matthews. New York: Simon & Schuster, 1971.
Teorema. Milan: Garzanti, 1968.
Trilogia della vita. Bologna: Cappelli, 1975.
Uccellacci e uccellini. Milan: Garzanti, 1966.

ROBERTO ROSSELLINI

Era notte a Roma. Bologna: Cappelli, 1960.
Viaggio in Italia. *Filmcritica* (Rome), nos. 156–157, 1965, pp. 294–313.
The War Trilogy (*Open City, Paisan, Germany, Year Zero*). Translated by Judith Green. New York: Grossman Publishers, 1973.

VITTORIO AND PAOLO TAVIANI

San Michele aveva un gallo, Allonsanfan. Bologna: Cappelli, 1974.
I sovversivi. *Cinema 60* (Rome), nos. 62–63, 1966, pp. 51–94.

LUCHINO VISCONTI

Gruppo di famiglia in un interno. Bologna: Cappelli, 1960.
Marcia nuziale. *Cinema Nuovo* (Milan), no. 10, 1953, pp. 256–58; no. 11, 1953, pp. 317–19; no. 12, 1953, p. 351; no. 13, 1953, p. 361.
Rocco e i suoi fratelli. Bologna: Cappelli, 1960.
Three Screenplays (*White Nights, Rocco and His Brothers, The Job*). Translated by Judith Green. New York: Orion Press, 1970.
Two Screenplays (*La terra trema, Senso*). Translated by Judith Green. New York: Orion Press, 1970.

LINA WERTMÜLLER

The Screenplays of Lina Wertmüller (*The Seduction of Mimi, Love and Anarchy, Swept Away, Seven Beauties*). Translated by Steven Wagner. New York: Warner Books, 1978.

PRESSBOOKS

L'arbre aux sabots. Rome: Italnoleggio Cinematografico, 1978.
Bye-Bye, Male. Rome: Anica-Unitalia, 1978.
Gesamtprogramm der Internationalen Filmwoche. Mannheim: Internationale Filmwoche, 1978.
L'Italie au XXXIe Festival de Cannes. Rome: Anica-Unitalia, 1978.
Il portiere di notte. Rome: Italnoleggio Cinematografico, 1974.
La villeggiatura. Rome: Italnoleggio Cinematografico, 1973.

Index of Names

Index of Films

383